The Which? Book of Saving and Investing

Published by
Consumers' Association and
Hodder & Stoughton

The Which?
Book of
Saving and
Investing

The Which? Book of Saving and Investing is published in Great Britain by Consumers' Association, 14 Buckingham Street, London WC2N 6DS and by Hodder & Stoughton, 47 Bedford Square, London WC1B 3DP.

Editor:	**Helena Wiesner**
Design and illustration:	**Banks & Miles**
Contributors:	**Jonathan Shephard** **Carole Slingsby** **Nigel Smith** **Dave Watts** **Sara Williams**

First Edition 1982
© Consumers' Association 1982

Typesetting by Vantage Photosetting Company Limited, Chandler's Ford, Hampshire.

Printed in Great Britain by Sir Joseph Causton and Sons Ltd, London and Eastleigh.

ISBN: 0 340 27488 3

The Which? Book of Saving and Investing aims to help you find the best investments for your money, taking into account your own particular needs and circumstances. It covers the details of the various choices open to you, and provides the framework within which to plan your investment strategy. The book is based on the knowledge and experience built up over 14 years of publishing **Money Which?** and on invaluable help provided by experts and consultants throughout its production.

Contents

1	Investment strategy	8
2	Investment choices	16
3	A bird's eye view	24
4	Getting professional advice	34
5	Tax	42
6	Your home	62
7	Alternative investments	70
8	Shares	78
9	Unit trusts	91
10	British Government stocks	102
11	Commodities	110
12	Local authority investments	117
13	Endowment policies	124
14	Unit-linked life insurance	133
15	Income and growth bonds	148
16	Annuities	150
17	Pensions from employers and from the state	156
18	Personal pension plans	164
19	Building society investments	180
20	Bank and finance company deposits	189
21	Index-linked investments	192
22	National Savings investments	198
23	Investing abroad	208
24	Investing for children	218
25	Saving and retirement	232
	Index	238

1 Investment strategy

Whether you're a small-scale investor, or looking for a home for many thousands of £££, your problem will not be lack of choice. The difficulty arises in making sensible choices among all the investments available – and, in some cases, finding out all the details needed to come to these decisions. Your aim should be to end up with a number of different investments, covering your differing needs. So before getting down to the nitty gritty of the different investments, we've set out a plan for working out your overall investment strategy. In the next chapter we give examples of different people putting their individual strategies into effect. In Chapter 3, we've given a bird's eye view of the different investments open to you – you'll find more details on each in the rest of the book. In the last three chapters of the book we deal with the particular cases of investing abroad, investing for children, and savings and retirement.

Of course, deciding now on a particular set of investments isn't the end of the story. It's important to keep a close eye on your investments and to review them periodically – see p15 for things to bear in mind.

Investment priorities checklist

Your personal circumstances are bound to affect your choice of investments. But no matter what your situation is, some things are worth considering *before* you start thinking about investments in detail.

? Are your dependants protected against financial hardship if you die early?
Would your mortgage be paid off if you died? Would your wife have to go back to work earlier than planned? Would your husband have a big enough income to pay someone to look after the children?

For most people, the solution to this protection problem is life insurance, not saving and investing. The type of life insurance which would suit you best is *term insurance* – see Box on p124.

? Have you put some money aside for emergencies?
Could you cope with an unexpected disaster (major car repairs or damage to your home,

say)? If not, concentrate on building up an emergency fund in some place where you'll be able to withdraw it at short notice (within a week, say). See p12, and Chapter 2 for investments to consider.

? Are you buying your own home?
Buying a home has proved a good long-term investment in the past. Buying your home also has tax advantages – under current rules, you get tax relief on the interest you pay on a mortgage of up to £25,000, and there's normally no capital gains tax to pay on the increase in value of your home. If you aren't buying a home (and don't already own one), pause for thought – and read Chapter 6 – before you go for any other long-term investment.

? Are you making some provision for your retirement?
Don't assume that the State pension on its own will safeguard your standard of living. In Chapter 17, we give details of pension schemes – both from the state and from employers. Try to work out how well off the State pension together with any employer's pension and income from your savings will leave you – see Chapter 25. If you're self-employed, or not in an employer's pension scheme, consider taking out a personal pension plan – see Chapter 18 for details.

Your next step is to choose the investments which are best for you – taking your own personal circumstances and aims into account. For example, how much capital have you got to invest and for how long? Are you saving for something in particular – eg a trip to the Bahamas in four years' time. Or just to accumulate cash? Do you expect your income suddenly to rise – or fall – in the near future? And so on. . . .

On this page, you'll find a personal investment strategy checklist of things to take into account when choosing your investments.

Personal investment strategy checklist

Some investments only make sense for people of a certain age (annuities for the over-70's, say); others (eg school fees policies) are obviously only suited to those with children to educate. These are extreme cases of the ways in which your personal circumstances can shape your investments strategy – but there may be less dramatic repercussions too. Most people will be saving and investing for a number of purposes. Different investments may be suitable for each purpose – so most people ought to end up putting their money into a variety of investments. It's worth thinking about the points below, and reading the sections on keeping up with inflation (overleaf) and on risk (see p12), before you decide on a particular investment. And when comparing interest rates on different investments, see p15.

Age
If you are 50, for example, you are more likely to be concerned with saving up for retirement and thinking about how to invest any lump sum you get, than with building up a deposit for your first home. Your children are likely to be off your hands too, and you may have more spare cash to save than you had in your thirties.

Health
If you have a weak heart, for example, you may find it difficult (or expensive) to get the right kind or amount of life insurance. You may want to supplement your life cover with additional savings. Investing through a life insurance policy is likely to be less worthwhile for you than for those in good health.

Family
You may want to save up (or invest a lump sum) for private education. And you need to think about how your assets will be passed on when you die. You may want to invest with an eye to building up a capital sum for your heirs to inherit.

Expectations
If you expect your income to drop at some point (when you start a family, perhaps, or when you retire), you may want to build up savings to draw on when you're hard up. On the other hand, if you expect a big rise in salary (when you get an additional qualification, say, or finish training) you may feel you can run down your savings a bit since you expect to be better off later. Or you may be coming into a large inheritance – and need to find a suitable home for it.

Tax
Some investments are unsuitable for non-taxpayers, while others may be particularly good for higher rate taxpayers. We cover tax in Chapter 4. Elderly people should look out for the effect of withdrawal of the age allowance – see p236.

What you want from your investments
If you want to build up a fund for next year's holiday, you probably need to consider a different range of investments from someone saving up for retirement, or to pass on a capital sum to their heirs. Similarly, if you are looking for a fixed income from your investments, you will select different investments from someone prepared to accept an income that varies with general interest rates. For more details, see p13.

How much you can invest
How much money can you afford to invest? Some investments are open to you only if you have a sufficiently large lump sum. And other investments are open only to those who can save a regular sum each month. Still others are more flexible and can take your savings as and when they arise.

How long you can invest for
Think carefully before you commit yourself to saving a definite amount each month for a long time (25 years, say), or locking up a lump sum for a lengthy period. All sorts of changes could happen over the period of the investment that might make it hard to continue, and most long-term savings plans penalise you if you cash in early.

Don't be taken in by ads

You may well come across advertisements similar to the one shown below.

The figures sound very attractive. The plan is worth £115,000 on retirement – providing you with a pension of £15,000 a year, or a lump sum of £35,000 plus a pension of £10,000 a year.

And the assumption about growth in your investment of 10 per cent a year may seem fairly reasonable.

But what will the money be worth when the plan ends in 20 years' time? Inflation could make mincemeat of the figures quoted in the advertisement. For example, if inflation averaged 10 per cent (the same as the assumed rate of growth) the £15,000 a year pension will be worth only £2,235 in 20 years. If inflation averaged 15 per cent, say, the £15,000 a year pension would be worth only £915.

Of course, the buying-power of your contributions will fall over the years and you could mitigate the effect of inflation, to some extent, by raising your contributions from time to time in line with inflation. And the value of your investment may grow by more than 10 per cent a year.

But looking behind adverts like this (and ones that tell you how a lump sum investment will grow) does illustrate the dramatic effect of inflation – something to be aware of when you're planning for some time in the future.

Keeping up with inflation

With some investments the value of the capital you invest stays the same – but, of course, this doesn't allow for the effects of inflation. If you invest £1,000 now, spend the income from the investment and get your £1,000 back in four years' time, it will be worth only £680 or so in terms of today's buying power if inflation averages 10 per cent or so a year. And (with the same rate of inflation) if you got your money back in 20 years' time, it would be worth only £150 in terms of today's buying power.

Looked at another way, an inflation rate of 10 per cent means that you have to see the value of your investments (after allowing for tax) rise by at least 10 per cent a year on average just for them to be worth the same to you in the future as they are now. That's a lot of running to have to do just to stay still.

The Diagram below shows the devastating effect of inflation – bear this in mind when considering how much your investments (or the income from them) will be worth in the future.

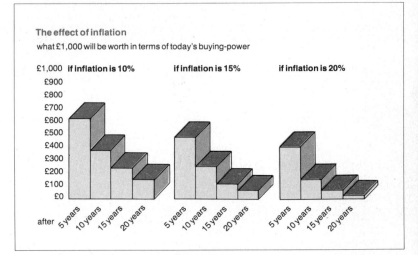

The effect of inflation
what £1,000 will be worth in terms of today's buying-power

There are three government-run investments which can give protection against rising prices. They all have limitations which mean that they're unlikely to meet all your investment needs. For details, see Chapter 21 and Chapter 10.

The main alternative is to take the risk of losing some of your capital in the hope that you will make a high enough profit to compensate for the effect of inflation.

The value of property, shares and *alternative investments* (such as stamps, antiques, diamonds and the like) should stand at least some chance of going up with prices in general. In the Diagram opposite, we compare the rates of return you might have got over different sample periods of time for various investments. You can see that – over the periods we've looked at – investments in 'things' (like your home, gold sovereigns, stamps) have done comparatively well. But bear in mind that with these types of investments, prices can go down as well as up. Read the section on *Risk* overleaf, for advice on how you can minimise the risks you are taking.

Of course, you may be prepared to put up with a drop in purchasing power because, for example, you're looking for a particularly 'safe' investment, or you want to be able to withdraw your money at short notice (eg for your emergency fund).

Investments compared

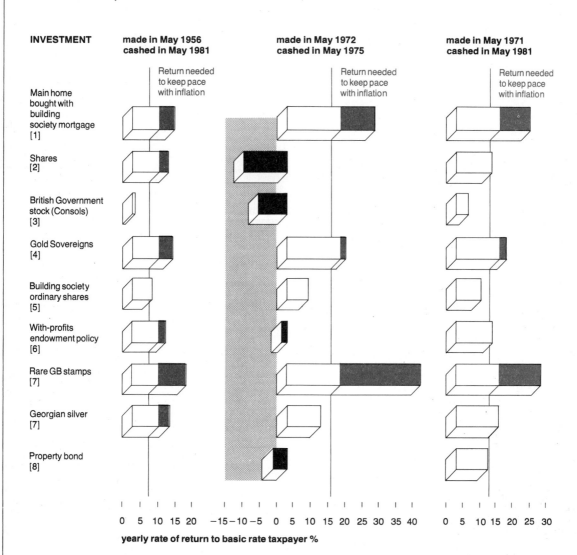

INVESTMENT	made in May 1956 cashed in May 1981	made in May 1972 cashed in May 1975	made in May 1971 cashed in May 1981
Main home bought with building society mortgage [1]			
Shares [2]			
British Government stock (Consols) [3]			
Gold Sovereigns [4]			
Building society ordinary shares [5]			
With-profits endowment policy [6]			
Rare GB stamps [7]			
Georgian silver [7]			
Property bond [8]			

Return needed to keep pace with inflation

0 5 10 15 20   −15 −10 −5 0 5 10 15 20 25 30 35 40   0 5 10 15 20 25 30

yearly rate of return to basic rate taxpayer %

Information provided by: Abbey Life Assurance; Bristol & West Building Society; Nationwide Building Society; Norwich Union Insurance Group; B A Seaby Ltd; *The Alternative Investment Report* (published by Robin Duthy)

[1] Based on average house prices. Allows for buying and selling costs. Costs such as maintenance, rates and insurance not included. Schedule A tax (payable by owner-occupiers before 1963) not taken into account. Assumes 25-year, 80 per cent repayment mortgage is taken out at the start of each period. Based on mortgage interest rates recommended by The Building Societies Association and tax relief at basic rate

[2] Based on The Actuaries' Investment Index and Financial Times Actuaries All-Share Index. Assumes income reinvested and allows for buying and selling costs. No allowance for capital gains tax
[3] Assumes income reinvested and allows for buying and selling costs
[4] Bought and sold via a dealer. Queen Victoria 1887 Jubilee sovereigns in exceptionally fine condition. No allowance for insurance and storage costs
[5] Assumes income reinvested
[6] Policy offered by particular insurance company. Taken out by man aged 29. Allows for tax relief (or premium subsidy) on premiums, and where applicable, terminal bonus.

[7] Based on yearly averages (not May-to-May) of prices fetched at auction for a selection of rare items in first-class condition after deduction of 10 per cent commission paid by seller to auctioneer. Includes some estimated prices where reliable data does not exist. No allowance for storage and insurance costs or for any buyers' commission
[8] Based on longest running property bond (introduced 1967). Allows for buying and selling costs and for capital gains tax.

Risk

One of the major risks you face is seeing the purchasing power of your investments drop over time as a result of inflation (see p10). This applies to practically any investment. But there are two additional risks you face.

Risk to capital

The value of what you've invested in shares, unit trusts, property and so on is likely to fluctuate. You may find that when you need to cash in your investment the value of, say, your shares or unit trusts is particularly low. Alternative investments (eg antiques, jewellery, Persian carpets) are at risk in this way too – when you want to sell, you may not be able to find a buyer at a price which gives you a reasonable return. And a dealer's mark-up may be particularly high.

Risk to income

The size of the interest (or dividend) you get may vary considerably, depending on the performance of the company, fund, investment or whatever. In the worst case, you might get no income from the investments at all.

What to do

The golden rule is to spread your money around. Decide first what proportion of your capital (if any) you are prepared to put into risky investments, what proportion you want in safe ones. Accepting a degree of risk is, in the main, a price you have to pay to stand at least some chance of maintaining the buying-power of your investments.

Aim to spread your money among different types of investments – eg property bonds, unit trusts, building societies. Particularly with risky-type investments, try to put your money with a number of different companies issuing each type of investment. Also try to stagger investing over a long period (at least a year, preferably longer). By spreading your investments in these ways you'll reduce your risk of doing very badly. Bear in mind though that you'll also reduce your chances of doing extraordinarily well.

If you decide to go for a relatively high-risk investment (like shares or alternative investments), don't be tempted to withdraw your emergency fund from its safe home and put it at risk too. This should cut down the risk of having to sell all your investments (because there's a hole in your roof) when prices are low. And steer clear of direct investment in shares unless you've got a substantial amount to invest – see p81.

If you know you'll need your money on a particular future date, be prepared to cash in investments beforehand – a few years in advance, if need be – ideally at a time when their value is high. If you wait until you need the money, you may find you have to cash your investments when prices are low.

Investing your emergency fund

When deciding on a home for this part of your capital, you want to look for three things:
- safety – no risk that when you cash in you'll get fewer £££ back than you put in
- instant accessibility – you don't usually get even two weeks' notice of an emergency, so you want to be able to get the money back on the spot, or at most in a couple of days
- highest possible return – but you'll have to be prepared to take less than you'd get for an investment that ties your money up longer.

See the Route Maps on pages 18 and 20 for some suggestions. Remember to update the amount of money you keep in reserve for emergencies regularly. Inflation will erode its buying power.

What do you want from your investments?

Most people want either income or capital gain from their investments – perhaps both. To some extent, the line between wanting income and wanting capital growth is an artificial one. After all, you can always cash in some of your investments from time to time to give you income. And if you reinvest income from your investments the value of your capital should go up over time. There are tax differences, though. For details, see Box overleaf.

Investing for income

You need to consider how long you're likely to go on needing the income from your investments. If it's for more than a couple of years, you can't afford to ignore the effect of inflation on the purchasing power of any income your investments produce. You'll need a rising income. To achieve this, you are likely to have to put some of your capital at risk. It may be sensible to invest part of your money for capital growth, with a view to cashing part of it in on a regular basis to provide income.

You have to make your own choice about how much of your capital to risk. Put the remainder in a place where the income from it will be safe – see the Route Map on p18 for suggestions.

If you don't anticipate having to rely on your extra investment income for longer than a year or two, you may well decide there is no point taking risks to get an income that will keep up with inflation.

If you don't pay tax, some investments may not give you such a good return as they do to taxpayers. We have marked these investments with ● in the Route Maps on pages 18 and 20 – but check that things have not changed since we went to press.

On the other hand some investments, where the return is tax-free, look more attractive the higher your rate of tax. These investments are marked with ○ in the Route Maps. Check in the Route Maps (and with current rates of return) that your investments are giving you as good a return as possible.

Investing for capital growth

You may want capital growth to give you:
● income later
● more to pass on to your heirs
● a fund to buy something.

Income later

If you're going to need your capital to give you an income later, you can't afford to risk all of it. But you do need to try to make up for the effects of inflation on its buying-power over the years between now and the time you plan to use it.

You should consider investing part of your money in National Savings Certificates (2nd Index-linked Issue). With this investment, the value of what you've invested is adjusted each

Cashing in investments to give income

With certain lump sum investments (eg single-premium bonds), it's possible to cash in part of the investment each year to give yourself an income. But note that with, for example, single-premium bonds or unit trusts which run a withdrawal scheme, because the value of your investment fluctuates, you may have to cash in a higher proportion of your investment from time to time – or else face a drop in your income. And if you cash in more than the growth of your bond, you'll be eating into your capital.

With other investments (eg shares, alternative investments etc) there are no special schemes. And you may get a poor price at the time you want to cash part of the investment to provide income.

Building capital by reinvesting income

As the tax system stands at present, if you invest for income with a view to reinvesting it to build up capital, you may pay more tax than if you had got an equivalent rise in value through a straight capital gain. Rates of tax on investment income in the 1982-83 tax year range from 30 to 75 per cent.

The first £5,000 of capital gains you make by disposing of assets in the tax year are tax-free – and above that the rate of capital gains tax is 30 per cent. So if you pay tax at higher rates or the investment income surcharge it may be sensible to invest for capital gain rather than income.

month in line with inflation (provided you've held the certificate for at least a year). You can invest up to £5,000 (April 1982). A married couple can each invest up to the maximum – ie up to £10,000 in all. You could also consider index-linked British Government stocks – see Chapter 10.

If you have capital left over, it makes sense to put some of your money into investments which may give a return high enough to make up for inflation. To minimise the chances of all your risky investments doing a nose-dive at once, follow the advice on p12.

More for your heirs

You may feel you can take risks with more of your capital for longer if your primary aim is to pass money on to your heirs.

What you need to be particularly aware of is the impact of capital transfer tax on what your heirs will get when you die – though it won't strike unless what you leave (together with taxable gifts made in the 10 years before your death) tops £55,000. To minimise the effect of capital transfer tax, consider:
- giving away each year as much as it is allowed without incurring any liability to capital transfer tax
- taking out life insurance with the proceeds going straight to your children
- leaving your possessions directly to the youngest generation (your grandchildren rather than your children) if you want the possessions to go to them eventually.

For more details on capital transfer tax, see p60.

A fund to buy something

If you are investing in order to buy something in the future, bear in mind that the value of some investments (eg shares, property, alternative investments) tend to fluctuate, so you may find that when you want to cash in your investments the return is not very good. It makes sense to steer clear of these if the time when you are going to want to use the money is very close at hand.

If on the other hand, you'll need the money in, say, 10 years' time, you could still go for investments which fluctuate in value – but be prepared to cash the investments *before* you need the money (preferably when they're doing well). Don't be forced into cashing your investment when its value is depressed – eg by a slump in the share or property markets.

And before you decide to take extra risks with your capital, in the hope of getting a greater gain, consider borrowing money to buy now rather than waiting until you have built up a larger fund.

Review your investments regularly

You can't assume that the best investments for you today will still be the best in a few months' time. For example, the rates of return offered by different investments will change. New types of investment may come on the market. Tax laws may change too. Inflation will mean that your investments need topping up. And changes in your circumstances, not to mention the effect of external factors (like political pressures throughout the world) could make a nonsense of your original choices. So it's vital to keep an eye on what's happening and change your investments when necessary.

Sorting out interest rates

The rates of interest quoted for many investments aren't strictly comparable, because they don't make any allowance for how frequently interest is paid out or re-invested.

The more frequently interest is paid out to you, the sooner you get the use of the money (to spend or re-invest) so the benefit to you is greater. If interest is re-invested it can start earning interest itself sooner – so your overall return is higher. A 'true' return allows for frequency of payment, so that if an investment pays interest more frequently than once a year, the true yearly return will be slightly higher than the quoted interest rate.

With most building society accounts (apart from subscription shares), most bank deposit and savings accounts, most local authority loans and most finance company deposits, interest is added twice a year (sometimes quarterly). And with some of these accounts you can ask for interest to be paid out monthly. Table 1 below shows the difference this would make if you had £1,000 invested for up to ten years.

Note that the true return is the same whether interest is paid out to you or reinvested – it's the frequency which matters.

For investments like those mentioned above which don't quote a true interest rate and which pay interest more frequently than once a year, use Table 2 to find the true interest rate. See next column for investments which do quote a true return.

How to boost your return

If you invest in something where there is a choice as to how often interest is paid out (eg with some building society accounts you can ask to have interest paid monthly instead of half-yearly) it's best to go for the most frequent interval. If you don't actually want to spend the money immediately you can re-invest it – in building society ordinary shares or subscription shares, for example. That way, the interest paid out from your main investment will itself start earning interest much sooner. For example, if you had £1,000 in a building society 2-year term share which paid 10% interest and re-invested it twice yearly, you would have £1215.51 after 2 years (a true rate of 10.25%). If on the other hand you asked for the interest to be paid out monthly and you paid it into a building society subscription share account paying 10½%, you would have £1220.63 after two years – an

overall true rate of 10.48%. Over longer periods of time, the difference would increase.

Which investments quote true returns?

The returns quoted on some investments are true returns – and can be compared directly with one another. This applies to National Savings Certificates, redemption yields on British Government stock and estimated returns on investment-type life insurance. And the rates quoted on investments where interest is added just once a year are also true – eg most building society subscription shares.

Note that with National Savings Bank accounts, interest is paid once a year, but only for complete calendar months – so if you pay in or withdraw money during a month the true return may be *lower* than the quoted rate.

Table 1: how £1,000 grows if interest at 10% is added

	yearly	half-yearly	quarterly	monthly
after 1 year	£1100	£1102	£1104	£1105
after 2 years	£1210	£1216	£1218	£1220
after 5 years	£1611	£1629	£1639	£1645
after 10 years	£2594	£2653	£2685	£2708
true return	**10%**	**10.25%**	**10.38%**	**10.47%**

Table 2: true rates of return

quoted rate	true rate		
	if interest is paid out or added		
%	half yearly %	quarterly %	monthly %
8	8.16	8.24	8.30
9	9.20	9.31	9.38
10	10.25	10.38	10.47
11	11.30	11.46	11.57
12	12.36	12.55	12.68
13	13.42	13.65	13.80
14	14.49	14.75	14.93

2 Investment choices

To help narrow down the choice of investments to those which would be most suitable for you, use the Route Maps on pages 18 and 20. One is for lump sums, the other for savings (either on a regular basis or piecemeal).

Follow the Route Maps for each sum of money you want to invest – eg your emergency fund, money you're willing to see fluctuate in value, money you know you will be able to invest for five years, and so on. You'll end up with a different shortlist for each sum.

Next, turn to the Table starting on p26 for a bird's-eye view of the investments on each of your shortlists. The columns of the Table are explained on p24.

For any investments which you think might suit you, read the relevant chapter in the book. Then find out what is happening to that investment at the moment. In each chapter, we tell you where to get more information. And check in the newspapers for the up-to-date rates of return being offered by the investments you have in mind.

Armed with these facts, narrow down the investments on your shortlists to those which suit you best. Don't forget that work on your investments doesn't end there – you'll need to keep them under review to make sure that they continue to suit you.

To show you how this can be done, we follow the investment decisions of Roger and Rose Steele who want to find homes for both a lump sum and for their savings. Their strategy and decisions will be followed through from start to finish. The remaining six examples look at only one of the problems each family faces. Three families have to invest lump sums of varying sizes; with the other three, it's savings of various amounts which are presenting difficulties.

Of course, your own final choice out of the shortlist each family ends up with, might – because of your own particular preferences – be different from that given in our examples.

Roger and Rose Steele have one child Alex. Roger earns around £10,000 a year at the local engineering works. They want to save for quite a few things – a holiday next year, and then a car, new furniture and so on. They don't want to lock their money away for too long. They've already got some money saved up in a building society ordinary share account and wonder whether that's the best place for it.

How Roger and Rose decide what to do with their money
They follow the investment priorities checklist on p8:

Both Roger and Rose have life insurance cover. They have policies which will pay out lump sums and a regular income if either dies
At present they have £2,100 put aside in a building society ordinary share account. But they feel that £500 is as much as they need in an emergency fund
Roger and Rose are buying their own home with a mortgage and don't intend to move in the next few years
Roger is in his employer's pension scheme – which offers quite good benefits
Roger and Rose would like to save something each month. So they've got to decide how to invest:
● their £500 emergency fund
● the additional £1,600 lump sum
● the money they manage to save.
They use the personal investment strategy checklist (see p9) to help sort out their investment plan.
● age – Roger is 34 and Rose 28. Rose is hoping to go back to teaching when Alex, their 3-year-old, goes to school – but of course teaching posts are much sought

after, so they're not going to rely on her getting one
● health – both are in good health
● family – apart from Alex, there are no immediate dependants. But they feel that if any of the parents were widowed or became ill, they'd like to help out. At the moment, this prospect seems unlikely, but it means they don't feel like committing themselves to very long-term savings – which they might not be able to keep up if they do have to help out. They don't intend giving Alex a private education. If they did, they would consider saving in a school-fees scheme
● expectations – Rose would like to work again, and if she can't get a job teaching, would like to consider some sort of retraining. This might involve some expense – they don't really know. There are no large inheritances coming their way – though eventually they will share in the proceeds from the sale of their parents' houses
● tax – Roger is a basic rate taxpayer, and any investment income won't put him into a higher tax bracket
● what they want from their investments – their main aims are: to pay for a holiday next year and later for a car and new furniture; to pay for any retraining that Rose may need in a couple of years or so; and to enable them to help out their parents should the need arise. They aren't looking for income from their investments
● how much they can invest – apart from the £2,100 in the building society, they reckon they can save about £50 a month – but most of this is earmarked for their holiday next year
● how long they can invest for – the Steeles have decided to keep £500 handy as an emergency fund. And

they need £40 a month of their regular savings available for their planned holiday. The other lump sum of £1,600 and £10-a-month regular savings can be invested for somewhat longer. But long-term investment clearly doesn't suit their needs.
As long as most of their money is safe, they don't mind taking a risk with some of it. Like everyone else, they're worried about inflation.
Once Roger and Rose have chosen their investments (see overleaf), they'll keep an eye on what's happening and may move their money around from time to time.

Route map for lump sums

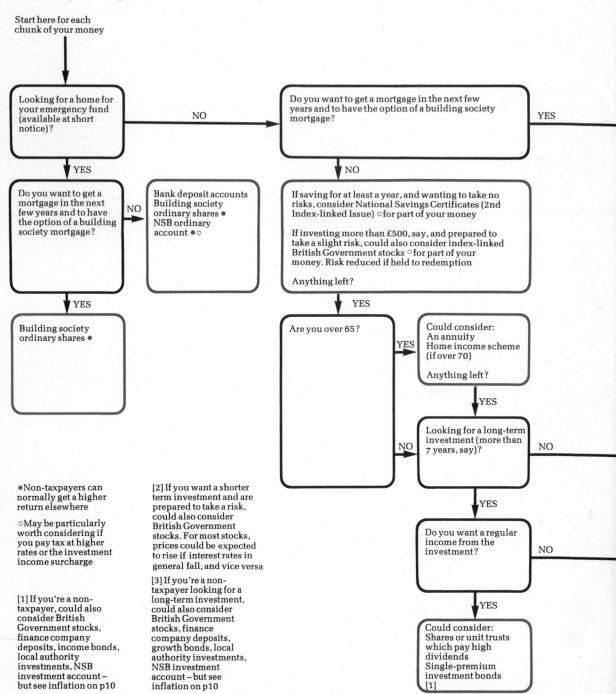

Start here for each
chunk of your money

Looking for a home for
your emergency fund
(available at short
notice)?

— NO → Do you want to get a mortgage in the next few
years and to have the option of a building society
mortgage?

— YES →

↓ YES

Do you want to get a
mortgage in the next
few years and to have
the option of a building
society mortgage?

— NO → Bank deposit accounts
Building society
ordinary shares ●
NSB ordinary
account ●○

↓ NO (from the right box)

If saving for at least a year, and wanting to take no
risks, consider National Savings Certificates (2nd
Index-linked Issue) ○ for part of your money

If investing more than £500, say, and prepared to
take a slight risk, could also consider index-linked
British Government stocks ○ for part of your
money. Risk reduced if held to redemption

Anything left?

↓ YES

Building society
ordinary shares ●

Are you over 65?

— YES → Could consider:
An annuity
Home income scheme
(if over 70)

Anything left?

↓ YES

Looking for a long-term
investment (more than
7 years, say)?

— NO →

↓ YES

Do you want a regular
income from the
investment?

— NO →

↓ YES

Could consider:
Shares or unit trusts
which pay high
dividends
Single-premium
investment bonds
[1]

(Are you over 65? — NO → Looking for a long-term investment)

●Non-taxpayers can
normally get a higher
return elsewhere

○May be particularly
worth considering if
you pay tax at higher
rates or the investment
income surcharge

[1] If you're a non-
taxpayer, could also
consider British
Government stocks,
finance company
deposits, income bonds,
local authority
investments, NSB
investment account –
but see inflation on p10

[2] If you want a shorter
term investment and are
prepared to take a risk,
could also consider
British Government
stocks. For most stocks,
prices could be expected
to rise if interest rates in
general fall, and vice versa

[3] If you're a non-
taxpayer looking for a
long-term investment,
could also consider
British Government
stocks, finance
company deposits,
growth bonds, local
authority investments,
NSB investment
account – but see
inflation on p10

How Roger and Rose choose their investments

Lump sum

First of all they try to sort out what to do with the £2,100 they have. They intend keeping £500 of this as an emergency fund and following the Route Map, they see there are three places they can put this money and get it out at short notice – a bank deposit account, building society ordinary shares, or an NSB ordinary account. They read about these and check on the rates of return currently offered by these alternatives. They choose building society ordinary shares – there's the added advantage of the society being open on Saturdays. They'll keep a close watch on rates of return in the future in case other investments offer a better return.

Now they follow the Route Map again to see what they could do with the £1,600. They decide they want to take no risks with part at least of this money, and see that they should consider National Savings Certificates (2nd Index-linked Issue). They're prepared to keep the money tied up for at least a year, and decide they'll put half of their spare lump sum in this investment. They'll look for something more speculative with

the rest. They decide to give index-linked British Government stocks a miss – being optimists, they're hoping for a return substantially better than inflation.

They arrive at the point on the Route Map where they're asked if they're looking for a shorter-term investment, and prepared to risk losing money for the chance of a capital gain on it. This suits them for the remaining £800 of their spare money. They see that suitable investments include shares, unit trusts and single premium investment bonds. Turning to the Table on p32 they see that they haven't got enough money to make a sensible investment in shares and they decide to choose between single-premium bonds and unit trusts – they feel they haven't enough to spread the money between the two. Roger believes that the prospects for commercial property are good – so they decide to plump for a single-premium bond specialising in property.

Regular saving

They follow the Route Map overleaf to see what to do with the £50 a month they reckon they'll be able to save. They come to the question – *Prepared to save a regular amount for 5 years or so?* – and decide they can commit the £10 a month they won't need for their holiday for this period. They choose to put it all in index-linked SAYE, but decide to split the money into two lots of £5 a month – so that if they can't keep up all their saving they'll still get index-linking on the half they can keep up. For their other £40 a month they end up with a shortlist of seven investments. After looking at the Table and checking on current interest rates, they decide that building society subscription shares will offer them the best overall return and the opportunity to withdraw their money at short notice without losing out.

Summary

They're going to invest £500 in building society ordinary shares, £800 in National Savings Certificates (2nd Index-linked Issue) and £800 in a property bond. They're going to save £40 a month in building society subscription shares and £10 a month in two index-linked SAYE contracts.

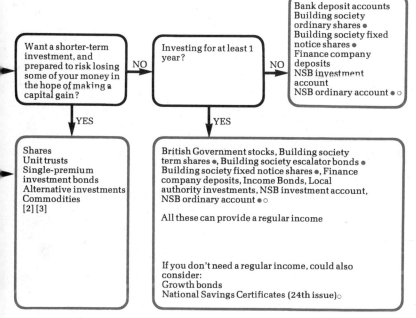

Route map for savings

Start here for each
chunk of your money

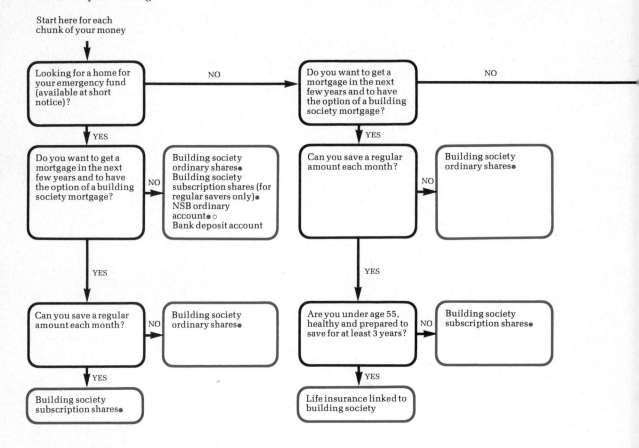

• Non-taxpayers can
normally get a higher
return elsewhere

○ May be particularly
worth considering if
you pay tax at higher
rates or the investment
income surcharge

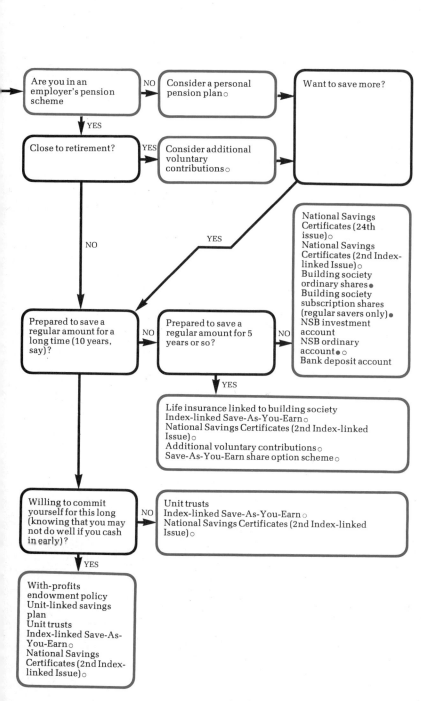

Are you in an employer's pension scheme
— NO → Consider a personal pension plan ○
— YES ↓

Close to retirement?
— YES → Consider additional voluntary contributions ○
— NO ↓

Want to save more?
— YES →

National Savings Certificates (24th issue) ○
National Savings Certificates (2nd Index-linked Issue) ○
Building society ordinary shares ●
Building society subscription shares (regular savers only) ●
NSB investment account
NSB ordinary account ● ○
Bank deposit account

Prepared to save a regular amount for a long time (10 years, say)?
— NO → Prepared to save a regular amount for 5 years or so?
— NO →

Prepared to save a regular amount for 5 years or so?
— YES ↓

Life insurance linked to building society
Index-linked Save-As-You-Earn ○
National Savings Certificates (2nd Index-linked Issue) ○
Additional voluntary contributions ○
Save-As-You-Earn share option scheme ○

Willing to commit yourself for this long (knowing that you may not do well if you cash in early)?
— NO → Unit trusts
Index-linked Save-As-You-Earn ○
National Savings Certificates (2nd Index-linked Issue) ○
— YES ↓

With-profits endowment policy
Unit-linked savings plan
Unit trusts
Index-linked Save-As-You-Earn ○
National Savings Certificates (2nd Index-linked Issue) ○

Anne Stevens is a basic rate taxpayer. She wants to go to Australia to see her daughter and her grandchildren. She finds out that the cheapest return fare is about £800. She can afford to save around £14 a month – and she's worried about how inflation will affect the air fare over the five years or so she reckons she'll have to save for.

She follows the Route Map until she comes to the question: *Prepared to save a regular amount for 5 years or so?* She sees she can choose between life insurance linked to building societies and index-linked SAYE. Looking at the Table on p28, she finds that index-linked SAYE guarantees to increase the value of her savings in line with the Retail Price Index – and decides to plump for this.

Anne realises that though the value of her savings will keep pace with inflation, she's likely to have to save for much longer than 5 years to build up enough money for the air fare. This is because the amount of her index-linked savings will start off at a much less than the air fare – ie £14 in the first month, £28 in the second month, and so on. So whereas she'll benefit from index-linking only on the amount already saved, inflation is likely to affect the whole of the £800 air fare from the start.

To try and make the saving period as short as possible. Anne decides that, whenever she has spare money she'll try to put it in something like building society ordinary shares – a suitable home for small, irregular sums of money. She also decides to approach her bank manager to see whether, once she's saved for some time, she could get a loan.

Paul and Sheila Plantin, in their late-40s, live in their own home, have an adequate emergency fund and enough insurance for their needs. They expect to pay tax on the top slice of their income at 45 per cent. Private school fees make a big dent in their income, and will continue to for some time. Sheila has just inherited £25,000. They want to invest £20,000 or so for their retirement and don't mind taking a bit of a risk. They'd like to get a regular income from this part of their investment, but are worried about extra income tax they might have to pay. They'll invest the remaining £5,000 with as little risk as possible (they're willing to tie this money up for five years or so).

First they follow the Route Map for their safe investment. They check investments with a ○ next to them carefully (these are particularly worth considering if you pay tax at higher rates or the investment income surcharge). They come early on to National Savings Certificates (2nd Index-linked Issue). They realise that the buying power of their money will be maintained; an added bonus is that after a year, they can withdraw some money (tax-free) if they need it. They see they should also consider index-linked British Government stocks if they're prepared to take a slight risk. They check on the current prices for the stocks, and find that for their rate of tax, the return should just beat inflation. They decide to put £2,500 into each of these index-linked investments, and resolve to try to hold the index-linked British Government stocks to redemption.

Next they follow the Route Map for their longer-term investment until they come to the question about whether they want a regular income – they see they can choose between shares, unit trusts and single-premium investment bonds. These are all investments which, hopefully, will rise in value in the long-term. They discover that if they invest in single-premium bonds, they can withdraw up to 5% of their investment each year for 20 years without paying tax. In 20 years' time, they'll have retired and are unlikely to be paying higher rates of tax – so may avoid paying any extra tax on this investment. They plan not to withdraw the full 5% each year – to leave themselves with a sizeable chunk of their investment when they retire. They decide to invest £10,000 split equally between a managed bond and a property bond.

They decide to invest £10,000 in unit trusts – ones that aim for capital growth rather than income. They plan to cash in some of their units each year, but to make sure that they don't make net capital gains of more than the £5,000 limit free of capital gains tax. As they approach retirement, they'll consider making additional voluntary contributions to Paul's pension scheme.

Mike and Sue English are in their late 20s, with one baby and another due soon. They pay no tax – and feel they've got little cash left over at the end of each month, what with food, rates, mortgage payments and so on. Mike is worried because they have no savings or life insurance.

For someone in Mike's position with dependants, life insurance should come before any attempt to save money. If Mike died, Sue would have to rely on social security to make ends meet. And if Sue were to die, Mike would have a hard time looking after the baby and going to work. They realise that investment-type life insurance is not really for them. With this firmly sorted out in their minds, they decide to go to an insurance broker to arrange protection-type life insurance, to cover them should one or other die.

They also decide to go to the local social security office and to their Town Hall to make sure that they're not missing out on any benefits available to them.

Next, they think about their emergency fund. They follow the Route Map on p20. They see that building society ordinary shares and NSB ordinary accounts each have ● beside them, indicating that non-taxpayers can normally get a higher return with other investments. That leaves bank deposit accounts. They check up on rates of interest and find that a bank deposit account currently offers a non-taxpayer a higher rate of return than the other investments. So they plump for that for any bits and pieces they can put aside.

Once they've built up a large enough emergency fund, they'll go through the Route Map again and look for a somewhat longer-term investment for their additional savings. They'll keep an eye on what happens to rates of return in the future – in particular, they'll keep an eye out for building society ordinary shares offering a higher rate of return to non-taxpayers than bank deposit accounts (which does happen from time to time).

Marianne Fortune, 21, has just inherited £3,000 from her grandmother. She's single, lives with her parents and has a large enough emergency fund. She's a basic rate taxpayer. She reckons that some time in the future she'll want to buy a home, and decides to put £2,000 towards this. She decides to try to turn the remaining £1,000 into something bigger – she's prepared to take risks with it.

She follows the Route Map for lump sums, and sees that if she wants to keep open the option of getting a building society mortgage, it might be wise to put the money ear-marked for her home in a building society account. She reads Chapter 6, and sees that she should check up on building society lending policies before she invests, and preferably split her money between two (or more) building societies. Since she already has her eye on the type of flat she'd like, she sorts out from a number of building societies the ones that seem most favourable. She feels she'll do best with fixed notice shares – and will be able to give the notice required.

She goes back to the Route Map, to see how she should invest the £1,000 she's going to gamble with. She's looking for a shorter-term investment but prepared to take a risk. She looks up the shortlisted investments in the Table and in the Chapters later in the book. She toys with investing her money in shares of just one company (a very risky strategy) or a commodity fund – but decides instead to put the £1,000 towards improving the 18th-century glass collection she started a couple of years ago.

Miss Simmons is aged 80, and lives alone. She lives on her pension and wonders what to do with the £5,000 she has to invest – which is at present in a bank deposit account. She's alarmed at the way inflation has made inroads into the buying-power of the interest she gets. She'd like to get a bit of extra income to allow herself a few more treats.

She realizes that she can leave some of her money in the bank deposit account to act as an emergency fund – but she reckons she won't need more than £300 for this. Thinking about it, though, she decides to leave twice this amount in her account – so that she can draw on it if she wants extra income.

Miss Simmons already owns her home, so doesn't need to worry about getting a mortgage. She's prepared to tie up her money for at least a year, and reckons that National Savings Certificates (2nd Index-linked Issue) will suit her very well. Although this investment does not pay out a regular income, she sees she could cash certificates to get an income. She realises that the value of what she invests will go up in line with

the Retail Price Index (though not if she cashes the certificates before a year is up). This index-linking seems a big plus to Miss Simmons. So she decides to put £2,000 into these and, after the first year, to cash bits of her investment if she feels particularly hard-pressed.

She decides not to put any money into index-linked British Government stocks – she wants to take no risks, and besides they don't pay a high income (nor can they be cashed cheaply in bits and pieces).

Since she's over 70, she could consider an annuity or cashing in on her home through a home income scheme. She's not really tempted by a home income scheme – she may want to move home later – so she decides to put the remaining £2,400 into an annuity. She realises that the income from this won't be protected against inflation. She decides to give more thought to moving to a smaller house, and investing any money from the sale to give her more income. She realises that there are heavy expenses involved in buying and selling property – and that she'll have to allow for these before going ahead.

Bob Mason, self-employed, earning around £7,000 a year, and his wife, Cathy, are in their mid-40s. Their 3 children have all left home and Cathy thinks it's time they started saving for Bob's retirement. They don't want to rely on their business for their retirement funds.

They already have an adequate emergency fund, and are buying their home with a mortgage. They follow the Route Map for saving to the question: *Are you in a employer's pension scheme?* Bob is self-employed – but neither is he contributing to a personal pension plan. He sees he'll get tax relief on the premiums he pays, and decides to put £20 a month into a scheme.

Cathy and Bob decide they'd like to save a bit more than this for their retirement – they reckon they could manage another £5 a month, and then bits and pieces less regularly. For their £5 a month, they're prepared to commit themselves for a long time, and consider the shortlist this leads them to: with-profits endowment policies, unit-linked savings plans, unit trusts, index-linked Save-As-You-Earn

and National Savings Certificates (2nd Index-linked Issue). They decide to go for regular savings in a unit trust. They realise this could be a risky choice – but they're hoping it may be worth it. They feel it's more flexible than a unit-linked savings plan. They decide to add odd savings to their building society ordinary share account (where they've got their emergency fund). When they've built up a big enough lump sum, they'll go through the lump-sum Route Map.

3 A bird's eye view

The hard work in putting your investment strategy into effect starts now. You'll have to get to grips with the nitty-gritty of what different investments offer and what their particular advantages and disadvantages are.

In this chapter we give you a summary of the main types of investment open to you, starting on page 26. The most important points about each investment are picked out in the Table (see below for why each column is important).

In the later chapters of the book you'll find much fuller details of each type of investment.

The columns in the Table

For regular saving or lump sum?

Some investments are very flexible. The minimum amount you can invest is fairly low – so they can be used as homes for lump sums, regular savings and odd bits of spare cash.

Bur some investments are open only to people who have a fair-sized lump sum of money to invest, and others only to people who want to save a regular amount each month or year, say. Of course, if you've a lump sum you can invest it bit by bit on a regular basis, if you like.

Minimum investment

This column tells you the minimum sensible amount you can invest. This isn't necessarily the same thing as the minimum amount you're *allowed* to invest. For example, you can invest as little as you like in shares, but the commission you have to pay makes an investment of less than £700 or so, less worthwhile.

Does it pay a regular income?

Some investments pay income direct to you at regular intervals. With others, the income is added to the value of what you first invested.

Of course, with some investments which don't pay an income out to you (eg single-premium bonds, index-linked National Savings Certificates), you may still be able to give yourself a regular income by cashing part of your investment at regular intervals – indeed, with some investments (such as single-premium bonds) there are often standard schemes to allow you to do this.

With some investments which pay out a regular income, the income is fixed when you take out the investment (eg local authority loans). With other investments (eg building societies) the income can vary after you've invested your money.

If you need to be sure of getting a regular number of £££ from your investment each year, go for one that pays out a fixed income – but see *Keeping up with inflation* on p10.

Note that if you go for a fixed income, you may regret your decision if interest rates in general rise – investments with interest rates which vary may turn out to have been better bets. On the other hand, if interest rates in general fall, you will feel pleased with yourself for putting your money in a fixed income investment.

How long is the investment meant to be for? This column tells you how long you should expect to have to leave your money invested in order to get the best return.

How quickly can you get your money back? In some cases, the answer is you can't. So don't put your money in one of these investments unless you're certain you'll be able to leave it there for the agreed period.

With other investments, you may be able to cash in early but not get back (or not be sure of getting back) what you paid in. So, if you want a certain amount of money at a certain time – eg to go on holiday in two years' time – you'd be wise to steer clear of these investments too.

Does value of capital fluctuate? Investments can be divided into two types:
● the value of the capital you invest stays the same (but see *Keeping up with inflation* on p10)
● the value may fluctuate. Unit trusts, single-premium bonds and Krugerrands are examples of investments where the value of the capital invested will fluctuate. With investments like these, you stand a chance of making a capital gain, but also run the risk of losing some of your money.

And because the value of the capital fluctuates, the success of your investment depends very much on *when* you invest and *when* you cash your investment. For more about how to reduce the risk of doing very badly see p12.

Points about tax This column picks out particular tax points for the various investments. More details on tax are given in Chapter 5, and in the chapters dealing with each investment.

Certain investments are more suitable for taxpayers than for those who don't pay tax – so non-taxpayers should beware of investments in the Route Maps on pages 18 and 20 which have ● next to them. Other investments, where the return is tax-free, look more attractive the higher the rate of tax. This also applies to investments where you get tax relief on the payments you make – for example, contributions to an employer's pension scheme, payments to a personal pension plan, interest on loans to buy your own home. All these investments are marked with ○ on the Route Maps.

Where you can get the investment This column tells you where to go to put your money in these investments.

Other comments This gives snippets of information about how some of the investments work, who might find it worthwhile to consider or to avoid a particular investment, and so on.

type of investment (and where to find more details)	for regular saving or lump sum?	minimum investment [1]	does it pay a regular income?	how long is investment meant to be for?	how quickly can you get your money back?
Alternative investments (eg stamps, oriental rugs, diamonds, gold . . .) *Chapter 7*, p70	lump sum	varies	no – in fact you have to pay for insurance etc. But see *other comments*	in the main, long-term investment	as quickly as you can find a buyer (with gold coin or bullion, relatively easy to find). But may get back less than you invested
Annuities *Chapter 16*, p150	lump sum	[2]	yes, normally arranged at time you buy the annuity. The older you are at that time, the higher the income – see also *other comments*	until you die	you can't – once you've made investment you can't cash it in
Bank deposit accounts *Chapter 20*, p189	either	often £1, but see *other comments*	no – but interest is added to capital at regular intervals and can be withdrawn. Interest can vary	any period – a home for emergency funds and a temporary home for other funds	in practice, with most banks at once – but may lose some interest
British Government stocks *Chapter 10*, p102 See also *Index-linked investments* overleaf	lump sum	none [4]	yes – income fixed at the time you buy the stock (except with a few stocks [5])	until stock due to be redeemed (paid back) by government – but some stocks can also be short-term speculation [6]	can sell stock at any time. Can take a day or two to get money if sold through stockbroker, a week or so through National Savings Stock Register
Building societies *Chapter 19*, p180 – escalator bonds	lump sum	normally £500 to £1,000	with some schemes, you can choose to have interest paid out to you. Otherwise reinvested. Interest can vary	up to 4 or 5 years; interest rate you get increases the longer you keep money invested	varies – may have to give up to 3 months' notice
– fixed notice shares	lump sum	normally £500 to £2,000	not normally	any period	normally 1 to 3 months' notice. May lose some interest if less notice given
– life insurance linked to building societies	regular saving	£3 to £8 a month	no	best return under 1982–83 tax rules is after 4 years	can cash in any time. But if cash in within 4 years, may have to pay back some of premium subsidy – see *other comments*
– ordinary shares	either	normally £1	you can choose to have interest paid out to you or reinvested. Interest can vary	any period – a home for emergency funds and a temporary home for other funds	in theory, with most societies, a month; in practice, on the spot or in a few days
– subscription shares	regular saving	normally £1 a month (maximum often £50 a month)	no	normally any period, but may get higher interest rate if save for more than certain period (eg 2 years)	see *ordinary shares* above
– term shares	lump sum	often £500 or £1,000	you can normally choose to have interest paid out or reinvested. Interest can vary	generally 2, 3, 4 or 5 years	with most societies you can't, until end of term (though your heirs get it if you die)

See p32 for footnotes

does value of capital fluctuate?	points about tax	where can you get investment?	other comments	
yes	No capital gains tax unless value of item at time of disposal more than £3,000 (post-1837 UK gold sovereigns free of capital gains tax). If count as trader, may have to pay income tax	auctions, dealers, other collectors.	need expert knowledge. Watch out for dealer's mark-up. With gold and diamonds can now invest indirectly through insurance-linked bond (can cash part for income). With gold, can invest directly on new gold commodities market	**Alternative investments** (eg stamps, oriental rugs, diamonds, gold . . .)
not applicable – can't get capital back	income made up of two parts – interest on capital and return of part of capital. Only interest part is taxable – normally paid after deduction of basic rate tax [3]	life insurance company or broker	only worth considering for older people (over 65, say). Man gets higher income than woman of same age.	**Annuities**
no	interest is taxable – but paid without deduction of tax	High-Street bank, National Girobank	you don't need a current account at the bank to open a deposit account – except with National Girobank. May get higher interest with special schemes, but minimum deposit can be high – £500, £1,000 or £5,000, say	**Bank deposit accounts**
yes – but if you hold stock until redemption, you know for certain what you'll get back	interest is taxable – paid without deduction of tax if bought through National Savings Stock Register, normally after deduction of basic rate tax if bought through stockbroker. May be liable for capital gains tax if stock held for less than a year	stockbroker, post office, High-Street bank or other agent (eg accountant)	best stock for you depends to large extent on rate of tax you pay. Get advice on which stock to choose – eg from stockbroker, bank. Buying and selling costs less for small investments if made through National Savings Stock Register	**British Government stocks**
				Building societies
no	building society pays tax on interest before it's paid out to you. If you pay tax at higher rates, or investment income surcharge, have to pay extra tax. If pay no tax (or less than deducted) can't claim tax back	building society	normally pays higher rate of interest than ordinary shares – say ½% higher in first year, 2% higher in fourth	**– escalator bonds**
no	see *escalator bonds* above	building society	normally pays ½% to 1½% more than ordinary shares	**– fixed notice shares**
no	return tax-free so long as pay tax at no more than the basic rate – always tax-free if keep policy going for at least 10 years, or three-quarters of its term, whichever is less	life insurance company, building society	government subsidises premiums (see p51) so more is invested in building society than premiums cost you. But policy is less worthwhile if you are 60 or more, or in poor health	**– life insurance linked to building societies**
no	see *escalator bonds* above	building society	also consider *fixed notice shares* above	**– ordinary shares**
no	see *escalator bonds* above	building society	normally pays 1¼% more interest than ordinary shares	**– subscription shares**
no	see *escalator bonds* above	building society	normally pays higher rate of interest than ordinary shares – say, 1% higher for a 3-year term. Also consider *escalator bonds* above.	**– term shares**

type of investment (and where to find more details)	for regular saving or lump sum?	minimum investment [1]	does it pay a regular income?	how long is investment meant to be for?	how quickly can you get your money back?
Commodities *Chapter 11*, p110 **– direct investment**	lump sum	[7]	no	in the main short-term speculation	can sell at any time
– commodity funds	lump sum	£1,000, say	varies with fund. Some pay an income – with others you can get income by cashing units	long-term investment or short-term speculation	varies with fund – a few days or a month
Endowment policies *Chapter 13*, p124	regular saving	£5 a month, say	no	10 years or more – period usually agreed at outset. *Flexible policies* have guaranteed cash-in value – usually after 10 years	can cash in policy at any time but what you get back is often at discretion of company (and in first year or two may get little or nothing)
Finance company deposits *Chapter 20*, p189	in the main, lump sum	[8]	yes – can choose to have interest paid out to you. Interest usually fixed if invest for agreed period. Otherwise can vary	[8]	with deposits made for agreed period, you can't. With other deposits, varies
Home *Chapter 6*, p62	either	normally at least 10% of price of home	no (unless you let it out)	any period	may take several months or longer to sell your home
Home income schemes *Chapter 16*, p154	lump sum [10]	[11]	yes – income (from an annuity) arranged at the time you take out the scheme (depends on age and sex)	until you die	you can't
Income and growth bonds *Chapter 15*, p148	lump sum	often £500	income bonds – yes growth bonds – no	fixed period, often 4 to 10 years	with some companies, at the end of agreed period only. With others, can cash in early – but return up to company
Index-linked investments – National Savings Certificates (2nd Index-linked Issue) *Chapter 21*, p194	either	£10 (maximum £5,000)	no – but can cash certificates to get an income	initially for 5 years (get bonus of at least 4% of original investment at end of 5 years). Can keep money invested	around a couple of weeks (but certificates not index-linked if cashed in before held for 12 months)
– index-linked Save-As-You-Earn (Third Issue) *Chapter 21*, p196	regular saving	£4 a month (maximum £50 a month)	no	5 years of saving – can leave money invested for further 2 years (can take out new scheme at same time)	around a couple of weeks (but if cash in before 5 years are up, no index-linking – get interest at 6% instead)
– index-linked British Government stocks *Chapter 10*, p107	lump sum	none [4] [17]	yes – and income increases in line with Retail Price Index	until stock due to be redeemed (paid back) by government – but can sell earlier	can sell stock at any time. Can take a day or two to get money if sold through stockbroker, a week or so through National Savings Stock Register [17]

See p32 for footnotes

does value of capital fluctuate?	points about tax	where can you get investment?	other comments	
				Commodities
yes	gain may be taxed as earned or investment income or as capital gain, depending on circumstances	commodity broker	investing directly in commodities not sensible for most people. Very risky	– **direct investment**
yes	see *Chapter 11*, p116	direct from fund, or through insurance broker, stockbroker etc	for legal and tax reasons, funds based offshore – Isle of Man or Channel Islands, say	– **commodity funds**
get at least a guaranteed amount at end of policy (or if you die) – more if policy is a with-profits one	return tax-free so long as pay tax at no more than the basic rate – always tax-free if keep policy going for at least 10 years or three-quarters of its term, whichever is less	life insurance company or insurance broker	government subsidises premiums on most regular-premium policies (see p51). Non-profit policies not recommended. With-profits policies better value	Endowment policies
no	interest is taxable. Depending on finance company, may be paid after deduction of basic rate tax	finance company or other company licensed to take deposits	[9]	Finance company deposits
yes	with only or main home, currently get tax relief on interest on up to £25,000 of loans to buy or improve it – and capital gain is normally tax-free.	estate agent, newspaper ads, *For sale* signs	proved a very good long-term investment in the past – see p64.	Home
[12]	get tax relief on mortgage interest, or if not a taxpayer, can get an option mortgage. For tax on annuity, see *annuities* p27	insurance broker	for how schemes work, see p154. Only worth considering for older people (over 70, say)	Home income schemes
no	tax treatment depends on how bonds work – can work in one of several ways. Check with company before investing.	life insurance company or broker	return can be lower if you're over 65 when you cash bond in (see p236 and 237)	Income and growth bonds
yes – but won't get back less than invested	return tax-free	post office, Trustee Savings Bank	value goes up in line with Retail Price Index – even after initial 5-year term is up.	Index linked investments – **National Savings Certificates** (2nd Index-linked Issue)
yes	return tax-free	post office High-Street bank, your employer	at end of 5 years, value of each payment increased in line with increase in Retail Price Index since payment made – continues to be index-linked if held for further 2 years (at end of which you get a bonus of 2 monthly payments). Will continue to be index-linked even after 7 years	– **index-linked Save-As-You-Earn** (Third Issue)
yes – but see *other comments* if stock held to redemption	see *British Government stocks* on p27	stockbroker, High Street bank or other agent (eg accountant) [17]	at redemption, government pays back *nominal value* (see p106) increased in line with Retail Price Index since time of issue. Get advice before investing	– **index-linked British Government stocks**

type of investment (and where to find more details)	for regular saving or lump sum?	minimum investment [1]	does it pay a regular income?	how long is investment meant to be for?	how quickly can you get your money back?
Local authority investments *Chapter 12*, p137 **– local authority loans** (often called bonds)	lump sum	£100 to £1,000, say	yes – interest fixed at the time you invest	agreed period – normally between 1 and 7 years	you normally can't (though your heirs may be able to if you die)
– yearling bonds and **local authority stocks**	lump sum	[13]	yes – income fixed at time you invest (except with a few stocks [5])	as for British Government stocks (but redeemed by local authority)	can sell on Stock Exchange. Takes a day or two to get your money
National Savings Bank *Chapter 22*, p206 **– ordinary accounts**	either	£1 (maximum £10,000)	no – but interest can be withdrawn. Interest can vary	any period – a home for emergency funds, a temporary home for other funds	£100 at once (about a week to withdraw all money)
– investment accounts	either	£1 (maximum £200,000)	no – but interest can be withdrawn. Interest can vary	any period over a month	1 month
National Savings Certificates (24th issue) *Chapter 22*, p199 (For 2nd Index-linked issue see *Index-linked* investments.)	either	£25 (maximum £2,500)	no	best return 5 years	around a couple of weeks (but return lower if cash in within first 5 years)
Pension schemes – employer's *Chapter 17*, p156	regular saving; can't stop paying as long as you're in the job	[14]	yes, from time you retire. Can often choose to have lump sum on retirement instead of part of pension	from time you join scheme until retirement (income carries on for life)	contributions must stay invested until retirement (unless you leave job within 5 years of joining scheme)
– personal pension plans *Chapter 18*, p164	either	varies – often £100 a year	yes – normally from any age between 60 and 75. Can choose to have lump sum on retirement instead of part of pension	from time you make payments until income starts (income carries on for life)	you can't cash investment in, but with some schemes you can get a loan (see p169)
– state *Chapter 17*, p159	regular saving	[15]	yes, from retirement age (later if you put off retirement)	you normally make payments until income starts (income carries on for life)	you can't cash investment in
Premium bonds *Chapter 22*, p203	either	£5 (maximum £10,000)	no – but might win prizes	any period – but can't win prize until bond held for 3 months	around a couple of weeks
Save-As-You-Earn share option scheme *Chapter 8*, p90	regular saving	£10 a month (maximum £50 a month)	no	5 or 7 years of saving	around a couple of weeks (but if cash in before 5 years are up, get lower return)

See p32 for footnotes

does value of capital fluctuate?	points about tax	where can you get investment?	other comments	
				Local authority investments
no	interest is taxable – normally paid after deduction of basic rate tax	local authority	doesn't have to be your own local authority that you invest in	**– local authority loans** (often called bonds)
as for British Government stocks	interest is taxable – paid after deduction of basic rate tax. May be liable for capital gains tax on any gain.	stockbroker (or local authority for stocks when stock first issued)	local authority stocks are alternative to British Government stocks – but normally give slightly higher return. Yearling bonds usually last a year or so. Some stocks difficult to sell	**– yearling bonds** and **local authority stocks**
				National Savings Bank
no	first £70 interest each year is tax-free – all interest paid without deduction of tax	post office	interest paid only for complete calendar months money is invested	**– ordinary accounts**
no	all interest is taxable – paid without deduction of tax	post office	worth considering if you don't pay tax. But interest paid only for complete calendar months money is invested	**– investment accounts**
no	return is tax-free	post office High-Street bank		**National Savings Certificates** (24th issue)
				Pension schemes **– employer's**
not applicable with most schemes	get tax relief on payments. Pension taxed as earnings, paid after deduction of basic rate tax	employer	Membership of scheme often compulsory. Can choose to make *additional voluntary contributions* (see p158)	
with some schemes – yes, with others – no	get tax relief on payments – see p178. Pension taxed as earnings *not* investment income	life insurance company or insurance broker	for self-employed and people who won't get a pension from their job	**– personal pension plans**
not applicable – can't get capital back	don't get tax relief on payments. Pension taxed as earnings, currently paid without deduction of tax	payments made through employer, or by stamp if self-employed	if you're earning, normally no way you can opt out of the State scheme	**– state**
no	prizes are tax-free	post office High-Street bank	prizes worked out to give return of 7% on all bonds held for 3 months or more. Chance of winning a prize in any year if hold £10 of bonds is around 1 in 120	Premium bonds
value of shares you can buy does – but there is a minimum guaranteed amount	return tax-free (but see p90)	your employer (but only about 100 approved schemes in existence)	at end of 5 years get bonus of 18 monthly payments (ie return of 10.5%). Can use money to buy shares in your firm at price agreed at start of 5 years (see p90)	Save-As-You-Earn share option scheme

type of investment (and where to find more details)	for regular saving or lump sum?	minimum investment [1]	does it pay a regular income?	how long is investment meant to be for?	how quickly can you get your money back?
Shares *Chapter 8*, p78	lump sum	£700 or £800, say, in each company	yes – most companies pay dividends. These can vary	in the main, long-term investment. But can also be short-term speculation	can sell shares and get money in 2 to 4 weeks – but may get less than you invested
Single-premium investment bonds *Chapter 14*, p136	lump sum	varies – normally between £250 and £1,000	no – but most companies have schemes which let you cash in part of investment (can cash up to 5% a year without paying tax at the time)	in the main, long-term investment	varies – can be straightaway, sometimes up to a week or month. May get back less than invested.
Unit-linked savings plans *Chapter 14*, p142	regular saving	varies – normally between £5 and £25 a month	normally no – but some plans pay income after 10 years	at least 10 years	can cash at any time – but may get back less than you invested (and in first year or two, may get little or nothing)
Unit trusts *Chapter 9*, p91	either	varies [16]	yes, with many trusts – amount can vary	in the main, long-term investment. But can also be short-term speculation	varies between trusts – can normally sell each day (but may get back less than you invested)

[1] Gives an idea of the minimum it's sensible to invest – see p24
[2] Depends on age and minimum income company will pay out – but minimum investment likely to be £1,000 or more
[3] Income from annuities you *have* to buy – eg as part of personal pension plan – is taxed as earned income
[4] If you buy stock on National Savings Stock Register (through post office). With a stockbroker, buying and selling costs make buying less than £700 or £800, say, less worthwhile
[5] The interest paid on a few stocks varies
[6] Stock prices tend to go up if interest rates in general fall, and to go down if interest rates in general rise. Some stocks tend to rise and fall more than others
[7] You need several thousand £££

[8] Usually two types of deposits. With one type you invest for an agreed period (often 1, 2 or 3 years): minimum investment varies – from £100 to £5,000, say. With others, you invest for any period but have to give notice to withdraw money. Minimum investment is often £100
[9] Under the Banking Act, companies must be licensed by Bank of England to accept deposits. A Deposit Protection Fund guarantees to pay 75%

does value of capital fluctuate?	points about tax	where can you get investment?	other comments	
yes	dividends are taxable – paid after deduction of basic rate tax. Liable for capital gains tax on any gain	stockbroker, High-Street bank or other agent (eg accountant)	buying shares of just one or two companies is very risky (see p79)	Shares
yes	when you cash in bond, may have to pay tax on the gain you've made (including any amounts you got earlier on, not taxed at the time) if you pay tax at higher rates or the investment income surcharge. Fund pays capital gains tax on gains	life insurance company or broker	value of investment depends on performance of fund of investments normally run by insurance company – eg property fund, equity fund, managed fund. Can switch between funds. Only way to invest small sum in property	Single-premium investment bonds
yes	return tax-free so long as pay tax at no more than the basic rate – always tax-free if keep policy going for at least 10 years, or three-quarters of its term, whichever is less. Fund pays capital gains tax on gains	life insurance company or broker	government subsidises premiums (see p51). Money invested in unit trust or insurance company fund (as for *single-premium investment bonds*). Go for high-investment plan – see p142	Unit-linked savings plans
yes	income is taxable – paid after deduction of basic rate tax. Liable for capital gains tax on any gain	direct from unit trust company or via insurance broker, stockbroker, High-Street bank	most unit trusts are authorised by the Department of Trade – this means, for example, the Department can lay down the rules about how prices of units are worked out, and so on	Unit trusts

of first £10,000 in your account, if company fails.
[10] Which you get by mortgaging your home (or with some schemes, selling part or all of it) to insurance company
[11] Varies with company – minimum value of home may be specified – eg £15,000
[12] With schemes based on loans, you still benefit in full from increase in value of home. With schemes where you sell part or all of your

home to the company, part or all of the increase in value of the home goes to the company
[13] £1,000 for yearling bonds. For buying local authority stock through a stockbroker, buying and selling costs make buying less than £700 or £800, say, less worthwhile
[14] Depends on scheme – some pension schemes are non-contributory (ie employee pays nothing); with others you pay a fixed % of your earnings

[15] You have to pay a percentage of earnings (up to certain limit) if employed and earning over certain amount; flat amount (and sometimes percentage of profits) if self-employed
[16] For lump sums often between £100 and £500; for regular savings often £10 a month
[17] At time book went to press, these stocks weren't available on National Savings Stocks Register (see p109). Check whether available now

4 Getting professional advice

Lots of people will give investment advice. But how good will the advice be? And does it matter whether you pay a fee or the advice is given free (or so it may seem)? In this chapter we look at the various sources of professional advice, what they might offer, and what charges will be made.

Investment advisers Various groups of people claim to give investment advice of one sort or another. For example:

- accountants
- bank managers
- bank investment departments
- insurance brokers
- investment consultants
- merchant banks
- solicitors
- stockbrokers

In fact, anyone can set himself up as an investment consultant or adviser. He needs no qualifications; there are no state controls.

Types of advice Investment advice falls into two categories:

- **general advice** – about how your money should be split between different types of investment
- **specialist advice** – about, for example, which shares to invest in, which kind of investment-type life insurance to buy.

Ideally, someone who gives general advice should know a lot about all types of investment and about the tax rules affecting them. He should find out all about your financial circumstances and what you want from your investments – eg a regular income or capital growth.

A specialist investment adviser may also need to find out a lot about your financial circumstances. But instead of knowing about all available investments, he should be an expert on one or two of them – insurance, or shares, for example.

If your adviser also manages your investments for you, you can often choose for the management to be *non-discretionary* (the adviser needs your prior approval to act) or *discretionary* (he doesn't). Most advisers prefer discretionary management – so that they can act quickly when necessary. If you make the management discretionary, it's normal to agree broad limits to the adviser's discretion – eg not more than 5% of your money to go into the shares of any one company.

Getting an adviser Investment advisers are easy to find. It's finding a good one that's difficult. Most general advisers – eg most accountants and solicitors – aren't fully trained in all aspects of investment, and normally give investment advice as a sideline to their main business. Some advisers, such as bank investment departments and merchant banks, claim that their employees are given the necessary training and experience to act as general advisers – but, in the main, they specialise in giving advice to those with a lot of money to invest (over £20,000, say).

On the whole, the people in a survey done for *Money Which?* seemed fairly happy with their advisers – although a fair number (21%) were unlikely to recommend their adviser to their friends. There were good and bad reports about all the groups of advisers in the *Money Which?* survey. So there may well be as much variation in the quality of advice given by advisers in the same group as there is between the groups.

As a first check on how good a general adviser is, see if he found out all the information about YOU that he needed – see Checklist.

Checklist

What an adviser needs to know about you to give general advice

Age

Health

Married/single

Number and ages of children/dependants

Size of family income (and how it's made up)

Prospects (eg job prospects/legacies)

Expenditure/commitments

Tax position

Pension

Investments

Home and mortgage

Insurance policies

How long you want to invest for

How important it is to you to:
● get a high income
● make a capital gain
● not lose money
● be able to get your money back quickly

Whether you're prepared to risk some of your money for the chance of a greater gain

Steps you should take

In general, you'll need to do a lot of the work of deciding how to invest your money yourself. Do your homework before setting off in search of investment advice. Find out what to expect from the different types of investment. And get clear in your own mind what you want from your investments – whether you are willing to risk losing money in the hope of a capital gain, whether you want your money available at short notice, and so on. This book should help you sort out your priorities.

Then, if you feel the need to talk further about your investment strategy in general, you could try your bank, an accountant or a solicitor (or all three). Make sure you tell them all they need to know about you – see Checklist.

Once you've decided on the types of investments you're interested in – eg investment-type life insurance, shares, building society investments – you could try contacting specialists in those fields. But get advice from more than one specialist in each field. And don't expect general advice from specialists.

With all advisers, check how much you're going to be charged. Whatever advice you receive, it's up to *you* to try to evaluate it – and decide whether to go along with it. After all, it's *your* money.

If you've got a lot to invest (£20,000 or more, say), you could ask a High-Street bank investment department, certain investment consultants, a merchant bank or a stockbroker to manage your investments for you – but see Verdicts on these advisers overleaf.

If you get bad advice, there is very little you can do apart from voting with your feet. It's an offence if an adviser dishonestly or recklessly makes a misleading statement to persuade someone to invest in certain investments, such as shares. But, except in this rare case, there's little that can be done about bad investment advice. If the adviser is negligent – eg you ask him to buy units in a particular unit trust and he buys the wrong ones –he is legally liable to compensate you for money you lose as a result. Many advisers have professional indemnity insurance to cover this.

If you want to complain about an adviser (or money-type organisation), you could try complaining to one of the trade associations or other bodies listed on p41.

Paying your adviser

Some advisers charge fees. Others get commission from the people they recommend you to invest your money with – so might not be as independent as they seem. See next pages for how each type of adviser is paid.

One of the problems with getting good, independent investment advice is that it doesn't come cheap. Unless you've got a lot of money to invest, independent investment advisers are unlikely to be willing to manage your investments for you – their charges would be too high a proportion of the money you have to invest.

Accountant

Getting in touch Most accountants will give existing clients investment advice and many will give it to anyone coming to them.

What they offer
● general advice (and a few accountants offer management of your investments too). Specialist advice will be taken from stockbrokers, insurance brokers and so on.

Investments they seem to consider Main emphasis is on building society investments, buying or improving your own home, investment-type life insurance.

Cost to you Sometimes advice is free. If not, may charge a fee based on time spent on you – at hourly rate between perhaps £15 and £60. Fee may be reduced if commission received.

Commission received Accountants may receive commission from building societies (say, 1% of money placed with them), unit trusts (1¼% of value of units sold) and insurance companies (much the same commission as *Insurance brokers* get). A few accountants share the stockbroker's commission if they arrange a share deal for you (for example, if you bought or sold £1,000-worth of shares through the accountant he would get £3.30, the stockbroker £13.20). Note that, if the commission is shared, for deals over £7,000 the overall commission is higher if you go through an accountant rather than to a stockbroker direct.
  Chartered accountants are supposed to tell you in writing of any commission they receive as a result of your investments. *Certified* accountants are supposed to deduct any commission received from their fee and show this on your bill. But, judging by some *Which?* readers' experiences, accountants often keep their clients in the dark about commission.

Qualifications Examinations taken by both sorts of accountants include personal taxation and the general principles of finance and investment (but not specifically investment for individuals).

Overall verdict
Worth considering for general discussion of investments. Came out very well in *Money Which?* survey for finding out about circumstances and needs of their clients.

What is meant by:
● *general advice*. The adviser looks at your finances and investments as a whole and suggests how your money should be split between different types of investment
● *specialist advice*. The adviser specialises in giving advice about one or more particular types of investment – eg shares, investment-type life insurance
● *management of your investments*. The adviser gives both general and specialist advice, claims to keep your circumstances and investments under review, and carries out administration (eg makes sure you get the share dividends you are entitled to).

Stockbroker

Getting in touch Ask your friends if they know a stockbroker they would recommend – and ask for an introduction. Or ask your bank for a recommendation. The Stock Exchange (address on p41) will provide you with the names of three stockbroking firms who will buy and sell for small investors. If you're a small investor, always ask a stockbroker what his minimum commission is before asking him to deal for you – minimum commissions for share deals seem to vary between £7 (£10 if you're buying shares) and £15 or so.

What they offer
● management of your investments. But there may be a minimum investment, varying between £5,000 and £25,000
● specialist advice on stocks and shares.

Investments they seem to consider In the main, stocks, shares, unit trusts.

Cost to you You pay commission on buying and selling stocks and shares (eg £16.50 for £1,000-worth of shares, £8 for £1,000-worth of British Government stock). A few stockbrokers also charge a fee for managing your investments – £10 or £15 a year, say.

Some stockbrokers may charge for a valuation (perhaps 50p a holding or £5 a valuation).

Commission received As well as getting commission from you for buying or selling stocks and shares, stockbrokers receive commission for buying unit trusts for you (normally 1¼% of the value of the units).

Qualifications For the last ten years or so, new stockbrokers have had to pass the Stock Exchange examination. Covers stocks and shares and unit trusts (and, in less detail, other investments and personal taxation).

Overall verdict

If you want to invest in stocks and shares, a stockbroker may be your best adviser. But don't expect him consistently to choose shares which do better than average. Some stockbrokers may not be very interested in dealing for you (let alone advising you on which shares to buy) unless you have a lot of money to invest.

Insurance Broker

Getting in touch No problem finding an insurance broker. Could ask among your friends, look in *Yellow pages*, or ask largest insurance broker association for the addresses of members in your area (write to British Insurance Brokers Association, address on p41). The difficulty is finding a good insurance broker. Personal recommendation may be your best bet.

What they offer
● specialist advice about investment-type life insurance (including pension schemes for the self-employed).

Investments they seem to consider Investment-type life insurance, building society investments, buying or improving your home.

Cost to you Nothing

Commission received Perhaps £72 in the first year for fixing up a £10-a-month endowment policy (ie up to 60% of first year's premiums); 3% or 3½% of value of single-premium bonds sold (eg property bonds); either 1¼% or 3% of value of units sold in unit trusts. May also get commission from building societies (say, 1% of money placed with society).

Qualifications May have passed examination of Charterered Insurance Institute. Covers insurance and includes such things as taxation and social security benefits.

Overall verdict

Worth visiting if you've already decided on investment-type life insurance. But don't expect general advice. Best to contact more than one.

Bank manager

What they offer
● general advice. Specialist advice, if you ask for it, will be taken from stockbrokers, insurance brokers and so on.

Investments they seem to consider   Building society investments, stocks and shares and National Savings investments.

Cost to you   Normally nothing.

Commission received   Bank normally shares stockbroker's commission (if you bought or sold £1,000-worth of shares through your bank, it would get £4.12, stockbroker would get £12.38). Note that, if the commission is shared, for deals over £7,000 the overall commission is higher if you go through your bank manager rather than to a stockbroker direct. If bank sells you unit trusts other than its own, it normally receives commission from unit trust (1¼% of value of units sold). Much the same commission for selling insurance policies as *Insurance brokers* get.

Qualifications   Nearly all bank managers are Associates of the Institute of Bankers (which can, though doesn't necessarily, mean they've had some training in personal investment). Some banks send managers on internal training courses which include personal investment.

Overall verdict
Worth considering for general discussion of investments.

Solicitor

Getting in touch   Nearly all solicitors will give existing clients investment advice; most will give it to anyone who comes to see them.

What they offer
● general advice. Specialist advice will be taken from stockbrokers, insurance brokers and so on
● management. Some solicitors will manage your investments, usually on a non-discretionary basis (see p34).

Investments they seem to consider   Most commonly building society investments, buying or improving your home, stocks and shares.

Cost to you   Sometimes advice is free. If not, usually charge a fee based on time spent on you – at hourly rate which varies, perhaps about £15 to £60.

Commission received   Much the same as *Accountants*. Solicitors are meant to take account of commission received when deciding what fee to charge.

Qualifications   Solicitors must pass Law Society examination. Covers tax law and legal aspects of investments and trusts (but not principles of personal finance and investment).

Overall verdict
Worth considering for general discussion of investments.

Investment Consultant

Anyone can call himself an investment consultant (or something similar). In practice, some of them seem to be either insurance brokers (see p37) or *licensed dealers* in securities. A licensed dealer is authorised by the Department of Trade to deal in investments such as shares. A licence doesn't really mean very much as far as the consumer is concerned – mainly that the holder hasn't been convicted of fraud or theft and agrees to conduct his business in accordance with government rules.

Getting in touch   In the *Money Which?* survey mentioned earlier, two in five readers whose most recent adviser was an investment consultant had answered an advertisement or been approached by the consultant direct.

What they offer
● some offer management of your investments – so long as you have a minimum amount to invest (varies between £5,000 and £100,000, but is commonly £20,000). These may be licensed dealers in securities.
● some give specialist advice on investment-type life insurance and unit trusts.

Investments they seem to consider   With licensed dealers in securities, main emphasis is on stocks and shares. With others, investment-type life insurance, building society investments, buying or improving your home, unit trusts.

Cost to you   For managing your investments, a yearly fee of perhaps 0.5% to 1% of the value of your investments.

Commission received   Most investment consultants share the stockbroker's commission if they arrange a share deal for you (as for *Accountant*). Usually get commission from unit trusts (either 1¼% or 3% of value of units sold) and from insurance companies (normally as for *Insurance broker*), and may get it from building societies (say, 1% of money placed with them).

Overall verdict
Such a varied bunch, we can't really give a sensible verdict. But be wary of a consultant turning out, in practice, to be just an insurance broker.

Other advisers?
Two other groups of advisers mentioned by readers in the *Money Which?* survey were:
● building society managers
● insurance company representatives.
   These are not usually regarded as investment advisers – because they are obviously likely to direct you towards investments run by their own employers. But it could make sense to contact a number of building societies or insurance companies direct if you've already decided the sort of investment you want and are trying to decide which society or company to go for.

Bank Investment Department

Getting in touch   Enquire at branch of bank – doesn't have to be your own bank

What they offer
● Management of your investments – either discretionary or non-discretionary (see p34) – if you've got a minimum of £10,000 to £20,000 to invest (depending on bank)
● general advice – may run a special service (separate from bank manager).

Investments they seem to consider   Most commonly stocks, shares, building society and National Savings investments, unit trusts.

Cost to you   For management of your investments, a yearly fee. Often around 0.75% each year of the value of your holdings.
    For general advice, there may be a fee based on time spent on you – perhaps, £30 to £35 an hour, or a one-off fee of perhaps £200.

Commission received   As for *Bank manager*.

Qualifications   Investment departments employ people with various qualifications – but give them training in personal investment.

Overall verdict
May be worth considering for general advice. And if you want your investments managed and have at least £20,000 to invest, bank investment departments are one alternative – though *Which?* readers have rated them worse than most other advisers for how well they understood their clients' investment problems.

Merchant bank

Getting in touch   Could ask the Issuing Houses Association (01-283 7334) for a list of members – but note that not all are recognised as banks. For what this means, see Chapter 20. Few merchant banks will consider advising you unless you have a large sum of money to invest (see below) – and some don't take on individuals at all. So you may need to get in touch with several.

What they offer
● management of your investments – usually discretionary – so long as you have a minimum amount to invest. This is commonly £100,000, but can be £250,000 or more.

Investments they seem to consider   In the main, stocks and shares, property, bank deposit accounts.

Cost to you   A yearly fee. Between 0.5% and 1% of the value of your investments.

Commission received   Very similar to High-Street banks (see *Bank manager*).

Qualifications   Merchant banks employ people with various qualifications – and normally give some of their staff training in personal investment.

Overall verdict
Only for the rich. Main emphasis on stocks and shares.

A who's who of money organisations

If you've got a complaint about a stockbroker or insurance company, say, and you've not been able to get anywhere by complaining direct, you could try the relevant organisation listed here. Most of them are trade associations, whose main role is to give information and promote members' interests, but they may help sort out your complaint.

Association of Certified Accountants
In general, won't deal with disputes over fees. May be able to help if accountant is being very slow or hasn't done something which he should have. Will look at complaints of general incompetence and inefficiency. Write to Legal Secretary, ACA, 29 Lincoln's Inn Fields, London WC2 3EE.

Association of Investment Trust Companies
Trade association for 200 investment trust companies. Gives general information and help with administrative-type problems. Write to the Secretary, Association of Investment Trust Companies, Park House, 16 Finsbury Circus, London EC2M 7JJ. Phone number 01-588 5347.

Banking Information Service
Main job is to give information about Barclays, Coutts, Lloyds, Midland, National Westminster and Williams & Glyn's, though may give help with administrative-type problems. Address: 10 Lombard Street, London EC3V 9AP. Phone number 01-626 8486.

British Insurance Association
Trade association for over 330 insurance companies, dealing with non-life insurance – eg car, house, holiday insurance. Established procedure for dealing with complaints. Useful leaflets on insuring home, car and so on. Write to Consumer Information Dept, BIA, Aldermary House, Queen Street, London EC4N 1TU. Phone number 01-248 4477

British Insurance Brokers Association
Trade association for insurance brokers (4,600 members). Has established procedure for dealing with complaints. Write to Consumer Relations Officer, BIBA, 130 Fenchurch Street, London EC3M 5DJ. Phone number 01-623 9043.

The Building Societies Association
Trade association for around 190 building societies. Main job is to give information though may be able to give help with administrative-type problems. Write to BSA, 3 Park Street London W1Y 3PF.

Corporation of Mortgage Brokers and Life Assurance Consultants
(around 300 member firms). Has established procedure for dealing with complaints. Write to PO Box 101, Guildford, Surrey GU1 2HZ. Phone number 0483-39121.

Institute of Chartered Accountants
In general, won't deal with disputes over fees. May be able to help if accountant is being very slow or hasn't done something which should have been done. Will look at complaints of general incompetence and inefficiency. Write to Secretary of Investigating Committee, ICA, PO Box 433, Chartered Accountants' Hall, Moorgate Place, London EC2P 2BJ.

Insurance Brokers Registration Council
Organisation with statutory power. Anyone calling himself an insurance broker has to be registered. A registered broker has to meet certain requirements and behave according to a Code of Conduct. The IBRC can investigate specific complaints. Write to the Registrar, IBRC, 15 St Helen's Place, London EC3A 6DS.

Insurance Ombudsman Bureau
An independent organisation set up to deal with complaints by disgruntled policyholders. Only certain insurance companies are in the scheme. Write to the Insurance Ombudsman, IOB, 31 Southampton Row, London WC1B 5HJ. Phone number 01-404 0591.

The Law Society
Won't look at complaints about incompetence or negligence. Will deal with allegations of professional misconduct. Runs a compensation fund which will compensate people who lose money because of the dishonesty of their solicitor or his staff. Write to the Law Society, 113 Chancery Lane, London WC2A 1PL. Phone number 01-242 1222.

The Life Offices' Association and Associated Scottish Life Offices
Trade associations for over 80 life insurance companies. Will help with problems about service, cash-in values, and so on. Write to LOA/ASLO Information Centre, Buckingham House, 62–63 Queen Street, London EC4R 1AD. Phone number 01-236 1101.

The Stock Exchange
Can go so far as to expel members in cases of serious misconduct. If you have a specific complaint about a stockbroker (eg negligence, dishonesty), write to the Secretary to the Council, The Stock Exchange, London EC2N 1HP. Public Relations Dept can give you general information and the names of three stockbrokers to choose from. Phone number 01-588 2355.

Unit Trust Association
Trade association for around 75 unit trust management companies. Gives general information and help with administrative-type problems. Write to the Secretary, UTA, Park House, 16 Finsbury Circus, London EC2M 7JP.

5 Tax

How the chapter is arranged

	page
Income tax	43
Tax and life insurance	49
Capital gains tax	53
Capital transfer tax	60

Why bother about tax? The short answer is that tax can affect the *return* you get on your investments. You can't know how good (or bad) an investment will be until you've allowed for tax.

Let's take an extreme example. Dave Grabber has a very high income, and pays income tax at 60%. He has a choice between two investments:

Investment A will pay him an income of 15 per cent a year

Investment B won't pay any income, but will – he hopes – show a capital gain of 10 per cent a year.

Both these figures are before tax – and, at first sight, Investment A looks more attractive. But after tax, Investment A will pay Dave only 6 per cent, whereas Investment B will pay at least 7 per cent. The reason is that, for someone like Dave, 60 per cent of any extra income is taken by the taxman, whereas capital gains are taxed at a maximum of 30 per cent, and up to £5,000 of gains in any tax year are tax-free.

This example shows how tax can affect the return on your investment. But it can also affect the cost – particularly with insurance policy premiums, pensions and mortgages. With most regular-premium life insurance policies, 15 per cent of the cost is paid for by the taxman – a considerable saving for you. With pension schemes – both employers' and personal pension plans for the self-employed or those not in an employer's scheme – tax relief can save up to 60 per cent of the cost. And of course most people qualify for tax relief on the interest they pay on their mortgages – which saves them tax at the highest rate they pay.

What are the taxes?

The most common tax you'll have to pay on investment income is income tax. The other main tax to watch out for is capital gains tax. Capital transfer tax doesn't directly affect the return you get on your investments – but we give the basic rules at the end of this chapter, and tell you how insurance policies can reduce your capital transfer tax bill.

Which tax hurts most?

People with high incomes are likely to be hurt most by income tax – which can take up to 75 per cent of the income they get from their investments. If you pay income tax at high rates, consider investing for capital gains: capital gains tax is charged at a flat rate of 30 per cent, and in each tax year you can make at least £5,000 of capital gains tax-free (see p55) – a fact which can benefit all taxpayers.

People who pay income tax should also consider tax-free investments where the return is tax-free – see the list on p44.

Income tax

Income tax is charged on your income for a tax year. Tax years run from 6 April in one year to 5 April in the following year. So your tax bill for the 1982–83 tax year will normally be based on your income from 6 April 1982 to 5 April 1983. But it's sometimes difficult to know in which tax year your investment income will be taxed. Sometimes your tax bill is based on the investment income you received in the tax year (current year basis), and sometimes it's based on the investment income you received in the previous tax year (preceding year basis). We tell you which basis applies to which types of income – and we tell you how you can sometimes juggle the figures to get a lower tax bill.

How much tax

All your income is added together, to arrive at your **gross income**	say, £9,000
From this you deduct your **outgoings** (certain payments you make – eg maintenance payments)	say, £1,500
This leaves what the taxman calls your 'total income'	say, £7,500
From this you deduct your **allowances**	say, £2,445
This leaves your **taxable income**	say, £5,055

Tax is charged on your **taxable income**.

Rates of income tax for 1982–83 tax year

The first £12,800 of your taxable income is taxed at the basic rate of 30 per cent. Anything more than £12,800 of taxable income is taxed at a series of higher rates – see Table below for details. In addition you may have to pay investment income surcharge – see overleaf.

Tax Rates for 1982–83 tax year

slice of taxable income	basic rate tax	so if your taxable income is	tax due
on first £12,800	30%	£12,800	£3,840
	higher rate tax		
on next £2,300	40%	£15,100	£4,760
on next £4,000	45%	£19,100	£6,560
on next £6,200	50%	£25,300	£9,660
on next £6,200	55%	£31,500	£13,070
on anything more	60%		

Investment income surcharge

You have to pay investment income surcharge if your 'total investment income' (see below for what this is) is above a certain limit. For the 1982–83 tax year this limit is £6,250. Anything over £6,250 is surcharged at 15 per cent.

If you're married, the investment income of both of you is added together, and the husband has to pay the tax on it. And the surcharge limit for a married couple is £6,250 (not £12,500).

In most cases, you can work out your 'total investment income' in the following way:

Step 1   take the gross (before-tax) amount of your investment income from all sources – including the grossed-up amount of building society interest received (see opposite), but excluding any investment income which is tax-free (see below for a list of what's tax-free) and excluding any covenant or maintenance payments you receive.

Step 2   take away from this figure any interest (eg mortgage interest) you pay which qualifies for tax relief, covenant payments to charities up to £3,000, and any alimony or maintenance payments you make under an enforceable arrangement – eg a court order or a separation deed.

The answer, for most people, will be their 'total investment income'.

But for some people this process won't work – for example if:
● the wife's earned income is separately taxed and the wife pays some outgoings (eg mortgage interest). In this case, what she pays will be deducted from her own earned income, and not from the couple's investment income. So the figure for 'total investment income' could be higher – and there could be a higher surcharge bill
● you make very large covenant payments during the tax year (excluding the first £3,000 of covenant payments to charities). If the gross payments *plus* three-sevenths of the net building society interest you get is more than the answer to Step 1, you must substitute this higher figure.

Example

Joe Sander has £9,000 of taxable investment income in the 1982–83 tax year, made up of £6,500 in dividends and tax credits, £2,000 (gross) from British Government stocks, and £500 gross (ie £350 net) in building society interest.

During the tax year, he pays £1,300 in mortgage interest which qualifies for tax relief. So his 'total investment income' is £9,000 *minus* £1,300 = £7,700.

He has to pay investment income surcharge on anything over £6,250. So his investment income surcharge bill is 15% of (£7,700 − £6,250) = 15% of £1,450 = £217.50.

Tax-free investment income

● proceeds from Save-As-You-Earn
● proceeds from National Savings Certificates (or Ulster Savings Certificates if you live in Northern Ireland)
● proceeds from regular-premium investment type life insurance policies (if held for at least 10 years, or three-quarters of the time the policy is planned to run for – whichever is shorter)
● premium bond prizes
● final bonus on British Savings Bonds
● first £70 interest each year from a National Savings Bank ordinary account
● interest you get in connection with delayed settlement of damages for personal injury or death.

Investment income taxed before you get it

Examples of this type of income are:
- dividends from UK companies
- distributions from unit trusts
- interest on certain loans – eg loans to local authorities or foreign governments
- interest on certain British Government stocks (normally all stocks bought through a stockbroker, except War Loan)
- interest on company fixed-income investments (loan stocks or debentures)
- interest from certain finance company deposits
- part of the income from annuities
- income from certain income bonds
- income from trusts and settlements
- income from a will, paid out to you during the administration period (ie while the details of who gets what under the will are being worked out).

Interest from building societies is treated in a special way – see below.

How it is taxed

This type of income is taxed on a current year basis – ie your tax bill for the 1982–83 tax year is based on the income paid (or credited) to you in that tax year.

There's no basic rate tax for you to pay on this type of income – because the basic rate tax (or something equivalent to it) has been deducted before the income is handed over to you.

With dividends from UK companies and distributions from unit trusts, each dividend or distribution is accompanied by a tax credit. Your gross (before-tax) income is taken to be the dividend *plus* the tax credit. For the 1982–83 tax year, the tax credit is 30 per cent of the gross income. So if, say, the dividend is £70, the tax credit will be £30 and the gross income £100.

You get a tax voucher from the company (or unit trust) showing the amount of the dividend (or distribution) and the amount of the tax credit. The tax credit should always equal tax at the current basic rate – so if the basic rate of tax changes, vouchers sent out early in the tax year (ie before the basic rate for the year is finally known) may show the wrong amount of tax credit.

Interest from building societies

Building societies pay tax at a special composite rate (fixed at $25\frac{1}{2}$ per cent for the 1981–82 tax year) before paying out interest to you. Because of this, you don't have to pay basic rate tax on interest you get from a building society. But you can't claim back the tax that the society has paid – even if your income is too low for you to pay tax.

If you pay tax at higher rates, or the investment income surcharge, you will have to pay extra tax on your building society interest. When working out your tax bill, the taxman includes the *grossed-up* amount of interest as part of your income. To find the grossed-up interest for the 1982–83 tax year, take the net interest, multiply it by 10, and divide the answer by 7. (If you've got a calculator, simply divide the net interest by 0.7).

You are liable for tax on this grossed-up amount at the highest rate of tax you pay (including the investment income surcharge, if you pay it). But you are treated as having already paid basic rate tax on the interest – so you only have to hand over the difference.

Example

Andy Smith got £350 interest from his building society in the 1982–83 tax year. As he pays some higher rate tax, he'll have to pay extra tax on this interest. He works out the grossed-up amount of interest – it comes to £500. He adds this to his other income, and finds that he's liable for tax at 40 per cent on the £500 grossed-up interest – ie £200 in tax. But he's treated as having already paid tax on this interest at the 30 per cent basic rate (ie £50 in tax). So he has to hand over an extra £200 – £150 = £50 to the taxman.

Points to watch

Annuities

If you've bought an annuity voluntarily with your own money (not, for example, as part of a personal pension plan), part of the income you get each year is treated as a return of capital, part as interest on the capital. Only the interest part is taxable – the insurance company will tell you how much this is.

Income bonds

There are several different types of income bond – which work (and are taxed) in different ways. Recently the taxman has clamped down on income bonds.

Discretionary trusts

For the 1982–83 tax year, discretionary trusts pay tax at 45 per cent on most of their income. This applies whether the income is kept by the trust or paid out to beneficiaries. If income is paid out to you by the trust, you get a tax credit of 45 per cent of the gross (before-tax) amount. If your income (including the income from the trust) is too low for you to pay tax, or if the highest rate of tax you pay (including the investment income surcharge) is less than 45 per cent, you can claim back some (or all) of the tax deducted.

Unit trusts

With the first distribution you get from a unit trust you're likely to get an equalisation payment. This is a return of part of the money you first invested, so doesn't count as income and isn't taxable. But see p58 for how it affects any capital gains you make.

With an accumulation unit trust (where income is automatically reinvested for you) the amount reinvested – apart from any equalisation payment – counts as income and is taxable.

With other types of income taxed before you get it, tax is deducted (usually at the 30 per cent basic rate) before the income is paid to you. Again, you normally get a tax voucher or a similar document from whoever pays you the money. This tells you the gross (before-tax) amount of income, the tax deducted, and the actual sum you get.

Keep any tax vouchers as proof that tax has been credited or deducted.

The outcome of all this is shown in the Diagram below. You can see that:

● if your income (including income of this type) is too low for you to pay tax, you can claim back all the tax that's been deducted or credited. And note that if your income is high enough for you to pay some tax, but not as much as has already been deducted, you can claim back the difference

● if you are liable for basic rate tax (but no more) on the whole of your income of this type, your liability for tax on this income is automatically met by the tax deducted or credited

● if you pay tax at higher rates, or the investment income surcharge, you will have to pay extra tax – calculated on the gross (before-tax) income.

Any extra tax on income received between 6 April 1982 and 5 April 1983 has to be paid by 1 December 1983 – or within 30 days of the date on your Notice of Assessment, if later.

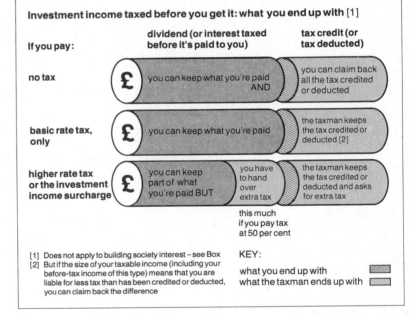

Investment income taxed before you get it: what you end up with [1]

[1] Does not apply to building society interest – see Box
[2] But if the size of your taxable income (including your before-tax income of this type) means that you are liable for less tax than has been credited or deducted, you can claim back the difference

KEY:

what you end up with
what the taxman ends up with

Investment income not taxed before you get it

Interest from the investments listed below comes into this category:
- National Savings Bank accounts
- Trustee Savings Bank accounts
- High Street bank and National Girobank deposit accounts
- certain finance company deposits
- certain British Government stocks bought on the National Savings Stock Register – eg through a Post Office – and War Loan
- British Savings Bonds, Co-operative Society deposits
- interest on loans you make to private individuals.

How it is taxed If you've been getting interest from one of these sources for a few years, it will normally be taxed on a preceding year basis – ie your tax bill for the 1982–83 tax year will be based on the interest paid (or credited) to you in the 1981–82 tax year. This bill must normally be paid by 1 January 1983, or within 30 days of the date on the Notice of Assessment you'll get – whichever is later. But if your interest doesn't vary much from year to year, and you pay tax under PAYE, the tax on your interest will probably be collected along with tax on your earnings.

Special rules Special rules apply to the first three and last two years in which you get interest of this type – see below for details.

If you get interest of this type from more than one source, the taxman may apply his special rules to each source separately – though he'll normally count all interest from banks (including National Savings Bank) as coming from a single source. But if there is a big change in the interest you get from a single source – eg if you

Interest not taxed before you get it: what your tax bill is based on

	Tax is initially based on:	but for some years, there's a choice:
First tax year in which you get interest from this source (year 1)	interest you get in first tax year (*current year basis*)	no choice this year
Second tax year (year 2)	interest you get in second tax year (*current year basis*)	no choice this year
Third tax year (year 3)	interest you got in second tax year (*preceding year basis*)	**your choice:** you can choose to have tax based on interest you get in third tax year (*current year basis*). Do so if this is less than interest you got in second year
Fourth and subsequent tax years . . .	interest you got in preceding tax year (*preceding year basis*)	no choice for these years
Until the last-but-one tax year in which you get interest from this source	interest you got in preceding tax year (*preceding year basis*)	**taxman's choice:** when you tell him, at the end of the next tax year, that you've closed your account, the taxman can revise your tax bill. He will base it on the interest you actually got in the last-but-one tax year (*current year basis*) if this comes to more than your original bill
Last tax year in which you get interest from this source	interest you get in this tax year (*current year basis*)	no choice this year

greatly increase or decrease the size of a bank deposit account – the taxman may treat such interest as coming from a new source, and apply his special rules.

You won't need to worry about these rules if your interest is much the same from year to year. But if it does vary, you may be able to reduce your tax bill.

If the amount of interest in year 3 is lower than in year 2, tell the taxman that you want your tax bill for year 3 to be based on the interest you actually got in year 3. (You can make this choice at any time within six years of the end of year 3.)

If the amount of interest in years 2 and 3 is high compared with the interest in year 4, consider closing your account (eg your bank deposit account) just before the end of year 4, and reopening it a week or so later (after the start of the next tax year). That way, your tax bill for year 4 will be based on the interest you actually got in that year, rather than on the higher amount of interest you got in year 3.

If you have more than one bank account, you may need to close them all – see previous page.

National Savings Bank Ordinary Accounts

You and your wife are each allowed £70 interest free of tax from an ordinary account with the National Savings Bank. But you are taxed on anything more.

Note that if you have, say, £100 interest and your wife has £20, you will have to pay on £30 of your interest, even though the combined interest isn't more than 2 × £70 = £140. If you and your wife have a joint account, however, you can have £140 interest free of tax.

Any one person is allowed only £70 free of tax – however many accounts he or she has.

All interest from National Savings Bank investment accounts is taxable; how much tax (if any) you have to pay depends on the size of your income.

Tax and life insurance

With most life insurance policies, you pay no income tax or capital gains tax on the proceeds. But there are situations where the taxman steps in:
- **tax on a policy gain:** this applies to single-premium policies, and in some circumstances other policies too – and may result in some higher rate tax and investment income surcharge
- **premium subsidy:** if you cash in a policy during its first four years, you may lose some or all of the subsidy you've had on your premiums – see p52
- **sale:** if you've bought (or been given) a policy which was taken out by someone else, you may have to pay capital gains tax if you sell it – see p56 for more details.

Tax on a gain from a life insurance policy

The proceeds of most life insurance policies are free of all tax. But you will have to pay some tax on any gain you make on a policy taken out (or altered) since 19 March 1968 if:
- you pay tax at higher rates or the investment income surcharge (or would do, if the gain were added to your investment income) and EITHER
- the policy doesn't qualify for premium subsidy (see p51) – for example, if it's a single-premium property bond or managed bond OR
- the policy does qualify for premium subsidy, but you cash it in or make it paid-up in its first 10 years (or within the first three-quarters of its term, if this is shorter).

Working out the gain When a policy comes to an end, the gain is normally the amount you get (including any amounts you got earlier on which weren't taxed at the time – see overleaf) *less* the total premiums paid (including the premium subsidy – see p51). If a taxable gain arises (eg on a single-premium policy) because the person insured dies, the gain is the cash-in value of the policy immediately before death (less premiums), if this is less than the sum insured.

How the gain is taxed Any gain is added to your investment income for the tax year in which the policy comes to an end. But you don't have to pay basic rate tax on the gain – only any higher rate tax and investment income surcharge. For example, if you would be liable for higher rate tax at 50 per cent (and no surcharge) you'd have to pay tax at $50 - 30 = 20$ per cent.

If adding the gain to your income means you pay tax at a higher rate than you would otherwise have done (including any investment income surcharge) the taxman should automatically

give you *top-slicing* relief. This will reduce your tax bill – so make sure you get it.

To work out your tax bill with top-slicing relief, first work out your *average yearly gain* by dividing the total gain by the number of *complete* years the policy ran for. Next, add this average yearly gain to your investment income for the tax year, and work out your tax bill on the average yearly gain. To get your tax bill on the total gain, multiply the tax bill on the average yearly gain by the number of years you have spread the gain over. For an example of top-slicing relief, see below.

Arnold Archer bought a £20,000 property bond in December 1976. He cashed it in for £30,000 in July 1981 – making a gain of £10,000. He already has a taxable income for the 1982-83 tax year of £14,600 including 'total investment income' (see p44) of £3,200. In the normal way, his tax bill on the gain would be worked out by adding the gain to his investment income for the year – see below.

But Arnold realises he should get top-slicing relief. With this, the average yearly gain of £2,500 (ie the £10,000 total gain divided by the four complete years the policy ran for) is added to his investment income for the year. His total tax bill on the gain is the tax on the average yearly gain multiplied by the number of complete years for which he held the bond. Top-slicing relief saves Arnold £2,792.50 − £1,400 = £1,392.50 – see below.

rate of tax %	income on which you pay this rate £	gain on bond £	amount of tax £
30	12,800		3,840
40	1,800		720
40		500	200
45		4,000	1,800
50		5,500	2,750
total gain		10,000	
basic and higher rate tax on gain			4,750
add investment income surcharge on gain [1]			1,042.50
			5,792.50
subtract tax at basic rate on gain (30% of £10,000)			3,000
total tax bill on gain			2,792.50

rate of tax %	income on which you pay this rate £	gain on bond £	amount of tax £
30	12,800		3,840
40	1,800		720
40		500	200
45		2,000	900
average yearly gain		2,500	
basic and higher rate tax on average yearly gain			1,100
add investment income surcharge on gain [2]			nil
			1,100
subtract tax at basic rate on average yearly gain (30% of £2,500)			750
so tax bill on average yearly gain is			350
total tax bill on gain (£350 × 4)			1,400

[1] Arnold's 'total investment income' (£3,200) plus his gain (£10,000) comes to £13,200. He pays the surcharge on £13,200 − £6,250 = £6,950. Investment income surcharge is 15 per cent of £6,950 = £1,042.50.

(2) Arnold's 'total investment income' (£3,200) plus the average yearly gain (£2,500) comes to £5,700. Since this is less than £6,250, the surcharge bill is nil.

If you cash in part of a policy

You get an allowance for each policy year – ie each period of 12 months since you took out the policy.

So long as the total amount you've had from the policy (including what you're getting this time) is less than the total allowances so far, there's no tax to pay. But if what you've had exceeds the total allowances so far, the excess counts as a gain (see opposite).

For each of the first 20 years of the policy, the allowance is 1/20th (ie 5 per cent) of the total premiums paid so far. For each year after the first 20, the allowance is 1/20th of any premiums paid in that year and the previous 19 years.

Note that policy years are counted from the date you take out the policy – but you don't get an allowance until the first policy year starting after 13 March 1975. So if you took out a policy before then, there will be some years for which you get no allowance.

Example

Tom Tupman pays tax at higher rates. He bought a single-premium policy in June 1975 for £10,000 and wonders how much he can withdraw each year without paying tax at the time.

For each of the first 20 years, Tom gets an allowance of 1/20th of the total premiums paid so far – ie 1/20th of £10,000 = £500. He can cash this amount each year without paying tax in that year. For the 21st year onwards, his allowance is 1/20th of any premiums paid in the year and in each of the previous 19 years – zero allowance in Tom's case since he paid for his policy with one premium at the outset. So if he uses up his allowance in each of the first 20 years he won't be able to cash any more of his policy without facing the taxman.

When Tom's policy comes to an end, the taxman will work out whether there's any tax to pay on his total gain. If he'd used up his £500 allowance in each of the first 20 years, he'd have had 20 × £500 = £10,000 from the policy. If he got another £5,000, say, when the policy ended, he would have had a total of £15,000. His total gain would be £15,000 *less* the £10,000 premium – ie £5,000. This would be added to his investment income in the tax year in which the policy ended – but he could get *top-slicing* relief (see example opposite).

If you cash in all (or part) of a life insurance policy, your 'total income' (see p43) is increased. For most people, this has no , significance at all. But if you get the special income tax allowance called age allowance for people who are 65 or over there could be problems – see p237.

If there's an excess

The excess is added to your investment income for the tax year in which the policy year you made the gain in comes to an end. Again, you don't have to pay basic rate tax on the gain – only any higher rate tax and investment income surcharge. And again, you get top-slicing relief (the gain is spread over the number of complete policy years since your last excess – or since the start of the policy, if you haven't previously had an excess).

When an excess is added to your income, your allowances for that and previous years are cancelled.

When the policy comes to an end, the total gain on which you may have to pay tax is:
● the amount you get at the end *plus* any previous amounts you've had from the policy, *less*
● the total premiums paid, any excesses, and any pre-14 March 1975 gains from the cashed-in part of the policy which the taxman was told of (by either you or the insurance company).

If, after making all these deductions you're left with a negative figure, you can subtract this from your 'total income' in order to reduce your higher rate tax and investment income surcharge bill. But you can't subtract more than the total of the policy's excesses and pre-14 March 1975 gains.

Subsidy on life insurance premiums

In general, you get a subsidy on the premiums you pay during the year on most regular-premium policies – eg an endowment policy or a mortgage-protection policy. But you can't normally get this subsidy on premiums you pay for a single-premium policy (eg a single-premium property bond).

The insurance company automatically allows for the subsidy. For the 1982–83 tax year, this is 15 per cent of your premiums. With most policies the premiums you've agreed to pay will be reduced to give this subsidy. The insurance company gets the balance from the taxman.

You get the benefit of this 15 per cent subsidy on premiums you pay on your own or your husband's or wife's life, or on your joint lives. But you won't get any subsidy on premiums in excess of £1,500 a year – or one-sixth of your 'total income' (see p43), if this is greater. For a married couple, the limit is £1,500 a year – or one-sixth of their joint 'total income' if this is greater.

Clawback

If you've got a regular-premium policy which qualifies for the premium subsidy (see previous page), and you cash it in or make it paid-up, the insurance company has to make a deduction from the cash-in or paid-up value if *all* the following apply:
- you took out the policy on or after 27 March 1974
- you cash it in or make it paid-up during its first four years
- you show a profit on the deal (ie the value of the policy is more than the *net* premiums you've paid – ie excluding the subsidy).

This deduction – called a clawback – is handed over by the insurance company to the taxman.

But with many policies, there won't be any clawback – because the value of the policy in the early years is generally less than the cost of the premiums. But there could be a clawback with unit-linked policies and life insurance linked to building societies.

The size of the clawback depends on when the policy is cashed in (or made paid-up) and on the rate of premium subsidy at this time. For example, if the rate of premium subsidy is 15%, the clawback in each of the cases below is A or B – whichever is less:

if cashed in during first two years
A = 15% of gross premiums paid so far (ie what you've paid plus the premium subsidy)
B = policy cash-in value *minus* 85% of gross premiums paid so far

if cashed in during third year
A = 10% of gross premiums paid so far
B = policy cash-in value *minus* 90% of gross premiums paid so far

A = 5% of gross premiums paid so far
B = policy cash-in value *minus* 95% of gross premiums paid so far.

Note – if B turns out to be a minus figure, there's no clawback. And, strictly, the clawback is calculated on the premiums you should have paid, not the ones you've actually paid.

If you cash in part of your policy

If, within four years of taking out a policy you cash in part of it, the same rules apply – and the clawback comes to just as much as it would have done if you had cashed in the whole policy. But the insurance company won't deduct more than the value of the part cashed in (so you can't get less than nothing!). Note that cashing in a bonus counts as cashing in part of your policy. And so in most cases does getting a loan on your policy from the company.

If, after cashing in part of your policy, you later cash in part or all of what is left, there may be more clawback. The rules for working out the clawback still apply, but:
- when working out B, add the value of the part you cashed in earlier to the current cash-in value of the policy
- take the smaller of A or B. From this, deduct any clawback made earlier. This gives the clawback that will be made this time.

Clawback after four years

If you cash in all or part of a policy *for the first time* more than four years after taking it out, there won't be any clawback. But if you've already cashed in part of it, there will be. The insurance company will deduct from the cash-in value an amount equal to either the premium subsidy on a year's premiums or the premium subsidy on the value of the part you're now cashing in (whichever is less).

Example

Leonard Quiller's gross premiums for a life insurance policy he took out in April 1980 are £10 a month. He decided to cash in his policy in December 1981 (after 20 months), when the rate of premium subsidy was 15 per cent. The insurance company tells him that the cash-in value is £180. Leonard works out the clawback:

The clawback is A or B – whichever is less:
A = 15% of gross premiums paid so far = 15% × £200 = £30
B = policy cash-in value *minus* 85% of gross premiums paid so far = £180 – (85% of £200) = £180 – £170 = £10.

So the insurance company will deduct £10 from the cash-in value of the policy and will pay Leonard £180 – £10 = £170.

Paid-up policies

Making a policy paid-up means you stop paying the premiums but don't take your money out. Making part of a policy paid-up means you reduce the premiums.

The clawback rules applying to the first four years of a policy apply if you make the policy paid-up or partly paid-up, in exactly the same way as if you cash in all or part of it – using the cash-in value at the time you make the policy paid-up, to do the sums. The clawback is deducted when the policy finally pays out. Note that there's no clawback on making a policy paid up more than four years after you take it out.

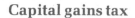

Capital gains tax

What is a capital gain?

You may make a capital gain (or loss) whenever you dispose of an asset, no matter how you came to own it. But you won't always be taxed on such a gain.

Anything you own (whether in the UK or not) counts as an asset – for example, houses, jewellery, shares.

You dispose of an asset not only if you sell it but also if you give it away, exchange it, or lose it. You also dispose of an asset if it is destroyed or becomes worthless, if you sell rights to it (eg grant a lease), or if you get compensation for damage to it (eg insurance money) and don't spend all the money on restoring the damage. But a transfer of an asset between husband and wife who aren't separated doesn't count as a disposal. Nor does the transfer of an asset you leave when you die.

Tax-free gains

You are not normally liable for tax on gains on the following:
- your own home (see p66)
- a second home lived in rent-free by a dependent relative
- private cars
- British money (including post-1836 gold sovereigns)
- foreign currency for personal or family expenditure (eg for a holiday abroad)
- British Government stocks held for a year or more, or which you inherited
- National Savings Certificates, British Savings Bonds, Save-As-You-Earn
- chattels – ie personal belongings, furniture, antiques, jewellery and other tangible movable objects – provided the value of each chattel at the time of disposal is £3,000 or less. A set – eg a silver tea service – is looked on as one object, unless the parts of the set are sold separately to unconnected people. If the value is over £3,000 but less than £7,500, there may be some relief from tax – see left.
- animals, boats and other tangible movable objects which are *wasting assets* (assets with a predictable life of 50 years or less).
- life insurance policies, if you are the original owner or if they were given to you (but you may sometimes be liable for income tax on the gain – see p49)
- betting winnings (including football pool dividends and premium bond prizes)
- gifts of assets liable for capital gains tax which you make during the tax year, provided their total market value is not more than £100
- gifts to charities and to certain national institutions – the British Museum, National Trust and National Gallery, for example.

Relief for chattels

If the value at the time of disposal is more than £3,000 but less than £7,500, the taxable gain is taken to be *either* your actual gain *or* five-thirds of the excess over £3,000, whichever is the lower. This can mean a saving in tax: if, say, you bought something for £1,500 and sold it a few months later for £3,600, your actual gain would be £2,100. But the taxman would treat your gain as being $5/3 \times £600 = £1,000$. Correspondingly, if you'd bought it for £3,600 and sold it for £1,500 your loss would be the difference between £1,500 and £3,000 (ie £1,500 not £2,100).

Working out your gain (or loss)

Capital gains tax was first introduced in 1965. After some years of relative quiet, a drastic change to the rules was proposed in the 1982 Budget: for the first time, people had some protection against being taxed on gains which were simply the result of inflation.

The result of the changes is that different rules apply, depending on when you first acquired the asset. Shares and unit trusts have always been a special case, and are dealt with on pages 56 to 58.

A gain you make on an asset is normally a taxable gain (and a loss is an allowable loss) unless the asset is one on which the gain is tax-free – see previous page.

Example

Matt Parsons owns two houses. His main home for capital gains tax purposes is exempt from capital gains tax – so there's no tax to pay when he sells it. He bought his second house for £10,000 (including allowable expenses) in 1970. He sells the second house in December 1985 for £40,000 (after deducting the cost of the sale).

Matt has already used up all his annual exemption from CGT (see opposite) and so can't deduct it from the amount of the gain.

Step 1

Matt deducts the purchase price (£10,000) from the sale price (£40,000). This shows a gain of £30,000. So Matt moves to *Step 2*.

Step 2

The £10,000 purchase price is indexed from March 1982. To find the indexed value of the purchase price, Matt divides the RPI in the month of sale by the index in March 1982, and multiplies it by £10,000. So if the RPI was 100 in March 1982 and 159.8 in December 1985, the calculation would be:
$159.8 \div 100 \times £10,000 = £15,980$.

To work out his gain, Matt deducts £15,980 from £40,000 – ie a gain of £24,020.

But suppose Matt had bought his second house in March 1982 at a price of £30,000, and sold it for £40,000 in December 1985. Here's what *Step 2* would look like:

Step 2

The £30,000 purchase price will be indexed from March 1983 (ie twelve months after the purchase). To find the indexed value, Matt divides the RPI in the month of sale by the index in March 1983, and multiplies it by £30,000. So if the RPI was 110.9 in March 1983 and 159.8 in December 1985, the calculation would be:
$159.8 \div 110.9 \times £30,000 = £43,230$

This is more than the sale price, so there's no gain. But under the new rules, neither is there a loss.

Assets bought after 28 February 1981, and sold after 5 April 1982 (other than shares or unit trusts).

Step 1
● take the value of the asset at the time of the disposal (ie the price you got, or the market value at the time you gave it away)
● deduct the value of the asset at the time you came to own it. This will be the price you paid (if you bought it); the market value at the time you came to own it (if you were given it); the value at the date of death (if you inherited it)
● deduct from the result any allowable expenses. These include the costs of acquiring and disposing of the asset (eg advertising, conveyancing, commission) and expenditure which has increased the value of the asset (eg improvements, but not ordinary maintenance).

If the result is a minus figure, you will have made an allowable loss – see opposite for how this affects how much tax you have to pay. If the result shows a gain you must move to *Step 2* to see whether the new index-linking rules will wipe out the gain. Note that index-linking won't either create or increase an allowable loss.

Step 2 (based on proposals in the 1982 Budget)
The value of the asset at the time you came to own it (see above) is linked to the Retail Price Index (RPI) from 12 months after the end of the month in which you acquired it. So if you bought something in March 1981, it will be linked to the RPI from March 1982. Similarly any allowable expenses (apart from disposal costs) are linked to the RPI, again with the 12 month delay. Expenses which increase the value of an asset are treated by the taxman as being made on the date when the results of the expenses are first reflected in the state and nature of the asset. So if, for example, you paid someone to frame a picture, the cost of the framing would be index-linked from 12 months after the month in which the framing was done. Expenses of acquiring the asset are treated as being incurred on the date on which the asset was acquired.

You take these index-linked figures, and add on the (unindexed) costs of disposal, and then deduct the result from the value of the asset at the time of the disposal. If the result is nil, or a minus figure, there's no capital gain and no allowable loss.

Assets bought after 5 April 1965 and before 1 March 1981, and sold after 5 April 1982 (other than shares and unit trusts).

Step 1 and Step 2 above still apply, but the value of the asset (and allowable expenses) won't start to be indexed until March 1982. So if, for example, you bought something for £5,000 in 1970, and spent £200 on restoring it in 1976, both the £5,000 and the £200 would be indexed from March 1982.

Assets bought before 6 April 1965 and sold after 5 April 1982 (other than shares and unit trusts)

You have the choice of two methods – both of which we explain. The idea behind both methods is to stop you paying tax on any gain made before 6 April 1965 – the day when capital gains tax was introduced.

Method 1   You work out your gain in exactly the same way as for assets acquired after 5 April 1965 and before 1 March 1981. If there's still a gain, you reduce the gain in the following way:
● divide the gain by the number of complete months you've held the asset (but count only the period since *6 April 1945*)
● multiply the result by the number of complete months between *6 April 1965* and the date of disposal. This gives the gain since 6 April 1965.

Method 2   You work out your gain in exactly the same way as for assets acquired after 5 April 1965 and before 1 March 1981, but for the original value of the asset you substitute its market value on 6 April 1965. If you want to use method two, you must tell the taxman within two years from the end of the tax year in which you disposed of the asset. Once you've chosen this method you can't change your mind – even if it means a higher tax bill for you. The taxman won't enter into discussion about the 1965 valuation until you've made the choice.

How much tax

Some gains are free of all capital gains tax – see p53. And you're let off paying tax on the first chunk of gains you make which are taxable. For the 1982–83 tax year, you pay:
● no tax on the first £5,000 of your *net taxable gains* (see below for what net taxable gains are). A husband and wife living together only get £5,000 free of tax – not £10,000
● 30% tax on all net taxable gains above £5,000.
    To arrive at your net capital gains for the year:

Step 1   Subtract your allowable capital losses on assets disposed of during the year from your taxable capital gains for the year

Step 2   If the answer to Step 1 is a minus number, your net capital gains for the year are zero and there's no tax to pay. You can carry forward the balance of your losses (together with any losses left from previous years) to future years
    If the answer comes to more than £5,000, any allowable losses you have left from previous years will be used to reduce your net taxable gains, but *not* to below the £5,000 level. If you still have allowable losses left, these can be carried forward to future years.

Example

Samuel Rider bought a holiday home on 6 October 1960 and sold it on 6 April 1982. He works out that he made a gain of £5,160 over the 258 months he owned the home – ie £20 a month. From 6 April 1965 to when he sold the home was 204 months – so his gain since 6 April 1965 works out at £20 × 204 = £4,080.

Example

Charles Harvey realises he can set some losses off against the £9,000 gain he made on his second home. In the 1982–83 tax year, he made a loss of £2,000 on some shares he sold. And he has £5,500 of allowable losses carried forward from previous years – from a disastrous investment in Sheepdip Enterprises. He works out his net capital gains for the year:

Step 1 Subtracting his allowable loss for the year from his taxable gain for the year leaves £9,000 − £2,000 = £7,000.

Step 2 This is more than £5,000, so the allowable losses brought forward from earlier years will be used to reduce his net capital gains to £5,000. This leaves him with £5,500 − £2,000 = £3,500 of losses to carry forward to the 1983–84 tax year.

Gifts – special rules

If you give an asset away, you may be liable for capital gains tax on the difference between its value when you acquired it (increased by the normal indexation rules) and its value now, *less* any allowable expenses you've incurred (increased by the normal indexation rules). For gifts made on or after 6 April 1980, there's a special form of relief available – called *roll-over relief*. The effect of this relief is to reduce *your* capital gain to zero – but it could mean a higher tax bill for the *getter* if he eventually sells, or otherwise disposes of, the asset. The getter is counted as acquiring the asset at its market value when you (the giver) first acquired it, *plus* any allowable expenses you incurred. He gets the benefit of the indexation rules up to the time he receives the gift. But there's no further indexation until 12 months after the month of the gift. Any capital transfer tax paid on the gift can be deducted when working out any capital gain eventually made by the getter – but only to the extent of reducing his capital gain to zero.

You and the person to whom you're giving the asset must apply jointly for roll-over relief – contact the taxman.

Don't claim this relief if you know your gains for the year (including the gain on the gift) won't exceed £5,000. You won't save tax, and the getter might pay more.

Life insurance policies

There's normally no capital gains tax to pay on proceeds from a life insurance policy. And if you sell a policy which you've taken out (or been given) there's again no capital gains tax to pay. But if you've bought a policy, the difference between the price you paid and what the policy pays you will count as a capital gain. And if you sell a policy which you've bought, the difference between what you paid and what the buyer paid you will count as a capital gain.

Shares and unit trust holdings

Rules for these have always been quite complicated. The changes proposed in the 1982 Budget add new complications. Below we outline the Budget proposals – these could have changed, so check with a professional adviser. As with other assets, the rules vary depending on when you first acquired the shares or unit trust holdings.

Shares and unit trust holdings bought after 5 April 1982

The basic rules are exactly the same as for other assets – you work out your gain and loss in the same way, and you get the benefit of indexation if you've held the shares for long enough. Problems begin when you've acquired two or more lots of shares of the same type: for example you might buy 400 Slagthorpe Ordinary shares in May 1982, and another 600 in July 1982. If you then sell some Slagthorpe shares, the taxman has special rules for deciding which of the shares have been sold (and therefore which buying price and date of purchase apply):

Step 1 If you sell some shares, the taxman looks at all the shares of that type which you've bought in the previous 12 months (but he won't, at this stage, look at shares bought before 6 April 1982). He will assume that you've sold the shares you bought in those twelve months *in the order in which you bought them*. So he'll look first at the earliest parcel of shares. If you've sold fewer shares than the number of shares in the earliest parcel he'll stop there. If you've sold more, he'll go on to the next parcel, and so on.

Step 2   If you've sold more shares than you've bought in the previous 12 months, the taxman will look at shares bought before then. (He still won't look at shares bought before 6 April 1982 – see later for how he deals with them.) He'll assume that you've sold your most recently acquired shares first – so he'll look first at the most recently acquired parcel of shares, and then at the next most recently acquired parcel, and so on, until he's used up all the shares you've bought since 6 April 1982.

The normal indexation rules (see p54) will then be applied to each parcel of shares.

Example

Sue Davis buys 400 Slagthorpe ordinary shares in May 1982; another 600 in July 1982; a further 800 in December 1982, and a further 1,000 in March 1983. She sells 2,000 of the shares in November 1983.
   The taxman looks at the shares in the following order:

2,000 shares sold	2,000
deduct 800 shares bought in December 1982	1,200
deduct 1,000 shares bought in March 1983	200
deduct 200 shares from the shares bought in July 1982	nil

Sue is left with the 400 shares she bought in May 1982, and a further 400 shares remaining from the 600 she bought in July 1982.

Shares and unit trust holdings bought after 6 April 1965 and before 6 April 1982

If, in this period, you've bought several lots of the same share (or unit trust) at different times, they're put into what's called a pool, and the cost of each share (or unit) is taken to be the average cost of buying them.
   So, for example, if you paid £700 for 250 shares in a company, and later pay £300 for another 250 shares, your total holding of 500 shares has cost you £700 + £300 = £1,000. This works out at an average cost of £2 a share.
   You have a separate pool for each type of share (eg voting and non-voting shares) you hold in each company. You also have a separate pool for each type of fixed income investment (eg loan stock, debentures, preference shares) you hold in each company.
   Each pool is frozen from 5 April 1982 – nothing can be added to a pool after that date. The acquisition cost of a pool is taken to be its cost to you at that date, and from then on the pool is treated as a single asset. You are treated as having acquired each pool on 6 April 1981 – and each pool is indexed from March 1982. Special rules may apply to any pool where any additions have been made in the 12 months before 6 April 1982.

Shares and unit trust holdings bought before 6 April 1965

Method 1   The general rule is that shares and unit trust holdings bought before 6 April 1965 are treated as if they'd been bought at their market value on that date unless this would lead to a larger gain or loss than you actually made. If one calculation shows you made a loss, the other a gain, you are treated as having made neither a taxable gain nor an allowable loss.
   If you bought shares in the same company, or units in the same unit trust, at different prices and dates before 6 April 1965, this method is applied to each purchase separately.
   If you're selling some of your shares, (or units), it is assumed that the shares you sell first are the ones you bought last.

Method 2   Few people can use this method – it's only for people who have sold NONE of their pre-1965 shares and unit trust holdings before a certain date (currently 6 April 1979; it will change to 6 April 1980 on 6 April 1983, 6 April 1981 on 6 April 1984, and so on). If you're within the time limits, you can choose to have the cost of *all* (not just some) of your pre-1965 holdings of shares and unit trusts taken to be their market value on 6 April 1965. It would pay you to do this if, for example, your holdings overall were worth less when you sold them than they were on 6 April 1965, *and* more on 6 April 1965 than when you bought them.

You can choose, separately, to have all your pre-1965 fixed-income investments (excluding British Government stocks, which would be exempt from capital gains tax) treated in the same way. Again, the same time limit applies. If a husband and wife both want to make the choice they must do so separately for their own holdings.

To make an election, fill in form CG28 and send it to your tax office. Bear in mind that once an election is made, it cannot be withdrawn. If you've already been assessed by the first method, but subsequently make an election within the two-year time limit, your earlier tax bill will be altered.

If part of shareholding bought before 6 April 1965, part after

You can apply *method 1* (see previous page) to those shares or units which you bought before 6 April 1965. The shares (or units) you bought after 6 April 1965 go into a pool and are treated separately. Shares bought after 5 April 1982 are treated as described on p56.

Or, if you're within the time limits, you can apply *method 2*, and choose to have your whole shareholding pooled – in which case the shares you bought before 6 April 1965 are taken into the pool at their actual cost, in the ordinary way. Remember though, that if you choose this method, it will be applied to all your holdings of ordinary shares and unit trusts (or all your holdings of fixed-income investments) bought before 6 April 1965.

Unit trusts and investment trusts

Gains or losses made on or after 6 April 1980 on unit trusts and investment trusts are treated exactly the same as those on shares – see p56.

Before that date, gains you made on unit or investment trusts came with a tax credit – which meant they were effectively tax-free for people who paid tax at the basic rate only.

Equalisation

With your first income distribution from a unit trust, you will normally be paid a small refund – called an equalisation payment – of some of the money you originally handed over.

This payment is not taxable, but must be subtracted from the buying cost when you calculate your capital gain or loss.

Accumulation unit trusts

With accumulation unit trusts, the income from your units is automatically reinvested for you.

Accumulation unit trusts work in one of two ways. The income can be used to buy more units for you, or the income is simply added to the value of the unit trust fund. Working out the cost of buying your units is complicated – and depends on the way in which the unit trust works. Check with the taxman for details.

In either case, keep all the tax vouchers you get from the unit trust – as evidence for the taxman, and to help with your sums.

Example

Sebastian Smith bought 1,000 units in Two Cities Unit Trust in June 1975 at £1 each	£1,000
In November 1975 he received an equalisation payment of	£5
So cost of buying units counts as	£995
He sold the units in September 1981 for	£2,095
His taxable gain is £2,095 – £995 = £1,100	

British Government stocks held for less than a year

Such gains are taxable. And there are complicated rules if you have held some of the stock for more than a year and some for less, or if you sell the stock and later repurchase it, or if you dispose of the stock before you acquire it. Ask your tax office for details.

Capital gains and marriage

A couple who are married before the start of the tax year, or who marry on the first day of the tax year, normally have their gains taxed jointly – ie the husband's losses are set off against the wife's gains and vice versa.

But a couple can choose to have their capital gains separately assessed – this will make the wife responsible for paying her share of the bill, but won't affect the total amount of the couple's bill. Whether assessed jointly or separately, either of the couple can ask for his or her own losses for any year to be set off against his or her own gains only (present and future). This can affect the couple's tax bill.

If either husband or wife has made net losses during the year while the other has made net taxable gains of £5,000 or less, the one who has made the losses should ask for them to be carried forward and set against his or her own future gains. That way there's no tax to pay this year – and there may be a tax-saving in future years.

Example

Paul Porter made a taxable capital gain of £4,600 in the 1982/83 tax year. His wife Shirley made an allowable loss of £1,200.

Paul and Shirley talk it over and realise that if they are taxed in the normal way, Shirley's loss will be set off against Paul's gain. They'll have no tax to pay – but will have no losses to carry forward.

If Shirley asks to have her own losses for the year set against her own gains only, however, there will still be no tax to pay (because their joint gains, ignoring Shirley's losses are less than £5,000). And Shirley will be able to carry her £1,200 loss over to set against her future gains.

How to avoid paying more CGT than necessary

● be sure to deduct from a gain, or add to a loss, all your allowable expenses

● if you have things which have increased in value and on which you will have to pay CGT when you sell them, you can avoid tax by keeping the gains you make each year below £5,000. It's worth making use of this £5,000 allowance each year if you can – it can't be carried forward to the next year

● if your losses for the year add up to more than your gains, you can carry forward the balance of the losses to set against gains you would have to pay tax on in later years. So keep a careful record of your losses

● if either husband or wife has made net losses during the year, while the other has made net gains of less than £5,000, the one who made the losses should ask for them to be carried forward and set against future gains. There'll still be no tax to pay that year, and there may be a tax saving in later years.

Capital transfer tax

Not a tax which affects investments very much. So we give a brief outline of the rules, and then home in on insurance policies – where a little care can keep capital transfer tax at bay.

Who's afraid of CTT?

You may face a capital transfer tax bill if:
- you give away a total of more than £55,000 within any period of ten years, or
- you die. When you die, the value of all your possessions is added to any gifts you've made in the previous ten years. If the total is more than £55,000, there could be a CTT bill.

But it's not as bad as it sounds. Some gifts are tax-free (see below) and are ignored by the taxman. For example, gifts between a husband and wife are normally tax-free no matter when they're made. So if you die worth £150,000, and leave the lot to your wife (or husband), the value of your estate, for CTT purposes, is nil.

Any gifts which aren't tax-free start to clock up on a running total. When your running total goes above £55,000, there will be a CTT bill. This £55,000 is known as the *nil rate* band. The nil rate band has been raised three times since 1974 – and will be increased in line with inflation in the future unless Parliament decides otherwise.

Under rules introduced in the 1981 budget, any gifts made more than ten years before the gift you're now making are knocked off your running total – so your running total can fall as well as rise.

Note: CTT began on 27 March 1974, so (with rare exceptions) all gifts made before then are exempt.

Tax-free gifts
- **normal expenditure out of income.** If you make regular gifts (to anyone) out of your after-tax income, all the gifts are ignored for CTT purposes, provided you can maintain your normal standard of living on the income you have left. There has to be a consistent pattern of gifts (eg gifts of similar amounts for, say, three years or more)
- **gifts of up to £250 each (in any tax year) to any number of people**
- **wedding gifts.** You can give up to £5,000 if you're a parent of the bride or groom, up to £2,500 if you're a grandparent or great-grandparent, and up to £1,000 if you're anyone else
- **gifts of up to £3,000 in any tax year which aren't tax-free for any other reason.** If you don't use up one year's quota, you can use it in the following year, as long as you've used all that year's £3,000 first.

Insurance policies   Regular premium life insurance policies are an excellent way of giving chunks of tax-free capital to your dependants – or indeed to anyone. You qualify for a government subsidy on the premiums you pay (within certain limits) – at 15 per cent for the 1982–83 tax year. To get the subsidy, the policies must be on your life (or your wife's or husband's life) or on your joint lives.

   The premiums will count as a gift, but there shouldn't be any capital transfer tax (CTT) to pay on them, since they'll normally be in one of the tax-free categories opposite.

What to avoid

Try to make sure that the proceeds of your policies don't count as part of your estate. If they do, they'll be added on to the rest of what you leave, and your CTT bill could rise.

How to avoid it

Get the policy written in trust so that the proceeds go to someone else. If a policy on your life is for the benefit of your wife (or husband) or children, the Married Women's Property Act provides a simple way of doing this. Otherwise, you'll need to get a declaration of trust written on the policy. Ask the insurance company what to do. Alternatively, you could give away the policy after taking it out. This would count as a gift for CTT purposes.

   The value the taxman puts on the gift of a policy is either the market value of the policy or the total amount paid in premiums, whichever is the higher. The market value will often be close to the surrender value, but, for example, the market value of a policy on the life of someone close to death will be almost as high as the amount the policy will pay out.

Types of policy

● **endowment policy** (see p124)
what it is: a policy which pays out a lump sum on a fixed date – or when you die, if this is earlier.
useful for: people who want to give tax-free capital away in their lifetime.
● **whole life insurance** (see p132)
what it is: a policy which pays out on your death.
useful for: paying the CTT bill when you die. A husband and wife who are going to leave everything to each other could take out a last survivor or joint life and survivor policy, which pays out on the second death (ie when the CTT bill will arrive). The premiums are lower than for a policy on a single life. A joint life first death policy is useful for paying a CTT bill on the first death
● **term insurance** (see p124)
what it is: a policy which pays out only if you die before the policy ends (within three years, or ten years, say). If you survive, it pays nothing.
useful for: someone who will be faced with a large CTT bill only if death occurs within a certain time. For example, someone who has received a lifetime gift may be caught by a CTT bill if the giver dies within three years

6 Your home

A house is first and foremost somewhere to live. But it can be
looked on as the largest single investment most people make.

The Diagram below shows that house prices have, on average,
increased more than tenfold over the past 25 years. On the Diagram
we've also shown the Retail Price Index (RPI), which measures
increases in prices in general. You can see that for most of the
period, house prices increased more quickly than the RPI. This
means that the real value of a home in terms of the buying-power of
what it's worth has, on average, gone up over this period. This can
be said of few other conventional investments. Of course, part of
the increase in house prices is due to better standards of housing –
eg more houses now have central heating than 25 years ago, many
dilapidated properties have been brought up to scratch. And there
were times – particularly after boom periods – when house price
increases haven't matched inflation – eg in 1980 and 1981.

Of course, not all houses have gone up by the amounts shown in
the Diagram. Some types of home and some areas will have risen
more than average, others less. The map opposite shows how
prices varied in the UK in the second quarter of 1981 – and the rate
at which they'd gone up over the previous five years. For each
region, we've shown prices for three different types of property –
detached, semi-detached and terraced.

Within the regions prices vary considerably – because of things
like size, number of rooms, how big the garden is and whether

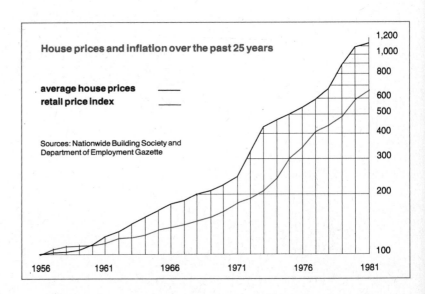

House prices and inflation over the past 25 years

average house prices   ——
retail price index   ——

Sources: Nationwide Building Society and
Department of Employment Gazette

1956   1961   1966   1971   1976   1981

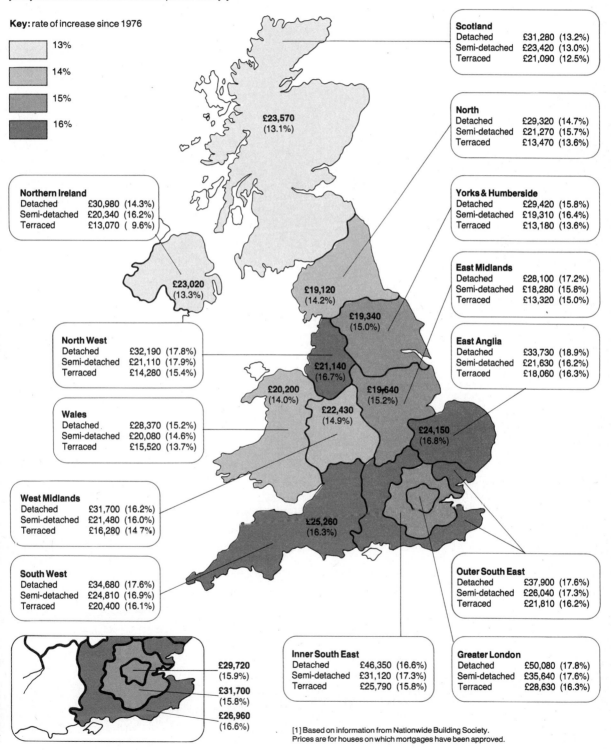

House prices in the UK
Average house prices in second quarter 1981 and average
yearly rates of increase since second quarter 1976 [1]

Key: rate of increase since 1976

- 13%
- 14%
- 15%
- 16%

Scotland
Detached £31,280 (13.2%)
Semi-detached £23,420 (13.0%)
Terraced £21,090 (12.5%)

North
Detached £29,320 (14.7%)
Semi-detached £21,270 (15.7%)
Terraced £13,470 (13.6%)

Yorks & Humberside
Detached £29,420 (15.8%)
Semi-detached £19,310 (16.4%)
Terraced £13,180 (13.6%)

East Midlands
Detached £28,100 (17.2%)
Semi-detached £18,280 (15.8%)
Terraced £13,320 (15.0%)

East Anglia
Detached £33,730 (18.9%)
Semi-detached £21,630 (16.2%)
Terraced £18,060 (16.3%)

Northern Ireland
Detached £30,980 (14.3%)
Semi-detached £20,340 (16.2%)
Terraced £13,070 (9.6%)

North West
Detached £32,190 (17.8%)
Semi-detached £21,110 (17.9%)
Terraced £14,280 (15.4%)

Wales
Detached £28,370 (15.2%)
Semi-detached £20,080 (14.6%)
Terraced £15,520 (13.7%)

West Midlands
Detached £31,700 (16.2%)
Semi-detached £21,480 (16.0%)
Terraced £16,280 (14.7%)

South West
Detached £34,680 (17.6%)
Semi-detached £24,810 (16.9%)
Terraced £20,400 (16.1%)

Outer South East
Detached £37,900 (17.6%)
Semi-detached £26,040 (17.3%)
Terraced £21,810 (16.2%)

Inner South East
Detached £46,350 (16.6%)
Semi-detached £31,120 (17.3%)
Terraced £25,790 (15.8%)

Greater London
Detached £50,080 (17.8%)
Semi-detached £35,640 (17.6%)
Terraced £28,630 (16.3%)

£23,570 (13.1%)
£23,020 (13.3%)
£19,120 (14.2%)
£19,340 (15.0%)
£21,140 (16.7%)
£20,200 (14.0%)
£19,640 (15.2%)
£22,430 (14.9%)
£24,150 (16.8%)
£25,260 (16.3%)
£29,720 (15.9%)
£31,700 (15.8%)
£26,960 (16.6%)

[1] Based on information from Nationwide Building Society.
Prices are for houses on which mortgages have been approved.

there's a garage, central heating and so on. But other things like the age of the house and its condition, architectural style, the area it's in may affect prices and the rate at which they change.

For example, in rural areas houses in a pretty village may become expensive because people increasingly want to buy them as second homes. But houses in a less attractive village a few miles away may be cheaper-than-average for the region because there are few jobs for the locals and people want to move away.

Local redevelopment could cause the price of your home to plummet. And if you have to sell your house quickly (because your job moves, say) you may also have to accept a cut in price.

When looking at the figures for average house prices bear in mind that price increases shown on the map have been averaged out over five years. During the 12 months to May 1981, house prices increased by very little, and in some cases, showed no increases at all – so price increases from May 1980 to May 1981 were substantially less than the averages shown.

What makes house prices change?

House prices are influenced by several factors – both in the long-term and the short-term.

Long-term factors include:
- people's earnings – particularly in terms of buying-power
- the availability of homes to buy
- the number of people wanting to buy
- trading-up (ie the tendancy for owner-occupiers to move on to more expensive homes).

In the short-term, relatively sudden increases in earnings (compared with prices in general) and in the numbers of first-time buyers, temporary shortages of houses to buy (eg not enough new houses being built), and speculation about house prices can fuel short, sharp booms of perhaps a few years' duration. Also the availability – or otherwise – of loan finance (eg mortgages from building societies and banks) can play a part.

A house as an investment

In the Diagram opposite, we've shown the rate of return you could have got by investing in a house over three different time periods. We've shown three yearly rates of return (allowing for buying and selling costs in each case):
- investing in your only or main home with an 80 per cent mortgage, allowing for mortgage repayments (after basic rate tax relief on the interest)
- investing in your only or main home bought outright with cash
- investing in a second home, bought outright with cash, and allowing for capital gains tax on the gain you make.

The Diagram also gives the rate of return you would have needed to keep pace with inflation.

For how investing in a house has compared with other investments, see the Diagram on p11. Bear in mind that, over the periods we've looked at, houses have improved in quality which artificially increases the return somewhat. And, of course, the gain on a house is not easy to get at – you'd have to sell and rent, or trade-down to see your money.

With a house, you have to pay various running costs – eg decorating, repairs, rates etc. If you weren't buying your own home, but renting one instead, you would be paying some of these costs anyway (perhaps indirectly in your rent). But with a second home, these running costs are additional ones (unless you can rent the home out to cover them).

For the periods we've looked at, you can see from p11 that when

Different ways of investing in a home

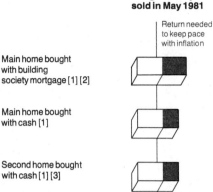

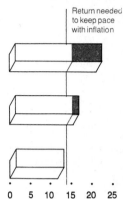

	bought in May 1956 sold in May 1981	**bought in May 1972 sold in May 1975**	**bought in May 1971 sold in May 1981**

Main home bought with building society mortgage [1] [2]

Main home bought with cash [1]

Second home bought with cash [1] [3]

Yearly rate of return to basic rate taxpayer %

0 5 10

0 5 10 15 20 25 30

0 5 10 15 20 25

[1] Based on average house prices. Allows for buying and selling costs. Other costs such as maintenance, rates and insurance not taken into account. Schedule A tax (payable by owner-occupiers before 1963) not taken into account

[2] Assumes 25-year, 80 per cent repayment mortgage is taken out at the start of each period. Based on mortgage interest rates recommended by The B S A and tax relief at basic rate
[3] Allows for capital gains tax since 1965.

compared with many conventional investments such as shares, building societies and British Government stocks, buying your main home with a mortgage has proved a very good investment. When compared with less conventional investments – eg gold sovereigns, rare stamps, Georgian silver – the picture is less clear. You might have done better with these investments or worse.

A hedge against inflation?

There is a traditional belief that investing in property – including private houses – offers protection against the ravages of inflation, as property tends to hold its value in real terms. The Diagram above supports this belief. Of course, when you invest and when you sell are crucially important. If, for example, you'd bought a house in 1972 (when prices were booming) and sold again in 1977, the return you'd have got would have been way below the increase in the RPI – especially after allowing for hefty buying and selling costs.

Why have houses done so well?
The main reason is that house prices have gone up by more than prices in general. But a number of other factors help to make housing an attractive investment. These include:
● tax relief on mortgage interest
● exemption from capital gains tax on your only or main home
● the effects of gearing.

Tax relief on mortgage interest

In general, you can get tax relief on the interest you pay on up to £25,000 of loans to buy or improve:
● your only or main home (normally the one you live in most of the time)
● the home of your former or separated wife or husband
● the home of a dependent relative who doesn't pay you rent.
To get tax relief on a loan you must, in general, be buying an

interest in the home – eg the whole of it, a half share, or buying out someone else. The home must also be in the UK or Ireland.

You can get tax relief for more than one home – eg the one you live in, one your ex-wife lives in. But the £25,000 limit applies to the total you pay interest on. For more details, see below.

Capital gains tax

Unlike many other forms of investment, your only or main home is, in most cases, exempt from capital gains tax when you sell. This helps existing owner-occupiers to trade-up – ie to move to a better house. The non-taxable profit from the first home can be ploughed back into the next home together with a bigger mortgage, in the hopes of reaping a higher capital gain. For more details, see below.

More about tax

What tax relief is worth.

For each £ of interest you get tax relief on, you pay tax on one less £ of your income. So if you pay tax at the basic rate only, each extra £ of interest you pay saves you 30p in tax (in the 1982–83 tax year). If, say, you pay higher-rate tax at 60%, each extra £ you pay saves you 60p in tax. This means that borrowing can be much cheaper than it seems at first sight. For example, tax relief means that a basic rate taxpayer who borrows money at 13.5% is, in effect, paying interest of only seven-tenths of 13.5% (ie 9.45%). And a 60% taxpayer, in effect, pays interest of only 5.4%.

Note that there are some loans you can't get tax relief on even if they are used for buying or improving your only or main home. These include option mortgages (available until April 1983) where you pay a lower-than-normal rate of interest, overdrafts and borrowing on credit cards.

What counts as improving a home?

A loan for improving your home can qualify for tax relief only if it is used for altering the home permanently. Ordinary repairs and decoration do not count as permanent – but converting your loft or insulating your home, building an extension or a swimming pool, or putting in fitted units do count. So does restoring a house bought in a dilapidated condition, converting your home into flats, or landscaping your garden. Installing central heating or double-glazing qualifies – but not portable radiators or night storage heaters, which aren't fixed.

The £25,000 rule.

The £25,000 limit applies to the total amount you and your wife owe. If you have more than one mortgage which qualifies for tax relief you get relief on the earliest loan first. If taking out a further loan takes you over the £25,000 limit, you get tax relief on only part of the interest you pay on the new loan – check with the taxman.

If you are 65 or over, you can also get tax relief on the interest on up to a further £25,000 of loans to buy an annuity, if the loan is secured on your only or main home – see p154 for more details. Note that the £25,000 rule has, since 6 April 1982, applied to loans taken out before 27 March 1974 (previously such loans counted towards the £25,000 limit only when working out tax relief on newer loans).

Moving home.

You may be faced with paying out on two loans at once – one on your new home, and one on your (unsold) old home. Under the normal rules, you get tax relief on £25,000 of loans on you new home (the £25,000 limit is reduced by pre-27 March 1974 loans, and by loans on homes of dependent relatives and former or separated spouses). But for a year (longer in deserving cases) you carry on getting tax relief as before on your old home too.

Capital gains tax (CGT)

If you (or you and your wife) have two or more homes, you can choose which one should count as your main home for CGT purposes. Make your choice within two years of acquiring the second home – otherwise the taxman can choose for you. You can alter the choice at any time, simply by telling the taxman (your new choice can be back-dated by up to two years).

In addition, one home owned by you or your wife and occupied rent-free by a dependent relative may be exempt from CGT (but, normally, not if the relative gave you the home in the first place).

But you may not get full exemption from CGT if any of the following apply:
- you let all or part of your home
- you use part exclusively for work
- the home wasn't your main one for capital gains tax purposes for all the time you owned it
- you were away from the home because of your work for periods totalling over four years (though you get full exemption for any period in which you were an employee working entirely abroad)
- you were away from the home for reasons unconnected with your work for periods totalling over three years
- you were away from the home for more than two years while you were trying to sell it
- your home is one of a series of homes you bought, or spent money on, in order to make a profit
- your garden is bigger than one acre.

For more details, see Inland Revenue leaflet CGT4 (1981) and CGT8 (1980) plus supplement – available free from your tax office. For how capital gains tax works, see p53.

Gearing

In the investment world, borrowing money to buy an asset, and only putting down a small part of the money yourself, is called **gearing**. This is a shrewd move, if the asset increases in value at a greater rate than the rate of interest you have to pay on your loan. If house prices go up by more than the after-tax relief interest on the mortgage, you'll get a relatively high return on your money.

You can see the effects of gearing from the Diagram on p65 – by comparing the rate of return for a main home bought with a mortgage with the return on a main home bought for cash.

Suppose, for example, that you had bought a home in May 1956 for £2,150 and sold it in May 1981 for £24,160. With an 80 per cent mortgage, your initial investment would have been 20 per cent of £2,150 – ie £430. Your gain in 1981 (after buying and selling costs) would be £21,240 – and the return on your investment (initial investment plus mortgage repayments – allowing for tax relief at the basic rate) works out at about 12 per cent a year. If you'd bought a home with cash, your investment would have been £2,150, and your rate of return 9.9 per cent a year. If you'd had a 90 per cent mortgage instead of an 80 per cent one, gearing would have been even more profitable.

In real life, people tend not to stay in the same house over a period of 25 years or so. Suppose you had three houses over our 25-year period –bought in 1956, 1961 and 1971 – always buying the most expensive you could afford, with the maximum mortgage a building society would give (which could mean mortgages of, say, 80 per cent, 70 per cent, and 50 per cent). Your rate of return (after buying and selling costs) would have been about 9 per cent.

But, be warned, your investment may come adrift if the after-tax relief mortgage interest rate exceeds the rate of increase in the price of your house. And if your house should fall in value, you'd feel the loss on your stake as dramatically as you'd feel any gain.

House prices in the future

We can only guess at how house prices will perform in the future, and whether the long-term trend for house prices to rise (even after allowing for inflation) will be maintained.

General economic uncertainty, worries about being able to afford mortgage repayments and worsening unemployment are likely to affect people's attitudes to house-buying. There seems little prospect of any major growth in the economy in the near future. On average, people's real earnings are unlikely to rise much over the next few years. This is not to suggest that an exodus from home ownership back to renting is heralded (or indeed, possible). But we might see a drop in demand for big houses with high maintenance and heating costs and increasing demand for smaller houses and flats. Regional differences might be accentuated by employment problems – eg areas where there are more jobs may attract more buyers and have the highest price increases.

Changes in the way building societies and other lenders operate would affect house prices in the future, though it's not entirely clear to what extent. Government action on mortgages could also influence the way house prices move. For example, the real value of the current £25,000 limit on loans qualifying for tax relief is being steadily eroded by inflation. If this continues, house prices may end up at a lower level than they would otherwise have been.

Increasing leisure time could make certain houses – eg those with gardens, close to sports centres, parks etc – more popular. High fuel costs could make homes with efficient insulation and heating systems sell at an even higher premium than they do now.

Extra expenses if you are going to buy

If you're going to invest in bricks and mortar, you'll also have to
find the money (perhaps three per cent or more of the purchase
price) for various incidental expenses at the time of buying. The
expenses you're likely to pay are listed below – we've given
example figures for a £25,000 house.

● **solicitor's fees.** Reckon on paying a solicitor between £250 and
£400 for conveyancing, etc. These figures include the lender's
solicitor's fee (for drawing up the mortgage deed) as your solicitor
will often be able to act for the lender too. Using a conveyancing
firm instead of a solicitor may be £50 to £100 cheaper

● **building society or other lender's valuation fee.** The cost varies
with the lender. With building societies, there is a fixed scale
depending on the price of the property. For example, the fee for a
house costing £25,000 is £41 plus VAT

● **own surveyor's fee.** A structural survey is optional, but usually
advisable. Charges vary quite widely (between £100 and £200, say,
for a three-bedroomed house). You may be able to save money by
asking the lender's valuer to do a structural survey when he does
the valuation, or by having an abridged survey done – such as
under the Royal Institution of Chartered Surveyors' scheme

● **Land Registry fee.** The fee, worked out on a sliding scale,
depends on whether the house has already been registered or not.
The fee for a registered house costing £25,000 would be £63.

● **stamp duty.** Payable (on sliding scale) for homes costing over
£25,000 – eg stamp duty on a house costing £30,000 would be £150

● **insuring the property.** Assume around £1.50 a year for each
£1,000 of cover (more if your home is of unusual construction)

● **removal costs.** If using a removal firm, get a few estimates first.
The cost depends on distance, how much furniture you've got, how
many flights of stairs are involved and so on. Do-it-yourself
removals (with hired van) normally work out cheaper.

Getting a mortgage

You'll probably need to get a mortgage to finance your investment.
Despite the presence of banks on the mortgage scene, you may want
to keep open the option of getting a building society mortgage. As
building societies, particularly if they're short of money, tend to
give priority to people who've been saving with them for some
time, it may be wise to start saving some time (two years, say) before
you intend to buy. Before you decide which building society to
save with, it's sensible to ask several about their lending policies.
See *Checklist* opposite for what to ask.

A bank, particularly if it's one you've got your account with, may
not insist on a minimum savings period before giving you a
mortgage. But it would be sensible to ask banks the questions on
the Checklist, too.

If you're a first-time buyer, take advantage of the Government's
Homeloan Scheme – see opposite.

Checklist: what to ask a building society before you invest

• how long you are likely to have to save for and how much you need to have in an account before the society will give priority treatment to a mortgage application. Also ask what restrictions have been applied in past periods of mortgage scarcity and what delays have been imposed on would-be borrowers

• how much money the society is likely to lend you. The maximum loan is usually based on what you earn ($2\frac{1}{2}$ times your pay, say; if you're married and husband and wife both work, possibly up to $2\frac{1}{2}$ times the higher of your incomes plus 1 times the lower). But you may find that when there's a shortage of mortgage money the society puts a limit (£25,000, say) on the amount it will lend any one borrower

• whether it will lend you money to buy the type of home you want – eg some building societies won't lend on converted flats, others view thatched cottages unfavourably, and many won't lend on properties with sitting tenants

• what proportion of the price of the home the building society will lend you (assuming the price is in line with the society's valuation)

• whether a charge will be made if you pay off your mortgage early

• what you can do if the mortgage interest rate goes up (eg with a straightforward repayment mortgage some building societies allow you to keep your monthly payments the same but increase the term of the mortgage).

Most of the answers you get will be qualified in some way since policies change over time and are conditioned by particular sets of circumstances. You should nevertheless be able to get a pretty clear picture on which to base comparisons.

Help for first-time buyers

The Government's **Homeloan Scheme** offers first-time buyers:
• a grant of between £40 and £110 to help with the cost of buying a first home
• a loan of £600 interest-free for five years.

The grant
To qualify for the grant (called the cash bonus) all the following must apply:
• you (and anyone who is buying with you) must not have owned a home before
• the purchase price must not be more than a certain limit – see next column
• you must be getting a mortgage
• the mortgage (including the government loan, if you get it) must be at least a quarter of the purchase price
• you must have been saving under the scheme for at least two years with an *approved savings institution* such as a building society, bank, or the National Savings Bank
• you must have at least £300 in your savings account throughout the whole of the 12-month period before you apply for the mortgage.

The amount of your grant will depend on the least that you have in your savings account in the 12-month period before you apply for the mortgage. It can vary from £40 if you've had at least £300, to £110 if you've had at least £1,000.

Maximum purchase price (April 1982)	
Greater London	£29,100
South East (except London)	£26,000
South West	£22,900
East Anglia	£21,400
West Midlands	£19,500
North West	£19,000
East Midlands	£18,400
Northern	£17,500
Yorkshire & Humberside	£17,100
Wales	£18,800
Scotland	£20,800
Northern Ireland	£21,500

The loan
If you qualify for a grant and you have at least £600 in your savings account when you apply for your mortgage:
• the amount of the mortgage you are offered can be increased by £600 (unless this would make the total loan more than the purchase price or the lender's valuation, whichever is lower), *and*
• £600 of your total loan will be interest-free for five years.

How to get the help
Open an account at an approved savings institution straightaway and tell them that you want to join the Homeloan Scheme (you must be 16 years old or more).

If you are applying for a mortgage now, but didn't register your savings under the scheme, all is not lost. Provided all the other conditions are met, you can still qualify for the grant and loan if you can satisfy the lender that you have been saving with the intention of qualifying under the scheme but were not aware of the requirement to register when you started to save. You also have to declare this on form HPA5.

7 Alternative investments

The struggle to stay ahead of inflation may lead you to look for less conventional investments to stake your money on in the hopes of showing a profit. And it's certainly possible to show that, over the last 25 years, an investor in certain *alternative investments* could have more than maintained the buying power of his savings.

The Diagram on p12 shows how gold sovereigns, rare British stamps and Georgian silverware have performed over three different periods since 1956 compared with investing in shares, buying a home and so on. We've given rates of return over different periods of time because the success of your investment depends very much on when you buy and when you sell. You can see from the Diagram that, in general, the return on these alternative investments have more than kept pace with inflation, and produced higher rates of return than most of the conventional investments we've illustrated. But presenting the investment potential of things such as Georgian silver, stamps and so on in this way can be misleading. In the main, the Diagram on p12 show things which proved to be successful investments. If *you* had been investing in 1956 or 1971, you might have chosen to buy things which didn't do nearly so well.

Which alternative investment to go for?

Limited supply plus growing demand is what to look for in an alternative investment. Things like old stamps, Georgian silver and Roman coins are available in limited quantities – there is no way that more can be produced (forgeries apart). So if more people want to own them – or the same number can afford to pay more (because of inflation, say) – prices will go up.

But limited supply, on its own, is not sufficient to make a good investment. For example, limited editions (see p74) are produced in quantities of a few hundred or a few thousand. But they are unlikely to prove good investments unless people will want to buy them in the future.

Nor is a high level of demand enough to make a good investment. For example, many collectors will snap up new issues of British stamps (eg the Royal Wedding issue was widely bought in July 1981). But if several million are issued, it's unlikely they will become valuable. For the investor, only stamps in fairly short supply and which are popular with collectors are likely to be wise buys.

Should YOU put your money in alternative investments?

If you're thinking of alternative investments, you should consider investing only part of your savings in this way – not more than 10 per cent, say – and certainly not your emergency fund or money you can't afford to lose. And bear in mind that:
● because of the expenses of buying and selling (eg auctioneer's commission, dealer's mark-up) you may not stand to make a profit

unless you keep your money invested a fairly long time – say, five years or more

● money invested in this way won't give you a regular income. And you may have to pay for storage, insurance and so on (see overleaf)

● fashions in collecting change; what may have been a steadily appreciating asset 10 years ago, may no longer be so much in demand now. You may even make a loss when you come to sell

● you may find it hard to decide on what price to ask when you sell – and, unless you sell at an auction, some haggling with buyers is likely to be involved. Going for a quick sale could mean a poor price.

Alternative investments have one advantage which most other types of investment lack – you can get pleasure out of finding and owning the things you invest in. Indeed, you're more likely to invest successfully if you do take an interest in them. And if your investments turn out to be unsuccessful, you at least have the consolation of owning a stamp collection, a set of prints or whatever.

On pages 73 to 76 we look at a few of the wide range of alternative investments available. Bear in mind that these are included as examples only – we are not suggesting that these investments in particular are ones you should go for. But reading pages 73 to 76 should give you hints on what to watch out for even if you decide to specialise in an area we haven't mentioned.

How should you invest?

The golden rule is **avoid investing from a position of ignorance.**

Here are a few tips:

● **find out about the things you want to invest in** *before* **you spend any money.** Read books and magazines on the subject, join societies for collectors of the things you are interested in, visit exhibitions, study auctioneers' catalogues and dealers' price lists, talk to experts. See p77 for a few details about societies, specialist magazines, useful addresses, and so on

● **start small.** Buy a few low-priced items in a narrow field, to get to know the things you are collecting. Develop your knowledge before spending more – and then stick to the field you are expert in

● **aim for items in very good condition.** You might have to settle for a poor quality item – to complete a set, say. But, in general, two or three items in good condition are likely to do better than several tatty ones

● **shop around.** Prices are likely to vary considerably between dealers – so don't be afraid to haggle over prices

● **be sceptical of 'guarantees'** (to buy back the things you invest in at double what you paid for them after five years, say). These

'guarantees' are only as good as the dealer who gives them – no good at all if he goes bust
● **invest in things which are collected world-wide** – so that the price you get when you sell won't necessarily be reduced if UK demand slumps.

Ahead of the crowd? You can make money if you invest in things which other investors haven't cottoned onto which subsequently become popular with collectors. You can't expect to be right every time (or even most of the time) with this sort of speculation. If you're only in it for the money, and other speculators do catch on, you may need to be good at spotting when a craze is reaching its height so that you sell before prices start tumbling.

Storage and insurance Careful storage may be important with things like stamps, port, paintings, say. Damp, sudden changes in temperature, sunlight, insects and so on could reduce (or even wipe out) the value of the things you collect.

You'll also need to insure your valuables against things like theft or fire. Typically, this might cost between £1 and £2.50 a year for each £1,000 of cover as part of a normal house contents policy (more if you live in a high-risk area). If you want all-risks cover (which includes cover against accidental damage, for example), this might cost between £15 and £20 or so a year for each £1,000 of cover. If your collection is worth a lot of money (more than a few thousand pounds, say), the insurance company is likely to insist on a safe, special locks and burglar alarms. The insurance company may ask for proof of your collection's value. A professional valuer (or a dealer) may charge perhaps one per cent of what he values your collection at. Remember to review the level of your insurance regularly – whatever the value of your collection.

Alternatively you could store your collection in a bank's strongroom – insurance may be less if you do this. The bank makes a charge for storage – from £1 a year for an envelope, say, up to £20 a year or more for a bulky item. Bank storage costs are considerably higher if you want to rent a safe deposit box – though these are difficult to get. Some dealers will also store and insure the things you buy from them – this may seem the simplest solution, but remember that you could have problems if the dealer you store with goes bust.

What about tax? Because there's no income from investing in things, there's no income tax to pay (unless the taxman decides you are carrying on a trade or business and taxes your profits as income).

You might be liable for capital gains tax if you make a gain when you sell or give away things you have invested in. But the first £5,000 a year of gains are normally tax-free. So are gains on things like antiques, jewellery and other tangible moveable objects which you sell for £3,000 or less, and if the gain is over £3,000 but less than £7,500, there may be some relief. Note that if you give things away you may not have to pay any tax that's due if you and the recipient apply for *roll-over relief*. For more details on capital gains tax, see pages 53 to 59.

You will normally have to pay VAT on the things you invest in if you buy from dealers.

Busted bonds

Collecting busted bonds is also known as *scripophily*. You collect old share certificates in companies which have collapsed, or government stock certificates issued by countries which have since had revolutions and repudiated their debts. Two distinct markets exist for busted bonds. You can still buy and sell some bonds – eg Russian or Chinese ones – on the Stock Exchange via a stockbroker. These are bonds where there is a chance (however remote) that some day the defaulting country may pay up on them. Recently, Rhodesian bonds have been redeemed by Zimbabwe, and Bulgaria has also redeemed some of its bonds. And in January 1981, the Chinese government invited people to register their claims on some £60 million worth of bonds defaulted on in 1949 (the year of the communist revolution). If you're tempted to sell such bonds, bear in mind that it might be more sensible to hang on to a rare bond which could appreciate as a collectors' item, rather than to redeem it at possibly less than face value.

The other market is for bonds or share certificates which certainly won't be redeemed. Their value lies in their appeal to collectors – because they are associated with a historic event (eg some were issued by the confederate states during the American Civil War) or because they're particularly attractive or rare. These can be bought from dealers, at auctions and so on.

Collecting busted bonds is a hobby of just a few dramatic years' standing. For about 10 years, interest – particularly in Imperial Russian and Chinese bonds – has been growing, but in 1978 and 1979 speculators suddenly caught on and started buying in a big way. Prices were forced up, and making a gain of 100 per cent plus in just a few months became commonplace.

Almost as suddenly, the bubble burst as the speculators began to offload their bonds – and there weren't enough genuine collectors to keep prices up. For example, one Chinese bond (the rare Deutsche-Asiatische Bank £500 1898 4½% Gold Loan) fetched £550 at auction in November 1978. Ten months later, the hammer price was £14,000. In June 1981, it could be bought from a dealer for around £5,000.

Recently, bond prices have started to pick up a bit. Genuine collectors are still on the look out for bonds to add to their collections. Demand in other collecting countries – eg US and Germany – didn't slump to the same extent as in the UK. In the longer term, bonds might turn out to be worthwhile. There are plenty around at low prices (£10 to £25, say) – perhaps too many.

Port

Laying down vintage port has, at times, been a highly profitable investment. Port suitable for laying down in 1961 (most probably of 1955 vintage) might have set you back £12 to £13 for a case of twelve bottles. If you'd sold that port at an auction in mid-1981, you could have expected to get somewhere between £150 and £215 (less auctioneer's commission) for it – ordinary individuals without a licence aren't allowed to sell or advertise alcohol except via a wine merchant or auctioneer.

If you'd paid a wine merchant to store the port for you, this might have cost £10 or more a case over the 20 years. But you could still have got a yearly return of around 12 to 14 per cent on your investment – free of tax unless the taxman reckoned you'd entered the wine trade and taxed the gain as your business profits. Since 1961, the cost of living has gone up by an average of around 9 per cent a year, so your investment would have kept well ahead of the rate of inflation.

But not all vintages have done as well as the 1955 one – and it's anybody's guess what will happen in the future. The most recent port suitable for laying down is the 1977 vintage. In mid-1981, a case of 12 bottles bought from a wine merchant would have cost around £75 to £100 (about 30 per cent less if you buy it and keep it in a bonded warehouse – because there's no VAT or duty to pay on it until it's taken out). Storage and insurance currently cost around £2 to £3 a year a case. Even if your investment doesn't produce a good cash return, at least you will have the consolation of drinking it.

Stamps

Apart from what they cost to use for postage, stamps are intrinsically worthless bits of paper. But they are avidly collected by very large numbers of people all over the world, some of whom are prepared at times to pay very large sums of money for stamps which are extremely rare, or of historical interest.

While there are many stamps which would have given you a good return on your investment over most of the last twenty years, some stamps have increased in value much more than others – and values can fall as well as rise.

Stamps which, in the past, have shown some of the largest increases in value have included examples (in fine condition) of rare nineteenth-century issues – sometimes called *classics*. This is because there is only a small – and known – number of these stamps in existence, and they have been sought by an increasing number of collectors.

But some investors have had their fingers burnt recently by innocently following the advice of a few unscrupulous dealers who have sold them 'investment' portfolios. The stamps turned out to be over-priced, and did not continue to appreciate at the rate that dealers claimed had applied in the past. The prices of many stamps fell dramatically between 1979 and 1980 making them difficult to resell – even back to the dealers they were bought from.

If you want to invest seriously in stamps, you will have to get to know a lot about them – through studying catalogues, going to auctions, joining a philatelic society and so on. Small differences in printing and watermarks – and even the sheet from which the stamp has been torn – can affect the

price drastically. The condition of the stamp is also very important. Moreover, forgeries and stamps with printing errors can be worth much more than legitimate stamps.

Buying special issues of commemorative stamps is unlikely to be a good investment because they are generally issued in very large quantities. Don't take catalogue prices as a guide to the values of stamps, or proof of how they have increased in value over the years. Catalogues show the prices at which a dealer would hope to sell stamps in first-class condition; he'd normally pay much less to buy the stamps. The prices fetched at auctions are a more reliable guide.

Limited editions

There are basically two ways to produce a limited edition:
● the number to be sold is specified at the outset – eg, 50, 500 or 5,000
● the number sold is the number ordered or bought by a certain date – eg 50 if only 50 are sold by that date, 50,000 if that is the number sold. With this method, the total number to be sold (important in evaluating scarcity) is normally known only after you've agreed to buy.

There are variations on these themes. For example, with some limited editions, the limit mentioned in the advertisements applies only to the UK, and more of the thing may be sold in other countries.

Of course, the investment potential of limited editions depends not only on the number produced, but also on the demand for them from collectors. And with many limited editions there's unlikely to be a big demand – so even if only a few dozen were

issued, you'd be unlikely to make a lot of money by investing in them. With some investments in limited editions, you may find that it's not the limited nature of the investment which makes it profitable – see below for an example of this.

Money Which? buys a limited edition

In 1979, as an experiment, *Money Which?* offered for sale a set of 50 hallmarked, sterling silver ingots. The ingots were part of a limited edition produced by *John Pinches* and commemorated 1,000 years of British monarchy. Each ingot had a portrait of one of the monarchs on it. John Pinches offered them for £350 in 1973. On 24 August 1979, Money Which? bought them from the original owner for £400.

In October 1979, Money Which? advertised the ingots in *Exchange & Mart* and contacted dealers. They were offered between £450 and £668 for them. A few offers were from people who said they were collectors, seven were from coin and medallion dealers, and one (the highest) was from a bullion dealer.

Money Which? stood to make a profit of over 65 per cent in just six weeks. But all the dealers stressed that what they were interested in was the scrap value of the ingots once they had been melted down – not their value as a limited edition. And no-one offered more than this scrap value.

It appeared that the timing of the Money Which? investment had been the crucial factor – prices of silver (and gold) had risen enormously over that six-week period. When Money Which? bought the ingots, their silver value was only around £420. In reality, the value of the ingots as collectors' items was minimal, but a very successful investment had been made in silver. In fact, by November 1981, after some periods of high drama on the world silver market, the scrap value of the ingots had declined again – to only around £435.

Diamonds

For the ordinary person there are three main ways of investing in diamonds: buying them over the counter, buying from diamond investment companies, or putting money into a scheme which in turn invests on the diamond market.

Buying diamonds over the counter

You can buy diamonds from a jeweller, or a diamond merchant, or at an auction; they may be loose or mounted in jewellery. When you want to sell, you can hawk the stones around dealers, or put them in an auction. But, as *Money Which?* discovered the hard way, there are serious drawbacks to investing this way. In 1970, *Money Which?* bought some diamonds (mounted in jewellery, and loose). Since then, they've hawked them around jewellers and dealers several times – most recently in August 1980. Each time, the prices they'd have fetched were very disappointing – a building society would have given a better return on the money involved.

Buying and selling loose diamonds over the counter seems to be a mug's game. Even if you get good value when you buy (and you've no way of being certain about that), the dealer's mark-up – which can be as high as several hundred per cent – is likely to make them a poor investment, even over a ten-year period. And particularly if you're looking for a sale on the spot, offers from dealers are likely to be on the low side. Most can't accurately establish the value of a diamond on the spot – though having certificates from a specialist diamond-grading laboratory might help in some cases.

As for diamonds mounted in jewellery, you're unlikely to show a profit on *new* jewellery for a very long time. The investment market for *antique* jewellery is more like that for antique furniture or porcelain, say, than for loose diamonds. Putting antique diamond jewellery into an auction may be the best way to sell.

Buying from diamond investment companies

These companies sell high quality, unmounted diamonds, usually with certificates describing the size and quality of each stone. You decide how much to invest and pay in advance. The company buys you diamonds as close as possible to that price (generally between £2,000 and £10,000 for each diamond). The diamonds are normally sent in sealed cases to a bank in the Channel Islands (to avoid VAT). Every so often the company lets you know its current prices for your diamonds.

When you want to sell, you contact the company again. They normally offer to try to re-sell your diamonds after two years or more, deducting commission of 10 to 20 per cent from the selling price. This means that unlike buying diamonds over the counter, the gap between buying and selling is normally fixed. Providing the company can find a new investor to buy your diamond, the price you get is the company's current list price less commission, and this gap is a lot smaller than a dealer's mark-up. And investing in diamonds from an investment company and selling them back later has produced high rates of return over some periods in the past. But over the recent past there has been little or no increase in diamond prices, and the high levels that diamond prices have reached could make it less likely that they'll increase much in the near future.

There could also be problems if the company can't find a new investor. If this proves impossible, and the company has instead to sell to the trade, you're unlikely to get it's current list price – and will probably get a lot less.

Before investing it's wise to compare list prices from several companies for diamonds of similar size and grade as there can be large variations.

Investment schemes

These are an alternative to buying diamonds directly. The money you invest is normally put into a fund and used to buy diamonds (usually owned by the fund, not by you). Broadly, the return you get when you cash in your investment depends on the rate at which the fund's diamonds have appreciated (or gone down) in value. There are several schemes around – all rather different from each other and all rather complicated. If you are tempted to invest this way, it's sensible to get professional advice first. By investing in a fund you can invest in a spread of diamonds for a relatively small amount. But the various charges involved can be higher than investing direct, and you don't usually own any diamonds. You could do well – but you would be unwise to place your faith in diamond prices going up a lot over any particular period of time.

Gold

For thousands of years, gold has been looked on as a store of wealth, and many people the world over believe that gold is a good asset to hold in times of political upheaval. But if you are tempted to invest in gold be prepared for a bumpy ride.

For example, in the twelve months to mid-January 1980, the gold price almost quadrupled – but by mid-April 1980 it had fallen by over 40 per cent. Even daily fluctuations can be alarming, so gold isn't suitable for the faint-hearted.

For an indication of how gold has performed over longer periods, see the Diagram on p11. Note that these show rates of return for gold sovereigns (ie not bullion (ie gold bars) because until exchange control was abolished in 1979, you were not allowed to own or to buy bullion. Nowadays, you can buy and sell gold in any form. Here we deal with buying coins (not to be confused with the rare coins that collectors go for) and gold bars. Other ways of investing include buying gold shares (eg the shares of companies that mine gold); buying units in a unit trust that specialises in gold shares or by dealing in gold futures. For how futures work, see p111.

The main ways of buying and selling coins and bullion are through banks, coin-dealers, jewellers and stockbrokers – or through the bullion-dealing companies that make up the London Gold Market (see opposite). It's probably advisable to steer clear of jewellers because they tend to have high mark-ups. Note that if you invest via intermediaries such

as stockbrokers, you will have to pay commission on buying *and* selling.

Bear in mind that the price at which a coin or bar is offered for sale will be higher than the current value of the gold in it. This extra cost over the gold value is known at the premium. The lower the premium, the more gold you'll get for your money. Premiums for particular coins fluctuate according to supply and demand, and it's possible for your investment to show a gain (or loss) without the gold price changing. Note that bullion and krugerrands (but not post-1837 sovereigns) are liable for capital gains tax – see p53.

Most of us couldn't possibly afford to invest in gold bars in the standard sizes in which they are traded (400 troy oz – around 12½ kilograms), though it is possible to obtain much smaller sizes – from 1 kilogram down to a 1 gram 'wafer'. But the very small bars are not at all

a sensible investment as the tinier the bar, the higher the premium. These small bars are often sold to be made up into jewellery. You can, of course, do this with coins too, but if you want to sell your pendant, or whatever, you may well get a very poor price.

In the Table below we show the prices at which you could have bought and sold single sovereigns, krugerrands and gold bars on 14 April 1982. Until recently, gold coins were often a better bet for the small investor than gold bars because they were normally exempt from VAT. But, from the end of March 1982, this exemption was withdrawn. Note that world trade in gold is transacted in US dollars – so the current exchange rate between the dollar and the pound will affect gold prices. When you sell, you may have to pay an assay fee – ie for checking that your bar actually is gold and doesn't just look like it.

Buying and selling gold at 10.30 a.m. on 14 April 1982 [1]

Gold price: U.S. $364.75 (£206.692) for a troy ounce

| | gold content | | prices | |
	troy ounces	grams	to buy [3]	to sell back
			£	£
Coins [2]				
Sovereign	0.24	7.32	63	50
Krugerrand	1.00	31.10	251	210
½ Krugerrand	0.50	15.55	138	113
¼ Krugerrand	0.25	7.78	85	58
⅒ Krugerrand	0.10	3.11	34	23
Bars				
1 kilogram	32.15	1000	7,660	6,630
½ kilogram	16.07	500	3,830	3,315
100 grams	3.22	100	775	660
20 grams	0.64	20	163	130
5 grams	0.16	5	46	30

[1] Retail prices for single bars and coins. Source: Johnson Matthey Bankers (London Gold Market member). Selling prices do not include any assay fee.
[2] Sovereigns are current issue (Queen Elizabeth II).
[3] Including VAT on buying prices.

A few sources of information

Books

Alternative Investment by Robin Duthy (Michael Joseph, but out of print – try a library)
Diamonds by Eric Bruton (NAG Press, £13.50)
Book Collecting – a beginner's guide by Seumas Stewart (David & Charles £6.50)
Miller's Antiques Price Guide 1982 (MJM Publications Ltd, £9.95)
Which? Wine Guide 1982 (£4.95 from Consumers' Association, Caxton Hill, Hertford SG13 7LZ)
Collecting Old Bonds and Share Certificates by Robin Hendy (Stanley Gibbons Publications Ltd 95p)
Coins and Banknotes for Profit by Peter & Mary Harrison (Barrie & Jenkins, but out of print – try a library)
Stamp Collecting for Profit by Peter & Mary Harrison (Barrie & Jenkins, but out of print – try a library)
The Antique Collectors' Club publish specialist books on art and antiques. (Write to 5 Church Street, Woodbridge, Suffolk IP12 1DX for a list).

Standard Catalogues

Stamps of the World 1982 (Stanley Gibbons Publications, £17.95)
Seaby's Standard Catalogue of British Coins (Seaby Publications. Sold in separate volumes – eg Vol I is *Coins of England and the United Kingdom*, price £7.50).

Societies

There are lots of societies – local and national. Here we give a very small selection. For societies near you, see *Directory of British Associations* or ask at your local library. This lists national societies and federations which may be able to put you in touch with a local society.
British Association of Numismatic Societies
Department of Coins and Medals, Manchester Museum, The University, Oxford Road, Manchester, M13 9PL (can put you in touch with local societies)
The Antique Collectors' Club
For address see entry under *Books* (can put you in touch with a local branch)
British Philatelic Federation
1 Whitehall Place, London SW1A 2HE (can put you in touch with local societies)
The Bond and Share Certificate Collectors' Society
PO Box 9, Tadworth, Surrey KT20 5DW
International Wine and Food Society
104 Pall Mall, London SW1Y 56W (can put you in touch with a local branch)

Magazines and journals

Too many to name. Look in a large newsagents (eg John Menzies, W.H. Smith) for magazines about your speciality – or see *Willing's Press Guide* or *Benn's Press Directory* at your local library.

Antiques and Collectors' Fairs

These are listed in **Exchange & Mart** – see under *Collecting* in the *Leisure* section. Details also given in specialist magazines.

Auctions

Here we list the largest auction houses in London. For local auction houses, see *Yellow Pages* (under Auctions), magazines for your speciality, and local newspapers.

W & FC Bonham & Sons Ltd, Montpelier Galleries, Montpelier Street, London SW7 1HH
Christie Manson & Woods Ltd, 8 King Street, St James's, London SW1Y 6QT
Phillips Sons & Neale, Blenstock House, 7 Blenheim Street, London W1A 0AF
Sotheby, Parke Bernet & Co, 34 & 35 New Bond Street, London W1A 2AA

Buying and selling gold

London Gold Market members prepared to deal with the public:
Johnson Matthey Bankers Ltd (01-481 3181)
Mocatta & Goldsmid Ltd (01-628 2825)
Sharps, Pixley Ltd (01-623 8000)

Banks prepared to buy back coins they've sold to you:
National Westminster Bank Ltd (ask at your local branch)
Standard Chartered Bank Ltd (branches in major cities. Ring 01-623 7500 for branch nearest to you).

8 Shares

It's less common these days for individuals to invest directly in shares. In 1963 over half of the value of all shares was owned directly by individuals; by 1980 this had fallen to around one-third. Nowadays, people tend to invest in shares indirectly – for example, through unit trusts (see Chapter 9), equity-linked life insurance (see Chapter 14), pension funds (see Chapters 17 and 18) or investment trusts (see p86). Should *you* invest in shares?

What you should expect

Investing in shares is a way of investing in the performance of a company. You can expect two sorts of return:
● income – the company will pay out an income (called dividends) to its shareholders. The hope is that this income will increase over the years as the profits of the company rise
● capital gain – the hope is that the share price of the company will rise over the years. This may happen if, for example, the company's

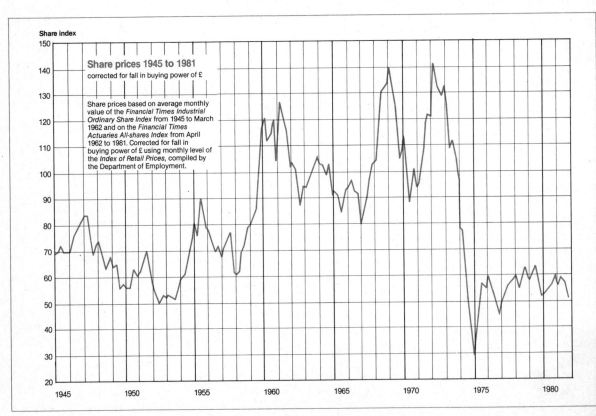

Share index

Share prices 1945 to 1981
corrected for fall in buying power of £

Share prices based on average monthly value of the *Financial Times Industrial Ordinary Share Index* from 1945 to March 1962 and on the *Financial Times Actuaries All-shares Index* from April 1962 to 1981. Corrected for fall in buying power of £ using monthly level of the *Index of Retail Prices*, compiled by the Department of Employment.

prospects improve. But you shouldn't expect that the share price will rise steadily.

Looking at what's happened in the past gives some sort of idea of the ups and downs of investing in shares. The chart opposite shows how the level of share prices (adjusted for the fall in the buying power of the £) has varied since 1945. As you can see it's been a bumpy ride. The success of your investment depends crucially on when you buy the shares and when you sell. And no one has a cast-iron method of forecasting the right moment to buy and sell.

But over the years the return on shares has, on average, been higher than with safer investments. Unfortunately, the past is not necessarily a guide to the future. The average investor should assume that investing in the shares of companies is a long term business.

Spreading your investment
If you invest heavily in just one company's shares, or in those of a very few companies, you could do very badly, or very well indeed. But if you invest in a wide spread of different shares, the results you'd get from your investment are unlikely to be far removed from the results for shares on average.

What are your chances of losing most of your money? Or of making your fortune? *Money Which?* has done some research to find out what might have happened if you'd invested in a different number of shares over a sample period of time – from the beginning of June 1969 to the beginning of June 1973. Note that even though the research was done for this particular period, its message applies to other periods too.

It was assumed that you had picked your shares from among those of the British companies whose names and prices were then listed in the back pages of the *Financial Times*. The shares of rubber, tea and mining companies (which are untypical, because they can involve extra risks) were excluded, as were the shares of investment trust companies (which are also untypical, in that they don't themselves run a business, but invest in a spread of different companies' shares – see p86). This left a list of 1,700 shares.

The value of £1,000 invested in each of these 1,700 shares was worked out four years after 'buying' them. To keep things simple, the expenses of buying and selling the shares (eg stockbroker's commission and stamp duty) were not taken into account, nor was capital gains tax or the dividends paid on the shares.

Results if you'd bought one share

The Diagram overleaf shows the results. Each red bar in the Diagram shows the proportion of shares whose value, at the end of the four-year period, came within the range of values shown on the left of the Diagram. For example, the third red bar from the bottom tells you that – with six shares out of every 100 – a £1,000 investment ended up worth between £500 and £750.

There was a wide spread in the results – £1,000 invested in just one share could have been worth from nothing to over £10,000.

A small proportion of individual shares did either very well, or very badly. With around three shares in every 100, you would have ended up with an investment worth £5,000 or more. And with nearly two shares out of every 100, you would have lost over three-quarters of your money – as shown by the lowest red bar on the Diagram.

By contrast, more than half the shares would have ended up with a value between £750 and £2,000 (you can check this by adding together the five longest red bars in the Diagram).

Results of a four-year investment of £1,000

if you held shares in 1 company

if you held shares in 16 companies

chosen from our sample of 1,700 companies' shares – see text. Investment made in 1969, cashed in 1973

value of £1,000 investment after four years

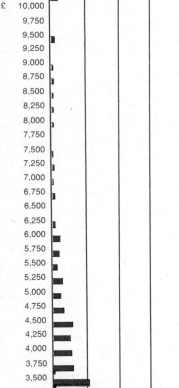

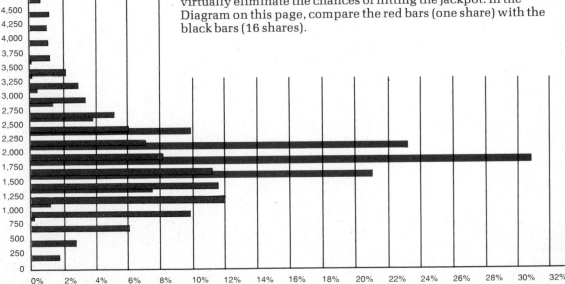

proportion of results in each range of values shown

Results if you'd bought more than one share

The Table opposite shows what your chances would have been of ending up with a particular result – say from £1,500 to £2,499 – depending on how many companies' shares you spread money over. The first column of the Table lists the range of possible values which an investment of £1,000 in June 1969 might have risen to – or sunk to – by June 1973. The second column – headed *comparative rating* – gives you a guide to how these results compare with the average for the period (close to £2,000).

The Table shows what the chances were if you had invested in only one company's shares, and how these chances changed if you had spread your £1,000 equally over the shares of two or more companies. Look, first, at the chances of ending up with a really handsome sum of money. You can see that someone investing in only one share had 0.4 chances in 100 of ending up with £10,000 or more. At the other end of the scale, the investor in one share would have had almost 3 chances in 100 of ending up with under £400 (ie less than one-fifth of the average result for the period).

By contrast, investors who spread their money over four or more shares had negligible chances of finding that their investment finished up in the top two or bottom two categories.

Now have a look at the results which fell in the range £1,500 to £2,499 – ie within about 25 per cent of the average for the period. You will see that an investor owning one share had about 33 chances in 100 of coming within this range. An investor with eight shares, on the other hand, had 72 chances in 100; and an investor with 32 shares was almost certain to do so (95 chances in 100).

Generally, the results suggest that going from an investment in one share to an investment in two makes a fairly big difference to your likely result. Thereafter, each additional share you include in your collection makes proportionately less difference to your chances than the previous share. Since spreading your money over the shares of 16 or so companies reduces the risk of a much-below average result to an acceptably low level – as the Table shows – there is little to be gained from buying more than this number.

But remember that, if you do buy as many as 16 or so shares, you virtually eliminate the chances of hitting the jackpot. In the Diagram on this page, compare the red bars (one share) with the black bars (16 shares).

Verdict The results show that the number of shares over which you spread your money can have a large effect on the outcome.

If you buy the shares of just one company, there's a small chance, but not a negligible one, that you might achieve either a much above-average return, or lose most or even all of your money. If you buy the shares of more than one company, your chances of an extreme result become much smaller.

If you spread your money over the shares of as many as 16 or so companies you'll be taking a very different sort of risk to that of an investment in the shares of just one company. The chances of all of them doing much worse than average are remotely small, as the Table shows. Unfortunately, the chances of a much above-average return are also extremely small.

It would be best to choose the shares of companies in different industries, because there's also the risk that a whole industry – and the shares of most of the companies in it – may hit the doldrums for a while. Similarly, it would be wise to spread your investments over different countries (see Chapter 23), so that the outcome of your investment doesn't depend entirely on the UK stockmarket.

But remember, share prices fluctuate – both individually and on average. So, even if you invest in a wide spread of shares, you can't be sure that the value of your share investment won't fall – particularly in the short or even medium term.

Because of buying and selling costs it doesn't make sense to invest small amounts in shares – less than £700 or £800, say. So to get a good spread – of, say, 10 shares – you'd need about £7,000 available for this type of investment.

Table: Results of a four-year investment of £1,000

value in June 1973	comparative rating	1	2	4	8	16	32
£10,000 or more	jackpot! more than *five times* average	0.4	0.1	—	—	—	—
£8,000 to £9,999	riches! from *four times* to *five times* average	0.4	0.2	—	—	—	—
£6,000 to £7,999	from *three times* to *four times* average	0.6	0,6	0.3	—	—	—
£4,000 to £5,999	from *twice* to *three times* average	5.0	2.6	1.3	0.1	—	—
£2,500 to £3,999	from *25% better* than average to *twice* average	16.4	16.9	14.2	10.4	6.0	1.7
£1,500 to £2,499	*within 25%* of average for period (taken as £2,000)	32.7	44.2	56.4	72.2	85.0	95.4
£1,000 to £1,499	from *half* of average to *25% below* average	23.7	25.7	24.3	15.7	8.9	2.9
£700 to £999	from *one third* to *half* of average	11.7	7.5	3.1	1.4	0.1	—
£500 to £699	from *one quarter* to *one third* of average	4.3	1.7	0.3	0.2	—	—
£400 to £499	near-disaster! from *one fifth* to *one quarter* of average	1.6	0.3	—	—	—	—
Under £400	disaster! less than *one fifth* of average	2.9	0.2	—	—	—	—

chances in 100 of £1,000 invested in June 1969 reaching the values shown — number of companies' shares held

Ways of choosing shares

If you've made the decision to buy shares, you are still faced with the problem of choosing which ones.

Often, the amateur investor won't do the choosing entirely himself, but will get professional advice (see Chapter 4) from a stockbroker, for example, or from the business pages of a newspaper. But in order to understand this advice, and to assess its worth, it would be helpful to know something about the different methods of choosing shares which may be used by advisers. There are four main ways of choosing shares:
- technical analysis
- fundamental analysis
- beta analysis
- hunch and inside knowledge.

Technical analysis (including chartism)

Technical analysis is concerned with the behaviour of the stockmarket – ie the rises and falls in share prices – rather than the details of a company's management, earnings, and so on. The method normally includes the study of charts ('chartism').

The underlying assumption is that investors, collectively, are in possession of all the available facts about companies, and that movements of share prices accurately – and quickly – reflect this knowledge. But technical analysts believe that share prices may not move instantly to take account of the information. And so analysts believe they can predict movements in price.

The method involves studying charts or graphs showing the range of prices at which each company's shares are bought and sold. The share price record of a company can indicate periods when investors have displayed confidence (or lack of it) in the company, and have built up (or sold) large holdings of its shares. Chartists argue that their graphs can tell them when such periods are about to recur – and they look for *trendlines*, for example, and for significant shapes like *tops* and *bottoms*. If the charts of the share price of a company has completed a top formation (see Chart below), a chartist would say this was the time to sell that share. And vice-versa for a bottom formation (see Chart) – a signal to buy.

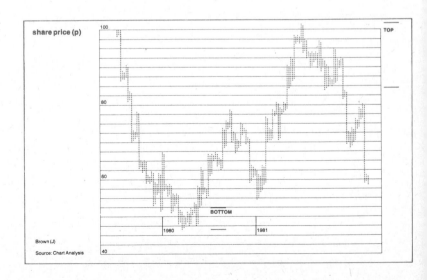

share price (p)

Brown (J)

Source: Chart Analysis

Fundamental analysis

A few examples of common terms and ratios

A few examples of common terms and ratios

Net working capital

First the value of what is owed by the company to suppliers, the taxman, shareholders (in the form of dividends), the bank (eg in the form of an overdraft) and so on is worked out. This value is then deducted from the sum of what is owed to the company by customers, cash held by the company or which the company can get at straight away and the value of items held as stock. This gives net working capital. A company needs to have sufficient working capital to keep going.

Profit margin

This is worked out by finding what the profit of the company is as a percentage of its sales.

Return on capital employed

This is worked out by finding what the profit of the company is as a percentage of its assets – ie the sum of the value of its property, its stock, what it is owed by its customers and so on.

The basic assumption here is that, at any given time, a company's shares have an intrinsic value. This value depends normally on the earning capacity of the company, which in turn depends on such things as the quality of management, and the outlook for the industry and for the economy as a whole. If the current market price of the shares is lower than what you suppose the intrinsic value to be, the share is one to consider buying.

Fundamental analysis will sometimes calculate a precise intrinsic value for a share, based on detailed estimates of the company's future earnings.

The analysis will use any information that can be obtained – in particular, by visiting companies, talking to the management and analysing the company report and accounts. Companies are obliged by law to publish the accounts of their business at least once a year, and to provide certain information. These accounts may reveal some important facts about the company's performance during the period covered by the accounts.

So specialists called investment analysts study and analyse these accounts with the idea of discovering how well the company is really doing. By working out the relationships between various factors (see Box for some examples) they try to build up a picture of the company's financial position, its trading record and prospects, and its financial management. This can be compared with other companies in the same industry to assess the company's performance and the performance of its management. In addition, by studying the economic background, this method is used to make predictions about how well, or badly, particular industries (eg heavy engineering) or even whole countries are going to fare.

But there are problems. The information available is far from comprehensive and not sufficiently standardised. And information in accounts is out of date. For example, after the most skilful reading of a company's account, one may still not know whether one part of the company's business is making losses and is being subsidised by more profitable parts.

Beta analysis

This is a method of share analysis which concentrates on the riskiness of a share. It doesn't look at the risk of investing your money in the shares of only one company which does badly or even goes bust – the section on *Spreading your investment* on p79 shows how you can reduce this risk. Beta analysis looks at the *market risk* of a share. This occurs because the UK stockmarket goes up and down, roughly speaking, as the prospect for the UK economy goes up and down. Some shares and unit trusts go up and down more than the average. These are called *aggressive* – ie when the FT-Actuaries All-Share Index goes up, the share or unit trust goes up relatively more, and when the index goes down, it goes down relatively more. The value of beta for such shares or unit trusts is more than one. Some shares and unit trusts are *defensive* – ie they go up and down less than the average (and the value of beta is less than one). Other shares and unit trusts fall somewhere between the extremes. The beta of a share is a measure of how much the rate of return on that share is likely to be affected by general stockmarket movements. It's normally worked out from the past performance of the share – which, of course, is not necessarily a good guide to the future.

Some people use this analysis so that, if they think the general level of prices in the stockmarket is going to rise, they can invest in shares with high betas – because their prices will (hopefully) go up correspondingly more. And if they think share prices in general are

going to fall, they will switch to shares with low betas, whose
prices should fall less than average. Another way of using this
analysis is to find the right investment for people – taking into
account the amount of risk they want to take.

Hunch and
inside knowledge

Of course, you could choose your shares by hunch – ie you have a
feeling that things are going to go well for a particular company.
Fortunes can be made or lost this way.

Investing as a result of a tip from an insider is a dodgy business.
And if *you* are the insider and you use your knowledge to invest
and make yourself or someone else some money, then it's probably
against the law and you could be convicted.

Verdict

There is no effective, reliable, proven, and generally usable method
of picking out which shares are going to be winners.

This does not mean, however, that you cannot make a sensible
choice of shares. A collection of shares which a person holds is
called a portfolio; and a portfolio chosen to match *your* objectives
and circumstances and preferred level of risk should certainly give
you better results than one which hasn't been so chosen. In broad
outline, choose your shares as follows:
● decide what your objectives are – because different shares are
likely to suit different objectives. For example, you may (or may
not) attach importance to drawing an income from your
investment. Or you may be speculating with your money – in the
hope of maximum gain, but accepting the possibility of a big loss
● if you're a higher rate taxpayer, you may do better trying to invest
for capital gain, rather than for income (see p42)
● try to choose the right time to buy and sell, because this can make
an enormous difference to how well your investment does – though
shares are regarded mainly as a long-term investment
● choose shares which carry the degree of risk you are willing to
accept. If you want to speculate, you could put all your money into
a collection of very risky shares. Alternatively, see p90 for other
ways of speculating in shares – in particular, *option warrants,
options* and *traded options*. On the other hand, if you are investing
for the long term, divide your money among the shares of a fair
number of companies and spread your investment over a number of
carefully selected different industries.
● consider reducing the influence of the UK stockmarket on your
investments by investing some of your money in other
investments, which are less risky – eg building society, British
Government stock or company loan stock (see p90); or consider
other risky investments – eg property bonds. And look at the
possibilities of investing some of your money overseas and giving
yourself a spread of geographical areas and currencies – see
Chapter 23.

Buying and selling shares

The great bulk of share dealing is done through The Stock Exchange. It is possible to buy shares in other ways – eg directly from someone who owns them, or from a dealer licensed by the Department of Trade – but The Stock Exchange is generally more convenient, and you are protected by The Stock Exchange itself against default by its members. You may be able to invest in the shares of the company you work for by saving in a special scheme – see Box on p90.

There is one Stock Exchange in the British Isles, but several trading floors – in London, Birmingham, Manchester and Liverpool, Glasgow, Belfast and Dublin.

Jobbers are the people who organise a market in the shares of a company. There are 17 jobbing firms (12 in London), all of which, during business hours, have representatives who stand on the trading floor of The Stock Exchange, buying and selling shares (and also other securities such as British Government stocks). The prices at which they buy and sell are determined, as in any other competitive market, by supply and demand. They make their money from what's known as the 'jobber's turn' – ie the difference between the price they'll pay to buy a share and the price they'll sell it at.

But a member of the public cannot just walk in and deal with a jobber. The only person who can do that is a stockbroker. A broker's job is to buy and sell shares on behalf of other people. He is responsible for providing you with share certificates when you buy shares, or with money when you sell them. He makes his living by charging a commission for this service.

You can either go to a stockbroker direct, or you can put your order through an agent – eg your bank manager, solicitor or accountant. For more details, see Chapter 4.

Buying shares

Suppose that you have found a broker to deal for you, and that you decide you would like to buy 500 *Slagthorpe Jam* shares. You look at the share price lists in your morning paper and see that they are quoted at 300p.

There are two points which must be made at once about this price. Firstly, it is normally yesterday afternoon's price – the price being quoted towards the close of Stock Exchange business. Secondly the price quoted in the newspapers is normally a 'middle' price. If the newspaper says that Slagthorpe Jam Co Ltd was 300p it probably means that, yesterday afternoon, jobbers were offering to sell Slagthorpe at 303p and to buy at 297p. The difference between the two figures is the jobber's turn.

You can give your order to your broker in either of two ways. One is simply to ring him up and say, 'Buy me 500 Slagthorpe Jam'. The broker will take this as an order to buy this number of shares at the best (ie cheapest) available price *now*. The broker will pass your order to his firm's dealer who will be on the trading floor. He in turn will ask one or more jobbers for a price for Slagthorpe. When he is convinced that he has found the lowest price available at that time, he will place your order by saying to the jobber 'Buy 500'. From that moment, your deal (technically, a bargain) is made and you have bought the shares.

The other way of giving a buying order is to give the broker a *limit*. Suppose that you decide that the shares would be a good buy

Investment trust companies

These are companies which don't run a business in the usual way, but invest in the shares of other companies which do. So an investment trust company is a convenient way of investing in a spread of shares. Unlike a unit trust – see Chapter 9 – it is quoted on the Stock Exchange in the normal way. The management of the investment trust company looks after its investments in the same way as a pension fund or unit trust manager – ie it buys and sells shares to get the best return.

An investment trust company differs from a unit trust in four main ways:

• in general, investment trust companies have a fixed number of shares that investors can buy. The number of units in a unit trust automatically increases or decreases as units are bought or sold by investors

• because the shares of investment trust companies are bought and sold on the stock market, the price can rise or fall depending on whether more people want to buy or sell. So the total value of the shares in the investment trust company is not always the same as the total value of the investments the investment trust company holds. Usually there is a discount – ie the total value of the shares of the investment trust company is less than the value of the investments it holds. With a unit trust, the price of each unit will always be based on the value of the investments in the unit trust divided by the number of units

• an investment trust can borrow money to invest in shares. This is known as *gearing*. The more that is borrowed, the higher the gearing – and so the more likely the share price is to change by relatively large amounts

• on average, the yearly management charges for an investment trust are lower.

Because of the gearing and discount, an investment trust can be regarded as a riskier investment than a unit trust.

at 295p but not a penny more. You ring up your broker and say, 'Buy me 500 Slagthorpe, at not more than 295p'.

The broker passes on this order, and the limit, to his dealer, who will note this down in his order book – and also pass it on to a jobber. As soon as the buying price falls to 295p – if it does – the shares will be bought on your behalf.

So you lose nothing by setting a limit, and you protect yourself from the risk of buying at a higher price than you expected. However, it is no use setting too low a limit; you won't get your shares, and will have wasted your time, and the broker's. And make sure your broker knows how long you want your limit to stand (he may have a standard time limit – eg one month).

At the broker's office, a contract note will be made out for the shares you have bought. You should get this on the following day, or soon after, and should check it at once to see that the details of what you have bought are correct. Keep this contract note carefully, as evidence of what you have paid for the shares. It will look something like the example opposite.

Selling shares

As with buying, so with selling, there are two kinds of order that you can give to your broker. You can simply ring up your broker and say 'Sell 500 Slagthorpe Jam'. Or you can set a limit – eg sell 500 Slagthorpe Jam if the price reaches 320p.

The contract note for a sale looks much like the contract note for a purchase. The commission, which is subtracted from the proceeds of the sale, is exactly the same as with a purchase, and with the same minimum charges. And there's VAT to pay on the commission. The contract stamp is for the same amount as it would be on a purchase of this size. But with a sale, there is no charge for a transfer stamp.

When the contract note for your sale has been made out, the broker will send it to you. He'll also send you a transfer form. All you will have to do is sign it at the place indicated, and send it back to your broker, with your share certificate. Don't date this transfer form – the broker will do this himself. You should keep the contract note as evidence of how much you have sold the shares for.

Provided you have sent in the transfer form properly signed, together with your share certificate, you should get the balance due to you from your broker on settlement day (see opposite).

Commission

If you buy or sell shares through a stockbroker, examples of the minimum commission rates (both for buying and selling) are:

on first £7,000	1.65%
on next £8,000	0.55%
on next £115,000	0.50%
on next £170,000	0.40%

But stockbrokers can charge more than these minimum rates. And there's a minimum charge – again your broker could charge more – of £7 for a sale, £10 for a purchase (except for deals under £300, when it's entirely at the broker's discretion). Check before you deal on what your broker will charge.

Tax

For details of how dividends are taxed, see p45. For capital gains tax, see pages 53 to 59.

1 Consideration

The name sometimes given to the amount you pay for the shares (or get for them if you're selling) before the various deductions are made. In our example, the consideration is £1,475.

2 Contract stamp

This is a stamp which, by law, has to go on most contract notes. Its amount depends on the amount of the purchase, and varies from nil to 60p.

3 Transfer stamp

This is the main government duty on the deal. It is for 2% of what you pay for the shares (taken to the nearest £50 upwards). In our example, the transfer stamp duty is 2% of £1,500 (ie £1,475 to the nearest £50 upwards).

4 Commission

The rate of commission varies depending on what you pay for the shares. On the first £7,000, the rate is 1.65%. For more details, see opposite. VAT at 15% will be charged on the stockbroker's commission.

CSI levy

If what you pay for the shares is over £5,000, an additional charge of 60p is made – this is a levy for the Council for the Securities Industry.

```
                         CONTRACT NOTE
                         ------------

                                           UNIQUE CODE NO.        DATE & TAX POINT
FREDERICK MURRAY ESQ.                         505050                 4 OCT 82

          WE HAVE TODAY BOUGHT FOR YOU, SUBJECT TO THE RULES AND REGULATIONS
                             ******
                 OF THE STOCK EXCHANGE, FOR SETTLEMENT ON 18 OCT 82

     500        SLAGTHORPE JAM CO. LTD ORD £1        295P      1      £1,475.00
     ------------                                                    ---------

     500                                                              1,475.00

                         CONTRACT STAMP   (O)      0.30       2
                         TRANSFER STAMP   (O)     30.00       3
                            COMMISSION    (T)     24.34       4
          VALUE ADDED TAX AT 15% ON £24.34         3.65
                          TOTAL CHARGES                                 58.29
                                                                    ---------

                              DUE TO US                              £1,533.29

                                                     CONTRACT NOTE STAMP
          (O) - OUTSIDE SCOPE OF V.A.T.                 DUTY PAID TO
          (T) - LIABLE TO V.A.T.                      INLAND REVENUE

U.K. RESIDENTS SHOULD RETAIN THIS CONTRACT NOTE AS THEY MAY REQUIRE      BGN NO.
        IT FOR CAPITAL GAINS TAX AND VALUE ADDED TAX PURPOSES           02040118

COMMISSION DETAILS
£1,475.00 AT 1.65%
```

Settling up

All share deals on the Stock Exchange are done within a period called an account, usually lasting 10 working days. An account normally starts on a Monday, and ends on the Friday of the following week. Settlement day, also frequently known as account day, is normally 6 working days after the final day of the account (ie on a Monday). On settlement day, the broker pays the jobber (or the reverse, for sellers) for all deals done during the account in question – and so the broker must have your money by that day.

So, following the end of an account in which you have done business with him, your broker will probably send you a statement. The statement will set out the totals from all the contract notes which have been sent to you during the account. If the statement shows that, taking purchases and sales together, you owe money to your broker, you should send him a cheque to arrive in time to be cleared by settlement day. If you are in credit, the broker should attach a cheque to the statement.

When you buy shares, anything from 10 to 21 days can elapse before you have to pay for them (but, of course, when you sell you may have to wait a corresponding length of time for your money).

The broker and jobber settle most of their purchases and sales through a system known as *Talisman*. The broker who has sold shares will deliver to the Talisman office, a transfer form and share certificate, and Talisman gives the company registrar details of the new holder of shares. The registrar will send a new share certificate to your broker who sends it on to you (or the share certificate can be sent direct to you).

How soon you get the share certificate depends on the company – can be six weeks, or longer. But your contract note is evidence that you have bought the shares. Should you want to sell them again before you have received the certificate, there should be no problem with shares in British companies.

The details

Ordinary shares

When you buy ordinary shares you are literally buying a share in the company, and a right to benefit from its earnings (if any). You can go to general meetings and vote on matters to do with the company.

Some companies issue ordinary shares only. The net (ie after tax) profits of such a company all count as earnings available to the ordinary shareholders (this does not mean, however, that all such earnings will actually be paid to the ordinary shareholders – see *Dividends*, in next column).

Many companies, by contrast, raise their capital in other ways – eg occasionally by issuing preference shares, more commonly by issuing loan stock or debentures. The company's first commitment is to pay the fixed income to its lenders and preference shareholders, which is why all such payments are commonly called prior charges. With such companies, the earnings available to the ordinary shareholders are the profits after deducting the prior charges and tax.

Nominal value of shares

If you had a share certificate for 500 shares in Slagthorpe Jam (see opposite), it would bear the words:
Slagthorpe Jam Co Ltd
Five hundred £1 ordinary shares
But this doesn't mean that you will get £1 each for the shares if you sell them. The shares of Slagthorpe Jam, like those of nearly all British companies, have a nominal value (sometimes called the par value) which in this case is £1. The total nominal value of all the shares which have been issued is the company's issued capital.

The nominal value of shares is of virtually no importance to the investor. Some companies use it, however, as a basis for expressing the amount of their dividends.

Price earnings ratio

A common way of looking at share prices is to say that in buying a share what you are really doing is buying a right to benefit from a corresponding share in the company's yearly stream of earnings. The price earnings ratio (or P/E ratio for short) is a way of saying how expensive (or how cheaply) you're buying that stream of earnings.

To work out a P/E ratio, first work out how much earnings there are for each share – ie divide the total after-tax earnings of the company by the number of shares. The P/E ratio is found by dividing the current market price by the earnings per share.

Take our Slagthorpe Jam example. Suppose the company's earnings in the last reported year were £1,800,000, which – since the company has five million ordinary shares (see opposite) – works out at 36p for each share. Each share actually costs 300p at current prices, so to buy earnings of 36p a year, you have to pay 300p. So Slagthorpe Jam would be said to have a P/E ratio of 300 divided by 36 = 8.3.

To inject more meaning into the P/E ratio, experts will contrast the historic P/E ratio (which is the kind usually quoted, and based on the last published accounts of the company) with, for example, an estimated P/E ratio (which would be one calculated on someone's forecasts of the company's earnings for the current year, and sometimes for the year after that).

Dividends

Shareholders receive their share of the company profits as dividends. Dividends will be sent to you at the address which your broker puts on the transfer form. Dividends come in the form of dividend warrants. These are in effect cheques, which can be paid into your bank account. Slagthorpe Jam last year declared dividends of 21p per share. There's no basic rate tax to pay on this – so it is equivalent to 30p per share before basic rate tax. For more details of how dividends are taxed, see p45.

Companies usually pay dividends twice a year (so long as they have earnings to distribute). About six to eight weeks before each dividend is paid, the company declares a dividend – ie announces what the next dividend will be. A week or two later, the company's shares go *ex-dividend* (and the share price is marked xd). Shortly after this, the register of shareholders is temporarily closed. The coming dividend will be paid only to those people who are on the register of shareholders on the day it was closed. Anyone who buys shares in the company after they have gone ex-dividend will not get the coming dividend.

A company normally keeps back part of its net profits (in our example opposite, £1,800,000 – £1,050,000 = £750,000) to finance expansion of its business, or to build up cash balances, or both. Amounts kept back are called retained profits or earnings, or retentions.

Dividend yield

The current market price of Slagthorpe Jam Company shares is 300p each. The dividend for each share is 21p. So you will have paid 300p to get a yearly income of 21p (provided future dividends are the same as last year's) with no basic rate tax to pay.

Now, 21p is 7% of 300p. Therefore the yield on your money would be 7% a year (with no basic rate tax to pay). This yield on your money is called the dividend yield. In practice, the dividend yield is usually quoted before-tax – and works out at 10% a year in this example.

Note that the dividend yield makes up only part of the return you hope to get from investing in shares – you also hope to get a capital gain.

When you see the dividend yield of a share published in a newspaper, there are two important points to be aware of. It applies to buying the share at the price indicated, and it is usually worked out on the basis of the last dividend – so has meaning only if the future dividend rate remains more or less unchanged.

New issues

If a company is not quoted on the Stock Exchange, it may be difficult to buy or sell its shares. You have to find an individual or an organisation who is prepared to deal with you. When the company decides it wants to make a better market in its shares, it may offer its shares to the public and become quoted on the Stock Exchange. Two well-known companies which have done this in recent years are J Sainsbury Ltd and Habitat Ltd.

The most usual method for marketing a new issue is an *offer for sale* by an issuing house – often a merchant bank. The issuing house puts advertisements in newspapers giving details of the company and offering a stated number of shares at a stated price (the prospectus). The advertisements normally include an application form. If you want to buy some of the shares, fill in the form saying how many you want, and send it with a cheque for the value of the shares you want to buy.

If the terms on which a new issue is made look attractive to the investing public, the issue may be over-subscribed – that is, more shares may be asked for than are on offer. In that case, the shares will be allocated by the issuing house (there is a variety of methods for doing this).

Scrip (or bonus) issue

A company may sometimes make an extra issue of shares to its existing shareholders. This is called a scrip or bonus issue. If, for example, you have 500 shares in Slagthorpe Jam and the share price is 300p each, your shareholding is worth £1,500. If the company makes a 1 for 1 scrip issue, you will get another 500 shares, making 1,000 in total. But the share price will instantly fall to 150p each, so your shareholding is still worth £1,500.

After a time, the share price will go ex-scrip, marked xc – this works in much the same way as ex-dividend, see opposite.

Rights issue

Occasionally, a company may decide it needs to raise more money from its shareholders – perhaps to finance some new investment. It usually makes a rights issue to its existing shareholders. This means

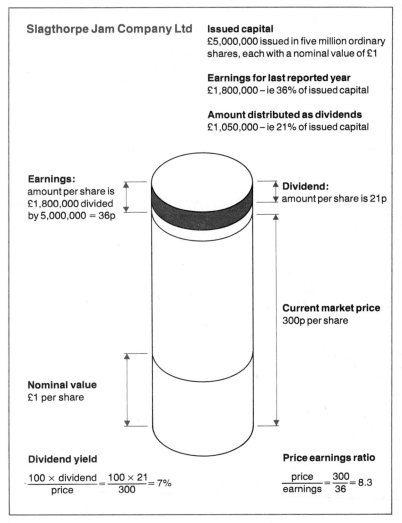

Slagthorpe Jam Company Ltd

Issued capital
£5,000,000 issued in five million ordinary shares, each with a nominal value of £1

Earnings for last reported year
£1,800,000 – ie 36% of issued capital

Amount distributed as dividends
£1,050,000 – ie 21% of issued capital

Earnings:
amount per share is £1,800,000 divided by 5,000,000 = 36p

Dividend:
amount per share is 21p

Current market price
300p per share

Nominal value
£1 per share

Dividend yield
$$\frac{100 \times \text{dividend}}{\text{price}} = \frac{100 \times 21}{300} = 7\%$$

Price earnings ratio
$$\frac{\text{price}}{\text{earnings}} = \frac{300}{36} = 8.3$$

the company offers you the right to invest more money in exchange for new shares it will issue.

You will know about this rights issue because the company will send you a document, telling you what it is raising money for and enclosing a form so that you can apply to take up some new shares. Do not ignore this document – it is valuable. If you don't understand what it is, ask a professional adviser.

There are four choices facing you as shareholder:
● you can do nothing
● you can pay up
● you can sell your rights to the new shares on the Stock Exchange
● you can sell part of your rights and take up part, so keeping your investment in the company at the same level.

Which you do, depends on whether you have the cash available and whether you want to increase your investment in the company.

Suppose, for example, you have 500 shares in Battendown Foods, the share price is 400p each and the company makes a one-for-one rights issue at 200p each. If the company has 3 million shares already issued, it is raising £6 million by the rights issue (issuing another 3 million shares for 200p each). The market value of the company before the rights issue is £12 million; afterwards it is £18 million. The share price after the rights issue will be:
£18 million ÷ 6 million = £3 each

If you do nothing, your 500

shares are now worth only £1,500, so on the face of it, you might have lost £500. However, many companies will sell rights which haven't been taken up and send you the proceeds. If you take up your rights, your investment is now worth £3,000 – but you've had to hand over another £1,000 to the company. Or you can sell your rights to the new shares on the Stock Exchange – in theory, for £500. This is worked out by taking the new share price from the old one – ie £4 − £3 = £1 per share.

Your fourth choice is to sell part of your rights and use the proceeds to buy the rest of the new shares.

After a while, the share price will go ex-rights (marked xr) – this works much the same as ex-dividend (see p88).

Mergers and takeovers

Occasionally, one company may decide it would like to acquire another company and it offers to buy the shares from the company's shareholders. For example, suppose Battendown Foods decides to take over Slagthorpe Jam. Battendown will send you a document offering to buy your shares. This document will contain a lot of information, including:
- what Battendown will pay for your shares. It may offer you cash, or some of its own shares in exchange, or a mixture of loan stock and shares and possibly cash
- why Battendown wants to buy Slagthorpe
- a profit forecast for Battendown
- the date on which its offer closes.

If Slagthorpe decides it doesn't want to be taken over, it will also send you a document telling you why you shouldn't accept Battendown's offer, probably giving a profit forecast for Slagthorpe, and so on.

Things can get very complicated after this, if, for example, a second company decides it would like to acquire Slagthorpe, or Battendown decides its first offer will not be accepted by the majority of shareholders and so increases its offer. You might end up with quite a few documents. Don't ignore them. You have to decide which is better – sticking with Slagthorpe or taking Battendown's offer. If you have a professional adviser, ask his advice.

Savings – related share option schemes

There are around 100 of these schemes which have been approved by the taxman.

If you've been working for your firm full-time for five years, you can agree to save a regular amount (between £10 and £50) each month. Your employer takes it out of your salary and puts it in a building society or a SAYE scheme (normally running for five or seven years).

At the end of five years you get back what you've saved plus a bonus of eighteen times your monthly savings. This gives a tax-free return of 10.5 per cent. You can then use this money to buy shares in the company you work for. You pay a special price for the shares which is fixed when you start saving – ie five years before.

The price could be as low as 90 per cent of the value of the shares at that time. So if the price of the shares now is higher than that, you get an immediate gain on top of the bonus you've already got.

Note that there's unlikely to be any tax due except possibly some capital gains tax if you sell your shares for more than you paid for them.

Any snags?

If you stop saving in the first year, you get your savings back but nothing else. If you change your mind after one year but before five years, you get tax-free interest of 8 per cent a year on your savings. The other snag is that you may find at the end of your saving period that your company's shares have fallen not risen – but you don't have to buy the shares if you don't want to.

Other ways of investing in companies

Companies can raise money by issuing *company loan stock* (also called *debentures*). They work like British Government stocks – they normally pay a fixed rate of interest and the loan will be repaid some time in the future. Because they are riskier than British Government stocks, you can expect the return to be higher. And if the company is in financial difficulties, the return may be very high indeed – though the risk is very high too.

A variation is a *convertible loan stock*. This starts out as a loan when the company first gets the money. But the person holding the loan stock has the right to convert it or part of it at a certain price into shares. If the share price of the company rises this may make the price of a convertible rise substantially too. If the share price falls, then it may not be worth converting the loan.

Some companies have *preference* shareholders, though these are getting less common. In many ways, these are like loans and a fixed rate of dividend is usually paid on them. There are different types of preference shares, but this is a highly specialised market – not usually for the average investor.

There are some very risky types of investments you can buy and sell on the stockmarket – *option warrants, options* and *traded options*. An option warrant is issued by the company, and is often tacked on to a loan stock – it can be detached and sold by the loan stockholder if he wants. A warrant gives you the right to buy shares in the company, usually during a fixed period and at a fixed price. If the shares of the company never reach that price, the warrant is worthless. But if the share price does rise, the price of a warrant will rise substantially.

An option is similar but is not issued by the company. Instead you pay a jobber (see p85) for the right to buy or sell shares in a company at a fixed price within a 3-month period. Once you've got the option you can't sell it – you can buy and sell only the shares of the company.

A traded option is a slightly different investment – and can itself be bought and sold. It lasts for a period of up to nine months and you can use the option to buy or sell shares at predetermined prices. Traded options exist for only a few companies.

9 Unit trusts

Investing in a unit trust is a way of investing in shares or, with some trusts, British Government stocks and the like. For many investors, investing in a unit trust is less risky and more convenient than investing direct in shares. If you invested directly, and put all your money in one company, say, you'd lose it all if that company went bust. But a unit trust invests in the shares of a lot of companies (around 60 or 70, say – though it varies widely). So if one company goes bust you lose only a bit of your money. Of course, you can invest direct in a lot of companies' shares but this involves more money and more work. For more details on investing in shares, see Chapter 8.

The return you get back from a unit trust comes in two parts:
- **income** – this is made up of dividends from the shares the unit trust invests in. It can normally be paid out to you
- **capital growth** – the hope is that the prices of shares which the unit trust has invested in will rise.

In practice, you can always reinvest your income to give more capital growth or cash in part of your investment to use capital growth as income – see p100.

Timing your investment in a unit trust

Investing in unit trusts is riskier than many other types of investment – eg building society accounts. But although there is a chance of you losing money with a unit trust, the hope is that you get a better return. You can see from the Diagrams overleaf that investors in unit trusts have had a bumpy ride over the years – doing very well in some periods, very badly in others. So the success of an investment depends very much on when you invest and when you cash your investment. If you'd invested in a typical general unit trust – see Diagrams overleaf – at the beginning of 1973 and cashed in two years later, you'd have lost nearly two-thirds of your money. But if you'd invested at the beginning of 1975 and cashed in two years after that, you'd have almost doubled it. Sadly, there's no foolproof way of forecasting when share prices are going to rise or fall.

For the long-term or short-term?

There are two schools of thought about how long you should invest in a unit trust for.
Either:
- you invest for a long time (at least seven years or so) and stick pretty well to the same trust (or trusts),
or
- you invest for a shorter time and move your money in and out of unit trusts or from trust to trust as the prospects alter.

For most small investors, the former is most probably the better strategy. Switching your money in, out or between trusts, could be expensive in charges – see p101 – and unless you're lucky or very knowledgeable you might time it badly. For example, suppose you'd switched a £1,000 investment between the general trust in the Diagrams opposite and building societies, and got it wrong every time (ie sold your units just as shares were about to rise and bought them back just as shares began to fall). You'd have around £400 after 10 years compared with around £2,500 if you'd stuck with the trust throughout. Of course, if you'd got your timing right, you'd have over £7,000. But unless you're prepared to do the work and take the chance of getting it all wrong, you should think of unit trusts as a long-term investment.

Size of investment

The minimum you can invest varies, but with most unit trusts it's in the £200 to £500 range – or, for regular saving, often £10 a month. Regular saving means less worrry about timing your investment. For more details, see p101.

Choosing a unit trust

There's no magic formula to tell you which trust will do best – we've tested several theories on p96. And you can't automatically expect that you'll get good advice from an investment adviser or newspaper. But the step-by-step guide on p98 should help you narrow down the choices.

What's happened in the past?

The upper Diagram opposite shows the outcome of a number of imaginary investments made at the start of 1971, and cashed at the end of 1980. £1,000 has been invested in each of:
• a typical general unit trust
• building society term shares (ordinary shares for the first couple of years)
• a British Government stock (2½% Consols)
• the longest running property bond.
From the Diagram you can see that the unit trust investment is worth more after ten years than, say, the building society, but has gone up and down a lot over the years. So you should only put your money in unit trusts if you are prepared to take the risk of losing money for the chance of greater gain.
From the lower Diagram opposite, you can see how the outcome of an investment in unit trusts could have varied depending on the trust you'd chosen. It shows what has happened to an investment of £1,000 in three different unit trusts made in January 1971. The middle line is the typical general unit trust from the upper Diagram, the others are typical specialist unit trusts in the best-performing and worst-performing sectors (for what a specialist unit trust is, see p95).

A general unit trust compared with other investments

Includes buying and selling costs; income reinvested after deduction of basic rate tax

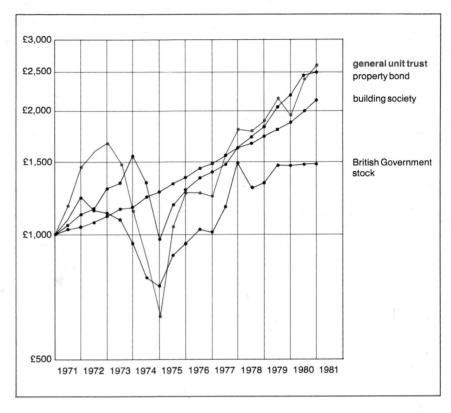

general unit trust
property bond

building society

British Government stock

A general unit trust compared with two specialist trusts

Includes buying and selling costs; income reinvested after deduction of basic rate tax

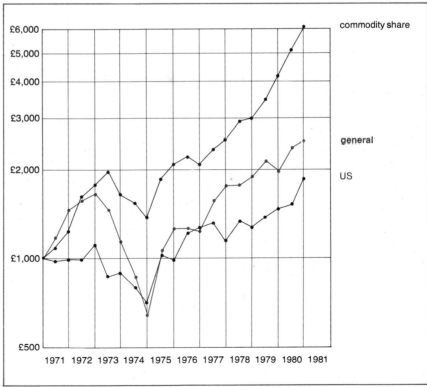

commodity share

general

US

Types of unit trust

Unit trusts vary in their aims and the kind of shares they invest in.
One way of grouping them is:
● general funds
● income funds
● capital growth funds
● specialist sector funds (eg commodities, energy)
● specialist regional funds (eg Japan, US).

General funds (or balanced funds)

The longest-running unit trust of most unit trust groups is likely to
be a general fund. The aim of the fund, as described in company
literature, might be something like:
*'The fund's objective is to produce steady growth of both income
and capital'.*

Most general funds invest mainly in the UK, but in several
different industries. You should expect the value of your
investment to go up and down as the UK stockmarket goes up and
down. But some general funds (often called *international funds*)
invest in several different stockmarkets around the world – so the
fortune of your investment is not so tightly tied to the fortune of the
UK stockmarket.

Income funds

These funds are often called *High Yield*, *Extra Income* and so on.
The objective of the fund might be described by the company as:
*'Designed for investors whose primary requirement is an above
average and increasing income. The fund's objective is to provide a
return about 60% higher than that of the FT-Actuaries All-Share
Index'.*

We looked at the size of the income for funds which have words
like *Extra Income* or *High Yield* in the name. And we found that
funds with this sort of name did pay out a higher-than-average
income (ie the fund was achieving what its name suggested).

There are now around 25 unit trusts which invest mainly in
British Government stocks – most of these aim to give a high
income.

Capital growth funds

The aim of these funds is to concentrate on getting increases in the
unit price, rather than pay out a high income. Many funds with
names like *Capital Growth*, *Special Situations*, *Smaller
Companies*, and so on, come into this category.

The aim of this type of fund might be described as:
*'The investment aim is maximum capital growth through the
active management of a small portfolio of shares. . . . Yield* (ie
income) *is not normally taken into account'.*

With *active management* the shares in the fund may be changed
more frequently than with other types of funds – so incurring a
higher level of costs, due to buying and selling shares.

Specialist sector funds These funds invest in particular industries (eg financial, energy). We looked at the shares held by these funds and compared the type of shareholdings with the name of the fund. In most cases, the name of the fund did give a clue to its content.

The aim of a specialist fund might be described as:

... *'The Fund's main objective is long-term capital growth, but there may be wider than average day-to-day price fluctuations. ...*

In other words, the managers are warning you that you could be in for a bumpy ride. This is because if a unit trust invests its money in one UK industry and the industry does particularly badly or well, then the unit trust will do badly or well, too. In fact, we found that the ride was only slightly bumpier with specialist sector funds than with general funds.

Specialist regional funds These unit trusts invest in certain overseas stockmarkets. A typical fund might have an objective like:

'This fund aims to achieve growth of capital through investment in the Far East covering countries such as Japan, Hong Kong, Australia, Singapore ...' In the main, these funds concentrate on getting increases in unit prices rather than income. Typically there are funds specialising in Europe, Japan, US, Far East, Australia.

You should not expect specialist funds to move in line with the UK stockmarket. This is why specialist regional funds and commodity funds often appear at the top – and the bottom – of tables showing unit trust performance. Look at the Table below – 17 out of 20 of the funds are either regional, commodity or energy funds.

Note that funds which invest overseas are also affected by the caprices of the currency market – the unit price of an overseas trust will tend to rise if the exchange rate of the £ goes down, fall if the exchange rate of the £ goes up.

Best and worst performing unit trusts

1979 TOP 5	% rise in unit price [1]	BOTTOM 5	% fall in unit price [1]	1980 TOP 5	% rise in unit price [1]	BOTTOM 5	% fall in unit price [1]
Britannia Minerals	109.5	Henderson Far Eastern	22.4	GT Far East	91.6	S & P European Growth	4.5
Britannia Gold & General	100.7	M & G Japan	23.9	M & G Australasian	87.4	Nelstar High Income	8.2
Britannia Universal Energy	75.3	London Wall Extra Income	24.7	Henderson Australia	75.4	Schroder Europe	10.7
Key Energy	61.9	Midland Drayton Japan	26.9	Gartmore Far Eastern	71.6	Murray European	10.9
S & P Energy	58.2	S & P Japan	31.0	Barclays Unicorn Australia	71.4	Choularton Income	15.8

[1] includes net income reinvested

Verdict on type of fund If you want to invest in a unit trust and hang on to it for a while, its probably best to choose a general or income unit trust. If you have enough money, spread it between two or more unit trusts, perhaps one general and one other – the other could be a growth or specialist fund. If you want to invest with the idea of shifting from fund to fund, then you can choose from the full range, according to your educated guess.

How to choose a unit trust

There is no magic recipe for choosing a unit trust. Below we look at some well-known systems for picking a winner – and put them to the test. We used details of unit trusts for the period 1 January 1973 to 30 October 1980. Note that our verdicts on the theories are general ones – there are always exceptions to any rule.

Theory 1
Small funds do best

It's argued that the managers can buy and sell investments more easily and so get the best return.

We divided funds up by size. Our results showed that, over the period, funds in the smallest size group (less than £2 million) had performed slightly worse than bigger ones. But over one year (1979) small funds did much better. So size doesn't seem to be a useful guide to picking a unit trust.

We also looked to see if small unit trusts were riskier than big ones – but there was no evidence for this.

Verdict: Size is not a particularly useful criterion for picking a unit trust.

Theory 2
The past is a guide to the future

This theory claims that trusts which have done well in the past will do well in the future.

We looked at the performance of unit trusts for the first half of the period (ie 4 years) compared with the second half.

We found that, in general, unit trusts which did worst in the first period did best in the next and vice versa. But this result could be because in the first period the UK stockmarket was plummeting down most of the time, while in the second period it was shooting up. So, for example, unit trusts invested overseas might do much better in the first period but those invested in the UK come out top in the second period.

We had a closer look at past performance by comparing the results of a fund in one year with its results in the next year for every year of the period we looked at. This time we found that the results gave no support to the theory.

Verdict: Past performance is not a good guide for picking a unit trust.

Theory 3
New is best

Because the managers will be giving a new unit trust lots of expert attention, it's claimed they'll do better than with old unit trusts.

We worked out the average return for new funds for the year after they were started and compared these returns with the average return on all unit trusts. We then compared the average return on new funds with the average return on existing funds of the same type. There was no evidence that new trusts performed better than old ones.

Verdict: No reason to believe that new unit trusts will perform better than old ones.

Theory 4
Winners turn to losers

Is it true that last year's winners are likely to be this year's losers, and vice versa?

We looked at what would have happened if, at the beginning of 1974, we had invested money in the six worst-performing unit trusts for the previous year, then sold at the end of 1974 and reinvested in the six worst-performing trusts for 1974 and so on until 30 October 1980. We then repeated this exercise six times, starting with 1975 and then 1976 and so on.

Then we turned to the six best-performing unit trusts and did the whole thing again.

The results are in the Table below. As you can see the winner – ie whether investing in the best, or worst, performing funds was the best idea – depended on the year you started in.

Verdict: Not a good guide for picking a unit trust.

Results of investing £1,000 in six worst-performing and six best-performing funds each year

Period of Investment	Six worst	Six best	THE WINNER!
1974–1980	£1,003	£1,133	BEST
1975–1980	£1,769	£1,412	WORST
1976–1980	£1,454	£1,195	WORST
1977–1980	£1,609	£1,413	WORST
1978–1980	£1,368	£1,757	BEST
1979–1980	£1,312	£1,662	BEST
1980	£1,140	£1,812	BEST

Theory 5
Pick a management company

It's claimed that some management companies do better than others.

We compared the average return of the different management companies' trusts for the first half of the period compared with what happened in the second half of the period.

We couldn't find any evidence that good performance in one period would mean good performance in the next. But this result has to be treated with caution as so many companies merged in the first four years.

Verdict: Evidence too slight to say that management company is good way to pick a unit trust.

A step-by-step guide to choosing a unit trust

Although there's no sure-fire way of choosing the unit trusts which will perform best, you can narrow down your choice amongst the bewildering number available by following the steps below. But be warned – it's a long job. You could ask advisers to do it for you – see opposite.

Step 1 Make sure a unit trust is a suitable investment for you – see Chapters 1 and 2. Don't feel that you have to invest **now** just because you've got the cash available now – bear in mind that the success of your investment will depend very much on when you buy and when you sell.

Step 2 If you have enough £££ (minimum investment is usually in the £200 to £500 range), invest in more than one unit trust.

Step 3 Decide which types of fund to go for – see p94.

Step 4 If you want to save a certain amount each month, only around a half of all unit trusts offer a savings plan. You could consider investing via a life insurance policy instead (see p142).

Step 5 Find out when you can deal. With around one quarter of unit trusts you can't deal daily, and this may be inconvenient.

Step 6 Still left with lots of unit trusts to choose from? Look at the investments the fund holds, whether they've been changed a lot (which can be costly) and so on. Ask the company to send you managers' reports (see opposite).

Step 7 Finally, choosing between these unit trusts will have to be based on your own hunches.

Example of using this guide
Jack and Jill Gander are in their late 40's with two children – one about to go to college and one about to take 'O' levels.

Step 1 They've already got a big enough emergency fund plus some other investments. Jack has just inherited £3,000. From reading newspapers and talking to people, they discover that the stockmarket is at a high level, although people seem to think that prices may still rise. They hum and haa, because they don't want to do what lots of small investors do – invest all their money in unit trusts just when share prices are about to fall. Finally, they decide to put only a bit of their money (£750, say) in unit trusts.

Step 2 £750 is enough money to split between two unit trusts.

Step 3 As they're looking for a long-term investment, they decide to go for a general unit trust. Because they're uncertain about share prices for UK companies (see Step 1), they decide to put their other money in an overseas fund and plump for a Far Eastern one.

Step 4 They want to invest a lump sum, so no narrowing down here.

Step 5 They're not that bothered about not being able to sell their units at once – but on balance would prefer to be able to do so.

Step 6 They decide to go for a general fund with some overseas investments. Looking at the brief details in the Unit Trust Year Book, they find there are about seven funds which match these needs. They get in touch with the companies and ask to see the latest managers' report on the particular unit trust and a current list of what investments are in the trust – they:
● look at what the investments are
● check that none of them are big holdings
● try to find how often investments are bought and sold – they'd prefer to go for one that's not too active
● look at the charges made.
They do a similar exercise with the Far Eastern funds, mainly looking at where the fund is invested and how much in any one region.

Step 7 Finally, they plump for the two unit trusts they're going to invest in.

Getting information

From the company

If you want information about a unit trust, ask to see the latest **manager's report**. The information in these reports varies somewhat. Nearly all tell how much is invested in the shares of which companies. But with a few there's little information except the name of the trust, its aim, the price, the yield, the shares the fund is invested in and the managers' view of the future. Other information given often includes a comparison of how the unit trust has done compared with, say, the FT Actuaries All-Share Index and, less frequently, what shares have been bought and sold since the last report.

The Department of Trade and the Unit Trust Association have produced recommendations on what should be in these reports. Any new unit trust set up will have to produce reports as recommended. But existing trusts can (end 1981) choose to alter their reports or not.

From newspapers and magazines

Details of most unit trusts are listed in several newspapers. An example entry might look like this: *Slagthorpe Income 55.6 56.1 – 0.3 6.7*. This tells you the name of the unit trust and (in order above), the price you can sell your units for, the price at which you can buy them, how much the price has changed since the previous day, and the yield (see p101). Magazines, such as *Money Management* and *Savings Market* give other details – eg what £1,000 invested five years ago would be worth now.

The Unit Trust Year Book gives lots of information about each unit trust and each management group. It is available from Minster House, Arthur St, London EC4R 9AX, price £12. Or try a library.

From investment advisers

In Chapter 4, we've looked at the various sources of professional advice – many of whom will help you in choosing unit trusts. But remember that it's up to *you* to evaluate the advice you get.

Most advisers get commission of 1¼% of the value of unit trusts they buy for you – but some get 3%.

The details

Units

When you invest in a unit trust you buy units in the trust from the management company. When you cash your investments, you sell units back to the management company (it *has* to buy them from you). The management company puts the cash you pay for units into the fund and it's used to buy investments, such as shares.

Prices

A unit has two prices. These prices are based on the value of the investments in the trust fund. The higher price (the offer price) is what you pay to buy units. The lower price (the bid price) is what you get if you sell units.

The prices are worked out using a method laid down by the Department of Trade (DoT). To get the offer price the company finds out the lowest price it would have to pay to buy the investments currently in the unit trust fund. It then adds various costs to this – eg stamp duty, management charges. The value it has after doing this sum is divided by the number of units the company has issued – and this gives the maximum offer price the company can charge.

The lowest bid price (ie the price the company has to pay you for your units) is worked out in a similar way. But this time the company has to find out what is the highest price it could get if it sold the investments currently in the unit trust fund.

The difference between these two prices is called the spread. The average spread quoted in the newspapers is around 7%, though the range is quite wide – from less than 1% to nearly 10%. If you want to sell a large number of units (eg over £5,000-worth), the management company does not

necessarily have to buy at the bid price quoted. Instead, it could offer to buy your units at a price nearer or equal to the minimum bid price as worked out in the DoT method.

In fact, it's possible for the unit price to rise or fall without the share prices of the investments in the unit trust rising or falling. This is because the spread the management company quotes is usually less than the spread it could quote under the DoT rules. So, for example, if lots of unit holders are selling, the management company can shift the unit prices downwards to discourage selling and attract buyers.

Prices for many unit trusts are worked out daily; some weekly, some fortnightly and a few monthly.

Buying and selling

You can buy or sell in several ways – eg over the 'phone, by letter, through an agent or broker. Note that an order over the 'phone is just as binding as one made in writing.

With some unit trusts you don't buy or sell at the price quoted in that day's newspaper, but at the price worked out when the fund is next valued. Not much of a problem if this is done every day, but it might lead to getting much less or paying much more than you expect if the fund is valued once a week, once a fortnight or even once a month. You can, of course, set a limit on the price you're prepared to pay for units or accept if you sell them – eg only sell at 65p or more.

When you have to pay for units and when you receive cash for a sale varies from company to company, but should generally be not more than a fortnight.

Charges

These used to be fixed by the Department of Trade, but since the beginning of 1980 management companies have been able to set charges for new unit trusts at any level they choose. Before raising charges in existing trusts, however, they have had to ask investors in the unit trust if they agree to the new level of charges.

There are two different sorts of charges. These are:
- **initial charge**. This is often 5% and is included in the spread between the bid and offer prices
- **regular charge**. This is often in the range ¾% to 1% a year. This charge is usually taken from the income of the fund.

Management of the unit trust

There may be three groups of people involved. First, a management company which does the administration and advertising. Secondly, there is an investment adviser. In many cases, this is the same company as the management company. But quite a few have advisers such as stockbrokers deciding how the fund should be invested. Thirdly, there is the trustee (see below).

Trustee

There are around 17 companies – mainly banks – acting as trustees to nearly 500 unit trusts. Trustees have several jobs. First, the trustee makes sure that no manager of a unit trust can run off with your money – the trustee keeps all the cash and investments of the fund in its name. Secondly, the trustee makes sure that the terms of the trust deed (see below) are stuck to by the managers. Thirdly, the trustee keeps an eye on the advertising done by the management company to make sure it doesn't give a false impression. For example, one of the Unit Trust Association rules is that all advertising should include a warning that unit prices can fall as well as rise.

Exactly how much the trustee does can vary, depending on how the trustee interprets the trust deed.

Trust deed

This lays down how the unit trust must be managed. The deed must, among other things:
- show how unit prices and income are worked out
- say what the management company's charges are
- say that unit certificates are not issued until the trustee is happy that the cash you pay has been put in the trustee's name
- put certain restrictions on advertising
- state that accounts of the unit trust will be sent to investors each year.

The trust deed also includes limits on how the fund can be invested. The fund cannot be invested, for example:
- directly in property. The fund can't buy offices, farms and so on – but it can buy shares in property development companies
- in such a way that more than 5 per cent of its value is in any one share (but there can be a few exceptions)
- so that it holds more than 10 per cent of the shares of any one company.

If the trust deed meets certain requirements and standards then the unit trust can be *authorised* by the Department of Trade. Most unit trusts are authorised ones, but it's worth checking before you invest. Only authorised unit trusts can be advertised to the general public.

Income

The investments which are held in the unit trust fund get income in the form of share dividends, interest from British Government stocks and so on. The management company takes its regular charge from the income and will usually pay out what's left to unit holders in the form of **distributions**. There are usually two distributions a year – but some trusts, which concentrate on producing income, pay out distributions once a quarter.

As the income comes into the fund, the unit price rises to take account of this, until it finally includes the whole of the distribution. On a certain day, the price will be marked *xd* (ie *ex distribution*) and will fall by the amount of the distribution. After that time, if you buy units, you will not get the next distribution to be paid; if you sell units, you still get the next distribution.

There are four different types of trust:
- accumulation trusts
- distribution trusts
- trusts with both accumulation and distribution units
- trusts where you can automatically reinvest income.

With accumulation trusts, the income of the unit trust fund is not paid to you in £££ – instead the unit price is simply increased to reflect the income. There are about 25 accumulation trusts.

With distribution trusts, the income of the unit trust fund must be paid out in £££ to each investor. There are about 150 of this type of trust.

With around 100 unit trusts, you can buy either accumulation units (where the income of the fund is used to increase the unit price) or distribution units (where the income of the fund is paid out to you).

With the rest of the funds, you can choose to have the income automatically reinvested (rather than paid out). This means the income is used to buy more units – and you have to pay an initial charge on these.

Tax

Distributions from a unit trust come with a **tax credit**. The effect of this is that if you're a basic rate taxpayer, there's no income tax to pay on the distribution. If you pay tax at higher rates or the investment income surcharge, you'll have to pay more tax. If you're a non-taxpayer, you'll be able to claim tax back. For more details, see p45.

The normal capital gains tax rules apply to unit trust investments. See p53 for details.

Size of income

If you are buying a unit trust as a way of getting an income, look at the **yield** of the fund. The higher the yield, the higher the income is compared to the £££ you invest.

To get the yield, the amount of the distribution per unit is divided by the unit price. This is then multiplied by 100 to give a percentage. For example, if the distribution per unit is two pence and the unit price is 40p, the yield is $2 \div 40 \times 100 = 5\%$.

Of course, if you bought units when the price was lower, say 30p, the yield on your investment would be $2 \div 30 \times 100 = 6\frac{2}{3}\%$.

Note that the yield usually quoted is the gross yield – ie based on the distribution *plus* tax credit (see above).

Another way of getting an income from unit trusts

The disadvantage of using the distribution from a unit trust to provide you with an income is that it can go up and down – because the dividends paid by shares held by the unit trust fund can also go up and down. It also alters because managers of the fund will buy and sell the investments of the fund. So some unit trust companies (around 20 covering about 100 trusts) have **withdrawal schemes**. With these you can choose to have as your income either:
● a percentage, say 5 per cent, of the original amount of £££ you invest. So you can be certain you get the same income each year. Or,
● a percentage, say 5 per cent, of the current value of your investment. In this case, the income would still go up and down each year.

If the distributions of the unit trust are not high enough to meet this income need, then some of your units are sold. But more units will have to be sold to make up your income when unit prices are low than when they are high – the opposite of what you want. And selling units can lead to you using up your capital increasingly quickly – the more units you sell, the lower your income from distributions in the future, so the more units will have to be sold in the future . . .

If you decide a withdrawal scheme could be useful, you'll need to check the minimum investment the company will take – it varies from £500 to £4,000.

Size of investment

For lump sum investments, all unit trusts ask for a minimum investment when you first invest – eg £250 or £500 – or you may have to buy a minimum number of units – 200, say. If you want to increase your investment you can usually do so by smaller amounts.

Nearly half the unit trusts will let you invest a regular amount, often £10 a month – but can be as little as £10 a quarter or £5 a month. This is known as a **savings plan**. For how this can be linked to a life insurance policy see p142. One advantage of a savings plan is that you don't have to worry so much about when you should invest as you would with a lump sum. But, you still have to worry about when you should cash your investment.

Pound-cost averaging is sometimes cited as being an advantage of a regular savings plan. What this seems to show is that you can get a bargain by investing regularly. This is because, if the unit price goes up and down, the average cost of your units will be less than the average of unit prices – when the unit price is low your fixed sum of money buys more units than when it is high. But there's nothing magic about this – it just shows the advantage of not having to worry about timing your investment correctly. Don't let this sort of advertising for savings plans persuade you that you are getting a bargain.

If you already hold shares, you could swap these for units – through a **share exchange scheme**. The unit trust company will usually do one of two things with your shares:
● put them in one of its funds, if the fund already holds that company's shares. In this case, in exchange for the shares, the company will often give you units equal in value to the price that it would have to pay in the Stock Exchange to buy the shares. As this is higher than you could get by selling the shares through the Stock Exchange, this seems a good saving
● sell them for you if the company does not want to put them in a fund. In this case, the company often pays the selling costs – eg stockbroker's commission.

Nearly all unit trust companies have a share exchange scheme – the details about minimum value of shares, number of shares and so on vary from company to company.

But don't let quite small savings push you into poor investment decisions.

Cost of switching

With the growth of more and more specialist funds and specialist advisers, there has been an increase in the number of companies which will let you switch your investment from one of their unit trusts to another for a lower-than-normal initial charge. They normally give you a discount of, say, 2% off the price of units in the trust you are switching to.

10 British Government stocks

The Government issues British Government stocks as a way of borrowing money. They can prove good investments. But they can also turn out to be very poor investments – as people who invested in War Loan in the 1940s, 50s and 60s know to their cost.

Conventional British Government stocks could suit three quite different categories of people:
- those who want a regular (normally fixed) income and who are confident that they won't want their money back in a hurry
- those who want to invest for a specific time period and want a fixed return over that period – and may not be too bothered how much of that return comes as income, how much as capital gain
- those who want to gamble that interest rates, in general, will fall (stock prices are then likely to rise, leading to a capital gain).

And now that index-linked stocks have been made available to private investors, these could be a way of protecting some of your money against inflation.

Below we describe how conventional stocks work. For more details on index-linked stocks, and on their pros and cons, see p107.

How stocks work

Most British Government stocks (commonly called gilt-edged securities or just gilts) pay a fixed amount of income each year. But with a few stocks, the income can vary – see Box opposite.

With stocks which are *dated*, the Government also promises to pay the holder of the stock a fixed number of £££, in a lump sum, at the time the stock comes to an end. With *undated* stocks no date is specified – so the Government need never pay off its debt.

Like shares, stocks are bought and sold on the Stock Exchange. And, as with shares, the prices of stocks fluctuate – so once you've bought some stock, the value of your investment can vary widely.

The Diagram opposite shows what has happened to the price of undated stocks since 1970. You can see, for example, that if you'd bought in January 1972 and sold three years later you'd have done very badly. You'd have got a before-tax income of 8.5 per cent a year on your original investment, but when you sold you would have got back less than half the money you originally invested – an overall loss of around 13.8% a year for a basic rate taxpayer.

If, on the other hand, you'd been lucky (or shrewd) enough to invest in January 1975 and sell three years after that, you'd have done very much better. You'd have got a before-tax income of 17.1% a year on your original investment and your investment would have increased in value by over 60% by the time you sold – an overall return to a basic rate taxpayer of around 27.4% a year.

So when you buy and when you sell is crucial to the success or failure of your investment. Of course, if you buy a dated stock and hold it until it comes to an end, you'll know from the outset what you'll get – both in income and capital gain.

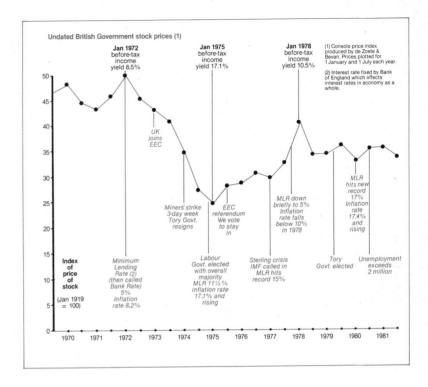

Undated British Government stock prices (1)

Jan 1972 before-tax income yield 8.5%

Jan 1975 before-tax income yield 17.1%

Jan 1978 before-tax income yield 10.5%

(1) Consols price index produced by de Zoete & Bevan. Prices plotted for 1 January and 1 July each year.

(2) Interest rate fixed by Bank of England which affects interest rates in economy as a whole.

UK joins EEC

Miners' strike 3-day week Tory Govt. resigns

EEC referendum We vote to stay in

MLR down briefly to 5% Inflation rate falls below 10% in 1978

MLR hits new record 17% Inflation rate 17.4% and rising

Index of price of stock

(Jan 1919 = 100)

Minimum Lending Rate (2) (then called Bank Rate) 5% Inflation rate 8.2%

Labour Govt. elected with overall majority MLR 11½% Inflation rate 17.1% and rising

Sterling crisis IMF called in MLR hits record 15%

Tory Govt. elected

Unemployment exceeds 2 million

What makes prices change?

In general, changes in interest rates in the economy as a whole. If interest rates rise, the price of stocks is likely to fall. If interest rates fall, stock prices are likely to rise. Why?

Suppose you invest £100 in an undated British Government stock which pays out an income of £10 a year. The yearly return is then roughly 10%. But now suppose that interest rates in the economy as a whole rise. New investors could then get a higher return on their money by investing elsewhere – so they'll hold off buying British Government stock. This means that the price of Government stock is likely to fall until the yearly return it offers is comparable to the return investors could get elsewhere. For example, if interest rates double the price of the undated stock which pays out interest of £10 a year may halve to £50 – so that the yearly return it then offers is roughly 20%.

Similarly, if interest rates as a whole fall, the price of British Government stock is likely to rise.

But it's not quite as simple as that with dated stocks because there are other factors at work. The main ones are:

● **how long to go until the stock comes to an end.** In general, the shorter the period left to run, the smaller the fluctuations in price. Take the example above of an undated stock paying interest of £10 a year and halving in price from £100 to £50. Suppose this stock was due to end in a year's time when the Government would pay the holder £100. If the price was £50, someone buying it now would get back £100 in a year's time plus £10 in income in the meantime –

Floating rate stocks (or variables)

Over the last few years a few British Government stocks have been issued which don't pay out a fixed amount in income each year. Instead, the coupon is linked to a rate of interest which itself varies – for example, ½% more than the rate paid on 3-month Treasury Bills.

Because the rate can vary, the price of the stock itself varies much less than the prices of stocks paying out a fixed income.

a return of around 120% in a year. The price needs to fall from £100 to only £90, or so, to give a return of around 20%
● **the stock's coupon** (see p106). In general, the higher the coupon, the smaller the fluctuations in the price. Take a stock with a coupon of 10%, for example, and five years to go before it comes to an end. If it is currently selling for its nominal value (see p106) of £100, the yearly return will be 10%. For the return (taking account of both income and capital growth over the next 5 years) to rise to 20%, the price of the stock would have to fall by around 28% to £72. But if the coupon was only 2%, the stock would have to be selling for around £71 to give a yearly return of 10%. For this return to rise to 20% the price would have to fall by around 32% to £48 or so.

What makes interest rates change?
A whole host of reasons. To take just two examples, the Government may increase interest rates to discourage people from borrowing, or to attract investors' money from abroad. See the Diagram on p103 for some of the events of the past ten years.

The price you pay

The price of British Government stocks is quoted as the price for each £100 nominal of stock. Prices are normally quoted in £s and fractions of a £, and shown to the nearest £$\frac{1}{32}$ (just over 3p) for short-dated stocks, and to the nearest £$\frac{1}{16}$ (just over 6p) for others.

Buyers normally pay about £$\frac{1}{8}$ more than the quoted price, sellers get £$\frac{1}{8}$ less. And if you buy a short-dated stock the price will be adjusted for something called accrued interest (see below).

Cum-dividend and ex-dividend
Most of the time, when you buy a stock, you buy it cum-dividend. This means you are entitled to a full half-year's interest when it becomes due, even if you haven't held the stock for that long.

However, some five weeks before the interest is due to be paid, the stock is declared ex-dividend. If you buy a stock ex-dividend, you are not entitled to the next interest payment – and therefore have a longer-than-normal wait for your first interest payment. The quoted price for an ex-dividend stock has xd after it.

With all but short-dated stocks and War Loan 3½%, there's an additional period of three weeks before the stock is declared ex-dividend, during which you can choose to buy or sell the stock either cum-dividend or ex-dividend; during this time, the ex-dividend version is called special ex-dividend. Because the cum-dividend version of a stock entitles you to the next interest payment, it costs more than the ex-dividend version. You'll find only the cum-dividend price quoted in the newspapers during this three-week period. Whether you should buy cum- or ex-dividend depends mainly on the rate of tax you pay – see opposite.

Accrued interest
This is the interest that a cum-dividend buyer gets for the period when he didn't own the stock, or which an ex-dividend buyer forfeits by getting his first interest payment late.

For short-dated stocks, the quoted price doesn't include accrued interest. So you have to pay a bit more than the quoted price when you buy cum-dividend, a bit less when you buy ex-dividend. For all other stocks, the quoted price allows for accrued interest.

The return you get

In income

A stock's coupon (see overleaf) tells you the before-tax income paid on each £100 nominal of stock. But it won't tell you how much income you'll get – because you are unlikely to pay £100 for each £100 nominal of stock. To work out the income you'll get (as a % of the amount invested), do this sum:

coupon × 100 ÷ price for each £100 nominal of stock

This is known as the income yield (or interest yield). Note that when doing this sum for a short-dated stock, you simply use the quoted price. But for any other stocks you first have to work out the accrued interest on the stock (for how to do this, see p107), and subtract this from the quoted price if the stock is cum-dividend, or add it on if it's ex-dividend.

In capital gain (or loss)

If you hold a stock until it comes to an end, you know you'll be paid its nominal value so you can work out the capital gain (or loss) you'll make. But with undated stocks or stocks sold before they come to an end, you don't know in advance what price you'll get, so can't be sure of what capital gain (or loss) you'll make.

The total return

With a dated stock, you can get some idea of the average yearly return on the stock if you held it until it was redeemed by looking at what's known as the redemption yield. It takes account of both income paid out and the capital gain (or loss) you make on redemption. But it doesn't normally take account of buying and selling costs and it assumes that the income paid out is reinvested at a rate of return equal to the redemption yield. Before-tax redemption yields are printed daily in the newspapers mentioned on p108.

Working out the after-tax redemption yield for any stock is not easy. It depends not only on the rate of tax you pay but also on how much of the return comes as income, how much as capital gain.

In general:

- stocks vary widely in redemption yields – in April 1982, before-tax redemption yields varied from 10.7% to 14.6%
- for stocks with about the same period of time left to run, people who pay a high rate of tax tend to get the best after-tax redemption yields from low-coupon stocks. By contrast, people who pay no tax tend to get the best redemption yields from high-coupon stocks
- when it's possible to buy the same stock in the special ex-dividend period, taxpayers normally get slightly better redemption yields if they buy ex-dividend. People who pay no tax may do slightly better if they buy cum-dividend.

New issues of stock

When the Government issues stock it usually advertises in the newspapers and includes in the advertisement a form for you to cut out and send in as your application for stock (along with your cheque).

Nowadays it's usual for only a minimum price to be quoted. You can offer what you like above that price.

If the whole issue (of, say, £800 million) is able to be sold at or above the minimum price the issue is closed. But don't worry about bidding too high – everyone who bids pays the price paid by the lowest successful bidder rather than the price they themselves bid. And issues don't normally sell out on the first day – so everyone who applies gets stock at the minimum price. After the initial offer, the stock that's left over is sold on the Stock Exchange through the Government broker over a period of time – and not necessarily at the price it was issued at.

During this period, the stock is commonly called a tap stock (because the supply of the stock is turned on and off like a tap, depending on the demand for it). When all this extra stock is sold, the tap is said to be exhausted. New short-dated stocks are lled short taps; new medium-dated stocks, medium taps; and so on.

Buying a stock direct from the Bank of England when it's first issued has the advantage that you don't have to pay any stockbroker's commission.

New issues of stock are often partly-paid. This means you don't have to pay the full cost of the stock when you first buy it – for example, you may have to pay 15% with your application, a further 15% one month later and the remainder the next month.

Details about stocks

Nominal value

British Government stocks are bought and sold in amounts which have a nominal value (sometimes called face value) of so many £ and pence. For each £100 nominal of stock you hold, the Government promises to pay you £100 in cash at an agreed time in the future – see redemption date.

But you don't have to buy stocks in multiples of £100 nominal. You could, for example, invest £125 in a stock costing £60 for each £100 nominal. You would then get: £100 × 125 ÷ 60 = £208.33 nominal of stock.

Name

Each stock has a name, like *War Loan* or *Treasury*. This is of no particular significance to investors, but helps to distinguish one stock from another.

Coupon

The percentage immediately after the name of each stock, eg 3½% after *War Loan*, is called the coupon. It tells you the before-tax income the stock pays out each year, expressed as a percentage of its nominal value – in the case of War Loan, £3.50 for every £100 nominal. Interest on nearly all stocks is paid twice yearly – in two equal instalments.

Redemption date

Following the name and the coupon is a year – eg 1995. The date on which the Government has promised to redeem the stock – ie to pay out the nominal value of the stock – falls in this year.

The date may be a range of years, eg 1995/98. In this case, the Government (but not the investor) can choose in which year out of this range to redeem the stock.

With a few stocks the coupon is

followed by a year and the words *or after*, eg *1923 or after*. This means that the Government can choose 1923, or any later year which suits it, to redeem the stock. These stocks, and a few others which have no year quoted at all, are called undated and need never be redeemed.

The life of a stock

Stocks are split into four groups, according to their life – ie the time left to go until redemption. They are called:
- short-dated if they must be redeemed in the next five years
- medium-dated if their latest redemption date is more than five but not more than ten years away
- long-dated if over ten years
- undated if no latest redemption date is given.

These are the groups used on the Stock Exchange; newspapers use others.

Turning interest into capital gain

Especially if you pay tax at higher rates (or the investment income surcharge) it can pay you to play a clever game. Here's how it works.

You buy a stock while it's in its ex-dividend period, hold it until shortly before the next income payment is due and then sell it cum-dividend. The cum-dividend price will be higher than the ex-dividend price to reflect the entitlement to the next interest payment. So you effectively make a capital gain rather than getting income – and the rate of tax on capital gains is only 30%, compared with a top rate of tax on investment income of 75% (and, of course, the first £5,000 of capital gains made in the 1982–83 tax year are tax-free).

A more sophisticated version of

this game is to buy ex-dividend during the three week special ex-dividend period, take the income payment in six months' time and sell cum-dividend in the special period after that. So long as you hold the stock for a year and a day, all gains will be free of CGT.

There are things to watch out for in this game. First, of course, the basic price of the stock may fall (eg because of rising interest rates in the economy as a whole). But this is a risk you take anyway. Secondly, beware of the taxman. If you try the game too often he may catch on to what you're doing and tax the capital gains as income. It will pay you to take the income sometimes.

Working out accrued interest

Correctly, accrued interest is worked out in a way that takes each day's interest into account. But you won't go far wrong if you do the sums in weeks.

For a cum-dividend stock: count the number of weeks since the last date interest was paid up to the date on which you want the accrued interest. Ignore odd days. For an ex-dividend stock, count the number of weeks still to go before the next interest date. The approximate accrued interest in pence is then:
coupon × weeks just counted × 2

Example What was the accrued interest on *Funding 6½% 1985/87* on 17 July 1981?

This stock was cum-dividend on 17 July 1981. The previous interest date was 1 May. Count the weeks from 1 May to 17 July – 11 weeks.

The approximate accrued interest is:
6½% (ie coupon) × 11 (ie weeks you've just counted) × 2
= 6.5 × 11 × 2 = 143p = £1.43.

Index-linked stocks

In his 1982 Budget, Sir Geoffrey Howe announced that anyone could now buy index-linked British Government stocks. Before then, they'd been sold only to pension funds and the like. Here we look at how they work and how they compare with other British Government stocks. We also look at how they compare with National Saving Certificates (2nd Index-linked Issue) – another investment suitable for a lump sum, which offers index-linking (see Chapter 21 for details of this investment).

How they work

There were four index-linked stocks when this book went to press – each with a different lifetime. The stock with the shortest life ends in 1988; the other stocks end in 1996, 2006 and 2111. When the life of a stock comes to an end, the person then owning it will be paid the nominal value (see opposite) of the stock *increased in line with inflation over the lifetime of the stock*. So someone owning £100 nominal value of 1996 stock issued in 1981 would get just under £420 if inflation averaged out at a constant 10 per cent over the life of the stock.

All the stocks also pay out a small income – their coupon (see opposite) is 2% or 2½% depending on the stock. The income is guaranteed to increase each year in line with inflation.

For technical reasons, inflation is measured by the Retail Price Index figures of eight months earlier.

What happens to the buying and selling price of the stocks?

The price of the stocks will tend to rise roughly in line with inflation. If the price is £100 and the Retail Price Index (RPI) goes up 10% a year, the price after a year might well be £110. But the price will also

be affected by people's views on the future rate of inflation and by the return they can get on other safe investments.

The price of stocks with a longer life may well fluctuate more than those with a short life.

Will your investment keep pace with inflation?

This depends entirely on the price at which you buy (or sell) the stock and whether or not you hold the stock to redemption. If you bought £100 nominal value of stock for £100 when the stock was issued, and if you then kept it throughout the lifetime of the stock, the increase in the capital value would exactly match the increase in inflation.

But suppose you had bought your £100 nominal value of stock for £90. Since it's the £100 nominal value which is index-linked, your capital gain at the end of the stock's lifetime would be more than the rate of inflation. If you'd bought at £110, your capital gain would be less.

If you want to buy stocks some time after they're first issued, you should compare the current market price with the nominal value *adjusted for the increase in the RPI*. If the RPI has increased by 10%, say, you should compare the market price with £110. If the price is higher, then your capital gain if you hold the stock to redemption will be less than inflation; if the price is lower, your capital gain will be more.

If you can't hold on to the stock until redemption, your gain will depend on the price you can sell at – see previous column.

Tax rules

These index-linked stocks are treated just like other British Government stocks for tax purposes – the income is liable for income tax and the gain is normally free from capital gains tax, unless the stock is held for less than one year.

How to buy?

At the time the book went to press you had to buy through a stockbroker or his agent – eg a bank. So a small investment (say less than £500) might not make sense – because of the costs of buying and selling. It's expected that the stocks

will appear on the National Savings Stock Register – where buying and selling costs (particularly for small amounts) are currently much lower.

How do they compare with other British Government stocks?

pro If you buy at the right price (see previous column) and hold them to redemption, you're guaranteed that the money you invest will at least keep pace with inflation.

con The coupon for all the index-linked stocks is low. And it could be costly to cash small bits to increase the income. So if you're after income, a high coupon stock may suit you better.

How do they compare with National Savings Certificates (2nd Index-linked Issue)

pro The return looks higher – an income of around 2% a year (which is taxed) compared with a tax-free bonus of 4% of the money you originally invested at the end of five years.

cons because the price of the stocks can fluctuate, you have to be careful about the price you buy and sell at. You can eliminate the second of these risks by holding the stocks until the end of their life. Don't forget buying and selling costs.

Worth it?

You have to decide whether you want to take a slight risk in exchange for the chance of a slightly higher return than with National Savings Certificates (2nd Index-linked Issue).

If you're a higher-rate taxpayer not looking for a large increase in income, you should consider putting some of your money into these stocks. And they're definitely worth considering for anyone who wants to keep a nest-egg on ice for a fairly long time.

If you need to sell stocks, the price should roughly match inflation over the time you've owned it – though fluctuations in price may work against you.

Choosing a stock

Which stock to choose depends on what you want from your investment.

A high fixed income?
Go for a high coupon stock. But beware of going for a stock which has a long time to go before it has to be redeemed – if you're forced to sell before then, you may lose heavily if the price of the stock has fallen meanwhile.

A known total return over a fixed period?
Go for a stock which lasts for the period you're interested in. If there's a choice, go for the one which gives the best after-tax redemption yield (see p105) for someone in your tax position. In general, a high rate taxpayer should go for a low-coupon stock, a non-taxpayer for a high-coupon stock.

Want to gamble on on interest rates falling?
Go for a stock with a long time to run, or for an undated stock. And choose one with a low coupon. But bear in mind that if interest rates rise rather than fall, you may end up losing heavily.

Protection against inflation?
Index-linked stocks might suit you. But bear in mind that you have to hold the stocks to redemption for index-linking to apply. And the extent to which your investment will be protected against inflation depends on the price you buy at. The stocks currently available are low coupon ones so may suit higher rate taxpayers best.

Where to get information and advice

Several newspapers give some information each day about British Government stock prices. But the most comprehensive information is given in The Times and the Financial Times.

To find the after-tax redemption yield for someone paying tax at the rate you pay it, and to get advice on which stock would suit your needs best, contact a stockbroker or your bank.

How to buy and sell

You can buy and sell British Government stocks through a stockbroker – either directly, or through a High-Street bank, solicitor or accountant, say. Around half the stocks are also listed on the National Savings Stock Register – you get forms for buying and selling these at a Post Office. There are important differences between buying and selling through a stockbroker on the one hand, and via the National Savings Stock Register on the other. In particular, except for large amounts of stock, buying through the National Savings Register is cheaper. Opposite we summarise the main differences.

Investing via a unit trust
There are now around 20 unit trusts specialising in British Government stocks and other fixed income investments.

Investing via a unit trust is generally more expensive than investing in stocks direct. The difference between the buying and selling prices of units is often around 4% – and there's a yearly charge.

From an income tax point of view, there's not a lot of difference between investing in a unit trust or investing direct. With capital gains tax, there is an advantage in investing direct. British Government stocks held for a year or more are not liable for capital gains tax, but gains on unit trusts are – though, of course, the first £5,000 of gains made by selling assets in the 1982–83 tax year is exempt.

Another problem with unit trust investment is that you have to accept the spread of stocks the trust chooses to invest in. By investing direct you can choose the particular stock which is best for your particular tax rate and investment aim.

Buying and selling British Government stocks

	Through a stockbroker or via a bank	Through the National Savings Stock Register
How much can you buy or sell?	no limits – but minimum charges make it expensive to buy or sell small amounts	you're not allowed to invest more than £5,000 in any particular stock on any one day. No limits on sales
– at what price?	you can set a price limit – eg won't pay more than £57½ for £100 nominal value of stock	you can't set a price limit
– can you buy cum- or ex-dividend if choice applies?	yes, you can choose which you want in special ex-dividend period (see text)	no, you have to buy cum-dividend in special ex-dividend period

What are the buying and selling expenses?

Through a stockbroker or via a bank: minimum rates of commission are laid down by the Stock Exchange and are based on the amount you invest (or sell for). VAT (currently 15%) is extra; also contract stamp (up to 60p) and an extra 60p on deals over £5,000

value of stock			minimum commission (as % of value)	
			if deal direct with stockbroker	if deal via bank, accountant etc
long-dated and undated stocks	first	£2,500	0.8	1.0
	next	£15,500	0.25	0.3
	next	£982,000	0.125	0.16
medium-dated stocks and new issues	first	£2,500	0.8	1.0
	next	£15,500	0.125	0.16
	next	£982,000	0.0625	0.08
short-dated stocks	no fixed scale but shouldn't be more than for medium-dated stocks			

Note: there may be a minimum commission of, say, £7 or even £10. Some examples, including VAT and contract stamp:

value of stock	commission [1]
£300	£8.15
£1,000	£9.50
£5,000	£30.79

[1] assuming minimum commission of £7

Through the National Savings Stock Register: commission (which includes VAT) based on the amount you invest (or sell for):

value of stock	commission
up to £250	£1 (but for *selling* stock worth £100 or less, commission only 10p for every £10 or part)
over £250	£1 plus 50p for every extra £125 (or part)

No contract stamp

Some examples of charges for different amounts invested (or sold)

value of stock	commission
£300	£1.50
£1,000	£4
£5,000	£20

	Through a stockbroker or via a bank	Through the National Savings Stock Register
How convenient?	a phone call or letter to your bank or stockbroker, say, is all that's needed. For a list of stockbrokers write to Public Relations Department, The Stock Exchange, London EC2N 1HP	you get special form from Post Office and post it off in the envelope provided (no stamp needed)
How quick?	stock should be bought or sold as soon as stockbroker gets your order (if in working hours)	stock normally bought or sold on day application received (probably day after posting)
Can you get after-tax redemption yields?	should be able to, quite easily	no
If buying, when must you pay?	on working day after the one you buy on, unless you've arranged otherwise – but in that case it may cost you a bit more	send payment with order (or can be taken from NSB ordinary account)
If selling, when do you get the cash?	as for buying – but first you have to give stockbroker your stock certificate with signed stock transfer form	you should get it within a week

11 Commodities

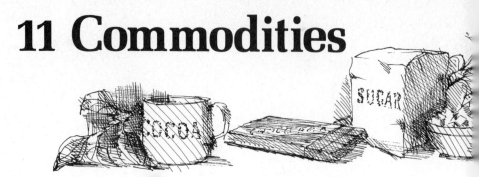

You might think that investing in commodities is a way of investing your long-term savings so that they stand a chance of keeping pace with inflation. Chapter 7 tells you about investing in things like stamps, antiques and wine. Here we deal with a different group of commodities – raw materials which can be bought and sold easily in large quantities on organised markets based in the City of London. The main raw materials which come into this category fall into two groups: *metals* such as copper, lead, silver, tin, zinc and *soft commodities* such as cocoa, coffee, rubber, sugar and gas oil.

How commodity markets work

Private investors can buy and sell commodities in two main ways:
- for delivery straight away
- for delivery on an agreed date in the future.

For delivery straight away

You can buy or sell copper, for example, which has already been mined, and is being stored in a warehouse. In the trade, this is known as buying or selling physicals or actuals; and the price you pay is known as a spot price. You have to pay – in full – for the commodity at the time you buy it. And you have to buy at least a minimum amount – 25 metric tons of copper, for example (which would have cost over £20,000 at the time this book went to press).

The commodity will be kept in a warehouse – and you'll have to pay charges for storing and insuring it.

If you buy a commodity for delivery straight away, you are hoping that the price of the commodity will go up and you'll eventually be able to sell it at a profit (after taking account of buying and selling costs, and storage and insurance charges).

For delivery on an agreed date in the future

This is the usual way in which private investors buy and sell commodities. You agree *now* to buy or sell a fixed amount of, for example, copper at a fixed price for delivery on some agreed date in the future. In the trade, this is known as dealing in futures and your agreement is known as a futures contract. There are rules about how far in advance you can arrange to buy or sell each commodity – eg up to three months with copper, and up to 17 months or so with cocoa. If you agree to buy or sell cocoa in December 1983, say, you are said to be dealing in *December 1983* cocoa.

If you buy a commodity for delivery in the future, you are hoping that its price will rise above the price you've agreed to buy it at – and that you'll be able to sell it at a profit before it is due to be delivered.

But you can also make a profit if you expect the price of a

Commodity options

A commodity option gives you the right to buy or sell a commodity futures contract at its current price at any time up to an agreed date. The amount you have to pay to buy an option varies widely – depending on what is expected to happen to the price of the particular futures contract you are interested in.

The advantage of taking out an option to buy a futures contract is that it gives you the chance of making a profit if the price of the commodity goes up – whilst at the same time limiting the amount of money you can lose if the price of the commodity falls, to the amount you paid for the option. The main disadvantage is that the price of the futures contract has to go up by at least the amount you paid for the option before you start making a profit.

commodity to fall. You can agree to *sell* rather than buy, December 1983 cocoa, for example, at a fixed price. You then have to buy – before December 1983 arrives – the cocoa you've agreed to sell. If the price of December 1983 cocoa does indeed fall below the price you've agreed to sell at, you will be able to make a profit on the deal. But if it goes up in price, you'll end up having to buy your cocoa at a higher price than the one you've agreed to sell at – and so make a loss on the deal.

You don't have to pay out the full cost of the futures contract you are dealing in – only a deposit (of perhaps 10 per cent of its value). But this doesn't mean that it's only your deposit you can lose. You will indeed lose a 10 per cent deposit if the value of a futures contract you've bought goes down by 10 per cent by the time you sell it. But if the price goes down by 50 per cent before you sell, you'll lose five times that amount. In practice, if the price falls, your broker (see p115) will ask you for more money (known as a margin call). If you don't hand over this extra money, he's likely to insist that you sell your futures contract straight away and accept the loss you've already made.

Trading in futures is not long-term investment

A private investor (often called a speculator) who deals in commodity futures is not making a long-term investment. He is gambling on what will happen to the price of a commodity over a relatively short period. If he buys December 1983 cocoa, for example, it's what happens to cocoa prices before then that decides whether he wins or loses his bet.

He may believe – quite correctly perhaps – that cocoa prices will double over the next five years. But he can't buy a futures contract which lasts that long. Buying December 1983 cocoa doesn't make sense unless he believes that cocoa prices are going to go up more than other people expect over the period before then.

How the markets are organised

London is one of the main centres in the world for commodity futures trading. There isn't one large market where all commodities are traded – there are several. For example, trading in aluminium, copper, lead, nickel, silver, tin and zinc is organised by the London Metal Exchange. Trading in soft commodities is organised by individual associations within the London Commodity Exchange (eg the United Terminal Sugar Market Association).

All the markets work in much the same way. Trading in each commodity takes place according to a set of rules – which lay down standards for the quality of the raw material, and fix things like the minimum amounts that can be traded.

Why futures markets exist

Futures markets enable people who trade in commodities – eg raw material producers (such as mine owners and farmers), manufacturers (such as chocolate firms) and wholesalers – to reduce the risk they face of losing money because of changes in the prices of commodities. Futures markets allow the raw material producers to get a guaranteed price for raw materials they haven't yet produced. And they allow manufacturers to know exactly how much they'll have to pay for raw materials they'll need in some months' time.

The private investor (or speculator), who has no intention of producing or using commodities, is one of the people who take on the risk that the producers and manufactures want to avoid. The private investor is the person who loses if, say, he has bought December 1983 cocoa and the price falls before he can sell it. But he is the person who gains if the price goes up before he sells it.

Commodity prices in the past

Commodity prices in general

The Chart below shows how the *Financial Times* index of commodity prices has changed between July 1952 (when it started) and October 1981. We've adjusted the index to take account of inflation – so the Chart shows what's happened to commodity prices, compared with UK prices in general. Note that when the index started, commodity prices were almost as high as they had ever been – due mainly to shortages caused by the Korean War.

The Chart is made up of a series of vertical lines. Each line shows what happened to commodity prices in a particular month. The top of the line is the highest level the index reached during the month, the bottom of the line is the lowest level.

The Chart shows two main things:
● compared with prices in general, the commodity price index fell fairly steadily between 1952 and 1972. And it's now back down below its 1972 level – at around 40 per cent of its 1952 level
● prices tend to go up and down quite quickly. A change of five per cent in a month is common.

Commodity prices since 1952 Index based on Financial Times Index of Sensitive Commodity prices, corrected for fall in buying-power of £, using monthly level of the Index of Retail Prices, compiled by the Department of Employment.

Index of commodity prices

Prices of individual commodities

The smaller Charts below show the average monthly prices of three commodities – cocoa, copper and sugar – since the beginning of 1976. This time, we haven't adjusted the prices for the fall in the buying-power of the £. You can see that all three commodities fluctuated in price enormously during this period.

The price of copper varied least. But even that almost doubled in price between the beginning of 1978 and early 1980. And by the beginning of 1981 it had fallen almost 40 per cent from its peak. Cocoa, on the other hand, more than quadrupled in price between the beginning of 1976 and mid-1977. By the end of 1980, it was almost back to its 1976 levels.

So to judge from what's happened in the past, it seems that you can expect a bumpy ride if you invest in commodities. Their prices may well double, or halve, in a year or two.

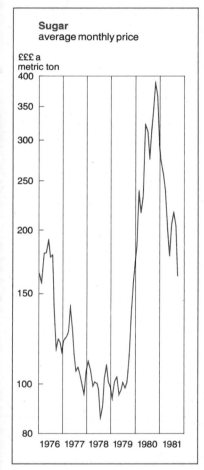

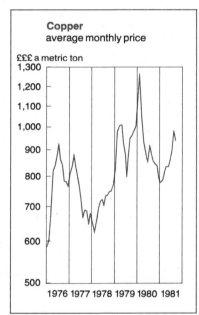

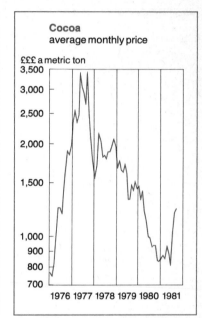

What commodity prices depend on

The prices of most commodities depend on supply and demand. In the end, the demand for a commodity comes from us – the consumers. To make the things which we want to buy, firms have to buy raw materials – for example, copper is needed for making electrical wire and copper pipes, cocoa for making chocolate.

If firms want to buy more of a commodity than is available, its price will rise. This may persuade producers that it will be profitable to produce more (eg start another copper mine, or plant more cocoa trees). But it may take some years before any more copper or cocoa is actually produced. The production of some other commodities – sugar, for example – can be increased within a year or so of producers deciding to produce more (weather permitting).

Prices in the long-term

There's no way of predicting with certainty, what will happen to commodity prices over the long-term – the next 20 or 50 years say.

If the world economy grows, and the total amount of goods and services produced in the world goes up, more raw materials will be needed. So you might expect commodity prices to rise, over the long-term. But if new and better ways of producing raw materials are found, or if cheap man-made alternatives to some raw materials are developed, some commodity prices may go down over the long-term.

Prices in the short-term

Commodity prices have fluctuated a lot from one year to another, and even from one month to another. These fluctuations can be the result of a number of things. The main ones seem to be:

● **natural disasters.** Droughts, floods, hurricanes, disease, and so on, may damage crops – and so lead to higher prices for commodities such as sugar, coffee and cocoa. Conversely, good harvests may lead to lower prices. Natural disasters can damage mining areas too – causing reduced production and high prices for commodities such as copper and tin

● **booms and slumps.** In the past, most economies have had periods of boom (with low unemployment and a high rate of growth of the amount of goods and services produced) followed by periods of slump (high unemployment, little – if any – growth in the amount of goods and services produced). In the boom, firms need to buy more raw materials in order to increase the amounts they produce – so raw material prices tend to rise. In a slump, firms cut back on the amounts they produce and the amount of raw materials they buy – so raw material prices tend to fall. In the last few years, much of the developed world has been in a slump at some time – and commodity prices have, in general, fallen

● **political problems.** For example, if a war breaks out, or a political revolution takes place, in an area of the world where a large proportion of the world's supply of a particular commodity is produced, the price of that commodity is likely to rise – as a result of fears that supplies of the commodity will be reduced

● **the exchange rate of the £.** Most of the world supply of commodities is bought by foreign firms – who naturally work out their cost in foreign currencies, such as US dollars and German marks. If they continue to pay the same price for their commodities, and if the exchange rate of the £ (ie the number of US dollars, German marks, and so on, you can get for a £) goes down, the price of commodities in terms of £££ will go up. Conversely if the exchange rate of the £ goes up, the price of commodities in terms of £££ will go down.

Commodity price agreements

With some commodities, the main producing and consuming countries have got together to try to reduce price fluctuations.

Most of these efforts haven't been very successful – there's always a temptation for some country to break an agreement by exporting more than it is supposed to. And not all producing countries may join an agreement in the first place.

The best known commodity price agreement is probably the one for oil, run by OPEC (the Organisation of Petroleum Exporting Countries) – but this depends on the co-operation of producing countries only.

How you can invest in commodities

You can invest in commodities in two ways:
● by buying and selling commodities directly through a commodity broker
● by putting money into a fund which has been set up specially to invest in commodities.

Buying and selling through a broker

Investing in physical commodities isn't a practical idea for most people. The minimum quantities you can buy are very large – for example 25 metric tons of copper (which would have cost over £20,000 at the time this book went to press), or 50 metric tons of sugar (which would have cost around £7,500). And with many commodities – such as cocoa and coffee – you run the risk of your commodity deteriorating in quality before you sell it.

If you deal in futures, you don't have to pay out such large sums of money, and you don't have to worry about the quality of your commodity. You have to put down only a deposit – perhaps 10 per cent of the value of what you're buying or selling. But the risk of losing a large sum of money is still there. Suppose, for example, you bought the minimum possible quantity of sugar for delivery in a year's time. You might have to put down a £800 deposit at the time you arrange the deal. But then if the price of sugar fell, you'd have to hand over more money to the broker. And if the price fell by 50 per cent before you decided it was time to get rid of your sugar, you would have lost around £4,000 (half of the £8,000 the sugar was worth when you arranged the deal).

You may be able to join a syndicate of people who pool their money and invest in commodities. Some commodity brokers run such syndicates. And, in some cases, there's a guarantee that you can't lose more than the amount of your original investment. But you might face problems about getting your money out when you want to. And there's still a fairly high chance of losing a lot of money.

Commodity funds

Putting money into a fund which has been set up specially to invest in commodities has three main advantages. First, it allows you to invest in commodities even if you can afford to lose only a more modest amount (£1,000, say). Secondly, you can be sure you won't lose more than the amount you put into the fund. Thirdly, most of the funds invest your money in a lot of different commodities – something you couldn't do yourself without investing a good deal of money. This means that if one commodity does particularly badly, it won't have a disastrous effect on the value of your investment.

For legal and tax reasons, the commodity funds which are available to the public are based outside the UK – often in the Isle of Man, or the Channel Islands. And they aren't allowed to send their booklets, prospectuses and so on, direct to members of the public. If you want these, you'll have to ask for them to be sent via a professional adviser – such as a bank manager or stockbroker.

How commodity funds work

Commodity funds work in much the same way as unit trusts. The fund is divided into a number of units – and your stake in the fund is represented by the number of units you own. The value of a unit is roughly the value of the fund divided by the total number of units.

But one major difference between these commodity funds and

Tax

How any profits you make from investing in commodities will be taxed is far from certain.

Profits from buying and selling *physical* commodities are likely to be treated as trading profits – and so taxed as earned income. A loss would count as a trading loss and you could set it off against the total of your income from all sources, but not against capital gains.

Just one isolated venture into the commodity *futures* market is likely to be treated as giving rise to a capital gain (or loss). But if you make a profit from a series of transactions, or invest as a member of a syndicate run by brokers or by a professional manager, this is likely to be treated as investment income – which means that you might have to pay the investment income surcharge on your profit, as well as income tax at basic and higher rates. In this case, a loss could be set off only against profits of the same kind, or against certain other income.

If the taxman looks on a commodity fund as being a managed syndicate, any profit you make is likely to be treated as investment income. But if he looks on a fund as more like a unit trust, your profit is likely to be taxed as a capital gain.

For more on tax, see Chapter 5.

most unit trusts is that most unit trusts are *authorised* by the Department of Trade. This means that the Department has looked at and approved the trust deed, which spells out how the trust works. And the Department lays down rules about how the prices of units should be worked out. There are no similar safeguards with these commodity funds. Also note that with unit trusts investing in the shares of companies which produce, deal in, or distribute, commodities, the value of a unit goes up and down with the share prices of the companies the trust invests in – it doesn't depend directly on commodity prices.

Most of the commodity funds can invest in both commodity futures and physical commodities. But a few invest only in physical stocks of just one commodity – eg copper or silver.

The performance of the funds which deal in just one commodity depend, on the whole, on what happens to the price of that commodity. But how your investment fares if you invest in a fund which deals in futures depends, to a large extent, on the skill of the fund managers. Over the six years or so since these funds started being formed there have been vast differences in performance. For example, assuming all income had been reinvested in the fund, if you'd invested £1,000 in 1976, it would have been worth over £7,000 five years later if you'd chosen the best performing fund. If you'd chosen the worst, £1,000 would have dwindled to £900 or so (worth less than £500 in terms of buying-power).

All the funds have minimum investments – perhaps £1,000. And all make charges – perhaps an initial charge of 5% of the amount you invest, a yearly charge of 2% of the value of the fund and, in some cases, a 'performance' fee of, say 10% of any increase in the price of units. Some of the funds pay out an income, but some don't. And the funds vary in how often the unit price is calculated and, therefore, how long you may have to wait to buy or sell units – with some this happens daily, with others you may have to wait a week, a fortnight or even a month. Some of the funds – but not all – have independent trustees who look after the fund's cash and the bits of paper which say what assets the fund owns.

For a list of some of the commodity funds, details of how they've done in the past and how to contact the managers, see *Money Management*, £2.75 from Minster House, Arthur Street, London EC4R 9AX. To find out more about any fund, ask the manager to send you details via your professional adviser.

Is commodity investment for you?

Buying physical commodities and storing them in the hope that their value will rise isn't a practical idea for most people. You have to invest several thousand pounds to buy the minimum possible quantity of just one commodity. And with commodities such as cocoa and coffee you run the risk of the stocks deteriorating in quality before you sell them. What's more, there's little reason to believe that commodity prices will, in the long run, rise as quickly as prices in general. They haven't done over the last 30 years or so.

Buying and selling commodity futures is a way of gambling on what's going to happen to the price of a commodity over a relatively short period – two years at the most. It could be a way of making, or losing, a lot of money in a short period. One large firm of commodity brokers estimated that 95% of commodity speculators who take their own investment decisions lose money.

If you decide that – despite the drawbacks – you do want to invest in commodities, putting your money in a special commodity fund has advantages. In particular, it cuts down the amount you have to be willing to risk losing.

12 Local authority investments

If you've got a lump sum to invest, and you don't mind locking it away for a time, putting it into an investment issued by a local authority could make sense. With these investments you can be sure of the number of £££ income you'll get each year and of how much you'll get back when the investment comes to an end.

But most local authority investments aren't suitable for money you're likely to need at short notice. Nor are they suitable for your long-term savings if you want to be sure of them keeping pace with inflation.

There are two main ways in which you can invest in local authorities:
● by lending money direct to a local authority for a fixed period. We call this type of investment a local authority loan. It's this type which is commonly advertised in newspapers, and often referred to (confusingly) as a bond – eg Scunthorpe Bonds.
● by buying local authority yearling bonds or local authority stocks – both of which can be bought and sold on the Stock Exchange.

Lending direct to a local authority

Local authority loans

How long for?
You have to agree to lend your money for a fixed period – normally between one and seven years. A few authorities offer to take money for longer – perhaps ten years.

Cashing in early
In general, local authority loans are not designed to be cashed in early. If you want to do this, you may have to convince the local authority that your circumstances have changed – eg if you've lost your job, and can't afford to live off the income you're now getting. If the authority agrees to your request it may make a charge. These loans can be transferred to someone else – but you may have difficulty in finding a buyer.

What happens if you die depends on the local authority. Some automatically repay the money, others insist on the loan being transferred – eg to your heirs.

Minimum investments?
Depends on the local authority – often £500 or £1,000. But some authorities will take as little as £100.

What rate of interest?

Rates vary frequently – in April 1982, most local authorities were offering interest rates of between 12½ and 14 per cent. The rate you get depends on:

- **when you invest**. Rates of interest offered by local authorities go up and down from time to time, in line with general movements in interest rates in the economy. But once you've invested your money, the rate of interest is fixed for the period of the loan – even if the rate to new investors soars or plummets
- **the amount you invest.** You may get a higher rate of interest if you invest at least £5,000, say, than you would if you invested only £500
- **how long you invest for.** If interest rates, in general, are expected to rise you might get a higher rate of interest the longer the period you invest for – for example, you might get ½ per cent extra if you invest your money for four years rather than two. But at times when interest rates in general are expected to fall, local authorities may well offer a lower rate of interest, the longer you want to invest for.

When is the interest paid out?

Normally half-yearly. A few loans pay all the interest at the end of the period of the loan. For this type of loan to be worth getting, it would have to pay you a higher advertised rate of interest to compensate for the delay in paying the interest out – at least ¼ per cent higher for a one-year loan, ¾ per cent higher for a two-year loan. For more details see p15.

Tax treatment

The interest counts as investment income for tax purposes. If the loan is for a year or more, the local authority has to deduct tax at the basic rate from the interest before paying it to you. If you don't pay tax, you can claim the tax back from the taxman. If you pay tax at higher rates, or the investment income surcharge, you'll have to pay extra tax.

Choosing a local authority

Local authorities wanting to borrow money from the public often advertise in newspapers, giving details of the rate of interest paid, the minimum amount accepted, and the length of time they want your money for.

The Chartered Institute of Public Finance and Accountancy runs a Loans Bureau. To find out which local authority is offering the best rate for the amount of money and length of time for which you want to invest, phone the Bureau on Monday to Friday between 3.30 pm and 5 pm on 01-828 7855. You won't be charged for advice given over the phone. Alternatively, you can write and ask for a copy of the weekly list they produce of the loans the different authorities are currently offering (see opposite for a sample of one). Address: CIPFA Loans Bureau, 232 Vauxhall Bridge Road, London SW1V 1AU. A single copy costs £2.50. Note that if you have a lot to invest (over £25,000, say) you may be able to get special terms – it's worth phoning the Bureau.

You may also be able to get help from, for example, a stockbroker. There's normally no financial advantage to be gained from investing in your own local authority – though there's nothing to be lost by asking.

Temporary loans

A temporary loan is for a period of less than a year. Most local authorities won't accept temporary loans unless you invest at least £25,000, say. But a few will take smaller amounts – perhaps £500 or £1,000.

With temporary loans, the local authority doesn't deduct income tax from the interest before paying it to you. So if you don't pay tax, you don't have the bother of claiming tax back from the taxman – but if you do pay tax, you have to settle up with the taxman direct. And the interest is quite often paid at the time the loan is repaid, rather than half-yearly.

Some temporary loans are, in fact, for periods of 364 days – ie virtually a year. But others are for shorter periods – for example, three months.

And some are arranged so that you can withdraw your money by giving an agreed period of notice – commonly seven days. With these, the interest rate can change – but the local authority must give you seven days' notice of any change.

Other local authority investments

You may come across two kinds of local authority investments not covered in this chapter – mortgage loans and local authority bills.

Mortgage loans are similar to – and to a large extent have now been replaced by – local authority loans.

Local authority bills aren't really suitable for small investors. They are normally issued in units of £25,000 or more, and are for fixed periods of three months.

How to invest

Contact the local authority direct. You can ask for an application form, fill it in, and return it with your cheque. Or you can write to the local authority, enclosing your cheque – and telling them your full name and address, the amount you want to invest, the period you want to invest for, and the rate of interest you expect to get. They'll write back to tell you whether or not they've accepted your money.

Verdict The main advantages of local authority loans are:

- your money is relatively safe (see p123)
- you know exactly how much income you are going to get, when you are going to get it, and how much you'll get back at the end of the period you invest for. Even if interest rates in general fall, your income will stay the same
- you need to invest a minimum of only £100 or so
- non-taxpayers, especially, get a relatively high return on their money – see Table on p123.

The main disadvantages are:

- you have to keep your money invested for an agreed period
- the return is fixed at the time you invest your money – so if interest rates in general rise, you may find that you could have done better by investing in, for example, a building society (where the rate of return you get can vary after you've invested your money).

AUTHORITY	1 YEAR		2 YEARS		3 YEARS		4 YEARS		5 YEARS		6 YEARS		7 YEARS		8 YEARS		9/10 YEARS	
		£		£		£		£		£		£		£		£		£
ROCHDALE M.B.C.	-		-		-		-		-		-		-		-		-	
ROCHFORD D.C.	-		9	500	10	500	11⅛	500	11⅛	500	11⅛	500	11⅛	500	-		-	
RUNNYMEDE B.C.	-		13	1,000	13	1,000	13	1,000	13	1,000	-		-		-		-	
RUSHCLIFFE B.C.	12¾	500	12¾	500	12¾	500	12½	500	12½ -	500	-		-		-		-	
ST. EDMUNDSBURY B.C.	-		-		-		13	500	13	500	13	500	13	500	13	500	-	
SALFORD CITY	-		-		-		13	500	13	500	-		-		-		-	
SALISBURY D.C.	-		-		-		13	100	13	100	13	100	13	100	13	100	13	100
SHROPSHIRE C.C.	-		-		-		-		-		12½	1,000	12½	1,000	-		-	
SANDWELL M.B.C.	-		11¼	250	11¼	250	11¼	250	11¼	250	11¼	250	-		-		-	
	-		12¼	500	12¼	500	12¼	500	12¼	500	12¼	500	-		-		-	
	-		13¼	1,000	13¼	1,000	13¼	1,000	13¼	1,000	13¼	1,000	-		-		-	
SCUNTHORPE B.C.	-		-		-		-		-		-		-		-		-	
SEFTON M.B.C.	-		12½	2,000	12½	2,000	12½	2,000	12½	2,000	-		-		-		-	
SEVENOAKS D.C.	-		-		-		-		-		-				-		-	
SHEFFIELD CITY	-		[illegible]			[illegible]	13	1,000	13	1,000	13						-	
								5,000	13½	[illegible]								

Buying a stock or a bond which can be bought and sold on the Stock Exchange

There are two main types of local authority investments which you can buy and sell on the Stock Exchange. Local authority stocks (often called corporation loans or corporation stocks) are generally issued for fixed periods of six or more years. They work in the same way as most British Government stocks (see opposite) – except that you are liable for capital gains tax if you make large enough gains.

Local authority negotiable bonds are often called yearling bonds because they commonly last for a year or so. Again, they work in a similar way to British Government stocks. Unlike most stocks they are issued at their *nominal value*, or very close to it (see p106 for what this means).

Local authority stocks

How long for?
Most stocks are issued for a fixed period of six or more years. Of course, you can buy a stock which has already been going for a number of years – and so has a much shorter period than six years to run. A few stocks are *undated* (see p106).

Cashing in early
You can cash in your stock at any time by selling it on the Stock Exchange – but there's no guarantee of what you'll get for it.

Minimum investment?
No fixed minimum. But the minimum commission charged by the stockbroker might make investing small amounts – less than £500 or £1,000, say – not so worthwhile.

What rate of return?
As with British Government stocks (see p105) the rate of return you get from your investment is a mixture of the income you get each year and the capital gain (or loss) you make when you sell the stock (or when it is *redeemed*).

When is income paid out?
Half yearly, on fixed dates which vary from stock to stock.

Tax treatment
The interest you get counts as investment income for tax purposes – and is paid out after basic rate tax has been deducted. Any gain or loss you make on the stock (after taking buying and selling expenses into account) counts as a capital gain or loss and is taxed accordingly – see p53. When working out any capital gain or loss, ignore any income that has been paid out to you.

Variable rate stocks

A few stocks pay out an income which can vary. The income paid out is linked to rates of interest in the economy in general. So you'll get a higher income from your stock when interest rates are high than you will when interest rates are low. Because the income varies, the price of the stocks (and, therefore, the cash-in value of your investment) changes very little.

How stocks work

Local authority stocks work in much the same way as British Government stocks (see Chapter 10).

They are issued for fixed periods – at the end of which an agreed amount is paid out by the local authority. Generally you have to pay less to buy a stock when it is first issued than the local authority agrees to pay out when it comes to an end (eg you may have to pay only £97.50 for each £100 paid out at the end). This means that you normally make a capital gain if you buy a stock when it is first issued and hold on to it until it comes to an end.

You also get a regular income. With most stocks, the income in £££ is fixed at the time the stock is issued.

Most local authority stocks are issued *partly paid*. This means that you don't have to hand over the full price of the stock if you buy at the time it's first issued. You pay an agreed amount straight away, and the rest at some agreed time in the future (normally within a couple of months) or in instalments on agreed dates.

After a stock is issued, it can be bought and sold on the Stock Exchange. The price of stocks can be expected to change if interest rates in the economy as a whole change. If interest rates go down, the returns offered by stocks which pay out a fixed income will look relatively attractive, people will buy them, and the prices of the stocks will rise. On the other hand, if interest rates in the economy as a whole go up, you would expect the prices of stocks to fall.

The total return you get on a stock is a combination of the income you get from it, and any capital gain or loss you make on it. If you buy a stock and hold on to it until it comes to an end, you know from the outset just what your return will be. But if you sell your stocks early, you don't know what the total return on your investment will be until you know what price you've sold your stock for.

Choosing a local authority

Choose a stock which suits you. If you want a high income each year, choose a stock which gives you one. If you are more interested in getting the highest possible return (taking both income and capital gain into account) over a particular period – again choose a stock which gives you what you want. A stockbroker should be able to tell you which stock suits you best. But make sure he takes your tax position into account.

Ask him to consider British Government stocks, too. The Table, on p123, shows how the returns on local authority stocks and British Government stocks compared towards the end of 1981.

You can see that, in general, local authority stocks came out slightly better. The figures don't take account of the commission you have to pay when buying a stock – but this shouldn't make much difference to your return unless you are buying a stock with less than two or three years to run, or you are investing only a small amount (less than £1,000 say).

If either of these apply, the minimum commission charged by a stockbroker might make buying a British Government stock through the National Savings Stock Register a better idea than it seems from the Table, because of the lower buying costs involved (see p109).

The same is true if you think you might have to cash your stock within a couple of years – because your selling costs will be lower and British Government stocks tend to be more *marketable* (with the result that the difference between the price you can buy the stock for and the price you can sell it for, is smaller than with many local authority stocks).

What about other stocks?

Some companies and foreign governments, for example, issue investments similar to local authority stocks (see p90 and p215 for details). With these, you have to take account not just of the after-tax return you can expect – but also of the possibility of the issuer being unable to pay up when the time comes.

How to invest

You have to buy (and sell) through a stockbroker – either contact one direct, or go through a bank manager, solicitor or accountant, say. For a list of stockbrokers, write to Public Relations Department, The Stock Exchange, London EC2N 1HP.

The commission charged on the deal is likely to be much the same as that charged on British Government stocks – see p109.

When a stock is first issued, you can buy it direct from the local authority. And when it comes to an end, the local authority pays you the nominal value of the stock. In both these cases, there's no commission to pay.

Yearling bonds

How long for?

Most yearling bonds are issued for a fixed period of a year or so. Two-year bonds are also fairly common.

Cashing in early

As for local authority stocks.

Minimum investment?

£1,000. And you have to invest in multiples of £1,000 – so you can't invest for example, £1,500.

What rate of return?

Bonds are issued once a week. On the day they are issued, all bonds lasting the same length of time pay the same rate of return. There's no difference between the rates paid by different local authorities. At the time we went to press you could expect to get a return of 14 per cent on yearling bonds.

When is the income paid out?

Normally half-yearly, on fixed dates which vary from stock to stock.

Tax treatment

As for local authority stocks.

Choosing a local authority

You can't choose a local authority. You put in your order with a stockbroker (see *How to invest*, below) and take what comes.

How to invest

Broadly, as for local authority stocks. But you have to buy through a stockbroker and there are no fixed rules about how much commission you'll be charged – you could expect to pay around $\frac{1}{2}$ or $\frac{3}{4}$ per cent of the cost of the bond (less if you're investing a few thousand £s). Again watch out for a minimum commission. There's no commission to pay when the bond comes to an end and the local authority pays up.

Note for devotees

As with British Government stocks (see p106), if you're a taxpayer it could pay you to buy a bond when it's first issued, or just after the interest is paid out on it, and sell it on the Stock Exchange five months later. This is because the price you can sell the bond for is likely to go up during this period, as the date for the next interest payment draws closer. You'll be liable for capital gains tax on your gain (see p53) – but there's no tax to pay on the first £5,000 of gains you make in a tax year, and only 30 per cent on anything more. If you waited until the interest was paid out, you'd have to pay tax on it at your highest rate of income tax. This tax saving could be worthwhile, even though you would have to pay commission to a stockbroker when you sold your bond. However, if the taxman catches on to what you're up to, he may put a stop to the tax saving by charging you income tax on the capital gains.

Verdict on local authority yearling bonds and stocks

Broadly, the advantages and disadvantages are the same as for local authority loans. But there's one main advantage of investing in a yearling bond or a local authority stock, rather than in a loan. You can cash in your investment early – though you can't be sure of just how many £££ you'll get if you do. With *yearling bonds*, you have to invest a minimum of £1,000. And with *stocks*, investing less than £1,000 or so may mean that your return is reduced because of the minimum commission charged by the stockbroker.

The Table opposite gives you an idea of how the returns from different types of local authority investment – together with British Government stocks – compared towards the end of 1981. You'll see that local authority stocks generally gave a somewhat higher return than British Government stocks if held until they come to an end. But if you buy and sell within a couple of years, local authority stocks may prove not such a good deal – because of extra commission and lower marketability (see p121).

Rates of return from local authority investments and British Government stocks
rates correct in November 1981

	return for someone paying			minimum investment needed to get this return
	no tax %	basic rate 30% %	higher rate 45% %	
Local authority loans for two to five years	12.0–14.5	8.4–10.2	6.6–8.0	commonly between £100 and £1,000
Local authority temporary loans	11.5–14.0	8.0–9.8	6.3–7.7	a few local authorities will accept £500 or £1,000
Local authority yearling bonds held to redemption [1] for one year	14.25	10.0	7.8	£1,000
Local authority stocks held to redemption [1] best short-dated (up to 5 years)	16.0	12.7	11.6	no fixed minimum – but minimum commission may make investing less than £500 or £1,000 or so less worthwhile
best medium-dated (over 5, up to 10 years)	15.9	12.5	11.0	
best long-dated (over 10 years)	16.8	12.2	10.7	
British Government stocks held to redemption [2] best short-dated (up to 5 years)	15.7	12.6	11.6	no fixed minimum
best medium-dated (over 5 up to 10 years)	15.8	11.6	9.6	
best long-dated (over 10 years)	15.7	11.3	9.5	

[1] But you normally have to pay commission when you invest, which reduces return somewhat.
[2] As for footnote [1] – but return reduced by less if you buy through the National Savings Stock Register.

How safe is your money? Money lent to local authorities is not guaranteed by the Government – but the Government has laid down rules which strictly control how much a local authority can borrow, and what it can use the money for. Broadly, a local authority can borrow money for periods of a year or more only to pay for capital expenditure – such as building council houses. It can borrow money to pay for day-to-day expenses (such as the wages and salaries of its employees) only on a temporary basis – and only to cover a temporary shortage of cash which will be made good when it has collected all the year's rates, Government grants and so on. Except with Government approval, a local authority isn't allowed to borrow on the strength of *next* year's rates to cover *this* year's spending. And this includes interest due on existing loans.

The Government also funds the Public Works Loans Board which acts as 'lender of last resort' to local authorities – the PWLB will lend money to any authority which needs to borrow immediately and cannot raise the money from other sources.

13 Endowment policies

An endowment policy is basically a long-term investment with life insurance tacked on. It's a way of investing in a mixture of British Government stocks, company loans, shares, property and so on – but you invest via a life insurance company.

How an endowment policy works

There are three main sorts of endowment policy:
● **non-profit**   You agree to save for a certain period – must be ten years or more. This kind of policy gives a poor, but guaranteed, rate of return. The average after-tax return offered by the insurance companies for a 30-year-old man paying into a policy due to last 25 years would be about 5% a year. The policy has to be kept going for the full 25 years to get this return – unless you die, in which case your heirs get the full sum guaranteed under the policy. If you had taken out a non-profit endowment policy in 1978 and cashed it in three years later, you would, on average, have got back less than you'd put in, even allowing for the premium subsidy (see p51). **Non-profit policies are not recommended**

● **with-profits**   You agree to save for a certain period – must be ten years or more. You can see from the Diagram opposite that, for the same premium, you're guaranteed a smaller sum with a with-profits policy than with a non-profit policy. But the guaranteed sum grows over the years as bonuses are added. And at the end of the period of the policy, you can expect very much more than you'd get from a non-profit policy. If current bonuses continue, a 30-year-old man paying into a 25 year with-profits policy might get an after-tax return of around 9.5% a year

● **flexible**   Similar to a with-profits policy, with a guaranteed cash-in value – often after ten years, with some policies sooner. You can usually carry on saving beyond this without having to give any information about your health. Because you have this flexibility, the return will not be as good as on a straightforward with-profits policy. A 30-year-old man could expect a return of around 9% if he cashes after ten years, around 8.5% after 25 years – if current bonus rates continue. For more details, see p128.

Bonuses

There are two sorts of bonuses. *Regular* bonuses (usually called reversionary bonuses by the insurance companies) are added to your with-profits or flexible policy. For how these bonuses are decided, see p127. Regular bonuses can be simple or, more commonly, compound depending on the company.

If, for example, the company announces a simple bonus of 4%, it adds 4% of the original guaranteed sum to your policy. So if the original guaranteed sum was £5,000, £200 would be added.

If the company announces a compound bonus of 4%, the

Life insurance for dependants

If what you want is life cover to protect your family from financial hardship in the event of your early death, you should take out *term insurance*.

With this sort of insurance, you insure for an agreed period. If you die within that period, the insurance pays out. If you survive, the policy pays nothing.

For a given amount of life cover, term insurance is very much cheaper than other types of insurance. For example, a 28-year-old man insuring his life for £20,000 for 20 years might pay £28 a year for term insurance, £900 a year for with-profits endowment insurance.

You can also take out term insurance policies which pay out a tax-free income if you die within the term. These are known as the family income benefit policies.

For more details, see *Money Which?* December 1979, p681.

How endowment policies work

(Our example is for a 30-year-old man with a 25-year policy and premiums of £20 a month. Figures would be different for other examples.)

start here

You agree to pay a premium of, say, £20 a month to the life insurance company but hand over only £17

£17
£3 premium subsidy

When you first take out a policy you decide how long you want it to last (25 years, say) and which type you want

EITHER

OR

AND
the company gets the other £3 from the taxman, because you get the government subsidy on premiums [1]

1. **Non-profit policy**
Provided you carry on paying the premiums, the insurance company guarantees to pay you a fixed sum – £9,500, say – at the end of the 25 years. If you die before 25 years are up, the policy comes to an end and your heirs get £9,500.

2. **With-profits policy**
Provided you carry on paying the premiums, the insurance company guarantees to pay you at least £5,600, say, at the end of the 25 years. If you die before 25 years are up, the policy comes to an end and your heirs get at least £5,600. But read on to see how this guaranteed sum may increase over the years.

The life insurance company puts the £20 into its long-term fund

Insurance company's long-term fund
£100 million, say

Your money is invested in British Government stocks, loans, ordinary shares, property and so on

Each year, the company announces *bonuses* for with-profits policy holders (based on the 'profits' made by its *long-term fund* – see text).

At end of YEAR 1
guaranteed sum is
£5,600 + bonus = £5,852

The sum guaranteed by your policy goes up by the amount of this bonus – so if the bonus is $4\frac{1}{2}$% each year

At end of YEAR 2
guaranteed sum is
£5,852 + bonus = £6,115

At end of YEAR 3
guaranteed sum is
£6,115 + bonus = £6,391

UNTIL

[1] Based on tax rules for 1982-83 tax year.

Expenses.
Each year, the insurance company deducts money to pay for office expenses, salesmen's commission, and so on

At end of YEAR 25 you may get back over twice as much as amount guaranteed at start of policy – £16,830 if rate of bonus continues to be $4\frac{1}{2}$%, say guaranteed sum increases by more (except in the first year of a policy). The bonus is worked out on the current guaranteed sum – ie the original sum *plus* bonuses already added. So in year 1, the company adds £200 (ie 4% of £5,000) to your policy, in year 2 it adds £208 (ie 4% of £5,200) and so on.

It's important to realise that there's no guarantee that a bonus will be added each year – though, in the past, it has been rare for a company to reduce its rate of bonus (let alone not to pay one).

Most companies pay a *terminal* bonus as well as regular bonuses. This is a one-off bonus announced at the end of the policy. Terminal bonuses have varied widely, depending on the current market value of the insurance company's investments – eg the shares it owns.

Comparing bonus rates with other rates of return

You can't compare them directly. First, you have to work out what a given bonus rate means in terms of the cash you get back at the end of the policy. Then you have to work out what rate of return this represents on the amount you save each month. Only then can you compare the rate of return you might get on an endowment policy with the rate currently offered by, say, a building society.

Premium subsidy

With these types of policy, you get a subsidy from the government on your premiums. If you agree to pay, say, £20 a month to the insurance company, you in fact hand over only £17 (at the rate of subsidy in the 1982–83 tax year). The insurance company gets the other £3 direct from the taxman. For more details, see p51.

Tax on the money you get back

There's normally no tax to pay on the money you get back from an endowment policy provided you don't cash it in (or make it paid-up – see p130) within its first 10 years – or within the first three-quarters of the period you insured for, if this is shorter. This makes endowment policies a more attractive type of investment, the higher the rate of tax you pay. For more details, see p49.

How with-profits policies have done in the past

On average, for a 30-year-old man taking out a 10-year with-profits policy coming to an end in 1981, with premiums (including the subsidy) of £20 a month, the return was around 10%. For a 25-year policy it was around 8%. For someone older, 45 say, the return was a bit lower (around 0.3% or less).

Only two flexible policies have been going 10 years – the average return for a man aged 30 when the policy was taken out and cashing it in after 10 years was about 7%.

Inflation over the last 10 years has been around 14% a year; over the last 25 years, 8% a year. So, in the main, these policies wouldn't have maintained the buying-power of your money.

Is an endowment policy suitable for you?

Non-profit endowment policies are not recommended – they offer a poor (though guaranteed) return.

If you're a taxpayer – especially if you pay tax at higher rates, or the investment income surcharge – a with-profits endowment policy is worth considering as a home for part of your long-term savings. But think carefully before committing yourself to saving a regular amount for as long as 25 years – the effects of pulling out early can be severe. And don't assume that the value of the money you invest will keep pace with inflation.

Flexible endowment policies have the advantage of giving a guaranteed cash-in value after a time. But they still involve a commitment of a number of years.

Where your money is invested

Your money goes into the life insurance company's long-term fund. The long-term fund is invested in a spread of different types of investment. For example, a company might have:
- 25 per cent of its long-term fund in ordinary shares
- 25 per cent in British and foreign government stocks
- 15 per cent in property
- 30 per cent in loan stocks, local authority loans, mortgages, etc
- 5 per cent in cash or other investments.

The idea of spreading the money around in this way is that it reduces the risk of the fund doing very badly. If all the money was invested in shares, for example, the value of the fund would plummet if shares as a whole plummeted. At the same time, of course, spreading the money around reduces the chances of the fund doing extraordinarily well. This, together with the way that the fund is valued (see below), means that an endowment policy should be regarded as providing a relatively safe, steady return on your money.

How regular bonuses are worked out

By law, an insurance company has to keep the money concerned with its *long-term business* in a *long-term fund* – separate from the rest of its money. Long-term business includes life insurance, permanent health insurance, annuities and pension schemes. The company has to get an actuary to value the assets and liabilities of its long-term business at least once every three years. The Government lays down rules about the valuation.

Assets
Some examples of the maximum values that can be given to assets are:
- land and property: its market value, estimated by a professional surveyor or valuer not more than three years before
- debts due to be collected in more than a year's time: what the company could expect to get if it sold the right to collect the debt
- ordinary shares, debentures, British Government stock and other investments quoted on a stock exchange: the average price on the day of valuation.

In addition, there are rules which limit the value that can be put on one particular investment – eg shares in one particular company. This is to prevent the fund becoming too dependent on that investment.

Liabilities
The liabilities are the benefits that the insurance company will have to pay out in the future – eg when policyholders die or their policies come to an end. The actuary estimates how much the insurance company will have to pay out in each of the next 35 years, or more.

But he also has to take account of the fact that £1 which has to be paid out next year is of greater concern to the company than £1 to be paid out in 10 years' time, say. This is because the company can earn interest on the assets of its long-term fund – so that less than £1 needs to be set aside now, to meet the debt in 10 years' time.

The value the actuary puts on future liabilities depends on the assumptions he makes about the future return on the assets. The higher the return he assumes, the lower the value he puts on the liabilities. In practice, the actuary tends to assume a much lower rate of return than the one currently being earned.

The actuary then values the premiums the company is going to receive in the same sort of way – allowing for office expenses, commission and so on. By taking away the value of the premiums from the liabilities, he gets a figure for net liabilities.

Surplus (or excess)
This is simply the amount by which the assets of the long-term fund exceed the net liabilities. Having worked out the surplus, the actuary decides how much of it should be added to the insurance company's reserves, how much should be paid out to the company's shareholders, and what rate of bonus should be paid on each type of with-profits policy – eg endowment, whole life and flexible endowment.

Note that once a bonus has been announced, it becomes part of the liabilities of the company, and cannot be taken away from the value of your policy (unless you cash the policy early).

Does the company have to pay a bonus?
There are Government's rules which require a company to notify the Secretary of State for Trade if it isn't going to give its with-profits policyholders their usual share of any surplus. And the Secretary of State has considerable powers to intervene in an insurance company's affairs – if, for example, he thinks that policyholders' *reasonable* expectations won't be met.

In practice, companies normally do add bonuses to with-profits policies each year.

Flexible policies

There are around 35 flexible with-profits policies available. The details of the policies vary widely between companies. But they all have two things in common:
● there is a guaranteed cash-in value – often after ten years, with some policies sooner than this
● you can cash in part of your savings, without having to cash in the whole lot.

How they work   Usually, these policies are made up of units (technically each unit is itself a small policy). You pay a monthly premium (£1 a month, say) for each unit you take out – and you may have to take out at least five units, say. Each unit pays out a guaranteed sum at the end of the policy (could be during the year before your 65th birthday, or after 10 or 25 years, say) – or if you die before then. Bonuses are added in the same way as with a standard with-profits policy.

Commonly, once the policy has been going for at least 10 years, each unit has a guaranteed cash-in value (ignoring bonuses) of:

original sum guaranteed at end of policy	$\times$	number of complete years policy has been going	$\div$	number of complete years policy was due to last in first place

On top of that you are entitled to a share of the bonuses that have been announced. Your share is worked out by increasing the answer to the above sum by the rate of bonus announced in each year of the policy.

Example
Joe Pepper bought 10 units at £1 a month each in a flexible endowment policy from Slagthorpe Life in 1971, when he was 29. Each unit guaranteed him £350 in 35 years' time. He decides to cash in one unit in 1981 – after it has been going for 10 complete years.

He works out what the guaranteed cash-in value of a unit is now. First he works out the guaranteed cash-in value ignoring bonuses:
£350 × 10 ÷ 35 = £100
Slagthorpe Life announced a bonus of 4% compound in each of the policy's ten years. Joe is entitled to these bonuses – worked out on the £100 basic sum he is now guaranteed. Over the 10 years, the bonus add up to £48.
So Joe is now guaranteed £148 for each unit.

Options   A flexible policy may have various options open to you. For example, you may be able to cash your policy after ten years and start another without having to give any information about your health. Or you may be able to increase the amount you're saving.

Table 1   How a company's standard with-profits and flexible endowment policies might compare

	return if policy cashed in after 10 years [1]	return if policy held for 25 years [1]	life cover at start of policy
flexible policy	9.0%	8.5%	£6,600
25-year policy	6.6%	9.5%	£5,500

[1] Figures are for 30-year-old man; premiums (including subsidy) of £20 a month. Figures also assume that current bonus rates will continue. Remember that cash-in value on a 25-year policy is *not* guaranteed

How flexible policies compare with standard policies

With both flexible and standard policies, there are usually no guarantees about cash-in values in the first 10 years – though some flexible policies give a guaranteed cash-in value sooner than this (at $7\frac{1}{2}$ years, say). After that, a flexible policy generally has a higher cash-in value than a standard policy. For examples of how the cash-in values might compare, see first column of Table 1 above.

A flexible endowment policy can be expected to give a somewhat lower return than a standard policy if the standard policy is seen through to its end. Look at the second column of the Table for a typical comparison.

Verdict

A flexible policy could be worth considering instead of a standard with-profits endowment policy. But you still have to hold it for quite a number of years before getting a guaranteed cash-in value.

Commission

Over three-quarters of the insurance companies sell at least some endowment policies through intermediaries – ie insurance brokers and people like solicitors and accountants. They pay them commission for making sales. The Life Offices' Association and Associated Scottish Life Offices – to which most companies belong – lay down the maximum commission their members are allowed to pay to intermediaries. For all except a few very small companies, the maximum is:
- **initial commission** (paid in the first year of policy) $2\frac{1}{2}$ per cent of yearly premium multiplied by the number of years the policy is due to run. But maximum initial commission is 60% of yearly premium.
- **renewal commission** (paid in each of the following years) $2\frac{1}{2}$ per cent of yearly premium.

In practice, most companies pay the maximum allowed. So if an insurance broker sells you a 20-year policy with a yearly premium of £200, he is likely to get £100 (ie $2\frac{1}{2}$% × £200 × 20) in the first year. In each of the following years, he might get £5. Note that these commission rules apply to some other sorts of investment-type life insurance.

There are no rules about the commission that companies are allowed to pay to their own salesmen.

What to do if you change your mind

To get the best return on a straightforward with-profits
endowment policy, you have to keep it going for the period you
originally agreed – often 15, 20 or 25 years. And even with a flexible
policy, you often have to last out for 10 years. But your financial life
could be drastically altered during this time (through marriage,
divorce, having children, moving home, being made redundant,
starting your own business, for example). So you may find yourself
wanting to end the policy early.

There's no doubt that a substantial number of endowment
policies are cashed in early (or simply allowed to lapse) – though
there are no reliable figures showing how many.

If you find that you need your savings back early, or you can no
longer afford the premiums, what are the alternatives?

**Cashing in
your policy**

Unless it's a flexible policy, the cash-in value of an endowment
policy is usually entirely at the discretion of the insurance
company. Note that this is also true of flexible policies in the first
ten years.

If a 30-year-old man cashed in a 25-year policy with premiums
(including the subsidy) of £20 a month, he would get back around
£300 if it had been going for exactly two years, around £2,750 if it
had been going for 10 years. This means a loss of around £120 for
the two-year period and a return of around 5.5 per cent a year over
10 years (allowing for the premium subsidy). Not very impressive.

Note that with most companies you get nothing back if you cash
your policy within its first two years.

Making it paid-up

You stop paying the premiums and the insurance company
reduces the guaranteed sum for which you are insured. This new
guaranteed sum – called the paid-up value – is paid out at the end of
the period you insured for (or when you die, if this is earlier).

Most insurance companies continue to add bonuses to the paid-
up value of a with-profits policy.

Getting a loan on it

Nearly all insurance companies will consider lending you money,
using your policy as security for the loan. Generally the maximum
loan is between 80 per cent and 90 per cent of the cash-in value.
Some companies will not make a loan of less than a certain amount
– usually £50 to £100. Interest charged is currently around 12 per
cent to 15 per cent a year, depending on the company.

Tax

You may have to pay tax on the gain you make on an endowment
policy if both the following apply:
● you pay tax at higher rates or the investment income surcharge
(or would do, if the gain were added to your investment income)
● you cash it in or make it paid-up in its first 10 years (or within the
first three-quarters of its term, if this is shorter).

The gain is normally the amount you get less the total of all the
premiums paid. For more details, see p49.

If you cash in your policy or make it paid-up, in its first four
years, the taxman may *clawback* some or all of the subsidy you've
had on your premiums. This will only happen, however, if you
show a profit on the deal (ie the cash-in value is more than the cost
of the premiums, after allowing for tax relief). For more details, see
p52.

What should you do?

If you need the cash, you'll have to choose between cashing in your policy and getting a loan on it. If you don't need the cash – but can no longer afford the premiums – you could also consider making your policy paid-up.

Which is the best choice for you will depend on the particular circumstances of your own case. The first thing to do is to ask the insurance company for:
- the policy's cash-in value
- details of any loan you can use your policy to get (eg rate of interest charged, how much you can borrow)
- the current sum guaranteed by the policy
- the current rate of bonus

and, if you don't need the cash
- the paid-up value and whether bonuses will continue to be added to this value.

Then you'll have to work out for yourself what the best course of action is. The example below will give you an idea of how to do this.

Example

Simon Smart has a 25-year with-profits endowment policy – for which he has been paying premiums of £20 a month for the last 15 years. He now finds he can't afford to carry on paying his premiums. He writes to his insurance company and finds:
- the cash-in value is £5,453
- he can borrow up to £4,640 on his policy. The rate of interest would be 13% at present, but could vary
- the current sum guaranteed by the policy is £10,318 (the original £5,276 plus £5,042 in bonuses)
- the current rate of bonus is $5\frac{1}{2}$% compound
- the paid-up value is £7,801 and bonuses will bontinue to be added.

Cashing-in

Simon doesn't need the cash. So if he cashed his policy in, he'd invest the £5,453. He finds that if he invested the money in a 10-year British Government stock, for example, he might (at that time) get a return of around 11% a year. He'd get a total of around £15,480 in 10 years' time (assuming he could reinvest the interest at 11% too – which, of course, may not be possible).

Making the policy paid-up

The paid-up value is £7,801. The company would add bonuses to this amount for the remaining 10 years of the policy. So, if the current $5\frac{1}{2}$% bonus rate continues, he'd get back around £13,325 in 10 years' time. The company may add a terminal bonus to this – say £1,330. This would make a total of £14,655.

Getting a loan

Though Simon doesn't need the cash at the moment, it might still make sense for him to get a loan on his policy and use this to help pay his premiums.

The amount his policy is likely to pay out if he continues to pay the premiums, and if the current rate of bonus continues, is £17,625 (ie the current guaranteed sum of £10,318 *plus* bonuses of $5\frac{1}{2}$% compound a year). And the company may add a terminal bonus to this. At current rates, it would be £1,760, making a total of £19,385. His £20 a month premiums actually cost him £17 after the premium subsidy (see

p51). So he'd need to borrow around £2,040 over the 10 years (ie 120 monthly payments of £17).

When his policy came to an end he could expect to get back £19,385 *less* the £2,040 loan – ie £17,345.

Of course, he'd also have to pay interest on the loan. This could be kept to a minimum if he borrowed the money in instalments, rather than borrowing the full £2,040 straightaway. In this case, the interest might work out at about £1,460 over the 10 years – rather than the £2,600 or so if he borrowed the full £2,040 now.

Deducting £1,460 interest from the £17,345 he'd get back from the policy, leaves a net amount of £15,885.

What Simon decides to do

Simon sees that, in this particular case, the best thing to do would appear to be to get a loan from the company to pay his premiums. If he can, he'll get a loan each year; if not, he'll get a loan now to pay all the premiums, and invest the money in a building society until it's needed.

The worst thing he could do at the moment is to make the policy paid up. He realises, however, that he can only make an estimate of the outcome. Things could alter in the next 10 years – interest rates and bonus rates could go up, for example.

How to choose a company

If you're taking out a with-profits policy, you'll be planning to pay money to a company for at least 10 years. So it makes sense to choose the company carefully. For a 25-year policy coming to an end on 31 March 1981, *Money Which?* found that the return on money invested with the best company worked out at almost double the return on money invested with the worst.

The return from a with-profits policy depends on several things – eg how successfully the management invests the long-term fund, how much of your premium goes in commission and expenses, how the actuary values the long-term fund, whether the company has any shareholders to share in the surplus made by the long-term fund, how many with-profits policyholders the surplus is to be split between.

So you can see that success at investing money (which is unpredictable) is only one of the important factors. This means that a company's past performance may be a guide to the future.

Probably the best way to choose a company will be to look at how the past performance of each company compares and how future performance might compare assuming current bonuses continue. Remember that terminal bonuses are generally thought to be less stable than regular (or reversionary) ones. So check how much of the return is forecast to be made up by a terminal bonus.

The latest *Money Which?* comparison of endowment policies is in *Saving for the future*, September 1981 p518. And you could check magazines like *Planned Savings* and *Money Management* which publish surveys of endowment policies at regular intervals.

Company safety

Insurance companies are closely supervised by the Department of Trade. The Secretary of State for Trade can intervene in the affairs of an insurance company if he thinks it's getting into difficulties. He can, for example, prevent it taking on any new business. Friendly societies are supervised in much the same way – but by the Chief Registrar of Friendly Societies (the head of a different Government department).

Insurance companies, but not friendly societies, are covered by the Policyholders Protection Act. If your company fails, the Policyholders Protection Board has to try to get another company to take over the policy. In this case, provided you carry on paying your premiums, the Act guarantees that at the end of the policy, you'll get at least 90 per cent of the sum guaranteed at the time your company went bust – unless the Board considers this amount to be *excessive.* You get no guarantee of what bonuses the new company will add.

So you may lose out on quite a lot of money if your company goes bust – it makes sense to be cautious when choosing a company. It would be prudent to avoid relatively new or small companies.

Whole life insurance

This is another kind of investment-type life insurance.

You agree to pay premiums for the rest of your life, or up to a certain age (65, say). The insurance company agrees to pay out a fixed sum (plus bonuses if they've been added to a with-profits policy) on your death, whenever that happens.

You can cash in your policy at any time, but in the first few years the cash-in value is likely to be little or nothing. Even after a very long time, the cash-in value is likely to be fairly low.

In general, this type of policy is unlikely to match your needs. If you want protection for your dependants, it would be better to go for *term insurance* (see p124), which is very much cheaper. If you're looking for an investment, you're likely to get a better return elsewhere – without being tied to such a long savings period.

But a whole life policy may be useful to pay a capital transfer tax bill on your death. The policy should be made out so that the proceeds go to your heirs, not to you (otherwise the proceeds could form part of your estate and become liable for CTT themselves). If you go for a whole life policy, *don't* take out a non-profit one.

14 Unit-linked life insurance

Despite its name, unit-linked life insurance is not really to do with insuring your life. But insurance companies enjoy certain privileges (mostly to do with favourable tax rules) which enable them to make unit-linking attractive to investors.

Unit-linking is suitable for both lump sum investors and regular savers who are prepared to take a risk with some of their money. To invest, you buy either a single-premium bond (eg an equity, property, managed bond) or a unit-linked savings plan. Both are technically life insurance policies – though normally you get only a small amount of cover.

In general, when you invest, your money buys you units in a fund of investments run by the insurance company. The price of each unit you buy is, approximately, the value of the investments in the fund divided by the number of units issued. The unit price goes up and down as the value of the investments in the fund (eg property, shares and so on) fluctuates.

When you sell your units, what you get back depends on the price of the units at the time. If the fund has been performing badly, you could make a loss. On the other hand, you stand the chance of making a large profit, if the fund is doing well when you sell.

The first part of this chapter deals with things which apply in general, whether you've got a lump sum to invest or want to save something each month. Information about single-premium bonds is on pages 136 to 141, and about unit-linked savings plans on pages 142 to 146. At the end of the Chapter we give brief details of somewhat more complicated schemes.

Where your money is invested
Your money goes into a fund of investments, usually run by the insurance company. Most insurance companies run a number of funds. The main types are:
● property funds – which invest in office blocks, factories, shops and so on
● equity funds – which invest in shares (either directly, or via unit trusts)
● fixed-interest funds – which invest in things which pay out a fixed income (eg British Government stocks, company loan stocks)
● managed funds – which invest in a mixture of things such as property, shares, and fixed-interest investments
● cash funds – which invest in bank deposit accounts, short-term loans to local authorities and other investments which pay out rates of return which vary along with interest rates in general. The value of an investment in a cash fund should increase steadily as the interest it earns is reinvested in the fund.

Some companies offer more than one of some types of fund – eg a choice of equity funds (including, perhaps, an international fund which specialises in foreign shares, or one which specialises in a particular region – eg Far East).

When you first invest, you decide which fund to go for. But with many of the plans, you can switch from one fund to another from time-to-time (from the equity fund to the fixed-interest one, say). You may have to pay a charge for switching ($\frac{1}{2}$ per cent of the current value of your units, say).

What should you expect if you invest

Property, equity and managed funds all aim at long-term growth. Traditionally, property and shares have been seen as more suitable long-term investments than things like building society and bank deposit accounts or British Government stocks, which pay out a rate of interest. By investing in property and shares you are investing in real things – so your investment should give you at least *some* protection against inflation.

The Diagrams opposite give an indication of how the value of £1,000 invested in a property, equity or managed bond might have varied since 1971. The black lines show the value of your investment in terms of £££, the red lines in terms of buying-power (taking account of rising prices).

You can see that the buying-power of your money would not have been maintained in any of these funds over the 10 years shown. If you'd bought an equity bond, your original £1,000 would be worth only around £550 in buying-power at the end of the period. The managed or property bond would be worth around £650.

But if you'd invested half way through the period instead, you would have made a profit in terms of buying power with all three bonds – a very slight profit in the case of the property bond, but well over £100 with the other two.

You can also see that unit prices in the managed and equity funds fluctuated quite a lot – look at the black lines to see this most clearly. Unit prices in the property fund fluctuated comparatively little – apart from the marked fall in 1974 to 1975 when the property market crashed (a bad time for the stock market, too).

The success of your investment, particularly with bonds, can depend very much on when you invest and when you cash your investment. Investing on a regular basis in a savings plan instead of putting a lump sum into a bond removes the danger of investing all your money at the wrong time. On the other hand, it also removes the chance of doing extremely well by investing all your money when unit prices are low. And the success of your investment will still depend very much on the price of units at the time you cash them.

How do you know how your investment is doing?

You can follow the fortunes of your investment by looking up the unit price in a newspaper (the Financial Times lists most companies' unit prices – look under the section headed *Insurance Property Bonds*). For more details see *Buying and selling* on p137.

How your investment might have done

property bond

in terms of £££
in terms of buying-power

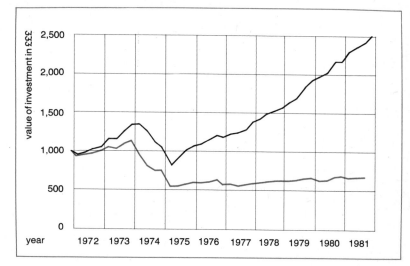

equity bond

in terms of £££
in terms of buying-power

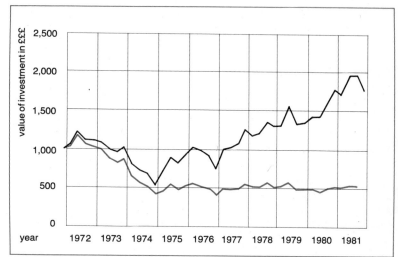

managed bond

in terms of £££
in terms of buying-power

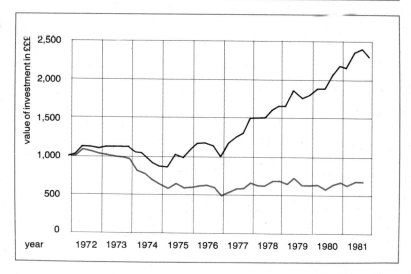

Single-premium bonds

With these policies, you hand over a lump sum to the insurance company. The company takes part of the money to cover its expenses and to provide you with life insurance. The rest of the money buys units in whichever fund you choose.

The Table below shows how the after-tax returns from building society term shares, British Government stocks held until the end of their term and typical property, equity and managed bonds have compared over 10, 5 and 1 years. You can see that none of the investments emerged as a clear 'best buy' over all three periods. For example, British Government stocks would have been the winner over the twelve month period, the equity bond over the five years.

Do you get an income? You can't get an income in the conventional sense of having interest paid to you. This is because you don't directly own the things the fund invests in. The income earned by the fund's investments is generally put back into the fund to buy more shares, property or whatever.

Instead, you can normally arrange to cash in part of your investment from time-to-time – on either a regular basis (under a withdrawal scheme) or an irregular basis. If you're a higher-rate tax payer, cashing in part of your bond could possibly lead to a bill for income tax (see p49 in Chapter 5), but in general paying tax on the gain you make can be avoided if you withdraw no more than five per cent of your original investment in any one year.

To make getting an income easier, bonds are often sold as a cluster or series of identical mini-policies so that you can cash in a whole policy – or several – at a time, according to your needs. The tax rules are simpler, too, if you cash in a whole policy rather than part of one. Of course, cashing units to get an income will start eating into the value of your investment if the unit price is increasing at a lower rate than the rate at which you are cashing units.

How approximate after-tax returns have compared

	yearly return [2] for someone paying basic tax rate, over:			yearly return [2] for someone paying tax at 45%, over:		
	10 years %	5 years %	1 year %	10 years %	5 years %	1 year %
British Government stocks [1]	6.7	8.2	10.1	6.0	6.4	8.8
building society term shares	8.5	10.2	9.8	7.3	8.5	7.7
property bond	8.9	13.5	7.8	8.0	11.8	6.4
managed bond	8.7	13.1	−2.7	7.8	11.5	−2.7
equity bond	5.6	17.9	−5.9	4.9	15.8	−5.9

[1] held until redemption   [2] to November 1981

You can normally choose for the income to be either:
● a percentage of the number of units you hold (in which case your income will go up and down with the price of units)
OR
● a percentage of the amount of your original investment (in which case your income in £££ will be fixed, but the number of units cashed in will go up when the unit price falls, down when the unit price rises).

Most companies insist on a higher-than-normal minimum investment if you want a regular income. For example, you might have to make an investment of at least £1,000 for yearly payments, £4,000 for quarterly payments, £12,000 for monthly ones.

Note that with a few companies you don't have to cash in units to get an income. Instead, the income the fund earns can be paid straight to you (in proportion to your unit-holding), rather than being reinvested in the fund.

Who should consider investing in these bonds?

You should *not* invest in bonds if:
● you are likely to want your money back at short notice (because the property or share market may be in a slump when you find you need to cash your bond)
● you object to the value of your investment fluctuating.

So long as neither of these things applies, you could consider putting some of your savings into one of these bonds. If you want to use the bond to provide an income, you'll probably do best with the sort which is a series of mini-policies.

Only an insurance company is allowed to offer the public a direct stake in a fund of investments which includes property. So if you want to invest in property other than your own home – and if you haven't got tens of thousands of £££ to invest – buying a property or managed bond may be the only way to do it. If you want to invest in shares, there are alternatives to equity bonds – see *Which way to invest in shares?* overleaf.

Single-premium bonds are suitable not only for people who are prepared to lock a lump sum away for several years in the hope that it will increase in value in the long-term. They are also suitable for people who will want to switch from one type of investment to another – property to shares, say – from time-to-time in the hope of putting their money where it will increase in value quickest.

Buying and selling

With about half the insurance companies you can buy or sell your units at any time at the going price. With the others, you have to wait until the next valuation of the fund (which could be in a week's or a month's time, say). Having to wait as long as a month for the next valuation isn't much use – and the value of the fund could change quite a lot meanwhile.

With nearly all property funds and some managed funds, the insurance company can, in theory, insist on a period of notice (six months, say) before allowing you to sell your units probably at the price ruling at the end of the notice period. But in practice, it's unlikely that the insurance company will insist on your giving notice.

Note that each unit normally has two prices. What you pay for the units (the offer price) is more than what you can sell your units for (the bid price). For example, the buying price of units might be £1 each, the selling price 95p. So if you invested £1,000 you'd get:
£1,000 ÷ £1 = 1,000 units.
If you sold these units immediately, you'd get back only:
1,000 × 95p = £950.

Life insurance
Single-premium bonds (and
unit-linked savings plans) are
technically life insurance
policies, so you can get a bit of
life cover.

With most of the companies,
the cover is related to the value
of your bond. For example, if a
29-year-old man dies, his
dependants might get about $2\frac{1}{2}$
times the current value. Some of
the companies give you a fixed
amount of cover from the time
you take out the bond – up to
four times the amount of your
original investment, say.

If what you need is protection
for your dependants should you
die, this type of policy is not for
you – see Box on p124.

The difference between the buying and selling prices is known as
the spread – and is effectively, the company's initial charge (see
Charges, opposite).

Note that when you finally cash your bond you may find the
insurance company makes a deduction from the amount you think
you're entitled to judging by the current unit price. This will be to
allow, to some extent, for future capital gains tax bills the company
may have to pay when it sells some of the investments in the fund.
The companies which don't make a deduction when you cash your
bond, take their future tax liability into account when fixing their
unit prices.

Minimum investment

All the companies set a minimum amount you can invest – between
£50 and £2,000. Note that if you invest a large amount in one go,
over £5,000, say, some companies give you extra units, eg one per
cent more, say, than someone investing £1,000 would get.

Age limits

Many insurance companies set minimum age limits for
bondholders – 18, say. And some set maximum age limits for new
bondholders – 80, say.

Adding to your investment

As the term implies, a single-premium bond bond is bought with
one lump sum payment. Recently, a few insurance companies have
started to issue bonds with an *additional premium facility*. This
means that you have the option of buying more units at any time by
paying an additional premium (subject to a minimum amount).
These units are added to the original policy you took out. The
advantage in doing this is that if you *are* liable to tax on the gain
when you cash the policy in, top-slicing relief (see p50) relating to
the additional premium can be spread over all the years since you
originally invested – and not just from the date you paid the
additional premium. This could reduce your tax bill.

Which way to invest in shares?
There are three main ways of
investing in shares. You could:
● invest directly in shares (see
Chapter 8)
● invest in a unit trust (see below,
and Chapter 9)
● invest in an equity bond (or
savings plan linked to an equity
fund). Your money will be put into
a fund run by the insurance
company (which may, in turn,
invest in a unit trust associated
with the insurance company).

The main advantage of investing
in a unit trust or an equity bond
rather than directly in shares is that
it allows you to spread your money
around a large number of different
shares – something you're unlikely
to be able to do if you invest
directly, unless you've got a lot of

money to invest (£7,000, say, for
this type of investment).

Unit trusts have advantages over
equity bonds for higher rate
taxpayers making capital gains.
Unit trusts don't pay capital gains
tax on their investments (insurance
companies have to), so the money
this saves can be used to buy more
investments for the fund. Instead,
you are liable for capital gains tax
when you sell your units. But your
tax bill for cashing a unit trust
holding may be quite low – and will
be nothing at all if, for example,
your net capital gains for a tax year
are no more than £5,000. For details
about capital gains tax, see p53.

On the other hand, higher rate
taxpayers have to pay tax on the
income of a unit trust (even if it is

reinvested for them). They don't
have to pay tax on the reinvested
income of an equity fund. If a
higher rate taxpayer wants to get an
income from an equity bond, he can
withdraw up to five per cent a year
and pay no tax on it at the time.
Because of the way gains on bonds
are taxed, they wouldn't be suitable
short-term investments for higher-
rate taxpayers.

Equity bonds or equity-linked
savings plans could be a cheaper
way for people to switch their
money around between different
types of investment from time-to-
time – see *Switching* on p140. You
can move your money from an
equity fund to a property fund, say,
without incurring the company's
initial charge again.

Cashing in part of your investment

Most companies allow you to cash (ie sell) part of your bond. But you often have to cash a minimum amount, and leave a minimum amount. The minimum amount you can cash is commonly £50 or £100 – and the minimum amount you must leave varies between £100 and £1,000 (but is commonly £500).

If you cash in part of your bond, watch out for the complicated tax rules – see p50.

If you already have shares

Most companies are prepared to give you units in their funds in exchange for your holdings of stocks and shares – though different companies have different rules about the size of the holdings they'll accept and the value they'll place on them.

Commonly, if the company is happy to put your shares into one of its funds, it will value them at the price it would have to pay to buy them on the open market (plus 1%, with some companies). This benefits you because if you sold them, you'd normally get a somewhat lower price and would have to pay commission to a stockbroker.

If the company doesn't want to put your holdings of stocks and shares in a fund, it will usually sell them for you (and with many companies, you pay no commission on the sale).

Note that exchanging your shareholdings counts as a disposal for capital gains tax purposes (see p53) – ie you may have to pay capital gains tax on any gain you've made. But there are ways in which the tax can be kept to a minimum, so get professional advice – particularly, if you are exchanging substantial shareholdings.

How bonds are sold

Bonds are sold by a variety of methods – through newspaper advertisements, by insurance brokers, by company salesmen, and by agents such as accountants and solicitors. Brokers, agents and so on normally get commission from the insurance company for selling bonds – the rate varies between $1\frac{1}{2}$% and 5% or so of what you pay for the bond.

Charges   The insurance companies normally make:
- an initial charge of around 5% of the amount you invest. This is usually included in the spread between the buying and selling prices (see opposite). A few companies have only one unit price at which you buy *and* sell – they deduct their initial charge from your investment before working out how many units you get.
- a regular charge. The insurance company deducts a charge from the fund at regular intervals to cover the costs of managing the fund. This charge might add up to between $\frac{1}{4}$% and 1% of the value of the fund each year.

Not all companies spell out in their policy documents the maximum charges they can make – so check up on charges before investing.

Switching   The majority of the insurance companies allow you to switch your money from one fund to another (eg from the equity fund to the property fund) without paying their initial charge again. This could prove a useful facility for investors who want to move their money around between different types of investment from time-to-time in the hope of keeping it in the type of investment which will increase in value quickest. But if you're tempted to use the switching facility, bear in mind that if you time your switches wrongly, you could end up doing very badly.

Note that switching your investment between funds doesn't count as cashing in your bond for tax purposes – so does not affect your tax position at all.

Most companies make some charge when you switch – typically ½% of the amount you move. But some companies allow you one free switch a year. Most companies set restrictions on how much you can switch, and there may be other restrictions – eg on the minimum amount you must invest in the first place to be allowed to switch, and restrictions about when you are allowed to switch.

Policy wording   The policy document is the contract between you and the insurance company, so it makes sense to see a copy before you invest. Check that most of the following points are spelled out:
● how the fund is valued. For examples, it might show that stocks and shares are valued at the market prices quoted on the Stock Exchange
● that property in the fund is valued by an independent valuer, such as a surveyor
● the maximum period between valuations
● how unit prices are worked out
● the charges the company makes – and the other costs it can deduct from the fund
● that you won't be double-charged if your fund invests in other funds run by the company
● what happens to the fund's income.

Tax   When you cash your bond, the gain you make is added to your investment income for the tax year. The gain is the amount you get (including any amounts you got earlier on which weren't taxed at the time) *less* the amount you paid for the bond in the first place. You may have to pay income tax on the gain you make. You don't pay basic rate tax on the gain (the insurance company has already paid tax on the income and capital gains of the fund), but you do have to pay any higher rate tax or investment income surcharge that is due – though your tax bill may be reduced by *top-slicing relief*. The tax rules are complicated (especially if you cash in only part of your bond), but can be used to your advantage, if you are careful over *when* you cash your units in. For more details, see p49.

Choosing a company   For details about the insurance companies and their funds, the following magazines do regular surveys (including details of past performance) – *The Savings Market, Money Management*. Remember, though, that past performance is *not* a reliable guide to the future. Try asking an insurance broker (or perhaps several brokers) for advice, but make sure he knows what it is *you* expect to get from your investment. Note that a few insurance companies don't pay commission to brokers, so these are unlikely to be suggested to you. Opposite is a list of things to check when deciding which company to go for.

Things to find out

● whether the company has a good choice of funds – and, if you want to switch between funds, includes a cash fund (which can be a useful temporary home for your money when prospects for shares, property and fixed-interest investments all look bleak)
● when you can buy and sell units. Some companies only allow dealing on certain dates – once a month, say
● what the company's charges are (and if these are spelled out in the policy document)
● how often the fund's investments are valued (see p137)
● whether the company makes any charge for cashing in the whole or part of your policy – some companies will charge if you sell units during the first year
● whether the company offers a *withdrawal scheme* (ie partial cash-in)
● whether income withdrawals have to be on a regular basis (ie a withdrawal scheme), or can be on an irregular basis to suit your circumstances. Check too if the bond is split into a series of policies to allow simple and tax-efficient income withdrawals
● if the company offers an *additional premium facility* so that you can add to your investment without having to take out a new policy each time (see p138), if you want to increase your investment
● if you can switch between funds at any time (with some companies, you can only switch on certain dates), what the company's switching charge is (one 'free' switch a year is fairly common), and whether you can switch just some of your units
● with a property fund, the size of the fund and how it is split between different types of property. Funds range in size from less than £1 million to over £30 million – you may feel happier to go for a larger fund. Also check that the fund is not too heavily invested in just one locality, or too dependent on one huge office block, say. (Some companies provide reports which list the properties in the fund)
● with a managed fund, the size of fund (see above), and how the investments are split between different sectors – though this, of course could change.

Company safety

It's important to realise that although the performance of your bond depends upon the performance of a fund of investments, *bondholders do not own the investments*. If the insurance company (or friendly society – a few offer single-premium bonds) were to go bust, bondholders would have no special rights over other policyholders.

Insurance companies, but not friendly societies (to which different legislation applies), are covered by the Policyholders Protection Act. This effectively says that, if your company goes bust, you'll get back 90 per cent of what you were owed when the company failed. But this amount will not necessarily be the selling value of the bond at the time. And if your policy has other benefits, such as a guaranteed cash-in value, which are considered *excessive*, you may get back less than 90 per cent of what you were owed.

Unit-linked savings plans

Unit-linked savings plans are somewhat different from single-premium bonds – though at first glance they may seem rather similar. With both, the insurance companies offer regular savers and lump sum investors the same choice of funds to buy units in (see p133 for what these are). And, as with bonds, the companies take part of the money you pay to cover their management expenses and to provide you with life insurance. The bulk of the money goes to buy your units.

But with savings plans, you agree to pay premiums to the insurance company at regular intervals (monthly or quarterly, say). The tax rules are also different – see Diagram opposite and p51.

Importantly, you get a government subsidy on your premiums (15 per cent of the amount you agree to pay for the 1982-83 tax year). In general, after the first few years of your plan (when the company's charges are normally highest), the subsidy comes to more than these charges. So more is invested for you than the plan actually costs you. However, the company makes some charges after your money has been invested – see p146 for details.

Types of plan   Unit-linked savings plans can be grouped into three broad categories, which we call:
- standard plans
- high-investment plans
- high-life-cover plans.

Look at the Table below, for how three fairly typical plans might compare. In general, compared with a standard plan, a high-investment plan has a higher minimum premium, invests a higher proportion of each premium in units and gives you less life insurance cover.

A high-life-cover plan, on the other hand, has a lower minimum premium, invests less of it in units, and gives you more life insurance cover.

A standard plan falls between the other two types – with more emphasis on investment, and less on life insurance protection than high-life-cover plans.

How typical plans might compare

	standard	high-investment	high-life-cover
length of plan	between 10 and 25 years	10 years	whole life
amount of life cover [1]	£7,500 for 25 years	£2,250 for 10 years	£15,000 for whole life
amount invested in units in first ten years [1,2]	£2,500	£2,850	£1,600
minimum monthly premium [3]	£10	£20	£5

[1] Figures are for a 29-year-old man paying premiums of £21.25 a month (with the premium subsidy of 15 per cent, the total premium comes to £25)
[2] Investor pays £2,550 but because of the premium subsidy, insurance company would receive £3,000 in total. Figures assume no change in unit price over period
[3] Including the premium subsidy. Cost to investor is less than this.

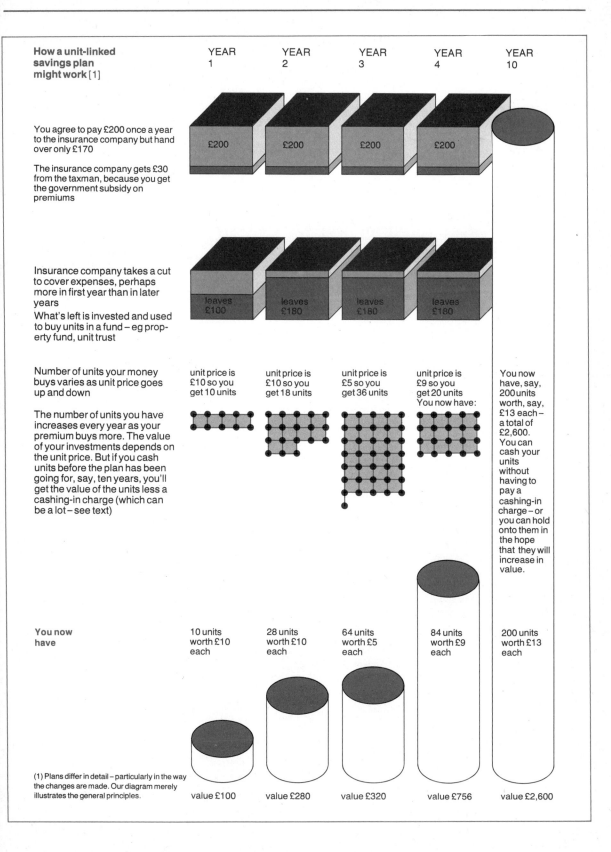

How a unit-linked savings plan might work [1]

YEAR 1 | YEAR 2 | YEAR 3 | YEAR 4 | YEAR 10

You agree to pay £200 once a year to the insurance company but hand over only £170

The insurance company gets £30 from the taxman, because you get the government subsidy on premiums

£200 | £200 | £200 | £200

Insurance company takes a cut to cover expenses, perhaps more in first year than in later years

What's left is invested and used to buy units in a fund – eg property fund, unit trust

leaves £100 | leaves £180 | leaves £180 | leaves £180

Number of units your money buys varies as unit price goes up and down

The number of units you have increases every year as your premium buys more. The value of your investments depends on the unit price. But if you cash units before the plan has been going for, say, ten years, you'll get the value of the units less a cashing-in charge (which can be a lot – see text)

unit price is £10 so you get 10 units | unit price is £10 so you get 18 units | unit price is £5 so you get 36 units | unit price is £9 so you get 20 units You now have: | You now have, say, 200 units worth, say, £13 each – a total of £2,600. You can cash your units without having to pay a cashing-in charge – or you can hold onto them in the hope that they will increase in value.

You now have

10 units worth £10 each | 28 units worth £10 each | 64 units worth £5 each | 84 units worth £9 each | 200 units worth £13 each

(1) Plans differ in detail – particularly in the way the changes are made. Our diagram merely illustrates the general principles.

value £100 | value £280 | value £320 | value £756 | value £2,600

In general, most high-investment plans last for 10 years; most high-life-cover plans – in theory – last for the rest of your life; and standard plans sometimes last until you reach a certain age (65, say) – or sometimes last for a minimum of 10 years and a maximum of (say) 25 years. But see *If you stop your plan early* below.

If your main aim is investment you should go for one of the high-investment plans.

If you're looking for both investment and life insurance, it may seem appealing to take out a standard or high-life-cover plan which achieves both these objectives. But, on balance, we recommend you try to keep your life insurance cover and your investments separate, as far as possible. By combining them, you lose flexibility. If, for example, you find you need to cash your savings plan in five years' time, and you need the life insurance cover it provides, you'll have to apply for life insurance all over again. In the meantime, you might have developed heart trouble or have become a fanatical pot-holer – so could have trouble getting the cover you need. You can avoid this problem by taking out a high-investment plan, together with term insurance to provide the life cover you need. Term insurance is the type of life insurance which pays out only if you die – see p124.

If you die In general, the insurance company will pay out the amount of life cover provided by the policy – or the value of your units at the time, if this is higher. With most plans, the life cover you get is based on the length of the plan and your premium. With a high-investment plan the cover might be three-quarters of the premiums you are due to pay during the plan. With a standard plan, the cover might be the total of the premiums you are due to pay – for example, a premium of £20 a month (including the subsidy) for a 25-year standard plan might get life insurance cover of £20 × 12 × 25 = £6,000.

The end of your plan When your plan comes to an end, you can normally choose between cashing in your units at the current price, or holding on to them. But with a few standard plans, you have no choice: you have to cash your units even if the price is very low at the time.

At the end of a high-investment plan, you may have the option of extending the plan – normally with a higher proportion of future premiums being invested for you.

And with some high-investment plans, you can arrange to get a tax-free 'income' at the end of your plan. In practice, this 'income' is usually provided by cashing units at regular intervals – so it's not 'income' in the normal sense of the word.

If you stop your plan early You should look on a unit-linked savings plan as a long-term investment. The way that most companies arrange their charges means that you lose out if you cash your plan early – and may get little or nothing back if you cash it in the first year or two.

With many plans, a lot of what you pay in the first couple of years goes in charges. The companies say this is to cover their expenses (eg the cost of setting up the plan, the commission they pay to salesmen or brokers who sell you the plan). And some companies make a special charge if you stop your plan early. In general, this charge goes down, the longer you keep your plan going (and may disappear once your plan has been going for 10 years, say).

If you don't need to cash your plan, but want to stop investing, you could make your plan *paid-up*. This means you stop paying your premiums, but the money you've already invested is left in the fund. In general, you are allocated the number of units which you could buy with the money you'd get if you cashed in your plan.

Alternatively, go for a plan which is broken up into a series of mini-policies. Then, if your circumstances change later you have the option of cashing just some of your units, keeping your plan going – and paying a reduced premium.

Not all companies' policy documents spell out how the plan's cash-in and paid-up values will be worked out. So you'd be wise to check the policy document before investing.

Tax Income tax and capital gains tax are paid by the fund (not by you) – though when you cash your units, some companies will make a small deduction from their value to allow for the fund's future capital gains tax liabilities.

But, if you cash your plan in early (or make it paid up), you may, if you pay higher rate tax or the investment income surcharge, be liable to pay income tax on any gain that you make. You may also have some or all of the subsidy on the premiums that the insurance company has received *clawed back* by the taxman. Full details about the subsidy on premiums, tax on the gain and clawback are given in Chapter 5 – see pages 49 to 52.

Should you invest? If all you want is life cover to protect your dependants from financial hardship if you die, a unit-linked savings plan isn't the right sort of insurance for you – you should buy term insurance (see p124).

If you are looking for a home for some of your long-term savings, a unit-linked savings plan is worth considering. But it's not suitable:
● as a way of saving up money which you know you'll need at a specific date in the future (eg to pay for a round-the-world cruise on retirement). You may find that when you need the money, the markets are in the doldrums and it makes sense to leave your money invested until unit prices rise again
● if you're not prepared to see the value of what you've already saved go up and down
● if you might need to cash in your plan in its first few years. Most plans are designed to be long-term investments and the company's charges normally penalise you if you cash in early.

Choosing a plan For where to go for information about the different unit-linked savings plans, see the first paragraph of *Choosing a company* on p140.

As we've said above, you should keep your life insurance and investment needs separate, so in general, steer clear of high-life-cover plans. Note that with these plans, the rate of return you get if you cash in after 10 years, say (see Table on p142) could be very poor compared to standard or high-investment plans – unless the company's funds have performed very well – as a much higher percentage of each premium goes towards providing life insurance.

So the choice is really between standard plans and high-investment plans. It may be wisest to go for a high-investment plan, provided you can afford the premiums (the minimum monthly premium can be as much as £50). A high-investment plan may be better because, normally, a higher percentage of the premium will be used to buy you units – typically 95 to 100 per cent unit allocation (compared to 90 per cent with a standard plan) after the first year or so – but check with the companies exactly what charges will be made. Although these plans usually last for 10 years, you often have the option to renew for another 10 years (paying, perhaps, the same premium, for an increased unit allocation).

As with single-premium bonds, some savings plans allow you to switch your investment around between the company's funds. So if you'd feel happier with the reassurance that you can move your units from say, the equity fund to the property fund, if say, the stock market crashes, check up on this before investing.

In general it makes sense to check the company's policy document to see if all charges (for cashing-in early, switching, managing the funds' investments and so on) are spelled out.

Finally, scan the checklist given on p141 (in the single-premium bonds section) as many of the points to watch out for which are given there, also apply to unit-linked savings plans.

Company safety

Like single-premium bonds, the success of your savings plan depends upon the performance of a fund of investments, but *you do not own the investments*. For what you'd get if your insurance company failed, see p141.

Charges

The companies make charges to cover the cost of setting up and running the plans, paying commission to salesmen and insurance brokers, and to pay for the life insurance cover they provide. Different companies make their charges in different, and sometimes complicated, ways – the main ways are listed here:

● **unit allocation** – not all of each premium is used to buy you units. With many plans, the proportion allocated to units is lower in the first year or two than in later years (perhaps 50 per cent in the first year and 90 per cent after that). It also tends to be lower the longer your plan is due to last and the older you are when you take it out. Women may get a slightly higher allocation than men of the same age. You may also get a higher unit allocation if the size of your regular premium is larger than normal (over £50 a month, say). And, with a few companies, a savings plan taken out by husband and wife together on a *joint-life and survivor basis* (see p150) may mean more units than normal.

● **initial charge** – often around 5 per cent of the money which is invested in units for you. Most companies have two prices for each of their units – the price you pay for a unit (the offer price) is higher than the price you get if you sell (the bid price). The difference (the spread) is the company's initial charge

● **regular charge** – the insurance company deducts a management charge from the fund at regular intervals, perhaps between ¼ and 1 per cent of the value of the fund each year. In some cases, the company issues two sorts of units. One sort (sometimes called initial or capital units) is issued to you for the first few years – and the insurance company deducts a higher regular charge (3½ per cent a year, say) from these

● **policy fee** – perhaps 50p a month or £5 a year is deducted from your premiums

● **the fund's income** – most companies reinvest the income of the fund. But a few companies keep the income; in general, these companies have a lower unit allocation charge

● **cashing-in charge** – see p144.

This variety of charges makes it very difficult to compare one plan's charges with another's. And it means that a plan that is cheapest in certain circumstances may well not be cheapest in others. For example, one plan may invest nearly all your premium in units but have a high yearly charge. Another may invest much less of your premium in units but have a lower yearly charge. Only those with calculators and extreme patience (or a home computer) will be able to work out how these different charges might affect your investment.

What makes things worse is that you can't necessarily compare one company's charges with another's from the illustrations the companies produce of how much you can expect to get back from their plans – because these illustrations may well be based on different assumptions.

For example, one company may assume that its fund will increase in value by 7½ per cent a year, another may assume 8 per cent, yet another 10 per cent. And the growth rate quoted may be before deduction of yearly charges, or it may be after.

More complicated unit-linked investments

Each year, the insurance companies come up with ingenious unit-linked schemes to exploit this or that aspect of the favourable tax rules for life insurance policies. Here we describe some of the schemes you may encounter. If you want to invest, *make sure you get professional advice.*

Flexible cover plans
These are plans offered by a few companies which can last for the whole of your life, but where the amount of life cover you have can be increased or reduced (within certain limits) once a year without altering the amount of your premium. So as your circumstances alter, a greater or lesser amount can be invested in units in the company's funds.

A feature of flexible cover plans (and a few high-life cover plans – see p142) is that the cost of the life cover is linked to the value of your units. If your units increase in value at a greater rate than the company predicts when you take the plan out, the life cover costs you less; if the rate is lower the cover costs you more. Instead of deducting a percentage from each premium to pay for the life cover, the cost of the cover is deducted from the value of your units. If your units perform very badly, you might have to pay an extra premium (though normally not within the first 10 years).

Capital conversion plans
You invest a lump sum (minimum £3,000 to £5,000, say), and after a period, can take income withdrawals free of tax. The simplest form of capital conversion plan means taking out a 9-year temporary annuity and a high-investment savings plan. Alternatively, you take out one or more single-premium bonds and a savings plan. Each year after the first (for nine years) you use the income from the annuity, or cash in single-premium bond units, to pay the savings plan premium – to which the premium subsidy is added. At the end of 10 years, you can start making income withdrawals from the savings plan without paying tax on them. The drawback with these plans though, is that you may be liable for tax on the annuity income or on any gain you make from cashing in the single-premium bond units.

Some plans are known as *flexible funding* plans as you can vary the premium into the savings plan to take account of fluctuations in the value of the single-premium bond units.

There are also more complicated capital conversion plans which mean that tax can be avoided entirely (even if you are a higher-rate tax-payer) and from which you can make cash withdrawals during the first 10 years. The minimum investment is high (£10,000) and the plans involve a high-investment savings plan and a series of investment-type policies for fixed periods (one of which expires each year for 10 years).

Index-linking
With flexible cover plans and a few high-life-cover plans, you can arrange to link the life cover you get to the Retail Price Index (RPI). Your cover can be increased in line with the increase in the RPI each year. If you do increase your cover, your premium will also go up, but the increase will depend not just on the increase in the RPI, but also on your age at the time you increase your cover.

Capital transfer tax schemes
With these schemes you invest a lump sum in a single-premium bond from which you can take cash withdrawals. If you die before a certain age (100, say) the lump sum passes to your heirs free of capital transfer tax. What your heirs actually get will depend on the value of your units at the time. If you do survive to the end of the period the plan lasts for, you get back the value of your units, but lose the capital transfer tax advantages. You need a lump sum of at least £10,000, say, to take out one of these plans.

15 Income and growth bonds

These are investments issued by insurance companies which are suitable for lump sums. You have to invest your money for a fixed period (perhaps five or ten years). In return you normally get a fixed rate of return for that period. They are often called guaranteed bonds.

With an **income bond**, the return is paid out as a regular income (usually yearly or half-yearly). With a **growth bond**, the return is left to accumulate, and paid out when the bond comes to an end.

If you die before the bond comes to an end, the insurance company normally pays out the amount you originally invested plus, with growth bonds, the return accumulated to date.

The insurance company normally arranges for the return from an income or growth bond to be free of basic rate tax – or to pay out enough to cover tax at the basic rate and leave you with the fixed return. If you pay tax at no more than the basic rate (even after adding what you make on the bond to the rest of your income) you should get the return quoted in the ads. But if you or your husband or wife are 65 or over (or approaching 65) see p236.

If you've got a lump sum to invest, *and* you don't mind locking your money away for a time, *and* you want a fixed return for this period, an income or growth bond may be suitable for you. Alternatives to consider include local authority loans, National Savings Certificates, and building society term shares. And don't invest in a bond if there's a chance that you'll need to cash it in early. Some insurance companies don't allow you to do this, and with the others, you may get back less than you originally invested.

If you don't pay tax – or pay more than basic rate tax

If you don't pay tax at all, you'll get more than the quoted return with some types of bond. But if you pay tax at higher rates, or the investment income surcharge, the return is likely to be lower than the rate quoted in the ads. To find out how you'd be affected, see *How to choose a bond* opposite.

How bonds work

Bonds are set up in different ways, often comprising one or more life insurance policies and one or more annuities. The mechanics needn't concern you at all, though your age or tax position may make certain types of bond a better buy for you than others. For devotees, *Types of bond* opposite gives brief details of how the types of bond most commonly available when this book went to press work. But note that bonds are normally available only for limited periods of time, and the mechanics of newly issued bonds change from time to time.

How to choose a bond

Company safety

For guidance on what happens if a company fails, see p132.

Tax rules – warning

Many of these bonds are set up to take maximum advantage of current tax rules. If the tax rules are changed, some or all bonds might become less attractive. This has already happened with some bonds – though bonds already issued have been treated in accordance with the rules in force at the time they were issued.

For a list of which companies issue which types of bond, get a copy of the most recent issue of *The Savings Market* magazine (see p154). But because bonds may be available for a short period only, the returns listed in such a magazine may soon be out of date.

Telephone the companies offering the best returns on suitable bonds and ask for details of their latest bonds. If you're not a basic rate taxpayer, ask them what someone in your tax position would get from their bond (after tax). Then choose the bond which gives the best return for the period you want to invest for. You could ask a couple of brokers to do this work for you.

In general, if you don't pay tax you're likely to get the biggest benefit from a *deferred annuity* bond. If you pay tax at higher rates you're likely to lose less of your return in tax with a *qualifying endowment*, but if you can arrange for the bond to end in a year when you pay only basic rate tax (after you've retired, perhaps), a *single-premium* endowment is likely to be best (or, with growth bonds, a *deferred annuity*).

Note that *deferred annuity bonds* generally give a better return the older you are.

Types of bond

Single-premium endowment bonds

Your investment buys a single-premium endowment policy which has guaranteed bonuses. You can choose whether to have these bonuses paid out to you as income or reinvested for growth (or you may be able to have part paid out, part reinvested). At the end of the term, you get back your original investment plus bonuses you haven't cashed in.

Deferred annuity bonds

Your money is used to buy a deferred annuity – an agreement which promises to start paying out an income at the end of the term. But there's a cash option, under which you can take a guaranteed lump sum instead.

With income bonds, part of your original investment goes to buy an immediate annuity – an agreement to pay out a regular income for the duration of the bond.

Qualifying endowment policy bonds

Your investment is divided between the first premium of a regular-premium endowment policy and a temporary annuity which pays you an income until the bond comes to an end. With growth bonds, you pay this income back to the insurance company to pay the rest of the premiums on the endowment policy. (Note that you are actually paid the income by the insurance company – and you have to make out a banker's order or direct debit authorisation to pay the premiums.) With income bonds, you keep some of the income and use the rest to pay the premiums.

At the end of the bond, the endowment policy pays out the amount of your original investment – plus, with growth bonds, the accumulated return.

With some companies, the endowment policy is a non-profit one – which means that the amount paid out at the end of the bond is fixed. Others use a with-profits endowment policy, so that what you get back isn't fixed – it depends on the bonuses added to the policy each year.

Annuity/endowment income bonds

Your investment is divided between a temporary annuity and a single-premium non-profit endowment policy. The annuity pays out a fixed income until the bond comes to an end, when the endowment policy pays out the amount of your original investment.

Tax

At the end of the term, proceeds from an endowment policy are taxed as a gain on a life insurance policy (see p49). Proceeds from a deferred annuity cash option are liable to tax at your highest rate (including the investment income surcharge) on the profit you make on the deferred annuity. The company deducts basic rate tax before paying you this profit and you can reclaim the tax if you're not a taxpayer.

Income you get from a temporary annuity is treated as income from any voluntarily purchased annuity (see p153). The company deducts basic rate tax before paying it out to you. Income from endowment policy bonuses are treated as cashing in part of a life-insurance policy (see p50).

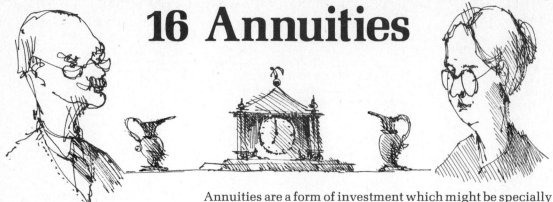

16 Annuities

Annuities are a form of investment which might be specially attractive to elderly people. With an annuity you hand over your money to an insurance company in return for a guaranteed income for the rest of your life. For example, in return for £10,000, a 75-year old man who paid tax at the basic rate could (in October 1981) have got an after-tax income of about £2,000 a year for life. On people who live for years and years, the insurance company will make a large loss. On those who die early, the company will make a handsome profit. People who buy annuities tend to be healthier than those who don't – the insurance companies allow for this in the income they offer. In this chapter we look at the various different types of annuity that are available, and their pros and cons. On p154 you'll find details of home income schemes – where you borrow money to buy an annuity, using your home as security.

Types of annuity   This chapter deals with immediate annuities. With these, the company starts paying you the income 'immediately' – which normally means half-yearly, starting six months after you buy it. There are also deferred annuities – where you pay a lump sum now and arrange for the income to start further in the future (in five years' time, say). Deferred annuities form the basis of many personal pension plans. The most common type of immediate annuity is a level annuity, where the income is the same each year. For a given outlay, this type gives you the largest income to start with – though, of course, inflation will erode its buying-power over the years. Another type is an increasing annuity, where the income increases at regular intervals by an amount you decide upon when buying the annuity. Unit-linked annuities are offered by a few companies – with these, your income is linked to the value of a fund (eg of property) and so goes up and down in amount.

The most common type of annuity stops when the person buying it dies – a single life annuity. But you can also get annuities which carry on until both the person buying the annuity and someone else, usually a wife or husband, are dead. These are called joint life and survivor annuities.

Variations   The figures we quote assume that you buy the annuity voluntarily with your own money – and not, for example, as a condition of a pension scheme. They also assume that the company pays you half-yearly, starting six months after you buy the annuity and that no payment is made after you die. You can, however, usually get any of the variations listed below. Some are fairly costly in terms of a reduced yearly income. We give examples for a 65-year old man:
● first payment to be made at the time you buy the annuity. The same outlay gives about seven per cent less income than the normal version. So for each £100 a year you'd get from the normal version,

you could expect about £93 if you went for this variation
● payments to be made more frequently than half-yearly (ie
quarterly or monthly). The same outlay gives a smaller yearly
income than an annuity paid half-yearly – about two per cent less if
the income is paid quarterly, three per cent less if paid monthly
● first payment to be made a year after you buy the annuity, then at
yearly intervals. The same outlay gives a yearly income about four
per cent more than an annuity paid half-yearly
● an extra, proportionate, payment (made after you die) for the
period between the date you receive the last half-yearly payment
and the date you die. The same outlay gives about one per cent less
income than the normal version
● some of the payments to be guaranteed – ie paid out by the
company for a minimum number of years even if you die early. The
same outlay gives you less income than the normal version – how
much less depends on your age and the length of the guaranteed
period (commonly, five or ten years). A 65-year old man wanting a
five-year guarantee would get about three per cent less income
● payment (made after you die) of the difference between your
outlay and the income paid out so far by the company. For a 65-year
old man, the same outlay gives about six per cent less income than
the normal version
● with a joint life and survivor annuity, less income to be paid after
the first person dies – often half or two-thirds of the amount paid
while both are alive. For a man aged 65 and a woman aged 60, an
annuity which reduces by half when one of them dies gives a
starting income about 13 to 14 per cent higher than normal.

The income   This depends on a number of things – in particular your age when
you get   you buy the annuity, the type of annuity you go for, and the level of
interest rates in general at the time you take the annuity out.

Insurance companies tend to vary their annuity rates frequently
and at short notice, but what you get stays at the rate that applied
when you bought the annuity. The Table overleaf gives you some
idea of the rates being offered on 13 October 1981 – when annuity
rates were relatively high. With the increasing annuity you'll find
two rates of return in the Table – one for the year in which the
annuity is bought, and one for the year to which the person buying
the annuity has a fifty-fifty chance of living.

The income you get from an annuity consists partly of interest
and partly of a return of the capital you invested, and each part is
treated differently for tax purposes – see p153. The older you are
when you take out the annuity the higher the capital part of the
income you get, and the higher the total amount of income. This is
because the older you are the shorter the period the insurance
company expects to have to pay the income for. A woman gets a
lower income than a man of the same age – women, on average, live
longer than men. Joint life and survivor annuities pay lower
amounts too.

For comparison, we have included in the Table the return
available on undated British Government stocks on 13 October
1981. Like annuities, these give you a guaranteed income for the
rest of your life – but unlike annuities, the money invested in stocks
is still yours to do with as you wish. You can leave the stocks to
your heirs when you die, or you can sell them at any time (though
there's no guarantee of what price you'll get for them). You can see
that the difference between the rates of return offered by an annuity
and by British Government stocks is larger the older you are and the
higher your rate of tax.

After-tax yearly return from annuities on 13 October 1981

age when you buy annuity	level annuities			increasing annuities (5% compound a year)	
	if you pay no tax	if you pay tax at basic rate of 30%	if you pay tax at rate of 45%	if you pay tax at basic rate of 30% first year	later year [1]
Man	%	%	%	%	%
60	17.2	13.7	12.0	9.9	24.0
65	18.5	15.1	13.4	11.3	22.3
70	20.5	17.1	15.4	13.2	22.5
75	23.3	19.9	18.2	16.0	23.6
80	27.4	24.1	22.4	20.0	26.8
Woman					
60	16.1	12.7	11.0	9.0	29.0
65	17.1	13.7	12.0	10.0	25.1
70	18.4	15.0	13.4	11.3	23.5
75	20.5	17.2	15.5	13.3	22.8
80	23.7	20.4	18.7	16.4	24.2
Man 65, woman 60	15.5	12.1	10.4	8.4	28.7
Man 75, woman 70	17.2	14.0	12.4	10.3	23.8
British Government stocks (undated)	14.5	10.1	8.0	10.1	10.1

[1] Year to which person buying annuity has a fifty-fifty chance of living – eg a man aged 70 has a fifty-fifty chance of living to be 82, and a woman aged 70 has a fifty-fifty chance of living to be 86

Inflation

When deciding whether to buy an annuity you should consider the effect that rising prices will have on the buying-power of your income . For example, a man of 65 who buys an annuity has a fifty-fifty chance of living for another 14 years. If prices continue to rise at the current rate of around 10 per cent a year, each £100 of income he gets at the start will be worth only £26 or so in 14 years' time. To see how rising prices might reduce the buying-power of an annuity, look at the Diagram opposite.

To protect the buying-power of your capital you should certainly invest part of your money in index-linked National Savings Certificates (see Chapter 21), cashing them in if you need income. You could also consider index-linked British Government stocks (see Chapter 10).

An annuity would then be worth considering for *part* of your remaining money – especially if you're over 70 or so.

Why an annuity is a gamble

Whether or not an annuity proves to be a good buy in the long run depends on:
● how long you live. Obviously an annuity will be a better buy if you live for years and years after buying it, than if you die soon after investing your money. If you are in poor health, you'd be wise to steer clear of annuities, and invest your money elsewhere
● what happens to interest rates after you have bought your annuity. The annuity income offered by an insurance company is related to the general level of interest rates at the time you buy. If, later on, interest rates go up, companies are likely to offer better annuities – but you'll be stuck with your relatively poor-value-for-money annuity. On the other hand, if interest rates go down, companies will offer poorer annuities – and you'll be sitting pretty

● the extent to which inflation will erode the buying-power of your income (see previous page).

But you don't know how long you're going to live, and you don't know what's going to happen to interest rates or to inflation – so you can't know if an annuity will turn out to be a good buy or not.

Should you buy an annuity?

Once you have bought an annuity – and handed over your money – you can't go back on the arrangement. So you shouldn't buy one without pausing for thought. You should first make sure your dependants would have enough to live on when you die. Then consider how much you want to leave your family (or favourite charity), how much you want to put by for a rainy day, and how much you want to leave available for holidays, replacing your car, colour television, and so on. You could consider spending part of what is left on an annuity – *provided* the extra income you get compared with what you'd get from another type of investment is large enough to compensate you for handing over part of your savings for good.

Which type?

For most people, a level or increasing annuity will be a better choice than a unit-linked one. With level and increasing annuities, you know just how many £££ of annuity income to expect each year. With unit-linked annuities, your income will vary from year to year – and may be very low in some years.

Choosing between a level and an increasing annuity is more difficult. An increasing annuity offers some protection against inflation – but not much, unless you're prepared to accept a low starting income. You can see from the Diagrams that in terms of buying-power it would take some six years for the yearly income from an increasing annuity to overtake a level one. It would take much longer (16 years at 10 per cent inflation) for you to receive the same *total* buying-power. And you may not live long enough to be any better off from the increasing annuity. It might be better to go for a level annuity, investing what you don't need at once to draw on later in retirement.

Tax treatment

Part of the income from an annuity is treated as your initial outlay being returned to you – and is tax-free. The remainder counts as interest – and is added to your investment income.

The amount of the tax-free part is worked out according to Inland Revenue rules. It is fixed in terms of £££, not as a proportion of the income from the annuity. For each type of annuity the tax-free amount is based on your age when you buy the annuity, the amount you pay for it, and how often the income is paid.

With increasing annuities, the tax-free amount normally increases at the same rate as the income from the annuity increases. With unit-linked annuities the tax-free amount stays fixed, whether the income rises or falls.

An annuity is treated in this special way only if you buy it voluntarily with your own money – eg if you use a lump sum from your employer's pension scheme.

The insurance company normally deducts tax at the basic rate from the taxable part of your annuity income before paying you. If you are liable for less tax than the insurance company deducts, you can claim tax back from the taxman. If you pay tax at higher rates (or the investment income surcharge) you'll have to pay extra tax.

If your income from all sources – including the taxable part of the annuity – is below certain limits, you can apply through the insurance company to have your annuity income paid without deduction of tax. Check with the taxman.

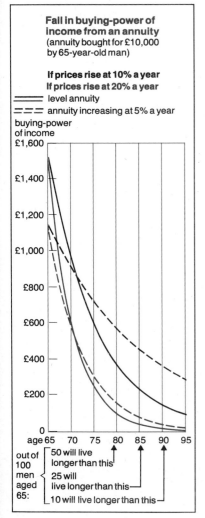

Fall in buying-power of income from an annuity (annuity bought for £10,000 by 65-year-old man)

If prices rise at 10% a year
If prices rise at 20% a year

level annuity
annuity increasing at 5% a year

buying-power of income

£1,600
£1,400
£1,200
£1,000
£800
£600
£400
£200
0

age 65 70 75 80 85 90 95

out of 100 men aged 65:
50 will live longer than this
25 will live longer than this
10 will live longer than this

From which company?

Our Table gives an indication of the sorts of return available on 13 October 1981. Companies' rates can change frequently. To choose a company yourself, get an up-to-date copy of one of the magazines which regularly compare companies' immediate annuity rates (be careful *not* to look up compulsory purchase annuities). These are:
Policy Market – £1.20 from Stone & Cox, 44 Fleet St, London EC4Y 1BS.
Money Management – £2.75 from Minster House, Arthur St, London EC4R 9AX.
Savings Market – £4 from Wootten Publications, 150/152 Caledonian Rd, London N1 9RD.

Company safety
The Policyholders Protection Act (see p132) gives you protection should your insurance company go bust. However, you'd still be faced with a lot of anxiety while it was all going on. To avoid this, you may do as well to avoid very new or very small insurance companies. Get your insurance broker to check for you.

If your age (and the amount of money you've got available) is close to those used by the magazine, get quotations from companies which do well for that age. But things may well have changed since the magazine went to press. So it might be as well to go to an insurance broker too. Some brokers subscribe to the *Quotel* computer system which lists annuity income offered by around 65 different companies (for a nearby Quotel broker write to Freepost, Quotel Insurance Services Ltd, 83 Clerkenwell Rd, London EC1R 5HP).

Home income schemes

If you're elderly and own your home, you may be able to boost your income with a home income scheme. A 70-year old man, for example, with a home worth £25,000 could boost his after-tax income by over £1,000 a year. A woman of 75 could do the same.

How the schemes work

You get a loan based on the security of your home. The loan is used to buy an annuity from an insurance company. While you live, you get the income from the annuity from which basic rate tax and interest on the loan has been deducted. When you die, the loan is repaid out of your estate (possibly by the sale of the home) before capital transfer tax is worked out. (Note that with some schemes, you sell all or part of your house to the company. Any increase in the value of the house then goes to the company, not to you.)

If you pay tax, you can get tax relief on the full amount of the loan interest. This means that if, for example, you pay tax at the basic rate of 30 per cent, you save 30p tax for each £ of interest you pay. See Diagram for an example of how this works out in practice.

If you pay tax at more than the basic rate your increase in income would be greater, because you'd get more tax relief.

If you don't pay tax, you can have an *option mortgage* on your home which, in effect, gives you tax relief at the basic rate. You'd end up with about the same income as a basic rate taxpayer. And if you remain a non-taxpayer – even when the extra income is taken into account – you'd end up with more than a basic rate taxpayer.

The nuts and bolts

The schemes are available for freehold houses, and for leasehold property with a substantial part of the lease still to run (50 to 80 years, depending on the company). When you apply for a scheme, your home will be valued by an independent valuer – you pay the fee, but it may be returned if you take out the scheme. The most you can usually borrow is a percentage (for example, 65 or 80 per cent) of the market value of your home. With one scheme, the annuity rate and the interest on the loan are fixed at an artificially low level at the outset. These rates don't change as time passes.

You may be able to take part of the loan in cash in return for a rather lower income. There's usually a minimum loan – commonly £10,000 or so.

If the house is occupied by two people – husband and wife, or brother and sister say – the annuity is arranged so that it continues for as long as either is alive. You generally have to be at least 70 to be eligible for this type of annuity (somewhat older if you're a woman, or a couple applying).

Pros and cons The value of your home is likely to go up year by year, after you've taken out the loan. You may be able to use the increase in value to get a further loan and buy another annuity. In this way you might be able to increase your income in line with inflation.

With an ordinary annuity, inflation reduces the buying power of your fixed income, and there's not much you can do about it. With these schemes, inflation still reduces the buying power of your fixed income, but it correspondingly reduces the value of your debt to the insurance company. So rising prices don't wholly work against you.

On the other hand, you'd be almost certain to get a better after-tax increase in your income by paying cash for an annuity (if you could do so) rather than mortgaging your home. And if it's likely you'll have to sell your home (to move in with relatives or into an old people's home, say) think twice before going for a home income plan. If you do move later on, you'll have to repay the loan, and may get left with a rather low fixed-income annuity.

Suitable for you? A home income scheme is worth considering if you need the extra income, provided you're at least 70 (or preferably older). But you'd almost certainly get a better after-tax increase in your income by paying cash for an annuity (if you could do so) rather than mortgaging your home. And remember that you can't cancel an annuity and get your money back.

How a home income plan works

[1] If you don't pay tax, you can have an option mortgage, which in effect gives you tax relief at the basic rate. Less interest would be deducted by the insurance company, and you'd end up with about the same income as shown above. If you still remain a non-taxpayer, you could claim the tax deducted from the annuity back from the taxman.

You mortgage your home to an insurance company and get in return an annuity of, say, £2,000 a year

The company also deducts mortgage interest you owe – say £1,200 [1]

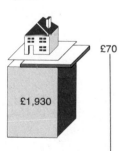 £70
£1,930

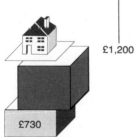 £1,200
£730

 £730
£360

 £1,090

Before paying you this, the company deducts basic rate tax of, say, £70 from the taxable part of the annuity – which leaves £1,930

So company hands you £730 [1]

But if you pay tax, you can claim tax relief on the mortgage interest – if you pay basic rate tax, for example, you can claim back £1,200 × 30% = £360 (provided you pay at least this much tax) [1]

So your income goes up by £360 from the taxman and by £730 from the company – a total of £1,090 [1]

17 Pensions from employers and from the state

You may feel this is an odd chapter to have in a book on saving and investing. If you're employed, there may be no choice about whether or not you can join the pension scheme. And anyone who earns over a certain amount has to make national insurance contributions, part of which is used to pay state pensions. However, unless you can work out roughly how much you'll get from these sources, you'll be ill-prepared to sort out your retirement finances (see Chapter 25).

A pension from your job

An employer's pension scheme may be contributory (you have to pay a proportion of your salary into the scheme each month – four or five per cent is common) or non-contributory. In either case, your employer makes contributions into the scheme on your behalf. Provided the pension scheme meets certain conditions, it gets very favourable tax treatment – you get tax relief on any payments you make, you pay no tax on contributions made by your employer, and the pension fund itself pays no income tax or capital gains tax.

To work out how much you'll get from your pension scheme, you need to know what kind of scheme you belong to. There are four main kinds – the commonest is a final pay scheme (see Box opposite for summaries of the less-common types).

Final pay scheme With a final pay scheme, the number of years you've been a member of the scheme, and the yearly amount you're earning at the time you retire – or in the few years before then – normally decide the size of your pension. Many schemes pay 1/60 of your final pay for each year of membership. Others pay, for example, 1/80 of final pay.

Under Inland Revenue rules, the maximum pension you can get at normal retirement age is 2/3 of your final pay – otherwise the taxman may insist that the scheme be changed. There's a lower maximum if you get a tax-free lump sum.

So if you reach normal retirement age after 40 years' membership of a scheme which pays 1/60 of your final pay for each year, you can retire on 2/3 final pay (and you still retire on 2/3 final pay if you reach normal retirement age after 45 years' membership). By contrast, schemes which work on eightieths would give only half final pay (40 × 1/80) after 40 years' membership.

Clearly, the higher your final yearly pay, the higher your pension from a given scheme. Different schemes have different rules, but most schemes are based on one of these definitions of *final pay*:
- average of the best 3 consecutive years' pay in the last 13
- basic salary in the last year before you retire (or last-but-one-year), plus – in some cases – average of overtime, commission and

bonuses during the last 3 years
- average yearly pay over the last few years (commonly 3 or 5).
Check with your employer exactly how your scheme works.

Taking account of the State pension

Some final pay schemes make a deduction *either* from the final pay used to work out your pension, *or* from the pension itself, to allow for the fact that you'll be getting some money from the State.

Commonly, the deduction made is 1/40 of the State pension for each year's membership of the scheme. But schemes vary, so check with your employer. If the normal retirement age in your job is earlier than 65 (or earlier than 60 if you're a woman), the deduction for the state pension should not apply until you reach the official retirement age for the State pension. It's particularly important that it does *not* apply if you're forced to retire early through ill-health. **Warning**: a scheme which makes little or no reduction to allow for the State pension isn't necessarily better than a scheme which makes a large deduction. What matters is the total amount of pension you end up with.

Inflation-proofing

Retirement can last a long time, particularly for women: on average, men retiring at 65 have 13 years of retirement, women retiring at 60 have 20 years. And you'll want an adequate pension not just at the time you retire, but later in your retirement too. If you need convincing about the devastating effect of inflation on a fixed income, look at the Table on p234.

A pension of, for example, only half your final pay, but inflation-proofed, can soon overtake an apparently better pension of 2/3 final pay which has no protection against rising prices.

But not many private sector schemes can promise that pensions will be fully inflation-proofed, because the cost of such a promise cannot even be guessed at. Many schemes, however, do promise to increase pensions by a certain percentage each year (commonly, an increase of 3 to 4 per cent a year is promised) and though much better than nothing, this falls short of today's rate of inflation.

Some schemes – particularly those run by large companies – have in practice given increases which don't fall far short of inflation. But how far companies can continue to do this – particularly if inflation takes another turn for the worse, and if companies' profits fail to improve – is uncertain.

Unless your pension is guaranteed inflation proof, you should make some allowance for a fall in its buying-power while you are retired.

Other, less common ways of working out pensions

Money purchase schemes

You and your employer pay contributions which are fixed as a percentage of your pay. The bulk of these contributions is invested for you and, on retirement, the proceeds are used to buy a pension. How much pension you'll get will depend on how the investments have done, and current interest rates.

Average pay schemes

With average pay schemes, your pension is based on your pay in each year you belong to the scheme.

The schemes are usually based on a graded scale of earnings. For each year that your pay is in a particular earnings band, you get a fixed amount of pension. As you move up the earnings scale, the amount earned in pension will rise (as will any contributions you pay). The yearly pension you're eventually paid will be the total of all the little bits of yearly pension you've earned in each earnings band.

For example, for each year your earnings are between £3,000 and £4,000, you may get £50 in pension a year. For each year your earnings are £4,000 or more, you may get £60 a year.

Flat-rate schemes

Flat-rate schemes provide a fixed amount of pension – say £5 a year – for each year's membership of the scheme.

Tax-free lump sums   You can normally choose to exchange part of the future income from your pension for a tax-free lump sum. But with some schemes, you automatically get a pension *and* a lump sum (part or all of which you may be able to exchange for extra pension).

If you have a choice, should you go for a tax-free lump sum or for a pension? If your pension is inflation-proofed this is so valuable that you should be wary of exchanging any of it for a lump sum. On the other hand, if you don't expect worthwhile increases in your pension after retirement, it might pay you to exchange as much as possible of your pension for a lump sum. If you then use this lump sum to buy, for example, an annuity (see Chapter 16), your after-tax income from the annuity may be more than the pension you've given up. It would be worth checking close to the time you retire on what income you'd get from an annuity.

Additional voluntary contributions   Some employers' pension schemes allow members to make additional voluntary contributions (over and above those they have to make to belong to the scheme) in order to get a higher pension at retirement. Your employer doesn't normally match your voluntary contributions by paying extra contributions on your behalf.

Before deciding to make additional voluntary contributions (AVCs), first check what will happen to them – will they build up solely on your behalf (eg via an account in your name with a building society) or will they go into the general pension fund (which may mean less for you). Next find out what you'd get for your AVCs – all you may get is a fixed amount of pension at retirement age which won't go up as time passes. With some schemes, you may be able to use your extra contributions to buy an addition to your basic pension (or the rate at which the pension increases), or to provide a pension for your widow.

Your extra contributions are normally treated in the same way as ordinary ones for tax purposes – ie you get tax relief on them at your top rate of tax, and they go into a fund which pays no tax on its income or capital gains. This applies if you keep making the payments for at least five years (or until you retire, if earlier), and if the total you are paying into your employer's scheme each year is not more than 15 per cent of your earnings from that job. So, particularly for higher rate taxpayers, and in the last few years before retirement, AVCs may be a very good way of saving. But note that you won't be able to get at your savings until you retire.

Retiring late   Generally speaking, under Inland Revenue rules, the maximum pension you can get from an employer's scheme at the time you retire is two-thirds of your 'final pay' (as defined by your scheme). If you work after the normal retirement age for your scheme you are allowed to get a higher pension than this. But how much extra pension you will get depends on the details of your firm's pension scheme (check with your employer). You may get about $\frac{3}{4}$ per cent extra pension for each month you delay retirement.

As an alternative, you may be able to go on building up one-sixtieths (or whatever your pension scheme works on) for each extra year of work. The detailed rules are complicated – check with your employer.

With many schemes, you and your employer stop making contributions when you reach retirement age for that scheme.

Other pension scheme benefits

Pension schemes can provide other benefits besides a retirement pension for you. They may also provide:
- a pension for you if you are forced to retire early because of ill-health
- a pension for your wife if you die first. Or if you are a married woman, a pension for your husband
- pensions for children or other dependants you leave on death
- an income for you if you have a long spell off work as a result of sickness or disablement (this starts to be paid when your employer stops paying you your normal pay). Note that with some employers, this may be provided for all employees – even those not in the employer's pension scheme
- a lump sum for someone you nominate should you die before leaving your job or retiring. (Again this may be provided for all employees, whether they belong to the employer's pension scheme or not.)

These benefits are mainly of importance when you are working out how much life insurance you need – see Box on p124.

Changing jobs

The Route Map below gives a broad indication of the options which might be put to you when you leave a pension scheme. Here we look in more detail at these options.

Deferred pensions

If you're in a final pay scheme, a deferred pension may well be pretty low, for two main reasons:
- the pension will be based on your pay (and years of membership of the scheme) at the time you left the job. For example, if you belonged to a scheme for 20 years and it paid 1/60 of final pay for each year, your deferred pension would be 20/60 (ie 1/3) of *your pay at the time you left*. Your pay at that time may well be very much lower than your final earnings on retirement
- with most private sector schemes, the pension is unlikely to be increased in line with inflation between the time you leave the job and the time you retire – so the earlier on in your career you change

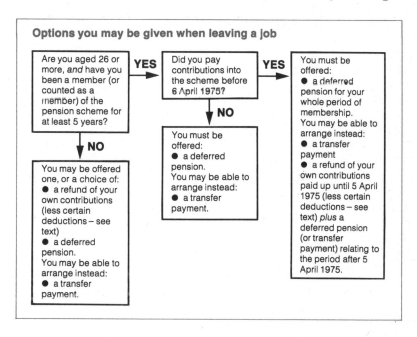

Options you may be given when leaving a job

Are you aged 26 or more, *and* have you been a member (or counted as a member) of the pension scheme for at least 5 years? **YES** → Did you pay contributions into the scheme before 6 April 1975? **YES** →

You must be offered:
- a deferred pension for your whole period of membership.
You may be able to arrange instead:
- a transfer payment
- a refund of your own contributions paid up until 5 April 1975 (less certain deductions – see text) *plus* a deferred pension (or transfer payment) relating to the period after 5 April 1975.

Did you pay contributions into the scheme before 6 April 1975? **NO** ↓

You must be offered:
- a deferred pension.
You may be able to arrange instead:
- a transfer payment.

Are you aged 26 or more...? **NO** ↓

You may be offered one, or a choice of:
- a refund of your own contributions (less certain deductions – see text)
- a deferred pension.
You may be able to arrange instead:
- a transfer payment.

Refund of your own contributions
You can get a refund of your contributions only in certain circumstances (see Route Map on p159) – and then only if the rules of your pension scheme allow it. You won't get back any of the contributions paid by your employer. The trustees of the pension scheme have to pay tax at 10 per cent on the refund, which they may deduct from the refund before handing it over to you. If your old pension scheme is *contracted-out* (see p162), there may be a further deduction from your refund to buy you back into the state scheme.

jobs, the less your deferred pension will turn out to be worth. If your employer's scheme is *contracted-out* (see p162), your deferred pension has to be at least a minimum amount.

For these two reasons, the final pension of someone who changes jobs a fair amount is likely to be much lower than someone with the same earnings over his working life, but who stayed in one job.

As you can see from the Diagram below, someone who changes jobs four times and accepts a deferred pension each time, could end up with a total pension of around ¼ his final pay. But someone with the same year-by-year earnings who works for one employer throughout, can end up with a pension of ⅔ final pay.

Transfer payments
You may be able to arrange for the pension scheme of your old employer to make a payment – called a transfer payment – into the pension scheme of your new employer (which will then take responsibility for your pension rights from your old job).

In return for this payment, your new employer will either:
● agree to pay you extra pension from retirement (normally fixed in £££ and not increased in line with future pay increases) *or*
● give you a credit of a number of years membership of his scheme. This will almost certainly be fewer years than you had been in your old employer's scheme – because the transfer payment will normally be based on your pay today, whereas your new employer's scheme will eventually pay you a pension based on your pay when you retire (after inflation and promotion have pushed your salary up). Note that if you're changing jobs in the public sector, special rules mean that you're unlikely to lose out.

If you are offered credited years, you should also negotiate a guarantee of the minimum pension in £££ from the transfer payment (which shouldn't be less than the preserved benefits you're giving up), in case you should change jobs again.

Even if you get a transfer payment, you're likely to lose out on pension as a result of changing jobs.

Trying to decide which to take

If you're changing jobs and can't decide whether to go for a deferred pension or a transfer payment get the *Money Which? Pension transfer calculator* (from Consumers' Association for £10) which will help you work out the sums.

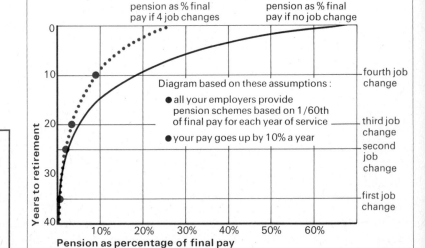

How your pension shrinks if you change jobs

pension as % final pay if 4 job changes

pension as % final pay if no job change

Diagram based on these assumptions :
● all your employers provide pension schemes based on 1/60th of final pay for each year of service
● your pay goes up by 10% a year

fourth job change

third job change

second job change

first job change

Years to retirement

Pension as percentage of final pay

A pension from the state

Your state pension may be made up of a flat-rate basic pension, an additional pension based on your earnings since April 1978, and a graduated pension based on your earnings from 1961 to 1975. These pensions are currently increased each year in line with changes in the retail price index. While this continues they should maintain their buying-power.

Basic pension

Anyone who has paid enough full Class 1, Class 2 or Class 3 national insurance (NI) contributions qualifies for this pension. There are complicated rules to work out whether you've paid enough in contributions. But you're pretty certain to qualify if you've paid contributions for 90 per cent of your 'working life' (broadly, between ages 16 and 64 for a man, between ages 16 and 59 for a woman). Note that, since April 1978, if you've stayed at home to look after children, or an elderly or sick person, the number of years needed to qualify are reduced. Even if you don't qualify for the full pension, you may qualify for a reduced one. Married women may qualify for a pension on their own contribution record, or may get one based on their husband's. If in doubt about how much pension you'll get, check at your local social security office.

Additional pension

This is a supplement to the basic pension for employed people who, since April 1978, have paid Class 1 NI contributions on earnings over a certain limit. What you get and what you pay depends on your earnings. The maximum in November 1982 is £9.59. If you belong to an employer's pension scheme which is contracted-out (see Box overleaf), you get no additional state pension – your employer provides the equivalent or more.

How it works

People earning below a certain level (£29.50 a week in April 1982) pay no contributions – so none of these earnings count towards the additional pension. If you earn over this lower limit you pay NI contributions on the whole of your earnings up to a given ceiling (£220 a week in April 1982).

The DHSS calculates for each year you work, how much of your earnings counts towards the additional pension. Your additional pension is related to the earnings recorded for all these years. But inflation might make your earnings of 25 years ago almost worthless. So these earnings are *revalued* each year – ie they are increased in line with the way average earnings have increased between the year you earned the money and the year you retire.

Contributions on earnings up to a lower limit count towards your basic pension. So an amount equal to the lower earnings limit for the tax year in which you're 64 (59 for a woman), is knocked off your revalued earnings. What's left is the amount of earnings which goes towards your additional pension. The best 20 years are picked out and added together (if you haven't been earning for 20 years, you make do with those you have). The yearly additional pension you get is 1/80 (ie 1¼ per cent) of your total.

Note that you won't be able to clock up 20 years' earnings before retirement age unless you were born after 5 April 1933 (for a man) or 5 April 1938 (for a woman).

The Table on the left shows how this works out for someone due to retire in 1983 (with 5 years' earnings counting towards his additional pension). And the Table on p233 shows how the additional pension will build up over the next 20 years or so.

How your additional pension is worked out

Suppose you have 5 years of earnings which count towards your additional pension

Revalued earnings	Part for basic pension	Extra for additional pension
£	£	£
5,534	1,534	4,000
5,684	1,534	4,150
5,984	1,534	4,450
6,284	1,534	4,750
6,534	1,534	5,000

Total for additional pension: £22,350

So yearly additional pension (1/80th of £22,350) is £279.39 a year – ie £5.37 a week

Graduated pension

In addition to your basic pension and additional pension, you may also get a *graduated pension* when you retire. Only people who were at least 18 and employed in a job between 1961 and 1975, and who earned more than £9 a week during that time, qualify for this type of State pension. The graduated pension scheme has now been abandoned – but you'll still get the meagre pension that your past contributions have earned.

Between April 1961 and April 1975, NI contributions were of two kinds: a flat-rate one paid by almost everyone in employment, and a graduated one paid by people who earned more than £9 in any one week.

For each £7.50 he had contributed, a man gets a pension of just over 4p a week (November 1982). If you're a woman, it will have taken £9 of contributions to earn that 4p a week (the rules were set this way because women retire earlier than men, and live longer).

Your graduated pension is increased in step with rising prices after April 1978. But it's still likely to be a small part of your total pension.

At most, a man's graduated pension worked out at £3.68 a week in November 1982, a woman's at £3.03 a week – and it's unlikely that many people will have earned even this much.

The Department of Health and Social Security keeps records of how many *units* of pension each person has earned (each unit producing a pension of just over 4p a week) – check with your local social security office.

Married women

If you pay full Class 1 or Class 2 or 3 NI contributions, you qualify for a basic pension (and, with Class 1 contributions only, earnings-related additional pension) in your own right in the same way as everyone else (see p161). And if you have had to spend time at home (caring for children for example) you can qualify for a basic pension with a shorter contribution record.

However, if you pay the lower Class 1 contribution or no Class 2 contribution (only possible for those married on or before 5 April 1977 and who had chosen to pay lower or no contributions) you can

---

What 'contracting out' means

When the new state pension scheme started in April 1978, employers who ran pension schemes for their employees could choose whether employees should belong to the new additional pension scheme, or not (ie to 'contract out'). If you are contracted-out of the state scheme, you pay lower national insurance contributions than employees who have stayed in the state scheme, and your employer's pension scheme takes over from the state the job of providing the additional pension. Broadly, a contracted-out scheme must guarantee that the pensions it pays (including deferred pensions) will not fall below the additional pensions members would have got from the state for their years of membership if the scheme hadn't been contracted-out. This guaranteed pension is called the *guaranteed minimum pension* (GMP).

The GMP will go up to take account of inflation both before and after retirement. After retirement, these increases are provided by the state. Before retirement, increases in the GMP part of deferred pensions may be provided partly or wholly by the pension scheme, the rest by the state. With some schemes which provide some or all of the increases in GMP, these increases may be offset against some (or even all) of the part of your deferred pension in excess of the GMP.

only qualify for a pension on your husband's record. You must be 60 or over and you will only get a pension when *your husband* starts getting his. The pension you get will be smaller than one based on your own contributions – around 3/5 the basic rate.

Widows
If your husband paid enough NI contributions, you qualify for a number of benefits, including state retirement pension when you reach retirement age. For details, get leaflets NP35 and NP36 from your local social security office. All widows' benefits except the state retirement pension stop if you remarry or live with a man as his wife.

Widows' benefits increase in the same way as the basic retirement pension.

If you're over 60 when your husband dies, you'll normally get the basic retirement pension. But if your husband was *not* getting a retirement pension at the time he died, you can normally get the (higher) widow's allowance for the first 6 months after his death, instead.

Earning extra state pension
You can earn extra state pension by putting off drawing your state retirement pension. You can do this for up to five years after retirement age.

For each 6 days (excluding Sundays) you postpone drawing your pension, your total state pension is currently increased by 1/7 of one per cent. But you have to put off your retirement for at least 42 days (excluding Sundays) to start increasing your pension. For each year you postpone your pension, the pension you get will be increased by about $7\frac{1}{2}$ per cent. Once you are 5 years over retirement age (ie 70 for a man, or 65 for a woman) your state pension is paid in full – and continuing to work won't increase it further.

A wife can't claim a pension on her husband's contributions until he starts drawing the state pension. If he puts this off, getting her part of the pension will be postponed too – and increased by the same percentage as her husband's.

Somewhat different rules applied before April 1979.

If you've already started drawing your state pension, you can cancel your retirement (once only), and earn increases in your pension from then.

The earnings rule
During the first five years after you reach the state retirement age, what's called the *earnings rule* applies (whether you are employed, or self-employed). You can earn up to a certain amount (£57 a week in November 1982) before your pension is reduced. After that, the earnings rule means that, broadly, your pension is reduced by half of what you earn between £57 and £61 a week, and by the full amount of what you earn above that.

If your earnings are likely to affect your pension, it may be to your advantage to defer drawing your state pension for a few years (building up a bigger pension – see above).

18 Personal pension plans

A personal pension plan (also called self-employed retirement annuity) is a pension scheme run by an insurance company for individuals who are either self-employed or in a job where they don't belong to the firm's pension scheme. You take out a personal pension plan by paying a premium (or agreeing to pay a series of premiums) to the insurance company. The company invests the money and, when you retire, it pays you a lump sum and a pension for life.

For example, if you started paying £1,000 a year into a scheme at age 40, you might get a pension of around £15,000 a year (after tax) from age 65. Or you could take a lump sum of around £42,000 and a pension of around £10,000.

What are the advantages?

Like other pension schemes, personal pension plans get much more generous tax treatment than most investments, and this can make them the best way of saving up for retirement. You get tax relief on your premiums (up to certain limits) at the highest rate of tax you pay. So if you paid tax at the basic rate of 30 per cent, the £1,000 premiums in the example above would cost you only £700. The insurance company doesn't have to pay any tax on profits it makes investing your money, the pension you get is treated as earned income, not investment income, and any lump sum you get is tax-free. This means that you're likely to get a higher pension (after tax) from a personal pension plan than from a comparable investment – eg by investing in investment-type life insurance and then at age 65 buying an immediate annuity (which also pays you an income for life).

Whether any pension scheme turns out to be a good investment for you depends mainly on how long you live. If you live to a ripe old age you'll obviously get much better value than if you die shortly after retiring. But what you're paying for is the certainty of having a regular income for as long as you live.

What are the disadvantages?

Unlike most other investments, once you've handed your money over you can't normally get any of it back until you're 60 – though with some schemes you can borrow back from the insurance company. Even when you're 60, you can take only a limited amount as a lump sum (the rest has to be paid out as pension). So if you decide later that another form of investment – eg shares, gold, a more expensive house – would give you a better return, you won't normally be able to switch.

Another real problem is inflation. The £15,000-a-year in our example sounds substantial – but if inflation averaged 10 per cent over the 25 years you'd been saving, your pension would be worth only £1,380 a year in today's buying-power in the year you retired. It could go down even further in value after that – by age 75 it would be worth only £530 if inflation continued at 10 per cent. So if you're some way from retirement, the pension you'll eventually need is likely to be much higher than would seem sufficient now. We tell you how you can try to allow for inflation on p171.

Who qualifies?

You can put money into a personal pension plan if:
- you have income from being self-employed (this includes being a partner in a partnership). But see also Box overleaf
- you have freelance earnings
- you have a job from which you won't get a retirement pension. This could be either because your employer doesn't run a pension scheme or, if he does, because you've chosen not to join it (but see Box overleaf), or because you don't qualify. If you have more than one job, the earnings from any job from which you won't get a pension qualify.

Are regular payments necessary?

The plans available are fairly flexible about when and how much you can pay in (but there are strict tax rules about this). With some plans, you can make one-off payments as and when you can afford to. With others, you agree to make regular payments each month or year – but even with these, you may be able to vary what you pay, miss out some payments or make extra ones. If you stop paying, the payments you've made already will stay in the company's fund and you'll get some pension from them when you retire.

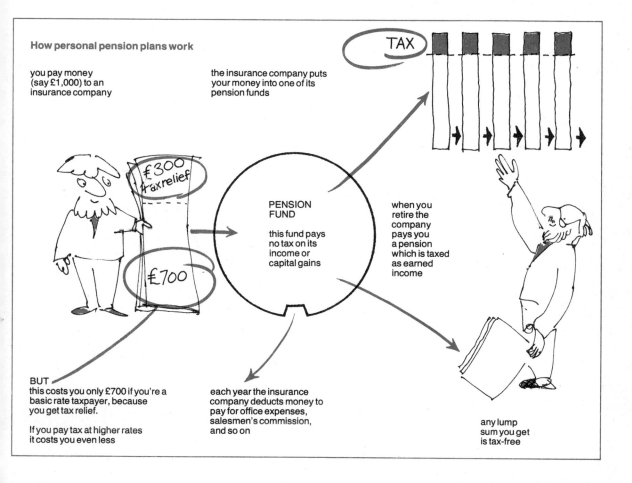

How personal pension plans work

you pay money (say £1,000) to an insurance company

the insurance company puts your money into one of its pension funds

TAX

£300 tax relief

£700

PENSION FUND

this fund pays no tax on its income or capital gains

when you retire the company pays you a pension which is taxed as earned income

BUT this costs you only £700 if you're a basic rate taxpayer, because you get tax relief.

If you pay tax at higher rates it costs you even less

each year the insurance company deducts money to pay for office expenses, salesmen's commission, and so on

any lump sum you get is tax-free

When should you start paying?

Generally, the earlier you start paying into a scheme the better – if you paid the same amount in premiums each year, starting just one year earlier could well increase the pension you get by over 10 per cent. See p172 for more details.

It is natural that many self-employed people are reluctant to pay money into a pension scheme when they feel that ploughing as much money as possible back into their business is the best investment they can make. Of course they may be right – but selling the business at the right time and price may not be easy and the business might fall on hard times before then. And there may be some capital gains tax to pay.

When can you start receiving the pension?

Generally at any time between the ages of 60 and 75 (though people in certain occupations can retire earlier, and you may be able to do so if you become too ill to carry on working). If you have several plans, you can start receiving the benefits from each at different times. You don't have to stop working if you don't want to. (Note that we use the word '*retire*' in this chapter as shorthand for '*start receiving the benefits of the plan*', regardless of whether or not you actually stop work at that time.)

Guide to the rest of this chapter

We start by telling you about the different types of plan available. Then on p170 we look at the things you need to decide before taking one out, and you'll find help in choosing a policy on p175. The choices open to you at retirement are covered on p176, and on p178 we give an outline of the tax rules about how much you can pay in.

Self-employed and thinking of forming a small company?

If you formed a limited company, you would have a wider choice of pension arrangements. You could still save for retirement through a personal pension plan. But there are other types of pension scheme for small companies and their directors which might prove more suitable.

If you are currently in a partnership, there are now schemes available which can give the partners control over the investments and which allow the partnership to borrow from the pension fund.

You would certainly need expert advice on whether forming a company would be best for you, and on the type of pension arrangements which could be made. An accountant or an actuary should be able to help.

Should you join your employer's pension scheme?

With many employer's pension schemes you won't be given the choice – joining the scheme is a condition of the job. When membership is voluntary, joining the scheme could give you a better pension than you'd get from a personal pension plan – because your employer will also contribute, and because your pension is likely to be based on your final pay. But you may lose out if you change jobs a lot – see p159.

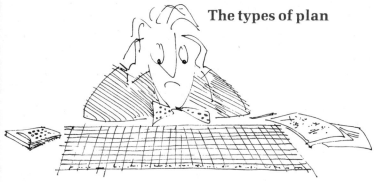

The types of plan

There are over 100 different personal pension plans available, but hardly two are the same. The main variations are in:
- how the pension you're entitled to is worked out
- your choice of investment
- how often you pay premiums
- whether the plan allows you to borrow money back from the insurance company.

How your pension is worked out

The way the insurance company works out how much pension you're entitled to from the payments you have made depends on how your personal pension plan is worded:
- **a deferred annuity** plan talks in terms of the pension you'll get at a certain age. This will be based on the amount you've paid into the scheme. For example, if you pay in £1,000 a year for 15 years from age 50, the company may quote you a pension of £6,000 a year if you retire at 65
- **a cash-funded** plan talks in terms of the amount of money that accumulates for you to buy your pension with. For example, your plan may say that if you paid in the same amounts as above, a cash fund of some £37,000 will have accumulated for you by age of 65.

When you retire, this cash is used to buy an immediate annuity which will pay you an income for life. The income you get will depend on the company's annuity rate for your age when you retire. This annuity rate will specify how much pension you get for each £ in your fund. In the example above, if annuity rates at the time you retired were at the level that applied in November 1981 ($17\frac{1}{2}$ per cent, say, for a 65-year-old man), your pension would be $17\frac{1}{2}$ per cent of £37,000 = £6,475 a year. But if annuity rates were lower your pension would be correspondingly lower.

Whether your plan is a deferred annuity or cash-funded, you're likely to have a further choice at the time you want to start getting your pension. Nearly all companies now offer an **open-market option** – ie they will let you shop around for a higher pension by switching your money to another company and getting your pension from them. (If your plan is a deferred annuity, the company will tell you how much cash you have available to transfer – see p176.) For example, in November 1981 you might have found that another company would offer you an annuity rate of, say, 18 per cent (rather than $17\frac{1}{2}$ per cent above). It's worth going for a plan that offers this option.

Your choice of investment

We give details below of the four main types of policy. For which type to choose, see p170.

Non-profit

Your premiums go into the company's pension fund which the company invests as it thinks fit – mainly in shares, British Government stocks, loans and property. Whatever happens to these investments, the amount of pension or cash fund you get is guaranteed by the company at the outset – it won't be more or less. Most non-profit policies are of the deferred annuity type – so that you know exactly how much your pension will be. (With a cash-funded plan it's only the amount of cash in your fund that's guaranteed – the amount of pension you get will depend on the company's annuity rate at the time you retire.) But these guaranteed pensions and cash funds are low, because the company must feel certain it can pay out the agreed amounts, whatever happens to its investments and to interest rates in the meantime.

With-profits

Your premiums are invested in the company's pension fund as above. The company guarantees from the outset the minimum pension it will pay you (if the policy is a deferred annuity one), or the minimum amount of money you'll have for buying an annuity with (if it is cash-funded). These minimum amounts are at first even lower than those from non-profit policies. But as the company makes profits on its investments, it announces increases in the minimum pension (or fund) you're guaranteed at retirement. These increases are called **reversionary bonuses**, and once they've been declared (usually every year or every three years) they can't be taken away. With most policies, a one-off **terminal bonus** may be added at the time you retire – though you've no idea how much this will be until that time arrives. As a result of these bonuses, you're likely to end up with a pension or cash fund which is considerably higher than you'd have got from a non-profit policy.

Unit-linked

Your premiums buy units in one of a number of funds offered by the insurance company. The most common types of fund are:
● **property funds** – which invest in office blocks, factories, shops and so on
● **equity funds** – which invest in shares (either directly, or via unit trusts)
● **fixed-interest funds** – which invest in things which pay out a fixed income (eg British Government stocks, company loan stocks)
● **cash funds** – which invest in bank deposit accounts, short-term loans to local authorities and other investments which pay out rates of return which vary along with interest rates in general
● **managed funds** – which invest in a mixture of things listed above.

Each fund is divided into a number of units. The price of each unit is, approximately, the value of the investments in the fund divided by the number of units that have been issued – so the unit price goes up and down as the value of the investments in the fund fluctuates (but with cash funds, most companies guarantee that the price of units won't go down).

In general, how well you do from a unit-linked policy depends a lot on *when* your money goes in, and out. If the unit price is at a peak when you pay your money in and in a trough when it's paid out, you won't do at all well. But if you happen to time things right, you would do better than with a with-profits policy.

With most companies there's a choice of funds to invest in, and you can switch from one fund to another (eg from the equity fund to the property fund). This could prove useful if you want to move your money around in the hope of getting the best return. But bear in mind that if you time things wrongly you could end up doing rather badly. There's often a charge for switching – perhaps $\frac{1}{2}$ per cent of the amount you move.

Nearly all unit-linked policies are cash-funded, so the amount of pension you get will also depend on annuity rates at the time you start taking the benefits. If – as is not impossible – both the value of your units and the level of annuity rates are low at the time you want to retire, you could find yourself having to make do with a low income, or putting off your retirement in the hope that they'll go up in the future.

A few unit-linked policies guarantee a minimum cash fund at retirement (eg not less than the total premiums paid), and some guarantee a minimum annuity rate – but these guarantees tend to be low (for example, much lower than you could be fairly certain of ending up with from a with-profits policy).

Deposit administration

These work rather like a bank deposit account. Your premiums are put into an account with the insurance company, and interest is added from time to time. The interest rate will vary, depending on the general level of interest rates, but there may be a guaranteed minimum rate (sometimes linked to The Building Societies Association recommended mortgage rate). The value of your fund (in £££) can't go down. With some companies you can switch between deposit administration and unit-linked policies.

All deposit administration schemes are cash-funded, and a few guarantee a minimum amount of cash fund you'll have at retirement. The amount of pension you get will depend on annuity rates at the time you retire – though many policies do guarantee a minimum annuity rate at retirement.

When companies work out estimates of how much pension you'll get from a deposit administration policy, they often assume that the interest rates and annuity rates they're paying at the moment will apply all the way through. This can make deposit administration policies look misleadingly attractive when interest and annuity rates are high – rather less attractive when they are low.

How often you pay the premiums

Most companies offer both regular- and single-premium policies. With a regular-premium policy you agree to make payments every month, quarter, half-year or year. With most companies, the terms you get (eg the amount of pension or cash fund you get, or the charges deducted from premiums) are decided when you first take out the policy, and apply to all your regular premiums.

With a single-premium policy, you pay in a lump sum which remains invested until you retire. The terms you get depend on when you pay the premium – so could be worse, or better, than for a regular-premium policy running at the same time.

Many schemes are fairly flexible – so the distinction between single- and regular-premium policies isn't always clear-cut. For example, having paid in your first premium, a scheme may allow you to make any number of payments of almost any amount at any time in the future. And with all schemes you can stop paying altogether at any time – see p172.

Single-premium policies give you the advantage of being able to decide with no constraints exactly how much you want to pay, and when – which may be useful if your income fluctuates a lot. And you have the chance to shop around each time for the company offering the best terms. The main advantage of a regular-premium policy is that with most companies the terms you get each year are the ones that were guaranteed at the outset – so you are protected against equally favourable terms not being available in the future. There is little point in going for a regular-premium scheme which does *not* have these guarantees – you'd be better off with single-premium policies. Of course, a regular-premium policy has the advantage of putting pressure on you to pay regularly.

You may do best to go for a mixture of single-premium and regular-premium policies – see overleaf. At retirement you can use the *open-market option* (see p167) to transfer all your policies to the company offering the best annuity rates.

Borrowing back from the insurance company

A number of personal pension plans introduced since 1980 have a *loan-back* facility which allows you to borrow from the insurance company up to the amount you've got in your pension fund. There is a minimum initial loan (usually £5,000) and you will need to be able to offer security for the loan – eg your house, business premises, or shares. With some companies there is a minimum regular premium you have to be paying – £1,000 a year, say. When you take a loan, part of your pension fund equal to the amount you've borrowed ceases to be unit-linked or have bonuses added to it. But you pay interest on the loan to the insurance company which, after deducting its charges, pays it into your pension fund – so you're effectively paying interest to yourself. If you use the loan for a purpose which qualifies for tax relief, you can get tax relief on the interest you pay. You could, for example, use the facility to pay maximum premiums to your personal pension plan in a year in which you wouldn't otherwise be able to afford to do so. You can repay the loan when you like – perhaps from selling your business when you retire, or with some companies, you can repay it out of the tax-free lump sum you get on retirement if this is sufficient.

In fact, there may be little advantage in borrowing from the insurance company whose scheme you've joined rather than, say, getting a loan from your bank. If the insurance company were getting a higher return from investing its funds than you were paying in interest, your own pension fund would be losing out. But the facility might be useful if, for example, you want to borrow at a time when the banks are operating a credit squeeze.

Index-linked schemes

A few companies offer funds which invest in index-linked British Government stocks, or lend the money out at rates of interest which are linked to the Retail Price Index.

But this does *not* necessarily mean that the value of your fund increases in line with the RPI – it may go up less quickly. The relationship between the RPI and the value of your fund is different with different schemes.

At present there is a relatively limited amount of index-linked British Government stock available and what happens to these schemes in the future depends on how much more is issued.

Planning your pension

Which type of policy?

Non-profit policies are the only ones where you know at the outset exactly how much pension (or cash fund) you'll get. But because of this guarantee, the return is comparatively low. We don't recommend them, except possibly if you happen to be very close to retirement and want to know pretty clearly where you stand.

Deposit administration policies and the cash funds of unit-linked policies are very dependent on levels of interest rates – so look good when interest rates are high but less good when they're lower. Because the value of your fund or the price of your units (in £££) can't go down, these policies could also be particularly useful for people nearing retirement who want to make sure they don't lose any money. And if you have a unit-linked policy, switching into the cash fund or into the company's deposit administration scheme shortly before retirement can be useful if you're worried about units going down in value. The pension you get will, of course, still be dependent on annuity rates when you retire.

For the long-term, the choice is really between with-profits and unit-linked policies. With-profits schemes are the less risky of the two. Although the guaranteed pension or cash fund is initially low, it is virtually certain to be increased steadily over the period to retirement. And if you go for a deferred annuity, your pension won't suffer if annuity rates are low at the time you retire (though some companies will bump up your pension if annuity rates are high). With unit-linked policies (apart from index-linked ones), the return you get is much more dependent on *when* you make your payments and *when* you start taking the benefits. While you may do very well with a unit-linked policy, you could do rather badly.

A good compromise would be to take out a regular-premium with-profits policy for an amount you can fairly easily afford, as young as you can – at age 30, say. It is probably worth going for a policy which allows you to increase the premiums on guaranteed terms in future years. But in years in which you could afford to pay a substantial extra amount, you could take out a single-premium policy – a unit-linked one, perhaps. As time passed, in order to protect your pension from inflation (see opposite) you would need to take out further policies (which would help to spread your risks) or to pay more into your existing policies.

Doing things this way should make sure that you have a reasonable pension from with-profits policies whenever you want to retire. So you'll be in a better position to choose a good time for taking the benefits of the unit-linked policies – eg when the prices of the units or annuity rates (or both) are high. Alternatively, in the few years before you intend to retire, if the prices of your units reach high levels or you think they may go down, consider switching into a cash fund or deposit administration scheme.

How much to pay in   With regular-premium policies, most companies set a minimum
regular premium, of say, £100 a year, £10 a month. The minimum
for a single-premium policy is normally £100 to £500 (but is £1,000
with a few companies).

In practice, the maximum you can pay in is the maximum
amount you can get tax relief on. For the 1982–83 tax year, the limit
is, broadly, $17\frac{1}{2}\%$ of your earnings from being self-employed or
from jobs where you are not in a pension scheme. For details, see
p178.

Companies produce very accurate-looking and impressive
figures showing the pension you'll get for each £ you pay in from a
certain age. Unfortunately these quotations are little use – not only
are they estimates, but they take no account of inflation which can
be devastating over long periods of time. For example, if you start
paying £500 a year into a regular-premium policy at age 35, you
may imagine yourself living in luxury on the £17,000 a year
pension the company quotes you. But if inflation averages 10 per
cent a year over the rest of your working life, the buying-power of
this pension at age 65 will be under £1,000 a year. Ten years after
retirement it would be worth only £375 a year, if inflation
continued at 10 per cent.

Inflation makes it extremely difficult to know how much pension
you should be aiming for, but you should consider the following:
● how much income you'll have after retirement from other
sources – eg from state retirement pension, from selling your
business, from part-time work
● the age you intend to retire at – the older this is, the more pension
you'll get for each £ you've paid in
● inflation after retirement. If you live to age 65, you can expect to
live to age 79 if you're a man, 82 if you're a woman. You'll still want
to be receiving a decent income in your old age, so the pension
you'll need in the first year of retirement will need to be much
higher in £££ than you'd think. Alternatively you could give up
some pension in the early years of retirement in order to have a
pension which increases each year – see p177
● inflation between now and retirement; over such a long period of
time, inflation can make mincemeat of your pension.

You can use the Table below to work out how many £££ pension
you'll need for various rates of inflation. For example, if you think
you'll need a pension of £6,000 a year (in today's money) in 30
years' time from the scheme, and you reckon inflation will average
10 per cent over that time, you'll need to get £6,000 × 17 =
£102,000 a year from the scheme to achieve this.

To take account of inflation both before and after retirement, use
the number of years up to your 70th or 75th birthday, say, even if
you intend to retire younger than that.

yearly rate of inflation	£££ you'd need to get, for each £ (in today's buying-power) of pension you want:				
	in 10yrs	in 20yrs	in 30yrs	in 40yrs	in 50yrs
5%	1.6	2.7	4.3	7	11
10%	2.6	6.7	17	45	117
15%	4.0	16	66	268	1,084
20%	6.2	38	237	1,470	9,100

You're likely to find, of course, that you can't possibly afford the premiums for a pension of the amount you've worked out. Your best approach may be to pay up to your limit for tax relief each year. But if you're close to retirement, you may find it impossible to achieve anything like enough pension, even if you do this.

When to start

If you were aiming at a pension at age 65 of two-thirds of your final pay (which is the most that someone in an employer's scheme could get) you'd need to pay the full $17\frac{1}{2}$ per cent of earnings allowed by the Inland Revenue every year from about age 37 onwards to achieve this (assuming an annuity rate of 14 per cent, and that the return the insurance company gets from investing your money equals the rate at which your earnings increase over the years).

But there are various reasons why you'd be unwise to leave joining a scheme as late as this: there may be years when you can afford to pay only a small amount in premiums; you may decide to use some of your premiums qualifying for tax relief to get life insurance or a pension for your dependants; you may need to retire before you're 65 – eg through ill-health; inflation may be very high in the first few years of your retirement. So, unless you are confident you would have substantial income from elsewhere, you should certainly start paying into plans by your early 30s.

If you had earnings which qualified in any of the last six (possibly eight) tax years, and haven't paid into schemes or haven't paid the maximum allowed, you can make payments in respect of those years now and over the next few years – if you can afford it. If you can't, a plan with a loan-back facility (see p169) may enable you to make these payments. See p179 for the detailed tax rules.

If you stop paying

If you think it's likely you may stop paying into a regular-premium plan (perhaps because you have no qualifying earnings in a tax year, or because you find yourself short of cash), you'll want to consider how the insurance company will treat the money you've paid in. Most regular-premium policies normally let you miss one or two payments, but there is likely to be a limit at which the policy has to be made paid-up.

This means that your money remains invested in the fund, and you'll get a pension when you retire (smaller, of course, than if you'd kept paying). Check with the company how they'd work out the pension you'd get.

You can often reinstate a policy within a year or so (maybe longer) of it being made paid-up. With with-profits policies, you'll normally have to pay all the premiums you've missed and, perhaps, a fee as well. But this could be worth doing if the guarantees on your old policy are better than they would be on a new one. Make sure you'll qualify for tax relief on the made-up premiums – see p179.

When you plan to retire

You must start to take the benefits from a policy sometime between your 60th and your 75th birthdays (70th with some policies), unless your job is one that is recognised as having a lower normal retirement age. For example, pilots, seamen and singers can start taking benefits at 55, while female nurses, midwives, deep sea divers and many sportsmen can start at 50. You don't have to have stopped working in order to draw your pension.

If you become too ill to work before the lowest age at which you can retire, you can start taking the benefits then. Of course, the sooner you start taking the benefits the smaller the pension you'll get, because you'll be paying in for a shorter period and drawing out for longer. If your policy hasn't been going for many years, taking the benefits even one year earlier will substantially reduce your pension.

With some policies, you have to say at the outset when you intend to retire, though you can change your mind later. Other policies have a standard retirement age, but you can still retire when you like within the age range allowed. If you don't know when you'll want to retire, but you have to name a date, check with the insurance company that you won't lose out by retiring earlier or later than the date you name.

Phasing your retirement

You may not want to stop work suddenly but would rather slide out gradually over a period of years. If so, you may want to supplement your earnings over this period by drawing a small amount of pension, increasing this year by year until you draw your full pension when you've stopped working altogether. You could do this by having several policies and taking the benefits from each at a different time. Or you could invest with companies which write their policies as a series of separate units, each of which can start paying out at a different time.

If you die before retirement

With most policies, a lump sum will be paid out to your heirs if you die before you've started taking the policy benefits. With some policies you have a choice as to how much will be paid out – for example, return of the premiums you've paid, or return of premiums plus interest on them.

Obviously, the more you want paid out on your death, the less pension you'll get. So it's probably better to get the biggest pension you can and arrange extra life insurance separately (see Box).

Instead of a lump sum, a few companies will alternatively pay out a pension for a dependant – but your dependant may get a better income by getting the lump sum and investing it.

For how these plans can be used to provide for dependants if you die after retirement, see p177.

This book on saving and investing doesn't cover the important subject of how much life insurance you need for your family. For more information, see *Protection-only life insurance, Money Which?* December 1979 p681.

Additional life insurance

If you qualify for a personal pension plan, you also qualify for special protection-only life insurance policies (known as *Section 226A* policies). With these, you get tax relief on the premiums at your highest rate of tax, instead of the normal subsidy of 15 per cent.

However, to get full tax relief, the premiums mustn't come to more than 5 per cent of your *net relevant earnings* (see p178), and these premiums together with your personal pension plan premiums mustn't come to more than $17\frac{1}{2}$ per cent of these earnings.

You don't have to get this life insurance cover from the same companies whose personal pension plans you're paying into – though they may give you a discount. Shop around for the cheapest or get a broker to do so for you.

Checklist for choosing a plan

The Checklist below should help you sort out the features you want when you're choosing a personal pension plan. Refer back to the appropriate bits of this chapter and then fill in your own personal Checklist. You could then take it to an insurance broker and ask him to find a suitable policy (or policies) – see opposite.

Tommy Tucker fills in the Checklist

Tommy is 31 and is a self-employed singer, and has just started thinking about saving up for retirement. He decides to start paying into a regular-premium policy – he feels he needs the discipline of having to pay each year. But this year he feels he can make a one-off payment into a single-premium policy as well. In later years, he may take out further policies. First he fills in the *Checklist* for his regular-premium policy.

Because Tommy wants the pension from this policy to be something he can depend on, not liable to go down in value and not subject to the level of annuity rates when he decides to start drawing the pension, he goes for a with-profits deferred annuity plan. So that he can get the best deal at retirement, he asks for an open-market option (see p167). Tommy can't see that he'll need to borrow large amounts from the company in the future – so he doesn't put a high priority on a loan-back facility. He wants a policy which guarantees at the outset how much pension he'll get for each £1 of regular premiums he pays in over the years. And as he's likely to want to increase the premiums (to help protect his pension from inflation) he wants a policy which will let him do so and guarantee the terms of these additional premiums as well. As Tommy has vague ideas about one day becoming employed as a singing teacher, he wants a policy which will see him right if he has to make it paid-up.

Tommy is a basic rate taxpayer. He sees from page 178 that, with his current level of earnings, he'll qualify for tax relief on about £2,000 of premiums. But for this policy, he doesn't want to commit himself to premiums of more than £1,200 a year – which would cost him £840 after tax relief.

Tommy doesn't know when he wants to retire – so he'll check that he won't lose out by retiring earlier or later than the age he nominates. He thinks it may be useful to be able to stagger taking the benefits on his regular-premium policy, in case he wants to retire over a number of years.

Next Tommy turns to his single-premium policy. He's prepared to take a bit more of a gamble with his one-off payment. He goes for a unit-linked policy which is cash-funded and fancies an equity fund – though he may switch later. This year he reckons he can afford £350 for his single-premium policy (ie £500 before tax relief). Tommy decides that it's not so important to be able to phase his retirement on his single-premium policy. He reckons that once he's 60 he'll keep his eye on the unit price and annuity rates, and draw his pension when either or both are favourable.

Tommy makes a note to check whether his wife Betty would have enough to live on (from his current life insurance, and what she'd get from his personal pension plans) if he should die before retirement. If not, he'll take out more insurance on a *Section 226A policy* – see p173.

Personal Pension Plan Checklist

THE POLICY	Your choices	Tommy's choices	
deferred annuity or cash-funded		deferred annuity with open market option	Cash funded with open-market option
non-profit, with-profits unit-linked or deposit administration		With-profits	Unit-linked equity funded
loan-back facility		not necessarily	not necessarily
single-premium or regular-premium		regular	single
if regular-premium:			
• do you want terms for future premiums guaranteed at outset?		yes	/
• do you want to be able to vary the premiums?		yes	/
• do you need a policy that is flexible if you stop paying?		yes	/
YOUR PREMIUMS			
if single-premium: amount (before tax relief) you'd like to pay in		/	£500
if regular-premium: yearly amount (before tax relief) you can commit yourself to		£1,200	/
RETIREMENT			
age you expect to retire at		don't know	don't know perhaps 60
do you want to be able to phase retirement on one policy?		if possible	no

IF YOU SHOULD DIE BEFORE RETIREMENT
be sure to find out what will be paid out if you die before retirement and consider taking out additional protection-only life insurance

Choosing a policy

There are over 100 different personal pension plans available, and choosing among them isn't easy. If this is going to be your main way of saving for retirement, you're likely to want to invest in several different plans. Use the Checklist opposite to sort out the features you want in each one.

If you want to find out yourself which policies offer which features, ask your library or a bookshop to get hold of the most recent edition of *Self-Employed Pensions* published by Financial Times Business Publishing Ltd. This gives useful comparative details on most plans. So too – though mainly for unit-linked policies – does a quarterly magazine, *The Savings Market* (£4 from Wootten Publications Ltd, 150/152 Caledonian Road, London N1 9RD).

You'll then want to try to find a company which will give you a better-than-average return on your investment. This is relatively easy for non-profit policies – simply get quotes. But for the other types of policy there's no sure way of knowing how each company will perform in the future.

With with-profits policies you could check on what pension you'd get from different companies if their current bonus rates were maintained, and on how they've done in the past (some companies have consistently achieved better-than-average results). The book mentioned above provides these figures in a broadly comparable way.

With unit-linked and deposit administration schemes, the past is little guide to the future – and neither are current growth rates. Companies use widely differing assumptions about future growth in working out estimates of pensions for the future. And the charges they make are worked out in complicated and different ways. It may be best to go for a company which keeps its charges down – though there's no guarantee that it will continue to do so in the future. The book above gives more-or-less comparable figures for the different plans with standard assumptions about future growth – usually, the higher the projected figure, the lower the charges.

If you get a broker to do the work for you, bear in mind that he might be tempted by the high commission paid by some companies – and is unlikely to steer you towards one which pays him no commission. Check with your broker what commission he'd get – he has to tell you if you ask.

It's particularly important to do some homework before you visit a broker. Brush up on your own knowledge of the plans available – it would help if you got brochures of different plans from a handful of companies. And increase your chances of getting good advice by going to more than one broker.

Your choices at retirement

When to retire

As long as you're of an age at which you can start taking the benefits under your plan (normally between 60 and 75 – see p172), you can write to the company at any time and tell them you want to start taking the benefits of the policy.

Shopping around for a higher pension

With nearly all policies, you don't have to take your pension from the company (or companies) you've been saving with. When you retire you can shop around to see if you can get a better deal from another company with the money that's built up for you – called the open-market option. First, you find out the value of your cash fund. If the policy is a deferred annuity, the company will have to work out (using what's called its *commutation* rate) the number of £££ of fund you're allocated for the pension you're entitled to. You then compare the benefits you would have got from this company with the benefits you could get if you switched this amount to another company. If, over the years, you've taken out a number of different personal pension plans, you could transfer them all to the company offering the best package of benefits.

With some companies, the cash fund you can transfer to another company is slightly lower than the one you'd be credited with by your original company.

To choose a company yourself, get an up-to-date copy of one of the magazines below which regularly lists companies' annuity rates:

Planned Savings (£2.50 from Wootten Publications, 150/152 Caledonian Rd, London, N1 9RD) – see *immediate compulsory purchase annuities.*

Money Management (£2.75 by post from Minster House, Arthur St, London EC4R 9AX) – see *substituted contracts* in the *Briefing* section.

Note that things may well have changed since the magazine went to press, so you'll need to check the best rates with the companies – or get a broker to do so. Some brokers subscribe to the Quotel computer system which lists the rates offered by around 40 companies (for a nearby Quotel broker, phone 01-242 0747).

Lump sum

When you retire you can normally choose to have a reduced pension and a tax-free lump sum. You may be glad to have a lump sum to spend at the start of your retirement. Or you could invest the money and draw on it later on. Even if you used the money to buy an immediate annuity you could end up with a higher after-tax income than the pension you'd given up. For more about immediate annuities, see Chapter 16.

Under Inland Revenue rules, the maximum lump sum you can have is three times the biggest remaining pension the company could pay you. Most policies allow the maximum lump sum to be worked out in this way. But some restrict the amount you get to three times the actual pension you're due to get in the first year – so if, say, you chose an increasing pension (see below) which started off at ¾ of the amount of a level pension, your lump sum would be proportionately lower.

Level or increasing pension

The buying-power of a level pension will quickly be eaten away by inflation. You could instead choose a pension which increases each year, but such a pension will, of course, be smaller to start off with. For example, a pension which increases by five per cent compound each year will start off at around ¾ of the amount of a level pension (for a man retiring at 65). Although the increasing pension would catch the level pension up in about six years, it would take 12 years before you'd actually received the same *total* number of £££ in pension. If inflation averaged 5 per cent over your retirement, it would be 14 years before you'd received the same amount in buying-power from the increasing pension; if inflation, averaged 10 per cent it would be 16 years.

A few companies offer pensions which are linked to an index – often the company's Index-linked gilt fund, which is loosely related to the Retail Price Index. But a pension which is increased in line with such an index is likely to start off much lower than a level pension. If it started off at half as much when you retired at 65, it would have to increase by an average of 20% a year if you were to have received the same total buying-power by the time you were 75, or by $12\frac{1}{2}$% a year if you were to have received the same total buying-power by the time you were 80.

With many unit-linked policies you can choose to have your pension unit-linked – so it will go up and down in line with the price of units in the fund. This could be a good idea for part of your pension, but we think you'd be unwise to link too much of your pension in this way, in case the fund hits bad times.

A pension for a dependant after you die

There are two ways you can provide an income for your husband or wife (or other person you name) if you die after you've started drawing the pension. The first way is to choose to have your pension paid as long as you or someone else is alive (called a joint life and survivor annuity). The pension may continue at the same level, or you can normally arrange for the pension to be higher while you are both alive. A joint-life pension (if you're both 65 and the pension stays level) might be around 15 per cent lower than a pension payable on one life only.

Alternatively, you can choose to have your pension paid for a certain period (often five or ten years) whether you live that long or not. As this removes the risk of getting virtually nothing back if you die soon after retirement, the pension you get at age 65 will be around 4 per cent less if it's guaranteed for five years, 10 per cent less if it's guaranteed for ten. Of course, if you died, your dependant would be left with nothing from the plan after the end of the guaranteed period – so don't look on this as adequate protection.

The tax rules

The rules about how much you can pay into personal pension plans each year are complicated. We give the main ones below, and you will find further details in the Inland Revenue's *Notes for Guidance on Retirement Annuity Relief, Finance Act 1980* – you can get a copy from: Enquiry Room, SFO, Lynwood Road, Thames Ditton, Surrey KT7 0DP.

Companies may refuse to accept premiums which are above the Inland Revenue limits. If you do exceed the limits, you won't get tax relief on the excess, and the pension that comes from it will be taxed as investment income rather than earned income. (But if you've exceeded the limits in the past, you may be able to correct this – see *Premiums paid in the past* opposite.)

How much tax relief?

You get tax relief at your highest rate of tax (but *not* including the investment income surcharge) on premiums of up to $17\frac{1}{2}$ per cent of your *net relevant earnings* for that year. Husband and wife each have their own $17\frac{1}{2}$ per cent limit worked out on their own net relevant earnings. See next column for how to work out your net relevant earnings.

People who were born between 1916 and 1933 can, from the 1982–83 tax year, get tax relief on up to 20 per cent of net relevant earnings. And people born before 1916 can normally get tax relief on an even higher proportion of their net relevant earnings – up to a maximum of $32\frac{1}{2}$ per cent if born in 1907. You can check the details with your tax office.

Premiums paid in, say, the 1982–83 tax year will, for tax relief purposes, normally be deducted

from the income that is used to work out your tax bill for that year (see Table). But there are a number of ways in which premiums paid in one year can qualify for tax relief in another year – see opposite.

How to claim your tax relief

When you take out a plan, the insurance company will send you a *Self-Employed Premium Certificate (SEPC)*. Send this to your tax office. Each year, enter the premiums you've paid in your Tax Return, and get *form 43* from the taxman to give details of your payments, and to tell him in which tax year you want them to qualify for tax relief.

Your net relevant earnings

Your net relevant earnings for a tax year will depend on the income used to work out your tax bill for that year. If you're in a job, your tax bill is worked out on a current year basis – ie your tax bill for, say, the 1982–83 tax year is worked out on your pay during that tax year. This normally also applies if you have freelance earnings. But if you're self-employed on a larger scale, and your business has been going for some years, you will be taxed on a preceeding year basis – ie your tax bill for the 1982–83 tax year will be based on the taxable profit your business makes in your accounting year ending in the 1981–82 tax year.

Your taxable profit from being self-employed is your takings (including debts to you) less certain costs you incur and deductions you can make:
- allowable business expenses
- stock relief
- capital allowances – for the cost of machinery and plant (eg car, equipment) used in your business

---

Before the 1980–81 tax year

For tax years earlier than the 1980–81 tax year, the definition of *net relevant earnings* was different. Stock relief was *not* deducted from your profits from being self-employed (but the other deductions in arriving at your taxable profits were). And in arriving at your total net relevant earnings, you had to deduct personal outgoings (such as mortgage interest, alimony) which could not be set off against other income.

For people born after 1915 the maximum premiums on which tax relief was allowed were the lower of 15 per cent of net relevant earnings for the year *or* the £££ limit given below:

Premiums paid in	£££ limit for tax relief
1974–76 tax years	£1,500
1976–77 tax year	£2,250
1977–80 tax years	£3,000

If besides being self-employed, you had a job which provided you with a pension, the £££ limit above was reduced by 15 per cent of your earnings from the other job.

Unused relief from last six years
You can get tax relief on premiums you pay on top of the 17½ per cent allowance a year (up to the whole of your net relevant earnings for the year) if you didn't pay the maximum premiums allowed in any of the previous six tax years. You have to use up the earliest unused relief first.

To work out if you've got any unused relief, use the limits that applied in the relevant tax year – see Box opposite.

Example
Willie Winkie is a self-employed private investigator and (conveniently) has had net relevant earnings of £10,000 each year for the last 10 years or so. He made no payments into a personal pension plan until the 1977–78 tax year – but from then on used up his full quota each year. He has unused relief from the 1976–77 tax year of 15 per cent of £10,000 = £1,500 to carry forward to the 1982–83 tax year.

In the 1982–83 tax year, Willie pays £2,750 into a personal pension plan. This is £1,000 more than his limit for 1982–83 (which is 17½ per cent of £10,000 = £1,750), but he tells the taxman on form 43 that he wants to use £1,000 of his unused relief from 1976–77. This means he'll get tax relief in the 1982–83 tax year on this extra £1,000. He'll lose £1,500 – £1,000 = £500 of unused relief from the 1976–77 tax year (since by the 1983–84 tax year more than six years will have gone by – but see *Looking over your shoulder* in next column).

Unused tax relief from longer ago
If an assessment becomes final for a tax year more than six years ago, you may be able to claim some unused relief from that year. The rules are very complicated – check with your taxman.

Premiums paid in the past
If, before 6 April 1980, you paid more in premiums than the *per cent* limit for a tax year, you could be allowed tax relief on these extra premiums (up to the £££ limit for that tax year) in your tax bill for either the 1980–81 or 1981–82 tax years – but not later – irrespective of your other payments. If this applies to you, check whether you've been given the tax relief in one of those years.

Example
Mrs Hubbard runs a boarding kennels, and pays £1,500 a year in premiums for a regular-premium policy. Her net relevant earnings for 1979–80 were £8,000, so she got tax relief on only 15 per cent of £8,000 = £1,200. But she gets tax relief on the extra £300 in her tax bill for the 1981–82 tax year.

Looking over your shoulder
You can ask in any tax year to have all or part of the premiums you pay in that year treated as if you'd paid them in the previous tax year. And, if you didn't have *any* net relevant earnings in the previous tax year, you'll be able to get the premiums treated as if you'd paid them in the year before that.

This means that if you can't afford to make payments this year to use up all the tax relief available to you, you may be able to catch up next year.

Example
Willie Winkie (see previous column) will – unless he does something – lose £500 of unused relief from the 1976–77 tax year. He can ask for £500 of premiums paid in the 1983–84 tax year to count as being paid in the 1982–83 tax year, and so use up this £500 of unused relief.

● **losses** – any business losses from earlier years which haven't been set off against other income.

For more details, see the section on *Tax for the self-employed* in the most recent *Money Which? Tax-Saving Guide*.

The Table below shows you what your net relevant earnings are for the 1982–83 tax year (see Box opposite for earlier tax years).

Example
Jack Horner is a self-employed baker. In his accounting year which ended on 31 December 1981 (ie in the 1981–82 tax year), his taxable profits were £5,400.

Jack also has a part-time job lecturing on pie-making. There's no pension with this job. In the 1982–83 tax year he earned £1,300 in this way. So Jack's total net relevant earnings for the 1982–83 tax year are £5,400 + £1,300 = £6,700. He can get tax relief on up to 17½% of £6,700 = £1,172.50 in premiums for his personal pension plan in the 1982–83 tax year.

	income taxed on	net relevant earnings for 1982–83 tax year
if you're in a job but not in an employer's pension scheme	current year basis	pay from that job in 1982–83 tax year
if you have freelance earnings [1]	current year basis	taxable profits in 1982–83 tax year
if you're self-employed	preceding year basis [2]	taxable profits [3] in accounting year ending in 1981–82 tax year

[1] If a substantial part of your income comes from freelance work, you may be taxed on a preceding year basis as if you were self-employed.
[2] In the first two and last three years of a business, there are special rules about what income your tax is based on – see *Tax-Saving Guide Money Which?* March 1982 p182.
[3] If your business makes certain payments (eg patent royalties, covenant payments, annuities), they must be deducted from your taxable profits when working out your net relevant earnings.

19 Building society investments

Over the last ten years or so, building societies have become the most popular places for people's savings. Over 20 million people have over £50,000 million invested in them. Building societies receive money – often quite small amounts – from people with spare cash, and lend it (usually in large amounts) to people who want to buy their own homes. But around 20 per cent of the money societies receive is put into investments which can be cashed in more quickly (like British Government stock) so that societies can meet large numbers of withdrawals if they need to.

With most building society accounts, when you invest you become a shareholder and a member. This gives you a right to receive the society's annual report and accounts, attend its annual general meeting and vote for its directors.

The investments they offer

In practice, most building societies offer much the same range of investment schemes. The scheme that will suit you best will depend on whether you want to invest a lump sum for a few years, save regularly (each month, say), or be able to pay in and withdraw bits and bobs whenever you want to. We tell you about the types of account under these three broad categories on pages 182 to 186. The Checklist opposite will point you towards types of building society account which may suit your needs – and will also remind you of some other investments to consider.

The interest you get

Apart from occasional fixed-interest investments, all building society investments have variable interest rates – ie they're likely to be changed from time to time. The interest rate for ordinary shares is recommended by The Building Societies Association, a trade association for the societies. Most of the largest societies follow this recommendation but many smaller building societies offer $\frac{1}{2}$ per cent or 1 per cent or so more.

Most societies offer a spread of interest rates through their different types of account – in general, the more you invest and the longer you are willing to tie your money up for, the higher the interest rate. The differential between one account and another (eg between ordinary shares and term shares) is generally fixed, so that when a society does change its interest rates, the rates on all its accounts normally go up or down by the same amount. On pages 182 to 186, for each type of account we give the extra you could expect over the ordinary share rate.

All interest from building societies is free of tax to a basic rate taxpayer, but if you pay tax at higher rates or the investment income surcharge you'll have to pay extra tax on the interest you get. If you don't pay tax you can't reclaim any of the tax which the building society has paid – so you'd most probably get a higher return elsewhere. For more on tax see p45.

CHECKLIST: will a building society account suit you?

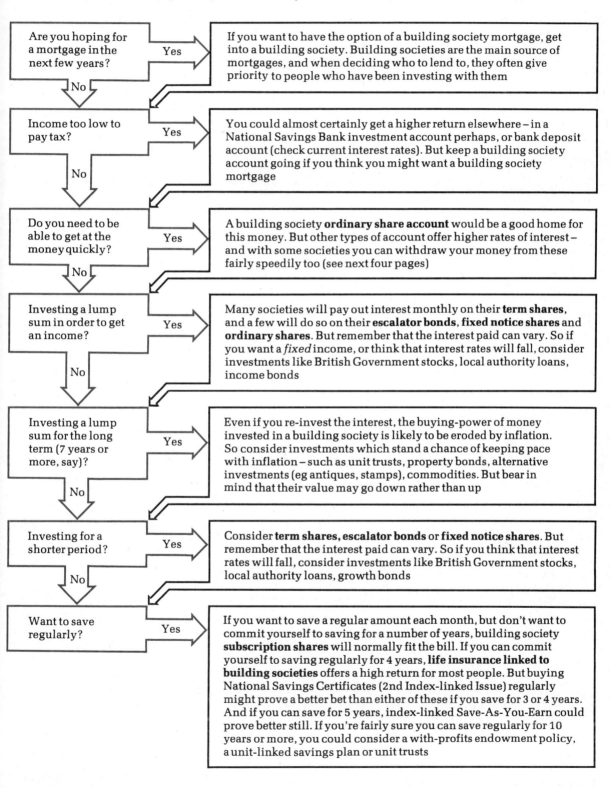

Are you hoping for a mortgage in the next few years? — Yes → If you want to have the option of a building society mortgage, get into a building society. Building societies are the main source of mortgages, and when deciding who to lend to, they often give priority to people who have been investing with them

No ↓

Income too low to pay tax? — Yes → You could almost certainly get a higher return elsewhere – in a National Savings Bank investment account perhaps, or bank deposit account (check current interest rates). But keep a building society account going if you think you might want a building society mortgage

No ↓

Do you need to be able to get at the money quickly? — Yes → A building society **ordinary share account** would be a good home for this money. But other types of account offer higher rates of interest – and with some societies you can withdraw your money from these fairly speedily too (see next four pages)

No ↓

Investing a lump sum in order to get an income? — Yes → Many societies will pay out interest monthly on their **term shares**, and a few will do so on their **escalator bonds**, **fixed notice shares** and **ordinary shares**. But remember that the interest paid can vary. So if you want a *fixed* income, or think that interest rates will fall, consider investments like British Government stocks, local authority loans, income bonds

No ↓

Investing a lump sum for the long term (7 years or more, say)? — Yes → Even if you re-invest the interest, the buying-power of money invested in a building society is likely to be eroded by inflation. So consider investments which stand a chance of keeping pace with inflation – such as unit trusts, property bonds, alternative investments (eg antiques, stamps), commodities. But bear in mind that their value may go down rather than up

No ↓

Investing for a shorter period? — Yes → Consider **term shares, escalator bonds** or **fixed notice shares**. But remember that the interest paid can vary. So if you think that interest rates will fall, consider investments like British Government stocks, local authority loans, growth bonds

No ↓

Want to save regularly? — Yes → If you want to save a regular amount each month, but don't want to commit yourself to saving for a number of years, building society **subscription shares** will normally fit the bill. If you can commit yourself to saving regularly for 4 years, **life insurance linked to building societies** offers a high return for most people. But buying National Savings Certificates (2nd Index-linked Issue) regularly might prove a better bet than either of these if you save for 3 or 4 years. And if you can save for 5 years, index-linked Save-As-You-Earn could prove better still. If you're fairly sure you can save regularly for 10 years or more, you could consider a with-profits endowment policy, a unit-linked savings plan or unit trusts

For lump sums

Term shares

Typical interest rates:

if you invest for	extra over ordinary share rate
2 years	+½%
3 years	+1%
4 years	+1½%
5 years	+2%

Notice of withdrawal:
Can't normally withdraw before end of term

Most societies offer term shares under a variety of names – such as *Capital Bonds, High Income Bonds, High Yield Shares.* You invest a lump sum for a fixed period – usually between one and five years. The longer the term, the higher the rate of interest. The minimum investment varies between societies – but is often £500 or £1,000.

With most societies none of the money can be withdrawn early (unless you die), so don't invest for longer than you're sure you want to tie your money up for. Some societies will, however, allow withdrawals in cases of hardship or genuine unforeseen need, and a few will let you withdraw for any reason. If you do, you normally have to give between one and six months' notice of withdrawal, and you may only get the ordinary share rate on what you withdraw.

When the term comes to an end, you normally have to close the account. But some societies are now offering *open-ended term shares.* With these, when the original term ends, you can leave your money invested indefinitely, usually at three month's notice – in which case it earns a higher rate of interest each year until it hits the highest rate being paid on the society's term shares. For example, if the original term is three years, you will get the 3-year interest rate for those three years, the 4-year rate in the fourth year, and the 5-year rate thereafter.

Verdict

Term shares are worth considering if you are happy to tie your money up for the necessary period. If it's possible that you'll want to leave it in for longer, go for open-ended term shares. And if you think you may want to withdraw your money early, choose a society which will let you (or choose another type of account).

How much you can invest

You aren't allowed to invest more than £20,000 in any one building society (though you can have up to £40,000 in a joint account – with your husband or wife, for example). This £20,000 covers all the money you have invested with the society, except in Save-As-You-Earn and life insurance linked schemes. But you can, if you wish, have up to £20,000 invested with each of any number of building societies.

Getting a monthly income

Building societies normally pay interest out (or add it to your account) half-yearly or yearly. But many societies will pay out interest monthly on ordinary shares or term shares – and some societies offer monthly income on open-ended term shares, escalator bonds and fixed notice shares too. A list of these schemes is in *Building Societies Gazette* (see p187). There may be a higher-than-normal minimum investment.

Tip: How to boost your interest rate

If you decide to invest a lump sum in a building society, and don't want to have the interest paid out to you, you may be able to get a higher overall return than simply having the interest compounded by asking for it to be paid monthly into a regular savings scheme such as subscription shares or life insurance linked to building societies. A few societies have formal schemes to do just this.

Fixed Notice shares

Typical interest rate: ½% to 1½% more than ordinary share rate

Notice of withdrawal: normally 1, 3 or 6 months

A fair number of societies offer fixed notice shares under names like *Extra Interest Accounts, Shares at Notice, Premium Shares.* You invest a lump sum – the minimum is often £500 to £2,000 – and you can add to this at any time. You have to give a fixed period of notice to withdraw – usually one, three or six months – in return for which you get a rate of interest higher than the rate paid on ordinary shares. If a withdrawal leaves less than the minimum amount in your account, it will probably be transferred to an ordinary share account.

A few societies ask for only one month's notice and some will let you withdraw without notice – but you normally lose some interest on money you withdraw.

Verdict

Interest is likely to be about the same as 2- or 3-year term shares, and your money isn't tied up for nearly so long – so generally a better bet. But if you think it's likely your money will be invested for several years, consider an open-ended term share or an escalator bond instead.

Escalator bonds

Typical average yearly returns

money kept in for	extra over ordinary share rate
1 year	+¾%
2 years	+1%
3 years	+1¼%
4 years	+1½%
5 years	+1¾%

Notice of withdrawal: varies

Escalator bonds are offered by a number of societies under names such as *Bonus Shares, Build-up Bonds, Progressive Interest Shares.* You invest a lump sum, normally a minimum of £500 or £1,000. If you withdraw it in less than a year, you normally get the society's ordinary share interest rate. But for each complete year you leave the money invested, you normally get additional interest. And the additional interest increases each year. For example, you might get ½% more for the first complete year, 1% more in the second, 1½% more in the third, 2% more in the fourth and 3% more in the fifth (but not all the schemes last five years). Obviously, the average return over the period is between the interest rate you get in the first year and the rate in the final year – see typical yearly returns on the left. At the end of the scheme your bond is normally repaid to you – though you may be able to leave your money invested at a higher-than-normal rate of interest.

With some societies you can withdraw your money only at the end of each complete year. With others, you can withdraw it at any time. In either case you may have to give up to three months' notice. If the scheme allows you to withdraw part of your money you must leave at least the minimum investment in your account.

Verdict

The best of these schemes offer yearly rates of return which are around the same as some of the best rates available on term shares – and you don't have to tie your money up for a long time.

Fixed interest schemes

Now and again some societies offer a scheme where the interest rate is fixed for a period (often one year). There is usually a minimum investment of perhaps £500 or £1,000, and there may be other restrictions. These schemes may be worth considering if you think interest rates are going to fall within the term of the investment.

For regular savings

Subscription shares

Typical interest rate: 1¼% more
than ordinary share rate

Notice of withdrawal: immediate
to one month

Most societies offer subscription shares, under names such as
Monthly Savings Plan, Regular Savings Shares. You agree to pay a
fixed amount each month – the minimum is often £1 a month,
maximum often £100. Although the rate of interest paid is higher
than the rate paid on an ordinary share account, most societies add
interest only once a year with subscription shares, twice with most
other investments. So the 'true' difference between the rates paid
on subscription shares and ordinary shares is more like 1%. See
p15 for more details. And with some societies, you get the extra
interest only if you keep up your payments for two or three years.

If you want to withdraw all your money, the notice you need to
give is usually the same as for an ordinary share account – see p186.
Some societies will let you withdraw part of your money once or
twice each year and keep the account going; with others, what's left
is automatically transferred to an ordinary share account.

Some societies will let you vary the amount of your regular
payments within certain limits. If you want to stop making your
payments (but not withdraw your savings) the money is normally
transferred to an ordinary share account.

With a few societies there's a limit – often several thousand £££ –
on the amount you can save in subscription shares. When you hit
the limit, your money is transferred to an ordinary share account.

Verdict

Worth collecting the extra interest if you can save regularly but
don't want to commit yourself to doing so for four or five years.

Life insurance linked to building societies

Return: varies according to your
age, levels of interest rates and how
long you save for

Notice of withdrawal: normally
around two weeks

These schemes are run by building societies in conjunction with
insurance companies under a variety of names – eg *Masterplan,
Top Ten Policy, Extra Growth Bonds.*

You take out a life insurance policy for which you pay regular
premiums. The government subsidy on life insurance premiums
(see p51) means that for every £85 of premiums you pay, the
taxman hands over another £15 to the insurance company. Out of
this £100, the company deducts, say, £5 to pay for your life
insurance and cover its expenses, and it invests the rest in a
building society. So you can get £95 invested for you at a cost to you
of only £85. This means that your return can be comparatively high
even though the interest rate paid by the building society is
generally lower than is paid on ordinary shares. For example, over
the four-year period from November 1977 to November 1981, one
life insurance-linked scheme gave a yearly return of 13.2 per cent,
compared with an overall yearly return of 10.3 per cent on the
larger societies' subscription shares. And you get some life
insurance cover – normally between 100 and 180 times your
monthly premium.

A policy normally lasts 10 years, though you can cash it in whenever you want to. You get the best return by cashing in after exactly four years (after paying the fifth premium, if you pay premiums yearly). If you cash in within the first four years, the return is lower because the taxman will take back some of the subsidy you've had (see p52). And if you wait longer than four years to cash in, the return falls because you're getting the subsidy only on your new premiums each year – and these form an ever-decreasing proportion of the total amount invested.

The return you get is tax-free, unless you pay tax at higher rates or the investment income surcharge and cash in the policy within its first $7\frac{1}{2}$ years (see p49). Even then, the extra tax is likely to reduce the return by only a small amount (1%, say).

The returns quoted for life insurance-linked schemes vary considerably, and it is worth choosing a scheme carefully – though remember that the returns quoted are only estimates and a company with a lower estimate could end up paying out more when the policy is cashed in. The return you get will be lower the older or less healthy you are, and lower for a man than for a woman of the same age – because the insurance company will deduct more for his life insurance cover.

Note that savings under life insurance linked to building societies don't qualify under the *Homeloan* scheme (see p69) aimed at providing those buying their first home with a grant and interest-free loan.

Verdict

The best schemes offer a high return for the under 60s in good health who can save regularly for four years.

Building Society Save-As-You-Earn (SAYE)

Return: fixed at 8.3% a year tax-free if you save regularly for five years, 8.6% if you leave savings invested for a further two years.

Notice of withdrawal: immediate

This scheme is exactly the same with all building societies. Note that it offers a fixed return, and is quite different from the National Savings Save-As-You-Earn scheme which is index-linked (see p196).

You can join the SAYE scheme of only one building society. You agree to make regular monthly payments of between £1 and £20. If you go on saving for five years, you get a tax-free bonus equal to 14 months' savings at the end. If you leave your money and this bonus invested for a further two years, you get a further tax-free bonus also equal to 14 months' savings when your investment is repaid to you.

You can stop making your payments and withdraw your money at any time. But if you stop in the first year, you get no interest at all. Any time after the first year you get interest of six per cent a year on your savings (eight per cent if the reason for stopping is the saver's death).

Verdict

In the past, the fixed return on building society SAYE has at times been higher than the interest rate paid on subscription shares, and at other times lower. Which is a better bet depends on what you think is going to happen to interest rates in the future – though higher-rate taxpayers have more to gain from SAYE. However, the return on National Savings index-linked SAYE or life insurance linked to building societies might be still higher.

For any spare money

Ordinary shares

Notice of withdrawal: immediate
to one month

Ordinary share accounts (also called *Shares* or *Paid-up Shares*) are
the basic accounts offered by all societies. You can pay into them
and withdraw money with few restrictions.

The minimum investment is often £1. Most building societies'
rules give them the right to insist on a month's notice for
withdrawals, but, in practice, you can normally get up to £250 or
so in cash or up to £2,000 by cheque on the spot. For larger
amounts societies may need a few days' notice. And you can't
normally withdraw money you paid in by cheque for 10 or 14 days.

In some ways you may be able to use a building society ordinary
share account much like a bank account. You may be able to have
your salary or pension paid into it direct. Most societies will make
cheques payable to other people (but be careful – you can't stop
such a cheque), and societies will even agree to pay out regular
amounts to particular people. However, one or two societies will
pay you less interest if the average amount in your account is low
and you make a lot of withdrawals, while a few other societies will
pay you more than the normal rate of interest if you keep a lot of
money in your account.

Verdict

A good home for your emergency fund – so long as you are a
taxpayer. And a flexible way of saving and spending.

Deposit Account

Typical interest rate: ¼% less than
ordinary share rate

Notice of withdrawal: immediate
to one month

A deposit account works like an ordinary share account. But
instead of becoming a member of the society you lend money to it.
Your money is extra safe – because if the society runs into
financial trouble, you're guaranteed that all your money will be
returned to you (whereas only 75% or 90% is guaranteed with
share accounts – see p188).

Verdict

It's extremely unlikely that your society will need bailing out – so
going for a deposit account probably isn't worth the slight loss of
interest.

Choosing a building society

With over 250 building societies, choosing which to save with can be bewildering. Before deciding which building society to invest with you should take the things listed below into account.

Rate of return Smaller societies tend to offer interest rates ½ per cent or 1 per cent or so higher than most of the larger societies. But these higher rates may not make a big difference to the amount of interest you get in £££. For example, 1% extra interest on £1,000 invested for a year will normally give you an extra £10.50. Or if you were saving £20 a month in subscription shares, an extra 1 per cent interest would give you an extra £1.30 in the first year.

One complication is that the rates quoted by societies are only 'true' rates if interest is paid out to you (or credited to your account) only once a year. Most societies pay interest yearly on subscription shares, but half-yearly on other accounts. The more often interest is paid, the sooner you get it, so the more it's worth to you – and the 'true' interest rate is higher. See p15 for more details. Take this into account when comparing small differences in the rates quoted by different societies.

Information on the savings scheme and interest rates currently offered by a large number of societies is published monthly in the *Building Societies Gazette* (£1.26 from 2 Burgon Street, London EC4 5DP). The financial pages in newspapers also give comparative information from time to time.

Convenience If you plan to open an ordinary share account and use it much like a bank account (but with the advantage of longer opening hours, including Saturday mornings) you will want a branch close to your home or place of work (or both). So shop around among the societies that are close by. If on the other hand you're happy to deal by post, you might consider one of the over-the-odds societies or a society offering a special scheme which suits your needs.

Hoping for a mortgage? When it comes to handing out mortgages, building societies usually give priority to people who have been investing with them for a time (often 2 years). If you want to keep open the option of getting a building society mortgage, you should be particularly careful in your choice of society. Before you pick a society, check with the branch manager that the society's lending policy will suit you – see the Checklist on p69. First-time buyers should also check that their savings will qualify under the *Homeloan* scheme (see p69). Beware of over-the-odds societies – they often charge over-the-odds for mortgages too.

One or two societies have special schemes in which you are guaranteed a mortgage if you fulfill certain saving conditions.

Safety   Building societies vary enormously in size. While the largest has assets of over £10,000 million, the assets of the smallest are under £1 million. A small society may have problems which a large society doesn't have to face. For example, it's more likely to get into difficulties if there's a sudden rush by investors to withdraw money – after the closure of a big local factory, for example. And its health may depend on the judgement and honesty of just one or two people who make all the decisions.

The few societies which have run into difficulties in recent years have generally been very small, but there are safeguards to try to prevent this happening, and protection if it does. All building societies must be registered with the *Chief Registrar of Friendly Societies*, who keeps an eye on how each society operates, and can temporarily stop a society advertising and stop it accepting money. He can even – as a last resort – get a building society wound up.

If a society does get into financial trouble, there is now a scheme run by The Building Societies Association to protect your money. The scheme covers all building societies – whether or not they belong to the Association. It guarantees to refund 100 per cent of any money in a **deposit account**. For **share accounts**, the amount guaranteed depends on whether your society is a contributing member of the scheme. If it is, you're guaranteed 90 per cent of your money; if it's not, you're guaranteed 75 per cent.

There are two features which should make for extra safety in a society:
● the society having *trustee status*. To qualify for this, a society has to meet certain financial requirements laid down by the government, and satisfy the Chief Registrar that it is a suitable home for the investment of trust funds
● the society being a contributing member of the protection scheme.

It would be sensible to stick to societies which qualify on both these counts (most do). As larger societies are less likely to run into difficulties than smaller ones, you may think it worth restricting your choice to them. And if you shop around amongst them you may find you lose very little interest by doing so.

20 Bank and finance company deposits

If you're looking for a way of investing your money so that its value in £££ can't fall, one investment to consider is a bank or finance company deposit account. A number of other companies which are not necessarily regarded as finance companies can also take deposits from the public as long as they're licensed by the Bank of England to do so – see Box overleaf.

Interest is paid on your money and the rate may be fixed when you invest or it may vary depending on the type of account you choose. In lots of ways, these deposit accounts are very similar to the range of accounts offered by building societies and are in most cases a better bet if you don't pay tax. However, if you do pay tax, you're likely to find you could get a better return elsewhere. Keep an eye on how the rates compare. *Money facts* in *Money Which?* can help and the financial pages of daily newspapers can keep you up-to-date.

Banks

Deposit accounts All the High-street banks offer deposit accounts in which you can save small sums – often a minumum of £1. You don't have to have a current account at the bank to open a deposit account. When you invest, you'll be given an account number, and a paying-in book. You can withdraw money at the branch of the bank which has your account, or you can arrange for the money to be transferred to your current account, or you may be able to go to another branch if you make special arrangements. You don't get a cheque book.

In theory, with most of these accounts you have to give seven days' notice if you want to get your money out. In practice, the banks will pay out on the spot, but will deduct seven days' interest.

Interest is usually added to your account twice a year – though it may be worked out every day. With Scottish banks, the interest is worked out on the minimum amount you have in the account during each month. The interest is taxable, although it's paid without deduction of tax. See p47 for details of how this type of interest is taxed. The rate of interest which is added to your money will vary with interest rates in general. You can invest as much money as you like for as long as you like – but it's best to use a bank deposit account as a home for an emergency fund and a temporary home for other money.

With the deposit accounts of some Scottish banks, you can make payments by direct debit or standing order. And with one Scottish bank, you get a cash dispenser card so you can withdraw cash from a machine.

Other bank investments

Nearly all the banks have other ways in which you can invest your money. There are four main types – not every High-Street bank offers them all. Note that if you've got a large lump sum, say £10,000 or £25,000, you may be able to arrange some sort of special deal with a bank – so ask around.

Regular savings schemes

Some of these are fairly similar to ordinary deposit accounts. Others are linked to the promise of being able to borrow money from the bank after a certain period of saving – eg guaranteeing or giving priority in getting a mortgage or getting a personal loan at a lower-than-normal rate of interest. There's usually a minimum amount you have to save (£10 a month, say) and you have to save for a certain time (1 year, say) to get a higher rate of interest than on a straightforward deposit account. With some schemes, you can withdraw part of the money during the year; with others you have to leave it untouched for a whole year. The rate of interest added could be, for example, 1% or 2% higher than the deposit account rate.

Fixed term; fixed rate of interest

You lock your money away for between one month and five years at a fixed rate of interest – you can't withdraw any of your money within the period you've agreed.

If you agree to invest for a fixed period you would normally expect that the longer the period you agreed to invest for, the higher the rate of interest you would get. This doesn't always happen. If the banks think interest rates will fall, you might get a lower rate of interest the longer you invest for.

With some schemes, the rate of interest offered for the period is closely linked to what's happening in the money market and so the rate of interest offered can change every day – check carefully before you invest. And ask all the banks offering this type of account – rates of interest vary from bank to bank. The minimum deposit ranges from £1,000 to £10,000.

Fixed notice of withdrawal

You invest a lump sum and have to give an agreed period of notice before you can withdraw your money. The period of notice varies from scheme to scheme – say 1, 3 or 6 months. These schemes offer a higher rate of interest than a deposit account – $\frac{3}{4}$% more, say. Rates can vary. Minimum investments range from £1,000 to £10,000.

Fixed term; variable rate of interest

If you've got a lump sum to invest (minimums range from £500 to £2,500) and you can invest for an agreed period of time, you can get a higher rate of interest than on a deposit account. The rate will vary during the period. The periods offered vary from scheme to scheme – can be as short as 6 months or as long as 7 years. Usually the rate of interest is guaranteed to be a certain per cent higher than the deposit account rate (or equivalent), or lower than the base rate – eg $1\frac{1}{4}$% higher than deposit account for a six-month period, $\frac{1}{4}$% below base rate for a four-year period.

Finance company (and other company) deposits

To be allowed to take deposits from the public, a company must be licensed as a bank or as a deposit-taking institution – see Box. The rates offered by different licensed deposit-takers vary, so check as many companies as you can before investing. As with banks, the interest is added twice yearly. The interest is taxable, although in most cases it is paid without tax being deducted. See p47 for details of how this type of interest is taxed.

These investments are, in general, for people with lump sums to invest and there are two main types (see below). A few deposit-taking institutions also offer other forms of accounts – for example, savings schemes, money funds (where the fund is managed and invested in the money market).

Fixed term; fixed rate of interest

You agree to invest for a certain period – say 1, 2 or 3 years, but could be only weeks or could be up to 10 years. In return, you get a fixed rate of interest. Normally you would expect that the longer you agree to invest for, the higher the rate of interest you'll get added or paid. But this may not always be so. If the company thinks interest rates will fall, you might find the longer you invest the lower the rate of interest added or paid.

Interest is usually added twice a year and you can often choose to have the interest paid out to you if you want. With a few accounts, interest can be added once a month or paid out to you as an income. Minimum investments needed for this sort of account range from £100 to £5,000. There's often a maximum too, say £25,000 or £50,000. You can't normally get your money out until the end of the period you agreed, although a few companies allow you to get out a small amount each year.

Fixed notice of withdrawal

You invest your money and agree to give a certain period of notice to withdraw it – 1, 3 or 6 months, or a year, say. If you choose this sort of account, the interest rate paid on it will normally vary with interest rates in general. The minimum amount you have to invest is around £100, but can be as high as £5,000 or as low as £1.

A bank versus a deposit-taking institution

Organisations which can take deposits from the public are divided into two groups
● a recognised bank
● a licensed deposit-taking institution (LDTI).

An LDTI is licensed by the Bank of England and is not allowed to call itself a bank – though there are certain exceptions for foreign companies. It has to meet certain conditions to get a licence but these are different from those required to be recognised as a bank. Only LDTIs and banks are allowed to advertise for, and accept deposits.

The Banking Act 1979, which set up the licensing system, also provided for a deposit protection fund to be set up. The fund will pay out 75 per cent of the first £10,000 in your account if your LDTI or bank goes bust.

Note that not all organisations are covered by these particular rules – for example, the National Savings Bank, and local authorities, among others, are excluded. And insurance companies and building societies are regulated in different ways.

Verdict If you're looking for a home for your emergency fund, you could consider a bank deposit account – particularly if you're a non-taxpayer. But check up on interest rates offered by other suitable alternatives. Taxpayers will generally do better with, say, a building society account, and non-taxpayers may find a National Savings Bank investment account offers them a better rate of return (though you have to give one month's notice to withdraw your money and you get interest only on money that is in your account for complete calender months). Keep a check on the variations being offered by banks and finance companies to see if there's a scheme which suits your needs and offers you a good rate of return.

21 Index-linked investments

This chapter tells you about two National Savings investments which guarantee that the buying-power of the money you invest will keep pace with rising prices.

One of them – National Savings Certificates (2nd Index-linked Issue) became available to people of all ages on 7 September 1981. Before that date, these certificates were available only to people aged 50 or over, and replaced the Retirement Issue (known popularly as Granny bonds because, when first issued, they were available only to people of retirement age). The other investment – index-linked Save-As-You-Earn – is suitable only for people who are able to invest a regular amount each month for five years.

For index-linked British Government stocks, see Chapter 10.

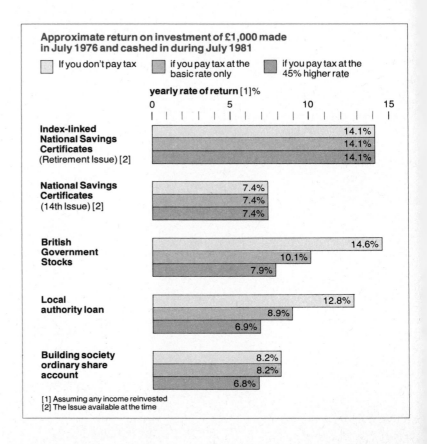

Approximate return on investment of £1,000 made in July 1976 and cashed in during July 1981

- If you don't pay tax
- if you pay tax at the basic rate only
- if you pay tax at the 45% higher rate

yearly rate of return [1]%

Index-linked National Savings Certificates (Retirement Issue) [2]	14.1% / 14.1% / 14.1%	
National Savings Certificates (14th Issue) [2]	7.4% / 7.4% / 7.4%	
British Government Stocks	14.6% / 10.1% / 7.9%	
Local authority loan	12.8% / 8.9% / 6.9%	
Building society ordinary share account	8.2% / 8.2% / 6.8%	

[1] Assuming any income reinvested
[2] The Issue available at the time

**Should you
invest in them?**
The Diagrams on this page and opposite will give you an idea of the
returns on these index-linked investments over the last five years.
They also show the returns on a number of other investments over
the same period. Note that we've given the return for the
Retirement Issue of National Savings Certificates, as this was the
one available in 1976.

You can see that, in the main, the index-linked investments
would have given higher returns than the alternatives.

Of course, there's no guarantee that what has been true in the past
will continue to be true in the future. But unless you are confident
that the rate of inflation is going to fall substantially (and stay that
way), or you expect after-tax rates of return on other investments to
exceed the rate of inflation, it makes sense to consider putting some
of your savings into these index-linked investments.

Note however, that to benefit from index-linking you have to
lock your money away for at least five years with SAYE, for at least
a year with the National Savings Certificates.

You may be tempted by index-linked British Government stocks
as an alternative to investing a lump sum in index-linked National
Savings Certificates. For more about this investment and the pros
and cons of taking this course, see p107. But for many people,
sticking to index-linked National Savings Certificates may be the
best course. You could, of course, consider putting some of your
money into each of these investments.

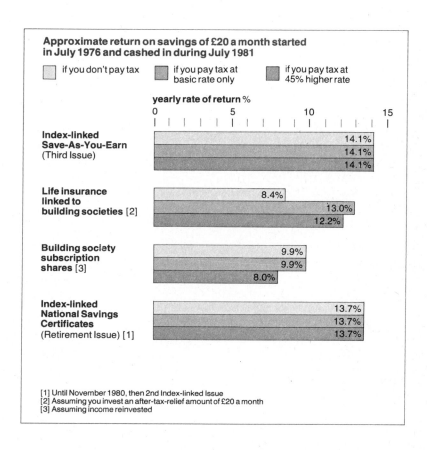

Approximate return on savings of £20 a month started
in July 1976 and cashed in during July 1981

☐ if you don't pay tax   ▨ if you pay tax at basic rate only   ▨ if you pay tax at 45% higher rate

yearly rate of return %

0   5   10   15

**Index-linked
Save-As-You-Earn**
(Third Issue)
— 14.1%
— 14.1%
— 14.1%

**Life insurance
linked to
building societies** [2]
— 8.4%
— 13.0%
— 12.2%

**Building society
subscription
shares** [3]
— 9.9%
— 9.9%
— 8.0%

**Index-linked
National Savings
Certificates**
(Retirement Issue) [1]
— 13.7%
— 13.7%
— 13.7%

[1] Until November 1980, then 2nd Index-linked Issue
[2] Assuming you invest an after-tax-relief amount of £20 a month
[3] Assuming income reinvested

National Savings Certificates
(2nd Index-linked Issue)

Who can invest?

Anyone, irrespective of age.

How much can you invest?

Anything between £10 and £5,000, in units of £10. A husband and wife can invest up to £5,000 each (ie up to £10,000 in all). If the certificates are in their joint names, however, they can invest only £5,000 between them. This investment is suitable for lump sums or savings (regular or a bit at a time). In some ways, it is more flexible for savings than index-linked SAYE (see p196).

How to invest

Go to a post office. If you're buying National Savings Certificates for the first time, you'll be asked to sign a holder's card and given a Certificate book with the certificates you've bought in it. If you already hold certificates, the new ones will be put into your book.

How index-linked certificates work

You can hold each certificate for up to to five years. If you cash it in within a year of buying it, you get back only the money you invested in the first place. But after a year, its value is increased in line with the change in the retail price index since you bought it. The certificate then continues to be revalued each month. And you get this increased value back if you cash it in. See example below.

At the end of five years a bonus which won't be less than four per cent of the original value of the certificate is paid. It may be more than four per cent if the Government feels at the time that more has to be offered to compete with other investments.

Which month's index applies when you buy a certificate?

The one announced in the second or third week of the previous month. And this, in turn, refers to the cost of living in the month before that. So in our example below of a certificate bought in July 1976, the index which applied when the certificate was bought was the one announced in June 1976 – ie the index for May 1976.

Which month's index applies when you cash in a certificate?

Again, the index announced in the previous month. In our example, you can see that the index which applied to a certificate cashed in July 1981 was 294.1. This was the index for May 1981.

Example: certificate bought for £100 on 15 July 1976

	retail price index which applies	increase in index over level which applied in July 1976	value of certificate	increase in value of certificate since July 1976
15 July 1976	155.2	—	£100	—
14 July 1977	155.2	—	£100	—
15 July 1977	181.7	up 17.07%	£117.07	up 17.07%
1 Aug 1977	183.6	up 18.30%	£118.30	up 18.30%
1 Jan 1978	187.4	up 20.75%	£120.75	up 20.75%
1 July 1978	195.7	up 26.10%	£126.10	up 26.10%
14 July 1981	294.1	up 89.50%	£189.50	up 89.50%
15 July 1981	294.1	up 89.50%	£193.50 [1]	up 93.50% [1]

[1] Including 4 per cent bonus

Example

Albert Hall bought a certificate in July 1976 for £500. The index which applied to his purchase was 155.2. In January 1978 he worked out how much he'd get if he cashed it in. The index which applied at the time was the one for November 1977 (announced in December). This was 187.4. So Albert worked out that his certificate was then worth:
£500 × 187.4 ÷ 155.2 = £603.74

Should Albert cash in his £103.74 gain?

Not unless he needs the money. The gain itself will be index-linked. So if, for example, the retail price index increases by a further 10 per cent, the value of Albert's certificate will also increase by 10 per cent – from £603.74 to £664.11.

Where to find the retail price index

The level of the retail price index for the previous month is announced on the second or third Friday of each month – and reported in the newspapers the following day. Some of them only report the rate of inflation – but the Financial Times normally prints the level of the index, too. When using a particular month's index, bear in mind that it applies to an investment made two months later – see the four questions beginning *Which month's index applies* . . . on pages 194 and 196.

Working out how much you'd get if you cashed in now

As long as you have held the certificate for at least a year, do the following sum:

original value × index which applies ÷ index which applied
of certificate   when you cash in   when you bought
                         certificate   certificate

If you're cashing in the certificate on its fifth anniversary, you have to add on the bonus you get (four per cent, or more if a larger bonus has been announced).

Alternatively, you can work out how much your certificate is now worth from a chart headed *Repayment Value*, which should be on display at post offices.

Should you cash in any old Retirement Issue certificates you've got?

You don't have to. You can keep it where it is, and your investment (including the four per cent bonus you'd have got if you'd had your money invested for five years) will continue to be index-linked. Alternatively, you could follow the Route Map on p18 to check on other investments to consider. Note that you can put up to £5,000 into the 2nd Index-linked Issue on top of what you've already got in the Retirement Issue.

Is there any tax to pay on the gain?

No. The money you get is free of both income tax and capital gains tax. This makes index-linked National Savings Certificates particularly attractive to higher-rate taxpayers, and those who pay the investment income surcharge.

What happens to your certificate if you die?

The certificate can be transferred into the name of the person who inherits them – even if he's already invested the maximum £5,000 in certificates of his own.

How to cash in certificates

Get form P576MA from a post office. Fill it in and send it off in the pre-paid envelope provided with the form. You shouldn't have to wait longer than a couple of weeks for your money.

Can you cash in only part of your money?

Yes. When you bought your certificate you bought a number of £10 units. You can cash in any number of units you wish.

The value of your certificate goes down in line with the fall in the retail price index. But it is guaranteed that when you cash your units in, you'll get back at least as much as your originally invested (plus the four per cent or more bonus if you held the certificate for five years).

What happens if the rate of inflation goes down?

Your certificate will continue to increase in value, but at a slower rate than before. A fall in the rate of inflation does *not* mean that the value of your certificate will fall. What's important from the point of view of your investment is how the rate of inflation compares with the rate of return you could get on other comparatively safe investments (eg building society accounts).

Save-As-You-Earn
Third Issue (Index-linked)

Who can invest?

Anyone aged 16 or over. You don't have to be earning to be eligible.

How much can you invest?

You have to make a regular monthly payment of a fixed number of whole pounds. The minimum monthly payment is £4, the maximum is £50. You aren't allowed to invest more than £50 a month – no matter how many different index-linked SAYE contracts you take out.

How to invest

Fill in an application form and send it off to the address on it. Get the application form from your bank if you want to pay by bank standing order, from your employer if you want the payments deducted from your pay, and from a post office if you want to pay cash each month, or by National Giro account standing order.

How does the scheme work?

You agree to make regular monthly payments for five years. If you pull out within a year, you get back only the money you invested – with no interest. If you pull out of the scheme after a year but before the five years are up, you get back the money you've invested *plus* interest at six per cent a year.

It's only if you keep your payments up for the full five years that your money is index-linked. Each payment is then revalued in line with the change in the retail price index between the time it was made and the end of the five-year period.

If you want to make regular savings of £10 or more a month, you could buy National Savings Certificates (2nd Index-linked Issue) each month instead – see p194. As soon as each payment has been held for a year, you'll benefit from index-linking, which might suit you better than the five years you have to commit yourself to with the SAYE scheme. (Of course, the return over five years isn't as good as with SAYE, as your last year's payments won't be index-linked – see Diagram on p193.)

When do you have to pay?

Each payment has to reach the Save-As-You-Earn office by the last day of each month – if it doesn't, it counts as a missed payment (see opposite). To make sure it gets there on time, it's safest to pay your money (or make your banker's order payable) by the 25th of each month at the latest.

Which month's index applies to each payment?

Confusingly, the payment you make in one month counts as the next month's payment. So, for example, the money you pay in June 1981 counts as the *July 1981 payment*. The index which applies to the *July 1981 payment* is the latest index available on 1 July 1981 – ie the one announced in June (which is the index for May).

Which month's index applies at the end of five years?

If, say, you made your first payment in June 1981, your contract will have started on 1 July 1981. The last payment will be due in May 1986 and you'll be able to cash your investment on 1 July 1986. The index that will apply when you cash it in will be the latest available at the time – ie the one for May 1986.

money paid in	is payment for	index which applies
June 1981	July 1981	May 1981
July 1981	Aug 1981	June 1981

first payment made in	contract starts on	index for first payment
June 1981	1 July 1981	May 1981

last payment made in	contract finishes on	index for end of 5 years
May 1986	1 July 1986	May 1986

Example
Joe Pepper made his first payment
for an SAYE contract in June 1976.
So the contract officially started on
1 July 1976. He pays £10 a month.
The index that applies at the end of
five years – on 1 July 1981 – is the
one for May 1981. This was 294.1.

To work out how much he should
get back if he cashed his investment
at that time Joe would have to do 60
different sums. One of these would
be for the *May 1977* payment. The
index which applies to that
payment is the one for March 1977
(which was 175.8). So the sum he
has to do for his May 1977 payment
is:
£10 × 294.1 ÷ 175.8 = £16.73
Joe would have to do similar sums
for each of his payments – then add
the answers to find out
approximately how much he
should get.

How much would you get back at the end of five years?
If you want to check the sums done by the National Savings
computer, you'll have to do some complicated sums yourself. For
each of the 60 payments you've made, do the following sum:
monthly payment × index which applies ÷ index which applies
at end of five years to that payment
Add together the 60 answers you get, and that's the amount you
should get back (give or take a few pence).

Do you have to cash in your investment after five years?
No. But you can't make any more payments on that contract. You
can leave your money invested for another two years. At the end of
the two years, your money is again revalued in line with the change
in the retail price index. And a 'bonus' of two monthly
contributions is added to the new total. You can then still keep your
money invested, and it will continue to be revalued, at three-
monthly intervals.

But be warned – if you cash your investment before the extra two
years are up you lose out. You get only the amount of money you
would have got if you'd cashed in as soon as five years were up.

Once the five years are up, you can take out a new SAYE contract.

If you miss a payment
The whole SAYE contract is postponed by a month. Each payment
you have already made is treated as if it had been made a month
later than it actually was – and it is the retail price index which
applies to that later month that will be used when working out how
much you get back in the end. The final payment will now be made
a month later than planned. If you miss more than one payment, the
contract is postponed by one month for each payment you miss.
But if you miss more than six, the contract is automatically ended.

Is there any tax to pay?
No. The money you get back is free of both income tax and capital
gains tax. This makes SAYE particularly attractive to higher-rate
taxpayers and those who pay the investment income surcharge.

What happens if you die?
No further payments can be made. Your heirs can cash in the
contract whenever they like. If they cash it more than a year after it
started, your payments will be index-linked from the time they
were paid to the month of repayment. But the payments will stop
being index-linked seven years after the contract started.

How to cash in your savings
Get form SA500 from a post office or bank. You shouldn't have to
wait more than a couple of weeks for your money.

Can you cash in only part of your savings?
No. You have to cash in the whole lot. So if you think you might
want part of your money back after five years, say, it makes sense to
split your monthly savings among two or more contracts.

What if the retail price index or the rate of inflation goes down?
As for 2nd Index-linked Issue – see p195.

Is this scheme the same as the building society SAYE scheme?
NO. With the building society scheme your savings are *not* index-
linked (see p185). Don't get the two confused.

22 National Savings investments

One way in which the Government raises money is to borrow it from the public. It offers various forms of investment in the hope that people will put their money in them. One such investment is the wide range of British Government stocks – dealt with in Chapter 10. Another form is the two index-linked national savings – see Chapter 21. Here we look at the remaining National Savings investments.

How interest is paid

National Savings Certificates

The first national Savings Certificates – then called War Savings Certificates – were issued in 1916. Since then, Governments have brought out a new issue whenever the rate of interest on the old issue seemed too high, or too low, in the prevailing circumstances. Normally, you can buy only one issue – the current one – at any one time. In all, various governments have brought out 24 issues of National Savings Certificates (by April 1982). Once you've bought a certificate you can in practice hold it indefinitely. Moreover, you don't have to have been alive and investing in 1916 in order to own some of the first issue – because certificates can be inherited. So you could hold quite a wide range of certificates.

With the early issues – up to and including the 6th – interest is added ad infinitum to the value of your certificates at a fixed rate of 5/12p a month (or, with some of these issues, $1\frac{1}{2}$p or $1\frac{1}{4}$p every three months). So the value of these certificates is growing (slowly) from year to year. But, because the amount of interest is fixed, it follows that the rate of interest – expressed as a yearly percentage return on the value of your investment – is going down, year by year. These certificates are now offering a miserly rate of return – around two per cent a year or less.

With more recent issues, the amount of interest varies in different years, and is fixed for only a certain number of years at a time – five or seven years, for example. Then, before this period is up, the Government announces how much interest will be paid for the next period of years, or even for just one year at a time. The interest is normally added at four-monthly intervals – though with the current 24th issue you get no interest at all until you have held the certificate for a full year. With the 7th, £1, 8th, 9th, 10th, 11th, 12th, Decimal, 14th and 16th issues there are bonus payments of interest – that is, an extra amount is paid at the end of certain years (counting from the date you bought the certificate). The effect of this is that there is a sudden jump in the interest rate in certain years – provided you hold the certificates until the end of the year in which the bonus is paid.

Note that with all National Savings Certificates, interest is not paid out to you – it's added on to the value of your certificate. You get the interest when you cash in the certificate. The interest is free of income tax, and capital gains tax doesn't apply.

Below we give details of the 24th issue, the one available when this book went to press. And then we look in detail at whether you should cash in any old certificates you have.

24th Issue of National Savings Certificates

Who can invest?

Anyone, irrespective of their age.

How much can you invest?

Anything between £25 and £2,500, in units of £25. A husband and wife can invest up to £2,500 each. If the certificates are in their joint names, however, they can invest only £2,500 between them.

How to invest

If you already hold other issues, take your Certificate book and holder's card to a post office. If you're buying National Savings Certificates for the first time, you'll be asked to sign a form and will be given a holder's card, showing your registered number which should appear on every National Savings Certificate you buy.

How does the 24th issue work?

Interest is added to the value of your certificate over the period of its life (which is 5 years at the outset). The amount of interest added increases as time goes by – giving an added incentive to hanging on to your certificates. Table 1 below gives the details, and shows the rate of interest for each year. Within any year, it's the rate of interest in the left column which you should compare with, say, the rate of interest on building society accounts. If you hold the certificate for the full five years, the overall yearly rate of return works out at 8.92 per cent.

Table 1   how a £25 unit of the 24th issue grows.

during year	£25 certificate increases by	for each complete	value at end of year	rate of interest for year
1	£1.80	12 months	£26.80	7.20%
2	£0.53	3 months	£28.92	7.91%
3	£0.63	3 months	£31.44	8.71%
4	£0.77	3 months	£34.52	9.80%
5	£0.95	3 months	£38.32	11.01%

How do you cash your certificates?

Get form P576MA from a post office. You shouldn't have to wait more than a couple of weeks for your money. You can cash in any number of units – for example, if you hold 100 units each bought for £25, you can cash in 50 of them.

What happens to your certificates should you die?

Your heirs can either cash in the certificates or transfer them into their own name. Form SB4 from most post offices will set things in operation.

**What about your
old certificates?**
Because interest is not paid out, but added on to the value of your
certificates, working out what return you are actually getting from
your investment isn't an easy matter. Moreover, besides needing to
know the rate of interest you are getting now, you need to know
what interest will be paid on them in the next year or two – in case
the interest, though low this year, should get better later on.

First, find your Savings Certificates. Next, check which issue (or
issues) your certificates are. This is printed on the certificates – eg
'*sixth issue*', '*decimal issue*'. Next, look at the date stamp on each
certificate to find out when it was bought.

Now look at the Table opposite (it continues overleaf). We
haven't included the first few issues as the return is so poor – the
figures for the 4th, 5th and 6th Issue will give you an idea of how
bad they are. Go first to the section of the Table which is concerned
with your issues, eg the *9th issue* – see column 1. This column also
tells you the issue price of each certificate. Then look at column 2
and find the *year* in which your certificates were bought.
Alongside the year, in column 3, you will find the value of each
certificate in 1982 on the anniversary of the date it was bought. For
example, a 9th issue certificate bought on 16 November 1955
would be worth £2.05 on 16 November 1982. This value,
incidentally, is of a single unit. The certificate documents you have
may in fact say that they are for multiples of 2, 3, 4 or more units – in
which case the value is the figure in column 3 multiplied by 2, 3, 4
and so on, as the case may be.

Interest now
Column 4 tells you the rate of interest paid for the year ending
during 1982 – on the anniversary of the date the certificates were
bought. If this anniversary fell before the date you are reading this,
this information is now of historical interest only. If the
anniversary is yet to come, the figure tells you the rate of interest
you will get if you hold on to your certificates until that date.
Because the interest is tax-free, this is, in effect, the after-tax rate of
return.

Interest next year
Column 5 tells you the rate of interest due to be paid next year – that
is, for the year ending during 1983 on the anniversary of the date
the certificates were bought.

Interest year after next
Column 6 tells you the rate of interest for the year ending during
1984.

Value for money
As we have said, all the early issues from the 1st to the 6th give a
deplorably low return, – it varies between 1.2 and 2.1 per cent.
Other investments can give a much better return. So if you've any of
these early issues, cash them at once and reinvest elsewhere.

With certificates of the later issues, you'll have to compare the
rate of return you can get with that available on other investments
(taking your rate of tax into account). Don't forget to look at the rate
of return next year, and the year after next before coming to a
decision. For example, with 19th Issue bought in 1980, although
the rate of return this year is 8.6 per cent, next year you'd get 9.2 per
cent, and the year after 13.3 per cent. So it may be worth hanging on
to them.

Table 2 National Savings Certificates

1 name of issue (and issue price)		2 year bought	3 value in 1982 (at anniversary) of date bought)	4 interest now	5 interest next year	6 interest year after next
				rate of interest for year ending at anniversary of date bought, in:		
			£	1982 %	1983 %	1984 %
4th	(16s)	1932	2.70	1.6	1.5	1.5
		1933	2.65$\frac{3}{8}$	1.6	1.6	1.5
5th	(16s)	1933	2.61$\frac{1}{3}$	1.6	1.6	1.6
		1934	2.57$\frac{1}{2}$	1.6	1.6	1.6
		1935	2.53$\frac{1}{3}$	1.7	1.6	1.6
6th	(15s)	1935	2.60	2.0	1.9	1.9
		1936	2.55	2.0	2.0	1.9
		1937	2.50	2.0	2.0	2.0
		1938	2.45	2.1	2.0	2.0
		1939	2.40	2.1	2.1	2.0
7th	(15s)	1939	3.81	9.8	10.0	[1]
		1940	3.47	7.3	9.8	10.0
		1941	3.23$\frac{1}{2}$	6.9	7.3	9.8
		1942	3.02$\frac{1}{2}$	6.9	6.9	7.3
		1943	2.83	6.8	6.9	6.9
		1944	2.65	7.3	6.8	6.9
		1945	2.47	6.5	7.3	6.8
		1946	2.32	5.5	6.5	7.3
		1947	2.20	4.1	5.5	6.5
£1	(£1)	1943	2.99	7.7	9.9	10.1
		1944	2.77$\frac{1}{2}$	6.9	7.7	9.9
		1945	2.59$\frac{1}{2}$	6.8	6.9	7.7
		1946	2.43	6.6	6.8	6.9
		1947	2.28	6.8	6.6	6.8
8th	(10s)	1947	1.95	8.6	9.7	8.4
		1948	1.79$\frac{1}{2}$	7.2	8.6	9.7
		1949	1.67$\frac{1}{2}$	6.7	7.2	8.6
		1950	1.57	6.1	6.7	7.2
		1951	1.48	7.6	6.1	6.7
9th	(15s)	1951	2.70	8.0	9.8	10.0
		1952	2.50	7.1	8.0	9.8
		1953	2.33$\frac{1}{2}$	6.9	7.1	8.0
		1954	2.18$\frac{1}{2}$	6.6	6.9	7.1
		1955	2.05	6.8	6.6	6.9
		1956	1.92	6.7	6.8	6.6

[1] Rate of interest not known (April 1982)

Table 2   National Savings Certificates – *continued*

1 name of issue (and issue price)		2 year bought	3 value in 1982 (at anniversary) of date bought)	4 interest now	5 interest next year	6 interest year after next
				rate of interest for year ending at anniversary of date bought, in:		
			£	1982 %	1983 %	1984 %
		1956	2.63½	9.8	8.5	[1]
		1957	2.40	7.4	9.8	8.5
		1958	2.23½	7.2	7.4	9.8
10th	(15s)	1959	2.08½	6.9	7.2	7.4
		1960	1.95	6.6	6.9	7.2
		1961	1.83	7.3	6.6	6.9
		1962	1.70½	6.6	7.3	6.6
		1963	1.60	7.0	6.6	7.3
		1963	2.63½	9.8	10.1	[1]
11th	(£1)	1964	2.40	7.4	9.8	10.1
		1965	2.23½	7.2	7.4	9.8
		1966	2.08½	6.9	7.2	7.4
		1966	2.49½	9.9	8.4	[1]
		1967	2.27	8.9	9.9	8.4
12th	(£1)	1968	2.08½	7.8	8.9	9.9
		1969	1.93½	6.6	7.8	8.9
		1970	1.81½	6.1	6.6	7.8
		1970	2.26½	8.6	[1]	[1]
Decimal	(£1)	1971	2.08½	9.7	8.6	[1]
		1972	1.90	8.9	9.7	8.6
		1973	1.74½	7.4	8.9	9.7
		1974	1.62½	6.9	7.4	8.9
		1974	1.85	8.5	[1]	[1]
		1975	1.70½	10.0	8.5	[1]
		1976	1.55	8.4	10.0	8.5
14th	(£1)	1977	1.43	6.7	8.4	10.0
		1978	1.34	9.4	6.7	8.4
		1979	1.22½	7.9	9.4	6.7
16th	(£5)	1976	8.51½	10.3	[1]	[1]
		1977	7.72	10.3	10.3	[1]
18th	(£10)	1979	12.24	8.8	10.3	11.1
		1980	11.25	7.1	8.8	10.3
19th	(£10)	1980	11.40	8.6	9.2	13.3
		1981	10.50	5.0	8.6	9.2
21st	(£10)	1981	10.75	7.5	7.8	8.5
23rd	(£25)	1981	27.25	9.0	9.6	10.3
		1982	25.00	–	9.0	9.6
24th	(£25)	1982	25.00	–	7.2	7.9

[1]   Rate of interest not known (April 1982)

Premium bonds

Who can invest?
Anyone aged 16 or over can buy premium bonds. And they can be bought in the name of someone under 16 by parents, grandparents or legal guardians.

How much can you invest?
Premium bonds cost £1 each, but you have to buy them in multiples of £5. You can hold up to £10,000 of bonds.

How to invest
You can get an application form from most post offices, High-street banks and Trustee Savings Banks. Premium bonds worth up to £10 can be bought over the counter. Over £10, they'll be sent from the *Bonds and Stock Office* (which keeps all the records).

How do you know if you've won a prize?
You'll be contacted by post at the last address the Bonds and Stock office has. So make sure you let them know if you move – get change-of-address forms from a post office. There's over £1 million in unclaimed prizes because the winners can't be traced.

How do you cash your bonds?
Get a form from a post office or bank. For each £1 invested you'll get £1 back (but, of course, if you've had your money invested for some time, inflation will have eaten away at its buying power).

What happens if you die?
Your bonds will remain eligible for prizes for 12 months after your death. To cash in the bonds, your heirs should get form SB4 from a post office.

How do premium bonds work?

You don't get interest on your money as such. Instead you get a chance of winning prizes. The total value of the prize money is equal to interest on all bonds that have been held for at least three months (over 1,400 million of them) calculated – in April 1982 – at a rate of 7 per cent a year.

Once you've held a bond for three clear months it has a chance of winning one of the monthly prizes, ranging from £50 to £250,000 and the once-a-week prizes of £100,000, £50,000 and £25,000. There are rules about how the total prize money is divided into prizes of different amounts. For example, in April 1982, the £7,787,350 prize money was split up as shown on the left.

All prizes are free of both income tax and capital gains tax.

1 prize of	£250,000
4 prizes of	£100,000
4 prizes of	£50,000
4 prizes of	£25,000
5 prizes of	£10,000
50 prizes of	£5,000
394 prizes of	£1,000
1,186 prizes of	£500
25,000 prizes of	£100
75,007 prizes of	£50

Your chances of winning

Each bond (once held for 3 months) has an equal chance of being chosen in each draw, irrespective of how long ago it was bought, and how many prizes it has won – or failed to win – in the past.

However, because premium bonds are a lottery, in any one year some investors will get more than the average in prizes, while most will get less. You would have to hold you bonds for hundreds, even thousands, of years in order to be reasonably sure of getting close to the average ration of prizes (which would give you a return of about 7 per cent).

So what are your chances of winning prizes in one particular year? We set a computer to work out the answers for people holding £10, £100, £1,000 and £10,000 of bonds. We assumed that the bonds had been held for the three months needed to qualify for prizes.

See opposite for the results. The chances of winning a particular amount include all the ways of winning. For example, £100 could be won as a single £100 prize, or as two £50 prizes, a total of £200 in prizes can be won as a £100 prize and two £50 prizes, or as two £100 prizes, or as four £50 prizes.

You can see that people who hold £10 of bonds stand very little chance of winning anything at all – overall, 99 out of 100 of them would win nothing in a year. And of those who hold £100 of bonds, 92 out of every 100 can expect to win nothing in a year.

Note that our Tables give your chances of winning in any one year. But what are your chances over a longer period of time? You can use the Tables to get an idea. For example, your chances of winning prizes if you hold £100 of bonds for 10 years are the same as if you'd held £1,000 for a year. Similarly your chances of winning if you hold £50 of bonds for two years are the same as if you'd held £100 for a year.

A worthwhile gamble?

First you have to work out what your stake is. What you're betting is not the money you've got invested. It's what you forgo by having your money tied up in premium bonds rather than earning interest elsewhere – eg in a building society account, local authority loan.

Your stake will vary as interest rates go up and down. When the prize money represented 7 per cent interest, you could have got an after-tax return of perhaps eight to ten per cent if you were a basic rate taxpayer. So you could look on your stake as being about 90p a year for each £10 of premium bonds you hold.

If you don't pay tax you'll be staking more than this (because you could get a higher return than eight to ten per cent). If you pay tax at higher rates, or the investment income surcharge, you'll be staking less (because your after-tax return on most types of investment will be lower than eight to ten per cent).

The small Table opposite gives you a rough idea of how premium bonds compare with some other forms of gambling in terms of the amount paid back to punters for each £100 staked.

The figure for premium bonds assumes that your stake is 90p for each £10 of bonds held. If your stake is lower, premium bonds will look a better bet. If your stake is higher, they'll look worse. To make the figures comparable, we've also allowed for the interest forgone on your stake if you bet on the dogs, craps and so on.

Verdict

Premium bonds should be looked on as a way of gambling rather than investing. If you fancy a flutter, you can see from the Table opposite that, at those levels of interest rates, premium bonds aren't a bad choice – much better than the football pools, say.

What you could win in any one year   your chances

if you have £10 of premium bonds
yearly stake: about 90p for basic rate taxpayer

nothing	about 99 in 100
something (ie £50 or more)	1 in 120
£50 exactly	1 in 160
£100 exactly	1 in 470
£200 exactly	1 in 440,000
£100 or more	1 in 450
£1,000 or more	1 in 33,000
£10,000 or more	1 in 620,000
£100,000 or more	1 in 2,200,000
£250,000 or more	1 in 12,000,000

if you have £100 of premium bonds
yearly stake: about £9 for basic rate taxpayer

nothing	92 in 100
something (ie £50 or more)	1 in 12
£50 exactly	1 in 17
£100 exactly	1 in 47
£200 exactly	1 in 4,100
£100 or more	1 in 42
£1,000 or more	1 in 3,300
£10,000 or more	1 in 62,000
£100,000 or more	1 in 220,000
£250,000 or more	1 in 1,200,000

money back for £100 staked
Blackjack	£91.01
Craps	£90.46
Roulette	£89.88
Premium bonds	**£77.78**
Horse and dog racing	£73.39
Slot machines	£66.97
Football pools	£25.69

if you have £1,000 of premium bonds
yearly stake: about £90 for basic rate taxpayer

nothing	1 in 2
something (ie £50 or more)	1 in 2
£50 exactly	1 in 4
£100 exactly	1 in 6
£200 exactly	1 in 33
£100 or more	1 in 3
£1,000 or more	1 in 330
£10,000 or more	1 in 6,200
£100,000 or more	1 in 22,000
£250,000 or more	1 in 120,000

if you have £10,000 of premium bonds
yearly stake: about £900 for basic rate taxpayer

nothing	2 in 10,000
something (ie £50 or more)	9,998 in 10,000
£50 exactly	1 in 820
£100 exactly	1 in 230
£200 exactly	1 in 47
£100 or more	999 in 1,000
£1,000 or more	1 in 12
£10,000 or more	1 in 620
£100,000 or more	1 in 2,200
£250,000 or more	1 in 12,000

National Savings Bank accounts

There are two types of National Savings Bank account – ordinary accounts and investments accounts. Investment accounts offer a higher rate of return – but you have to give one month's notice to withdraw your money.

National Savings Bank ordinary accounts

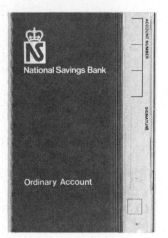

Who can invest?

Anyone aged 7 or over can open an account. If aged under 7, the account can be opened by a relative or friend.

How much can you invest?

You must invest a minimum of £1 to open an account. Maximum is £10,000, no matter how many ordinary accounts you have.

How to invest

You can open an account at most post offices – you'll be sent a bank book where a record is kept of all your transactions.

How much interest?

The rate of interest on ordinary accounts is 5 per cent a year (April 1982), but the government can vary the rate. Interest is worked out on each complete £1 in the account for a full calendar month. Money in your account doesn't start earning interest until the start of the month following the one in which it is deposited. And it stops getting interest from the start of the month in which it is withdrawn. This means that you could have your money invested for almost three months and get just one month's interest. You'll get most interest if you put your money in on the last day of a month, and take it out on the first day of a month.

Interest is added to your account on 31 December. The first £70 of interest is tax-free (so at 5 per cent rate of interest, you can invest up to £1,400 and pay no tax on the interest).

Getting your money out

You can withdraw up to £100 at once by taking your bank book to most post offices. If you want more than £100, you have to apply in writing on an application form available from most post offices – getting your money could take about a week. If you withdraw more than £30, your bank book has to be sent to the Savings Bank headquarters (the limit is a £100 if you have a *Regular Customer Account* – check at your post office).

What happens if you die?

If you're aged 16 or over, you can nominate all or part of the money to go to one or more people – get the form from the National Savings Bank, Glasgow G58 15B.

National Savings Bank investment accounts

Who can invest?
As for ordinary accounts.

How much can you invest?
You must invest a minimum of £1 to open an account. Maximum is £200,000, no matter how many investment accounts you have.

How to invest?
As for ordinary accounts.

How much interest?
The rate of interest varies depending on how much the government feels it needs to offer to attract investors (in May 1982, the rate was 13 per cent a year). As for ordinary accounts, interest is worked out for complete calendar months – so beware of losing out on interest.
   Interest is added to your account on 31 December. All interest is taxable, but is paid without tax having been deducted.

Getting your money out
You have to give one month's notice to withdraw your money. You can get an application form from most post offices. You'll have to send your bank book in with your application form.

What happens if you die?
As for ordinary accounts.

Save-As-You-Earn (Fourth Issue)

This scheme is available only in conjunction with an approved savings-related share option scheme run by your employer. The rate of return over the five year period for which the scheme lasts is 10.43 per cent (10.64 per cent if you keep the money invested for a further two years). For more details see p90.

British Savings Bonds

These bonds are no longer available, but you may still hold some as the last date on which some of the bonds reach maturity is 15 August 1984. Once your money has been invested for six months, it earns interest (which is taxable) at 8½ per cent a year. If you keep your money invested for the full five years that these bonds run for, you get a tax-free bonus of four per cent of the amount you invested. The before-tax rate of return over the full five-year period works out at 10.4 per cent. Once the five years are up, no further interest will be added. You can cash the bonds at any time but you have to give one month's notice to withdraw your money.

National Savings and premium bond gift tokens

You can get gift tokens worth £5, or in multiples of £5 up to £30, from most post offices. These can be deposited as if they were money in National Savings Bank accounts, or can be used to buy premium bonds or National Savings Certificates.

Any old National Savings stamps?

Remember them – 10p each (or 6d and 1/-in pre-decimal days)? They were withdrawn on 31 December 1976, but you can still cash in any you've got knocking around.

23 Investing abroad

Exchange control restrictions were lifted on 23 October 1979. Although it was possible to invest overseas before that date, there were all sorts of barriers to doing so – for example, you had to get Bank of England permission to transfer money abroad to buy a house, you had to change money via the dollar premium (which could have meant a poor rate of exchange). While there's no guarantee that exchange controls won't be re-imposed, at present you are free to invest world-wide.

You may decide to invest abroad for two main reasons:
- you reckon that you'll get a better return on your money than with a UK investment – taking account of the return (both income and capital growth) in terms of local currency and the effect of changes in the exchange rate of the £
- you want to spread your money around different countries in the hope of cutting down the risk of your investments, as a whole, doing very badly.

Below we look in more detail at these reasons, and at how different countries' investments have performed in the past. But bear in mind that investing overseas should form only part of your overall investment strategy. The first three chapters of this book give general advice on how to plan your investments – and can be applied not just to UK investments, but to overseas ones too.

Better return abroad?

Just as you might compare different investments in the UK to check which would give you the best return, so you should consider overseas investments as alternatives to UK ones. For example, you may have decided that a British Government stock paying a high income meets your investment needs. It would be worth checking whether a similar foreign investment could offer the prospect of a better return. The same goes if, for example, you are looking for a capital gain in unit trusts, or want to put money in a bank deposit account.

When comparing the returns don't look at the return in local currency only (eg the rate of interest you'd get on your deposit account). You must also consider how changes in the exchange rate will affect your total return.

Exchange rate of the £

Suppose, for example, you invest £100 in the US, at an exchange rate of $2 to the £ – ie you invest $200. If you get interest of 16 per cent, at the end of the year you'll have $232 (ignoring, for simplicity, any tax and any cost of buying and selling the investment). You discover that the £ has gone down a lot in value over the year compared with the $ and that the exchange rate is now $1.60 to the £. In this case, you'd get back £145 (ie $232 ÷ 1.6), giving you a total rate of return of 45 per cent – substantially more than the 16 per cent you get in local currency.

Of course, things may not work out in your favour in this way. For example, you may find at the end of the year that the £ has gone up in value and that the exchange rate is now $2.40 to the £. In this case, you'd get back about £97 (ie $232 ÷ 2.4), which is less than the £100 you originally invested, despite the 16 per cent your money has been earning.

In short, it's good for your overseas investment if the exchange rate of the £ goes down against the currency concerned. It's bad if the exchange rate of the £ goes up.

Cutting risks It's all very well to go for the best return on the money you invest, but few people are willing to face the risk of losing a lot of it in the process. One way of cutting down this risk is to spread your money around different types of investments – eg putting some in British Government stocks, some in shares, some in a building society and using some to buy a house. The chance of *all* these different investments doing extremely badly is lower than the chance of just one of them turning out to be a dud. Of course, reducing your risk of loss in this way also reduces your chance of winning the jackpot.

Spreading your investments around different countries is another way of cutting down your risk. Although the economies of (and the health of investments in) some countries may, at times move up and down more or less together (eg Canada and US, Singapore and Hong Kong), this is not true of all countries. For example, the problems faced by the Far East are quite different from those faced by Germany, and different again from those faced by South Africa.

By choosing investments in a cross section of countries you reduce your risk of all of them doing badly at once.

And although short-term fluctuations in exchange rates can have a dramatic effect on the value of your investment, in the long-term you can look on an investment overseas as a hedge against the £ going down relative to the other country's currency.

Where to invest Overseas, as in the UK, there is a wide range of investments – for a summary of the main types, see pages 214 to 216.

Giving details of how all the different investments available have performed in a wide range of countries would take the whole of this book. So we've concentrated on how interest rates and share prices have varied in six different countries and in the UK, over a sample period – from 1972 to the end of 1979. But first let's look at what's happened to the exchange rate of the £ over that period.

Exchange rate of the £

You can see from Diagram 1 that, over the period in question, the exchange rate of the £ tended to go down against the other currencies we looked at. Diagram 2 shows the gain you would have made (ignoring buying and selling costs and the interest you might have got) if you had bought £100 worth of each of the currencies in Diagram 1 at the end of 1971, and changed it back into £££ at the end of 1979. Diagram 2 also shows the yearly rate of return these gains represent. You can see that you could have achieved a rate of return of nearly 14 per cent a year – simply by turning your money into Swiss francs. And even with Australian dollars, you'd have ended up with a small positive return.

Warning   Just because these large gains were made over the period shown, doesn't mean the same will apply for different periods. Indeed one of the major problems in choosing where to invest is trying to predict what will happen to exchange rates in the future. From the end of 1979 to when this book went to press, the exchange rate of the £ against most of the currencies shown, went up – and then, in mid-1981, down again.

In the long term, one key factor affecting exchange rates is inflation – if the rate of inflation in one country is considerably higher than in another, the first country's exchange rate is likely to fall relative to the second. You can see from Diagram 3, that over the period when the exchange rate of the £ tended to be falling, the inflation rate in the UK was generally higher than in the other countries we looked at.

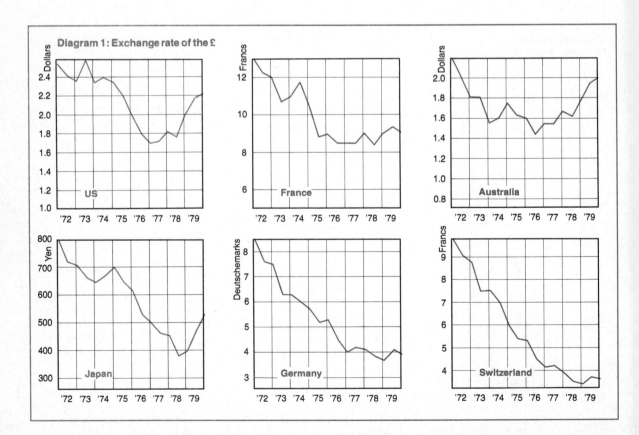

Diagram 1: Exchange rate of the £

Inflation isn't the only factor though. You can see from Diagram 1, that around 1977 to 1978, the drift down in the exchange rate of the £ tended to slacken – and with some countries (eg US, Japan), the process was even reversed. Why this turnaround?

It's at least partly due to North Sea oil. As the oil gradually became available, the UK had to import less oil and was able to sell some of its own. Both factors helped to strengthen the exchange rate of the £. It's difficult to estimate how long North Sea oil will continue to have a significant effect on our exchange rate.

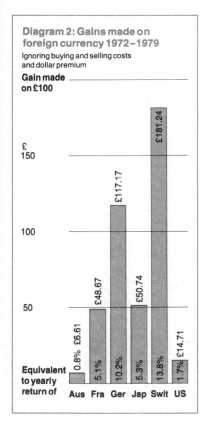

Diagram 2: Gains made on foreign currency 1972–1979

Ignoring buying and selling costs and dollar premium

Gain made on £100

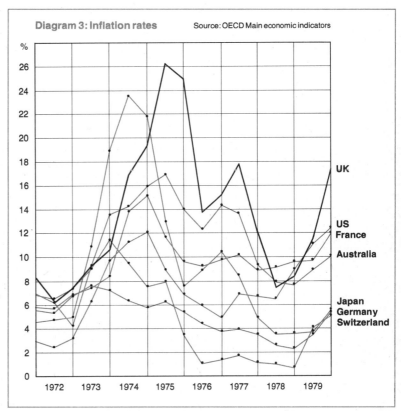

Diagram 3: Inflation rates   Source: OECD Main economic indicators

The return in local currency

Diagram 4 shows how the returns on stocks issued by the governments of the different countries compared over the period 1972 to 1979. You can see that the UK consistently offered higher interest rates than the other countries.

This was at least partly because the interest rate a country has to offer to attract foreign investors must reflect, to some extent, how people expect that country's exchange rate to move in future. And, over the period, foreign investors tended to be wary of the UK's record of high inflation rates and a falling exchange rate.

Diagram 5 looks at share prices. You can see that, whatever the country, you'd have had a bumpy ride with an investment in shares. If you'd been clever (or lucky) enough to buy and sell at the right times, you could have made a bomb. But if you'd got your timing wrong, you'd have lost a lot. In most countries, even if you'd kept your money invested throughout the eight year period, your shares would have been worth little more (even ignoring inflation) at the end than they were at the beginning. Only Japan showed a fairly marked increase.

The total return

Exchange rate changes, and the return in the local currency, are the key factors in working out what an overseas investment is worth to you. Diagram 6 draws these factors together, and gives the average yearly rate of return for government stocks and shares bought at the end of 1971 and sold at the end of 1979. The red bars give the return in local currency, the black bars the return adjusted for the changes in the exchange rate. Our figures take account of both changes in the capital values of the investments and the income from them.

You can see that, especially with government stock, although UK investment came out quite well in terms of local currency, other countries did better when changes in exchange rates were taken into account. This applied particularly to countries with 'strong' currencies, such as Germany and Switzerland.

Warning The graphs we've shown are for a sample period to show how exchange rates, local rates of return and total returns are interrelated. Future rates of return may be quite different.

Should YOU Invest? If you've got several thousand £££ to invest, putting some of it abroad is worth considering. Though you can't rely on getting a better return than in the UK, spreading your money among different countries could cut down the risk of your investments, as a whole, doing badly. Bear in mind that the outcome of your investment depends not just on how well it does in terms of local currency, but also on what happens to exchange rates. And what will happen to exchange rates over the next few years – in the light of what happens to relative inflation rates, how long North Sea Oil lasts, and political developments throughout the world – is anyone's guess.

Because your investment depends so much on exchange rates, investing abroad is not the place for money where you want to be quite sure of how much you'd get at short notice – so not a home for your emergency fund, say. If you travel a lot in a particular country, a foreign currency bank deposit account may be particularly suitable for you. Investing indirectly – eg through UK-based unit trusts or investment trusts – would cut down on administrative problems, and would be less risky than direct investment (in foreign shares or foreign government stocks, say).

Diagram 4:
Return on government stocks [1]
Source:
Morgan Guaranty Trust Company of New York

[1] held to
redemption

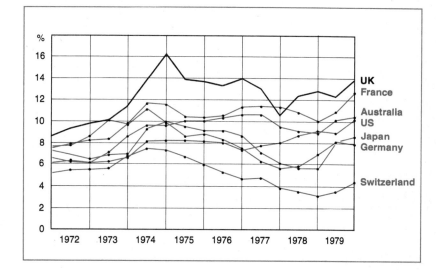

Diagram 5:
How shares have done

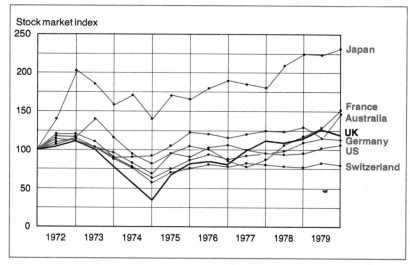

Diagram 6:
Average yearly return 1972–79
Ignoring buying and selling costs
and dollar premium. Income reinvested
Source:
Phillips & Drew and Capital International indices

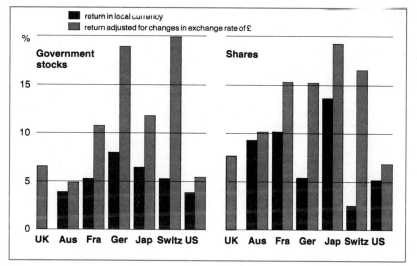

Details of investments

Foreign currency bank accounts

High-street banks will open foreign currency accounts for UK residents. These can be either current accounts (ie you can draw cheques on them), or deposit accounts (where interest is paid). You don't need to have a UK account with a bank to be able to open a foreign account.

Interest rates vary from day to day. In general, the more you invest the higher the rate of interest you can get. If you have to give notice to withdraw your money the rate of interest is normally fixed for this period. Note that interest rates – and the minimum amount you have to invest – vary from bank to bank. For example, in mid-October 1981, the minimum investment for seven days' notice of withdrawal ranged from the equivalent of US $1,000 to £20,000. And the interest rate for such deposits ranged from $6\frac{1}{2}$ per cent to $12\frac{1}{2}$ per cent for Australian dollars, from $2\frac{3}{4}$ per cent to $7\frac{1}{4}$ per cent for Swiss francs. There were similar variations for other currencies, so shop around before opening an account.

Points to watch

● current accounts don't normally pay interest – and you may pay charges for operating them. So it's not worth having one unless you travel a lot in a particular country, or plan to live there part of the time
● some foreign banks with branches in this country will also open accounts for UK residents. They tend to offer rates of interest similar to (or somewhat lower than) those given by our High-street banks. You could also open an account direct with a bank abroad.

Points about tax

Interest on UK-based accounts is normally paid without any tax being deducted – either in the UK or abroad – but is liable for UK tax. You must declare the interest you get on your Tax Return.

Unit trusts

Many unit trusts invest overseas rather than in the UK. Some of these are based in the UK, some in places like the Channel Islands and Isle of Man (known as offshore funds). And, of course, many other countries have their own unit trusts. Some trusts spread their investments internationally, others specialise in particular areas – eg US, Far East, Australia. Most invest in shares, but some invest in government stocks, Eurobonds or put money on deposit. A few specialise in investing in foreign currencies. Investing through a unit trust means that you can get a stake in a spread of investments in an overseas country for a relatively low minimum investment (say £500) – and that you don't have to get involved in the administrative problems associated with investing directly in overseas stocks and shares (see p217). See Chapter 8 for more details about unit trusts.

Money Management (£2.75 by post from Minster House, Arthur St, London EC4R 9AX) gives lists each month of which UK unit trusts invest where and how they've performed in the past (though, of course, this is no guide to the future).

Points to watch

● not a home for money you might need at short notice. Should be considered, in the main, as a long-term investment (7 years or more, say) – though can also be short-term speculation
● if you invest via authorised UK unit trusts (but not offshore funds), you get the protection of the Department of Trade as a watchdog.

Points about tax

Distributions from UK-based unit trusts are paid with only UK tax deducted, distributions from most offshore funds with little or no tax deducted. So no problems with reclaiming tax held back by foreign governments. With foreign-based unit trusts, distributions are normally paid with some tax withheld by the foreign government. You'll have to arrange to get a credit for any tax deducted – see p217.

Investment trusts

Investment trusts are companies which, in turn, hold the shares of other companies (see p86 for more details). Many UK investment trusts hold overseas shares (perhaps specialising in particular areas of the world too – eg US, Far East, Australia). UK investment trust shares can themselves be bought and sold on the London Stock Exchange. Details of UK investment trusts are published in the *Investment Trust Year Book* (£12.50 for 1982 issue from Minster House, Arthur Street, London EC4R 9AX). Monthly statistics of where the companies invest, and how they've performed are printed on the fourth Saturday each month in the Daily Telegraph and the Financial Times.

Investment trusts also exist in other countries – and a few of the major foreign ones are quoted on the London Stock Exchange.

Points to watch
● as with unit trusts, investing through a UK investment trust spares you the administrative problems faced with overseas shareholdings
● not a home for money you might need at short notice. Should be considered, in the main, as a long-term investment (7 years or more, say) – though can also be short-term speculation.

Points about tax
As for unit trusts.

Foreign currency funds

These offer a means of investing in a range of currencies without opening individual bank accounts. You invest your money in the fund, and the investment managers then shift it around among a range of currencies, in the hope of taking advantage both of high interest rates and exchange rate movements. So, in effect, you are staking your money on the skill and luck of the managers. Some of the funds are based in the Channel Islands (off-shore funds), and operate like unit trusts. Others are UK-based and are linked to life insurance.

Government stocks

Just as the UK government raises money through issuing British Government stocks, so there is a wide range of stocks issued by foreign governments and bought and sold on foreign stock exchanges. Some of these are also traded on the London Stock Exchange. Note that many companies, including foreign ones, also issue fixed interest securities which work in a similar way to government stocks. These normally pay a higher rate of interest, reflecting the fact that a company has more chance of going bust than most governments.

Points to watch
● as with shares, there is a certain amount of administrative hassle, and extra cost in dealing in foreign stocks on foreign stock exchanges (see overleaf). May be simpler to invest through a unit trust that specialises in foreign stocks.

Points about tax
Gains on foreign stocks are liable to capital gains tax – unlike gains on British Government stock held for a year or more. Interest payments are generally made after deduction of some foreign tax. You may have to arrange to get a credit for the tax deducted – see p217.

Points to watch
These funds give the opportunity of investing in currencies for a relatively low outlay – the minimum investment ranges from £500 to £1,000. But the funds haven't been going long enough to tell how well they'll do.

Points about tax
Income from the Jersey-based funds is paid without any tax being deducted – but is liable for UK tax. You must declare this income on your tax return. With the funds linked to life insurance, the normal tax rules apply – see p49.

Shares

Shares in foreign companies can be bought and sold on their appropriate stock exchanges. And some foreign companies' shares are traded on the London Stock Exchange too. For foreign dealings done abroad, you have to pay the commission rates applying in the relevant country (as well as UK commission if you use a UK broker). Not a suitable way of investing in foreign companies unless you've got enough money to get a good spread of companies (and preferably of countries) – say £10,000 to £20,000 or more set aside for investment in foreign shares. The rest of us would be better advised to invest via unit trusts or possibly investment trusts.

Points to watch
● not a home for money you might need at short notice. Should be considered, in the main, as a long-term investment (7 years or more, say) – though can also be short-term speculation
● some countries' protection for shareholders is less extensive than ours – may be as well to stick to large, well-established stock markets (eg US, Japan, Canada, UK, West Germany, Switzerland, France, South Africa, Netherlands, Australia)
● it's likely to be difficult for you (or your adviser) to have detailed knowledge about a lot of foreign companies, and the economic environment in which they're functioning. Even those in the know may find it harder to keep up to date than those on the spot. And there are likely to be administrative hassles in collecting your dividends, and so on – see overleaf.

Points about tax
Dividends are normally paid with some tax withheld by the foreign government. So you'll have to arrange to get a credit for the tax deducted – see p217.

Eurobonds

Eurobonds are a way in which international borrowers (for example, governments, companies, international institutions like the World Bank) raise money. The bonds – which pay interest – are generally issued in a particular currency (eg dollars, deutschemarks) and are quoted on various stock exchanges. But nearly all trading takes place *over-the-counter* through a variety of agents (including banks), rather than through the stock exchanges. Eurobonds issued by companies (rather than governments, and so on) normally pay a slightly higher rate of interest, reflecting the higher chance of them going bust.

Points to watch
● Eurobonds come in fairly large units (eg $1,000) – and you may find it difficult (or costly) to buy or sell a small number of units. You may do better to go for a unit trust specialising in Eurobonds
● the interest rate may be fixed, or may be changed at set intervals
● interest rates on Eurobonds generally reflect interest rates in the country of the currency they're issued in.

Points about tax
As with foreign stocks, capital gains on Eurobonds are liable to capital gains tax. Interest is paid without any foreign tax being deducted. But the interest is liable for UK tax, and you must declare it on your Tax Return.

Property

Buying property abroad is full of pitfalls for the unwary. For example, the costs of buying and selling are usually considerably greater abroad than they are in the UK: perhaps 10 per cent on both buying *and* selling. There may be severe restrictions on taking your money out of the foreign country again if you decide to sell. And there's always a chance that, at some time in the future, the political climate in the country might change and foreigners won't be welcome. You should certainly get professional advice before contemplating an investment in property abroad.

Points to watch
● *always* visit a home before buying – don't rely on glossy brochures. Try to spend a fair bit of time in the area, and see the house at different times of the day, and even in different seasons
● check carefully on things like the reliability of local water, electricity supplies, sewage; and on the structure and surroundings of the house you have in mind
● planning permission for new buildings is easier to get in many countries abroad than in the UK; your idyllic country retreat may become the centre of a concrete jungle
● if you are planning to retire abroad, be particularly cautious. And check on medical facilities.

Points about tax
Gains you make on selling property abroad are liable to capital gains tax. Income you get from letting property is taxed as investment income, and you must declare it on your Tax Return. You can deduct any expenses incurred abroad in managing and collecting the income (eg paying an agent). If some foreign tax has been deducted, you'll have to arrange to get a tax credit.

Investment-type life insurance

Some life insurance companies run funds which invest abroad. These work a bit like unit trusts. For details of how single-premium and regular-premium policies work, see pages 136 and 142.

Cost of buying and selling foreign currency
Unless you're investing in UK-based foreign investments (eg a unit trust) you're likely to have to exchange the £££ you want to invest for foreign currency. And when you cash your investment, you may have to turn your foreign currency back into £££ again. In both cases, you'll be charged for the transaction (the charge may be hidden in that different exchange rates are likely to be used depending on whether you're buying or selling foreign currency). If you're changing a lot of money – several thousand £££, say – you may get a better deal than with smaller amounts. And if you're dealing through a stockbroker or other agent you may be able to benefit from favourable exchange rates he can get.

Administrative problems
If you have foreign investments you have to make arrangements in the foreign country for the share certificate (or whatever) to be held by an agent (eg a bank, stockbroker) and passed on to the new owner when you sell, and for dividends, interest, and so on, to be collected and sent on to you. You could make these arrangements yourself or ask a UK agent (eg a stockbroker) to make them for you. Either way, there'll be a fee to pay.

Tax on overseas investments

The tax treatment of investments held abroad (as opposed to UK-based foreign investments) can be extremely complicated. But even if you plan to hand over your tax affairs to an adviser, a bit of background knowledge would help you to understand what he's up to.

Income tax

In general, if you're a UK resident all your income is liable to UK tax, whether or not it is brought into this country. So if, say, you have a bank deposit account in Switzerland, you have to declare the interest you get from it in your Tax Return, even if you keep the interest (or spend it) abroad. When converting foreign income into £££, use the exchange rate applying at the time it was due to be paid to you (not when you actually changed it into £££).

Income from overseas investments is often taxed in the country in which it originates – so two lots of tax could be charged on one lot of income. The UK government has made agreements with a wide range of countries to limit the extent to which income may be taxed twice. Under one of these *double taxation agreements* the amount of tax which a foreign government deducts from income before it reaches you is reduced. And the tax actually deducted is allowed as a tax credit against the UK tax charged on the same income.

Suppose for example, that you're entitled to £1,000 in dividends from the US. Tax at 30 per cent would normally be held back by the US taxman before paying over the dividends to non-US residents.

However, because of our double taxation agreement with the US, only 15 per cent is withheld – ie you get £850. If, say, you're liable for tax in the UK at 40 per cent on your £1,000 gross dividends, there'd be £400 tax to pay. But the £150 you've paid in tax to the US would be allowed as a credit against the £400 of UK tax you're liable for – so you'd have to hand over to the taxman £250 not £400.

If you are liable for no UK tax (or less than has been deducted under a double taxation agreement) there'll be no further UK tax to pay – but you can't claim back the extra foreign tax you've paid.

In general, double taxation agreements mean that tax on dividends is withheld at a rate of 15 per cent. With interest payments the rate at which tax is withheld varies more between countries.

For more details of how double taxation agreements work, see Inland Revenue leaflet IR6 (available free from your tax office).

How to get your relief

If your foreign income is paid to you through an agent (eg a bank) in the UK, who passes it on to you after deducting basic rate tax, the agent should allow for any double taxation agreement when doing his sums.

But if the income is paid direct to you from abroad, you have to apply for double taxation relief yourself – and until you do so, you may find the income arrives with substantial amounts of foreign tax withheld, and no credit against UK tax allowed for it. To get the foreign tax reduced, get an application form from the Inland Revenue, Inspector of Foreign Dividends, Lynwood Road, Thames Ditton, Surrey KT7 0DP. To get the foreign tax withheld allowed as a credit against your UK tax bill, apply to your Tax Inspector.

When UK tax is due

Your tax bill is normally based on the foreign income you get in the preceding tax year – ie your tax bill for the 1982–83 tax year would be based on the foreign income you got in the 1901–82 tax year. Special rules apply in the first three and last two years in which you get foreign income of this type – as for UK income not taxed before you get it (see p47).

Other tax deducted

In certain countries, foreign dividends are paid after deducting tax other than personal income tax. And non-residents may not be able to reclaim this tax. So before investing in a particular country, check that the return you hope to get allows for *all* the tax deducted.

Capital gains tax

Gains you make on overseas investments are liable for UK capital gains tax in the normal way (see p53). In general, you'll be taxed on gains whether or not you bring the sales proceeds into the UK. Your capital gain will be the difference between the value of the asset in sterling when you acquired it, and its value in sterling when you disposed of it – using the exchange rates that applied at the relevant times. Note that gains you make on foreign currency – eg held in a bank deposit account – are liable for capital gains tax in the normal way (unless you got the currency for holidays or living expenses abroad).

There's normally no foreign capital gains tax to pay if you're a UK resident. However, gains on selling a foreign home may be taxed in the country where the home is. And if you have a permanent home in certain foreign countries (eg a country cottage in California) or spend substantial parts of the year there, you may find that you're treated as a resident of that country and are liable for local capital gains tax. Any foreign tax you pay is allowed as a credit against your UK capital gains tax liability.

Capital transfer tax

UK capital transfer tax is charged on foreign assets given away during your life or left on your death, in the normal way. A similar tax is likely to be charged by the country in which the assets are situated.

The foreign capital transfer tax (or its equivalent) is normally allowed as a credit against UK capital transfer tax.

Note that there are likely to be delays (perhaps lengthy ones) and complications in obtaining probate for assets held abroad in your name, on your death – it may be better to have them held in the name of a UK agent (eg a bank).

24 Investing for children

Choosing an investment for a child's money is much the same as choosing one for an adult's – you have to take account of how much there is to invest, how long you want to invest it for, what rate of tax will be paid on the income, and so on.

In the first three chapters of this book we looked at ways of sorting out your investment strategy, and finding investments which will suit your needs. Following the Route Maps and explanation in those three chapters should lead you to a short-list of investments suitable for your child.

Which alternative to choose will depend very much on the child's (or, in some cases, the parents') tax situation. Some investments which may be best for a non-taxpayer, can give a poor return to someone who does pay tax (and vice versa).

For details of how a child's income is taxed, see p230. In general, income of more than £5 a year which comes from gifts from the parents is taxed as the parents' income – and will be taxed at the highest rate of tax they pay. Any other income will be taxed as the child's own income – so it won't be taxed at all unless his income exceeds the single person's allowance (£1,565 for the 1982–83 tax year).

The Table opposite shows the main types of investment available, the age at which a child is allowed to invest in them in his own name, and the minimum investment needed. You can see that there is quite a wide range of investments available from birth – though a child generally has to reach seven to withdraw money.

Example

Samantha (who is 12) is saving up for a new disco outfit costing £35. She reckons she can save 25p a week out of her pocket money and plans to do a week-end paper round, bringing in £1 a week. Her godmother is giving her £10 for Christmas, which she plans to put towards the outfit.

She works her way through the Route Map for savings on p20, and whittles her choice down to a National Savings Bank account, bank deposit account or (but only for her regular savings) a building society subscription share account. She doesn't pay tax – and the interest from her pocket money savings won't come to more than £5 a year, so there's no need for her parents to worry about paying tax on her interest.

She sees from the Route Map that with building society subscription shares, a non-taxpayer could normally get a higher rate of return elsewhere. When she checks on current interest rates she finds that, for a non-taxpayer, a National Savings Bank investment account offers the best return – both for regular savings and for lump sums. She sees from p207 that she'd have to give a month's notice to withdraw money – and regards this as a good thing because it will discourage her from frittering the money away.

type of investment	age child can invest in own name [1]	minimum investment
Bank deposit account	from birth, but normally no withdrawals until 7	none
British Government stocks bought through Post Office [2]	from birth, but not normally cashable until 7	none [3]
National Savings Certificates [2]	from birth, but not normally cashable until 7	£10
National Savings Bank ordinary account [2]	from birth, but normally no withdrawals until 7	£1
National Savings Bank investment account [2]	from birth, but normally no withdrawals until 7	£1
Trustee Savings Bank ordinary account	from birth, but normally no withdrawals until 7	5p (but £1 to earn interest)
Trustee Savings Bank investment account	from birth, but normally no withdrawals until 7	£1
Building Society ordinary shares	varies – often 7	often £1
Building Society subscription shares	varies – often 7	10p to £1 a month
Building Society term shares	varies – often 7	£500 or £1,000
Finance company deposits	varies – often 18	often £100 to £1,000
Life insurance policies	varies widely – often 16 to 18, can be younger	often £5 to £10 a month; lump sum, £250 to £1,000
Premium bonds [2]	16	£5
Save-As-You-Earn	16	£4 a month
Local authority loans	must be 18 when loan matures	often £250 to £500 – sometimes more
Shares	18	none [3]
Unit trusts	varies – often 18	often £250 to £500
British Government stocks bought through stockbroker	18	none [3]

[1] See p222 for ways of investing on behalf of a child, if the child is too young to invest in his own name.

[2] National Savings gift tokens (value: £5, or in multiples of £5 up to £30) can be used. These tokens can't be exchanged for cash.

[3] You have to pay commission each time you buy or sell so investing or withdrawing small amounts may not be worthwhile.

Trusts

If you're planning on giving substantial amounts of money to a child, you may be worried that he or she might squander it. You could, of course, keep the money in your own name and hand it over when the child reaches 18, say. But doing this has disadvantages. For example, *you* may be tempted to squander the money, it might mean more capital transfer tax to pay if you were to die, and so on.

A way out of this problem is to set up a trust for the child. A trust is managed by *trustees* for the benefit of those for whom it was set up (the *beneficiaries* of the trust). The people setting up the trust – the parents, say – can act as trustees; or they can appoint friends or relatives; or a professional adviser (such as a solicitor or accountant) can be appointed as one of the trustees. Below we give brief details of how a trust is set up – and opposite look at some short-cuts you can take.

A trust can have more than one beneficiary – so you can, for example, set up a trust for the benefit of all your 10 grandchildren (plus any more that come along). In this chapter we normally assume a trust has only one beneficiary – but what we say holds equally well for trusts with more than one.

When a trust is set up, the trustees may be given the power to invest in specified investments, or to invest *as they think fit*. If they aren't given these powers there are special rules about how they can invest the money.

When the child is 18, he can ask the trustees how the money has been invested. In extreme cases, he may be able to sue the trustees if it's clear that they have failed to invest the money in his best interests.

Putting money into a trust could mean a capital transfer tax bill, though – see p230.

Setting up a trust   The rules about trusts are extremely complicated so we recommend you ask a solicitor with experience of setting up trusts to draw up a **trust deed** for you. This will specify who the trustees are, who is entitled to benefits from the trust, when income and capital are to be paid out, ways in which the trustees can invest the money and so on.

Even a fairly straightforward trust might cost between £100 and £300 to set up – and there could be a charge each year from the trustees for running the trust (as much as £100 or more say). So it's probably not worth setting up a trust unless you plan to give a lot of money to your children (at least £5,000; possibly as much as £20,000, say) – and feel the cost of setting up and running the trust is worthwhile, or would be outweighed by tax-savings.

There are two basic types of trust:
- **fixed trusts** (often called **interest in possession** trusts) where a

particular person (or people) has the right to the income from the trust (or the equivalent of income – eg the right to live in a rent-free home). The trustees have no choice but to hand over the income to the beneficiaries at the times stated in the trust
● **discretionary trusts** where it is left to the discretion of the trustees which of the possible beneficiaries should be paid income. They may also be free to decide which should get capital. The trustees may be given the power to accumulate income – ie not to pay it out at all (until the trust ends). This type of trust is an *accumulation trust.* An *accumulation and maintenance trust* is a type of accumulation trust from which income can be paid out only for the maintenance, education or benefit of the beneficiaries (until the beneficiaries get an interest in possession, that is).

The trust deed may say that a beneficiary shouldn't get any payments (or other benefits) from the trust unless some event happens – eg he gets married, or reaches the age of 25. This type of trust may be fixed or discretionary.

The distinction between **fixed** and **discretionary** trusts is important because there are special income tax and capital transfer tax rules for the different types of trust – see p230.

Broadly, the current tax rules mean that:
● setting up a fixed trust for your own child won't normally save you income tax – the income from the trust will be taxed as yours
● **but** if you set up an accumulation trust, income which is accumulated will be taxed at 45 per cent (in the 1982–83 tax year) and there'll be no further income tax to pay so long as it isn't paid out until your child reaches 18. So this could be worthwhile if you pay tax at more than 45 per cent.

Note of warning
Once you've set up a trust, you can't normally change your mind and take the money back. However, trusts can be set up so that the person giving the money can, in certain circumstances, get some or all of the capital back without losing tax advantages. These trusts – not covered in this chapter – are known as **power of appointment trusts**. If you think you might be interested in this type of trust, check with a solicitor or other professional adviser.

Short-cut trusts There are ways of making sure that money you invest for your children is held in trust for them without going to the expense of setting up a tailor-made trust.

Life insurance policies
You can take out a life insurance policy (on your, or your wife's life) with the proceeds made payable to your child. Perhaps the simplest way of doing this is to get a policy worded according to the *Married Woman's Property Act.* In this case, the policy (and any money it pays out) is held in trust for the child until he reaches an age you specify when taking out the policy.

The policy can be a single-premium one (eg a managed bond, property bond) or a regular-premium one (eg a unit-linked savings plan, an endowment policy).

The premiums you pay count as gifts for capital transfer tax purposes (but will probably come into one of the tax-free categories – see page 60). There's no capital transfer tax to pay on money paid out by the policy. And if the policy is handed over to the child after he reaches 18, any taxable gain on the policy is taxed as the child's, not the parents'. But if the policy ends before it is handed over, the gain is taxed as the parents' – though the trust pays the tax.

Unit trusts

A few unit trust management companies run schemes which set up accumulation and maintenance trusts if people want to invest for children.

The minimum investment ranges from £100 to £500, and there's sometimes a small fee for setting up the scheme. Get a stockbroker to check on which companies run these schemes, or contact the Unit Trust Association (address on p41). Check whether the unit trusts available would be suitable for your child – see p98.

Investing on behalf of the child

With many of the investments in the Table on p219 (eg shares, premium bonds, building society accounts) you can invest in a child's name, even if the child is too young to do so himself. Money invested in this way can be used only for the benefit of the child – and he can ask for it to be handed over to him at the age you specified when investing the money (18, if no age was specified). It can be handed over earlier (with your agreement) once the child exceeds the minimum age for holding the investment.

Example

Leslie and Lucretia Lime pay tax on the top slice of their income at 50 per cent. They've got £5,000 from a with-profits endowment policy, and want to invest it for their 10-year old daughter, Sally. They don't want her to have the money until she's 18.

They consider whether to set up an *accumulation and maintenance* trust (which could save them income tax) – but they decide that the amount they're investing doesn't justify the expense of setting up a tailor-made trust. So they put £3,000 into a single-premium managed bond, taken out on Leslie's life, but with the proceeds payable to Sally and the policy being handed over to her when she is 18 – so that any gain on

it will count as hers for tax purposes. They invest the remaining £2,000 in unit trusts on behalf of Sally – the income from this will count as Mr and Mrs Lime's for tax purposes (though any gains will be taxed as Sally's).

The £5,000 will count as a gift for capital transfer tax purposes. But Mr and Mrs Lime have not used their tax-free quota of £3,000 each for this year (ie they have £6,000 tax-free in hand). So they can invest the money for Sally without fear of capital transfer tax. And there'll be no capital transfer tax to pay when the investments are handed over to Sally.

Tax-saving tips

We give details about tax as far as children are concerned on p230. And there's yet more on tax in Chapter 5. Here we point out the main things to bear in mind, and some ways you can take advantage of the income tax, capital transfer tax and capital gains tax rules to keep tax bills when investing for children to a minimum.

Giving money to your children won't normally save you any income tax
Income of more than £5 a year which comes from gifts made to a child by his or her parents counts as the parents' income for tax purposes – and, if it's taxable is taxed at their highest rate of tax (including investment income surcharge if they pay it).

Giving money to your children during your lifetime could save capital transfer tax
In general, you have to pay capital transfer tax on anything over £55,000 that you give away during any 10-year period in your lifetime, or on your death. But some types of gift are tax-free and don't count towards the £55,000 limit. It makes sense to take advantage of these tax-free ways of handing money to your children during your lifetime. For a list of the main tax-free gifts you can make, see p60.

And in general, gifts which are taxable are taxed at a lower rate if you make them at least three years before your death rather than leaving them in your will.

Note that husband and wife are taxed separately for capital transfer tax purposes – and can each make their quota of tax-free gifts.

If you want to invest money for your child without him being able to get his hands on it for the time being, consider taking out an insurance policy where the proceeds are made payable to your child – see Short-cut trusts on p221

If you pay income tax at more than 45 per cent, want to give your children large amounts of money and don't want to put the money into investment-type life insurance, consider setting up an accumulation trust
Income which is accumulated is taxed at a flat rate – 45 per cent for the 1982–83 tax year.

Giving money to your grandchildren (or any other children who aren't your own) could mean less tax to pay on the income it produces
Income which comes from gifts made to a child by anyone other than his parents counts as the child's own income for tax purposes. A child can have income of at least as much as the single person's allowance (£1,565 a year in the 1982–83 tax year) before starting to pay tax.

If you want to give money to your grandchild (or any other child who isn't your own) who doesn't pay tax, and you don't mind him being able to spend it, consider setting up a deed of covenant
For more about covenants, see overleaf.

Covenants

These may be a particularly effective way of handing over money to a child not your own – eg a grandchild. And they could also help you in paying money to your own student child, once over 18 (or married).

A deed of covenant is a legally binding agreement under which one person promises to make a series of payments to another. Covenant payments to an individual qualify for tax relief provided:
- neither the person making the payments, nor his wife, gets any benefit from the money
- the covenant does not benefit the children of the person making them unless they are at least 18, or married
- the agreement is for more than 6 years.

How a covenant works

Suppose you agree to pay a *gross* amount of £100 a year under a covenant – to your grandson, say. You deduct tax from this gross amount at the basic rate (30 per cent for the 1982–83 tax year) and hand over £70 (£100–£30). Note that you deduct tax at the *basic rate* – even if you pay tax at higher rates. You're allowed to keep this £30 tax provided you pay tax at the basic or higher rates on at least as much of your income as your gross covenant payments.

If your grandson's income – including the £100 gross amount of the covenant – is low enough for him not to pay tax, he can claim £30 from the taxman. So at a cost to you of £70 a year, your grandson can get a total of £100. To claim tax back, your grandson should get form R185(AP) from you – get this from the taxman.

If your grandson pays tax at the basic or higher rates, he can't claim any tax from the taxman – so there is no tax saving in using a covenant. But covenant payments received are not liable for higher rate tax or the investment income surcharge – so there is no extra tax to pay either.

Is it worth making a covenant?

If the person making the payments can get tax relief on them, there continues to be a tax advantage as long as the child getting them pays no tax on his income (including the gross amount of the covenant payments). For the 1982–83 tax year it would be worthwhile to use a covenant to make a child's taxable income up to £1,565 a year (the amount of the single person's allowance).

Covenants for students

A parent can get tax relief on covenant payments to his own children provided they're 18 or over, or married. The same rules about tax relief and so on as above apply, so this could be a very effective way of paying a child's maintenance while at college.

A child's income may affect his student grant. The rule for undergraduate grants is that if a child has after-tax income above a certain level (£345 for 1982–83), his grant is reduced by £1 for every £1 of income over the limit. But the following do *not* count as income for this purpose:
- earnings from holiday jobs
- covenant payments from parents, unless the child is 'independent' (broadly, aged 25 or more, or had supported himself for at least 3 years before starting the course).

Check the rules for other grants.

Covenants and life insurance policies

Premiums for most regular-premium life insurance policies qualify for a subsidy from the taxman (at 15 per cent for the 1982–83 tax year) – irrespective of whether or not you pay tax. A child can get this subsidy on premiums paid for a policy to insure his own life when he is 12 or over (in Scotland, girls can't take out policies until age 12, boys age 14). Some companies won't issue policies until the

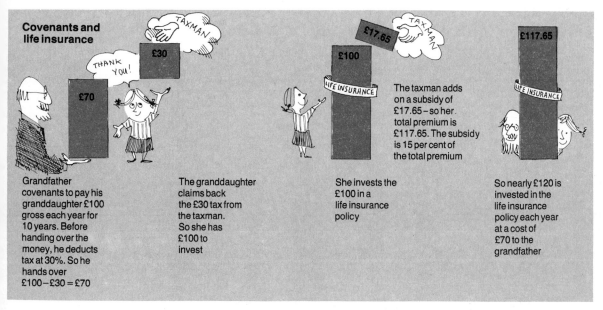

Covenants and life insurance

Grandfather covenants to pay his granddaughter £100 gross each year for 10 years. Before handing over the money, he deducts tax at 30%. So he hands over £100 − £30 = £70

The granddaughter claims back the £30 tax from the taxman. So she has £100 to invest

She invests the £100 in a life insurance policy

The taxman adds on a subsidy of £17.65 – so her total premium is £117.65. The subsidy is 15 per cent of the total premium

So nearly £120 is invested in the life insurance policy each year at a cost of £70 to the grandfather

child is 16 or 18. Policies taken out by a child can't normally be cashed in until the child is 18 or over.

By combining a covenant with a life insurance policy, you could get the result shown in the Diagram above. The overall rate of return depends, of course, not just on the help from the taxman, but also on the rate of return on the insurance policy in the scheme.

A number of insurance companies market schemes of this type. Or you could do-it-yourself, and make your own choice of insurance policy. It would be simplest for a bank account to be opened in the child's name, to receive the covenant payments, and pay the insurance premiums.

Drawing up a covenant

You can draw up your own deed of covenant without getting professional help, by following the wording in our example below. The covenant we've illustrated would be suitable for a student child. You can modify it for a non-student by leaving out the phrase *or until she ceases to be receiving full-time education at any university, college, school or any other educational establishment.*

You must date the deed, sign it, and get someone (not the person you are paying) to witness it. The deed must also be sealed – you can do this by sticking on a disc of paper (lawyers use red). You can make a thorough job of delivering it by putting the tip of the first finger of your right hand on the seal saying *'I deliver this as my act and deed',* and then handing over or sending the deed to the person you are paying. The first payment must be payable *on or after* the date the deed is signed, sealed and delivered.

In Scotland, if the deed is not in your own handwriting – eg if it is written by someone else, or typed – you must write the words *adopted as holograph* above your signature, and on each of the preceding pages (if any).

A covenant is normally worded so that the payments automatically come to an end if either the person who gives the money or the person who receives it dies before the covenant ends. A covenant can usually be cancelled at any stage by mutual consent – but not by children under 18, and it must not be agreed in advance that it will be.

I, George Shrewd, of Hill Cottage, Slagthorpe, covenant to pay my daughter, Sara, of the same address, a gross amount of £140 on each of the following dates in each year, namely 1 October, 1 January and 1 April, for the period of seven years, or for the period of our joint lives, or until she ceases to be receiving full-time education at any university, college, school or any other educational establishment (whichever is the shortest period), the first payment to be made on 1 October 1982.

Dated 1 June 1982

Signed, sealed and delivered by George Shrewd:

George Shrewd .... SEAL ⬤

in the presence of:

Tom Observer Brian Patch Slagthorpe

(witness's signature and address)

Planning for school fees

If you've decided to send your child (or children) to a private school, you're going to be faced with substantial bills.

School fees for a boarder might currently work out at about £2,500 a year for a prep school, for example, £3,900 a year for a public school.

You may well find paying fees out of your current income hard going. So if there's time in hand, it's worth looking into ways of saving now for school fees in the future. When working out how much you might need, don't forget that school fees – along with prices in general, and your earnings – are likely to rise over the years, due to inflation.

Various insurance companies and brokers specialise in arranging schemes to provide the money that's needed for fees at the time it's needed. In the main, these schemes are based on investment-type life insurance policies and annuities.

We give details of the main types of school fees schemes opposite. Broadly, they fall into two groups:
● **capital** schemes were you invest a lump sum now to provide fees in the future
● **income** schemes where you save on a regular basis to build up the money needed to pay school fees.

Depending on your circumstances a mixture of the different types may suit you best.

Note that these schemes do not *guarantee* to pay a child's school fees whatever they are – they simply pay out sums of money at various intervals (which may turn out to be less than, or more than, enough to pay the fees).

It's worth bearing in mind that there's nothing magical about school fees schemes. They are simply a way of investing money in order to make a set of payments some time in the future – and they use the sorts of investment which you might well choose to invest in yourself if you were arranging to save up for school fees independently. However, there has to be careful timing of the investments to make sure there's money around when the fees are due, and there are tax complications which have to be taken into account. So rather than going it alone, you may decide it's best to make your investments through a special school fees scheme.

Where to go for school fees schemes   Your bank or a reputable insurance broker should be able to help you – or put you in touch with an insurance company or broker specialising in school fees schemes. Or you could try *Independent Schools Information Service* (tel 01-222 7353) for help. But get quotes from more than one source – different schemes suit different people, and you could save money by shopping around.

How school fees schemes work

Capital schemes   You pay a lump sum to an insurance company or broker. How it's
invested depends on the type of scheme. Some schemes (which we
call **annuity trust schemes**) can have income tax advantages – see
below. With these, the money is held in trust and invested in an
annuity on the child's life. The annuity starts paying out at the time
the child is expected to start at the fee-paying school, and stops
when the child is expected to leave. The annuity payments are
made to the school.

With other schemes, a range of investments might be used to
provide the fees – including British Government stocks, building
society accounts, annuities, life insurance policies. If you wish,
these investments may be held in trust for the child.

Most trust schemes include an option to cash in the scheme if
you decide you don't want to send your child to a private school
after all. If you keep this option, or if the investments aren't held in
trust, you can cash in the scheme at any time. But see below for a
possible capital transfer tax complication if you keep the option to
cash in a trust scheme. The amount you get back normally depends
on the value of the annuity, British Government stocks, or
whatever, at the time. Some schemes guarantee that you'll get back
at least 90 to 95 per cent of what your originally invested; a few
guarantee a rate of interest (up to four per cent) on top of this.

If you've given up your right to cash in a trust scheme, then
what's paid out (and to whom) is left to the discretion of the
trustees. If you said at the outset that the money invested was to be
used for maintaining, educating or training the child – so avoiding
capital transfer tax, see below – the trustees have no choice but to
use the money in this way.

How much do you need to invest?

With most schemes there's a minimum investment – usually
£1,000. Beyond this, the amount you need to invest will depend on
how long there is until the fees start and what the fees are expected
to be. If you have a just-born child, you would need to think about
investing a lump sum of £23,000 or more to pay fully for private
boarding education (assuming fees went up from current levels by
10 per cent a year).

Tax

With annuity trust schemes (see above) there's no income tax to pay
on the money paid out for school fees. This can make such schemes
attractive for higher rate taxpayers.

With other schemes (whether in trust or not) there may be some
income tax to pay on money paid out by the scheme, if the parents
(or the child if the scheme was set up by anyone other than the
parents) pay tax at more than the basic rate.

How much capital transfer tax has to be paid and when, depends
on who gives the money – see overleaf.

If the parents give the money   Payments made by the parents solely for the *maintenance, education or training* of their children are free of capital transfer tax. So there's no capital transfer tax to pay when the money is first invested, nor when the fees are paid. But if the money is not held in trust – or if it is held in trust and the parents keep the right to cash in the scheme – there may be capital transfer tax to pay if the parent who gives the money dies. The cash-in value of the investment will form part of his or her estate, and will be taxed in the normal way. If the parent gives up the right to cash in a trust scheme, the money will remain in trust for the child and will be used for his maintenance, education or training – the money won't form part of the parent's estate.

If someone else (eg grandparents) give the money   If the grandparents (or whoever) don't set up a trust scheme, the money they eventually pay over for school fees will count as gifts for capital transfer tax.

  If they do set up a trust scheme – and they give up the right to cash in the scheme – the money they invest in the first place counts as a gift for capital transfer tax purposes. If they keep the right to cash in the scheme, what counts as a gift is the cash-in value of the scheme when fees start being paid (which will almost certainly be higher than the value of the original investment).

  Grandparents (or others) may be able to avoid capital transfer tax in the following way:

  The grandparents make an interest-free loan (repayable on demand) to the parents of the child, who immediately invest the money in a trust for the education of the child (so the parents don't have to pay capital transfer tax). The grandparents let the parents off the loan at a rate of £3,000 a year (£6,000 if *both* grandparents made the loan), until the debt is wiped out. A disadvantage is that the grandparents could ask for the outstanding loan back at any time, and if they were to die the money would count as part of their estate. And the taxman may not look kindly on such a scheme – so before trying anything on these lines, ask the Inland Revenue Capital Taxes office what they think.

Composition fees
You can, with many private schools, pay school fees in advance by what's known as a **composition fee**. In this case, the school then invests the money, often in an annuity which starts paying out when the child goes to school. The amounts you have to invest will vary from school to school but are broadly similar to those involved in capital schemes.

Income schemes   There are a number of different ways in which these schemes can be set up – but most involve saving regularly by taking out investment-type life insurance policies, ending year by year as the fees become due.

  For example, suppose you plan to send your child to public school in 10 years time for five years. You could take out five with-profits endowment policies which end after 10, 11, 12, 13 and 14 years respectively. For the first 10 years, you'd pay a flat amount (the premiums for all the policies). From the eleventh year onwards, the premiums would start to tail off, as each policy ended.

  If you expect your income to go up over the years you might prefer to pay premiums which increase rather than decrease. In this case, it may be best to take out five 10-year policies in successive years. Your premiums will increase each year up to the fifth year, stay level for the next five years, then tail off as policies end.

Some companies use unit-linked policies (see chapter 14) to provide part or all of the fees. With these, there's the risk that when you want to cash in a policy, the value of the units may be particularly low and you might get less than you'd hoped for.

If you change your mind about sending your child to private school, what happens depends on whether or not the policies are being held in trust for the child. If they are being held in trust (which gives a possible capital transfer tax advantage – see below) the money from the policies must be used for the benefit of the child. If they are not being held in trust you can either cash in the policies, or keep them as a form of saving.

How much do you need to invest?

As with capital schemes, the amount you need to invest will depend on how long there is to go before your child is going to private school and what the fees are expected to be. If you were hoping to provide private boarding education for a just-born child (assuming fees went up from current levels at 10 per cent a year) you would have to think about investing around £1,000 in the first year, rising to £6,500 in the year in which the child starts school, staying at that level for two years, then decreasing.

Tax

There's normally no income tax to pay on the money paid out by these schemes (except, in certain circumstances, when a life insurance policy has to be cashed in early).

If it's the parents who pay for the scheme there's no capital transfer tax to pay on the premiums or on the money paid out by the policies. If people other than the parents pay for the scheme, there's no capital transfer tax to pay so long as the premiums are paid out of their normal income – or count as tax-free for some other reason (see p60). If the policies are being held in trust for the child, there's no capital transfer tax to pay if the person who set up the scheme dies. But if the policies are not being held in trust, the proceeds on death count as part of the person's estate.

Failed to plan? If you've left it too late, or the fees are more than you anticipated – don't despair. All may not be lost:
- try your bank manager. If you've got security – eg investments you don't want to cash, or a home with no mortgage (or only a small one) – you may be able to get a bank loan
- a specialist school fees broker may be able to arrange a loan based on the security of your home
- if you have an investment-type life insurance policy, you may be able to borrow from the insurance company on the strength of it
- some banks will lend you the money for school fees if you agree to take out an investment-type life insurance.

Children and tax

Income tax

Children's income

If the child gets investment income of more than £5 a year which comes from gifts or trusts *provided by the parents,* it is normally treated as the parents' income for tax purposes. They will pay tax on it at their highest rate of tax, including the investment income surcharge if this applies.

If the child gets investment income which comes from gifts, trusts or inheritances provided by anyone other than the parents, or from money he has saved out of his own earnings, it is treated as the child's own income for tax purposes. The child gets his or her own Tax Return, and can claim the single person's allowance (£1,565 for the 1982–83 tax year) and any other allowances for which he or she qualifies.

Trust income

A *fixed* trust pays tax at the basic rate on its income. Any income paid out of the trust comes with a tax credit of the amount of tax deducted (30 per cent of the before-tax income for the 1982–83 tax year).

If the trust was set up by the parents, the income counts as the parents' (see above), and they get the 30 per cent tax credit. If the trust was set up by anyone other than the parents, the income counts as the child's and the child gets the tax credit. If the parents (or child, as the case may be) don't pay tax, or pay less than the tax deducted, they can claim tax back.

If the highest rate of tax the parents (or the child) pay is 30 per cent, the tax liability on income from the trust is automatically met by the tax credit.

If the parents (or child) pay tax at a rate of more than 30 per cent (including the investment income

surcharge, if they pay it) they will have to pay extra tax – calculated on the income paid out plus the tax credit.

Discretionary trusts These pay tax on their income at the basic rate (30 per cent for the 1982–83 tax year) plus investment income surcharge (15 per cent) – ie at a rate of 45 per cent for the 1982–83 tax year.

As with a fixed trust, any income paid out is taxed as either the parents' income (if the trust was set up by the parents) or the child's income (in any other case). But with a discretionary trust, the income comes with a tax credit of 45 per cent of the before-tax amount of income. Whether or not there's more tax to pay (or whether a rebate can be claimed) depends on whether the parents' (or child's) top rate of tax is more or less than 45 per cent. If the top rate is *less* than 45 per cent, it would be worth asking the trustees to pay as much income out as possible – as tax could then be claimed back from the taxman. With an accumulation trust, if the income is accumulated and not paid out until your children are 18 or over, there'll be no further income tax to pay – but neither you nor your children will be able to claim tax back.

Capital transfer tax

For brief details of how capital transfer tax works, see pages 60 and 61 in Chapter 5.

If you make a gift to your child (or set up a trust under which he or she benefits) it normally counts as a gift for capital transfer tax purposes.

But some gifts you make are free of capital transfer tax – we summarise the main ones to bear in mind on p60.

Below we tell you some of the special capital transfer tax rules which apply to trusts.

Capital transfer tax on trusts

The taxation of trust funds and settlements can be very complicated – one reason for getting professional advice if you're setting up a tailor-made trust.

In general, with trusts set up after 26 March 1974, the value of the money, property (or whatever) you put into the trust counts as a gift at the time you make it – and is taxed in the ordinary way. In the main, gifts into trusts count as tax-free if they would be tax-free when made to an individual.

With a fixed trust, anyone with the right to income or the equivalent of income (eg the right to live in a rent-free home) from the trust is considered to own the trust's capital – or part of the trust's capital, if the rights to the benefits are shared among several people. When a person's right to the trust's benefits goes to someone else, he's considered to be making a gift. For example, your child may have the right to income from a trust once he reaches 18. If this right passes to his younger sister when she reaches 21, he is considered to make a gift at that time. The gift is valued as the share of the trust's capital which he is considered to own, at the time the right to the income is transferred, and is added to his running total of taxable gifts and taxed in the normal way – this tax is paid by the trust.

When the trust finally comes to an end, and the capital is handed over to beneficiaries who until that time had the right to the income, there's no further capital transfer tax to pay.

Discretionary trusts (other than accumulation and maintenance trusts – see next column).

A discretionary trust may be charged capital transfer tax even if payments aren't made out of the trust. Capital transfer tax is automatically charged every 10 years on everything in the trust at that time. The rate of tax is based on the running total (see p60) of the person who first set up the trust immediately before he set it up, and also on the amounts that have been paid from the trust in the previous 10 years on which tax has been charged. Tax is charged at 30 per cent of the rate which would apply to this person. The 10-year periods are calculated from the date the trust was set up, but no trust will have to start paying this 10-yearly charge until its first tenth anniversary after 31 March 1983.

When payments are actually made from a discretionary trust's capital (or if fixed interests are created), the trust is also charged capital transfer tax. The value of what's paid out (or turned into a fixed interest) is scaled down in proportion to the time since the last 10-yearly charge – eg if it's one year since the 10-yearly charge, the value is taken as one-tenth of what's paid out. Tax is charged on this scaled-down amount at the rate which applied for the last 10-yearly charge. If the payment from the

trust is made within three months after a 10-yearly charge, there's no tax to be paid.

Note that these rules were under discussion when this book went to press. Check with your professional adviser on the final rules.

There are special rules for discretionary trusts set up before 27 March 1974, and rules to allow the trustees to reorganise these trusts without incurring massive capital transfer tax bills. But these rules end on 31 March 1983 – so if they affect you, get advice now.

Accumulation and maintenance trusts Payments of capital from certain accumulation and maintenance trusts are free of capital transfer tax. And these trusts are also free of the 10-yearly tax bills. To qualify, a trust must be for the benefit of one or more people under the age of 25, who must get the capital of the trust (or at least the right to the income, or use of the trust property) on or before their 25th birthday. If any income is paid out from the trust before this, it must be used only for the maintenance, education or training of the beneficiaries.

If the trust was set up after 14 April 1976, it will be free of capital transfer tax only if the children who benefit have a grandparent in common or the trust is less than 25 years old.

Capital gains tax

If you hand over assets (such as shares, or your second home) to your children, or put them into a trust, you *dispose* of what you've given – and there may be some capital gains tax to pay (as well as capital transfer tax) unless *roll-over relief* is claimed. The asset is valued at its market value at the time you make the gift. For the rules about capital gains tax, see pages 53 to 59 in Chapter 5.

Bear in mind that the first £5,000 (for the 1982–83 tax year) of net capital gains you make from disposing of assets during a tax year is tax-free.

Once a gift has been made, how much capital gains tax has to be paid on any further gains depends on whether the child controls the investment, or whether it's in trust.

Gains made by a child

Capital gains made by a child are taxed as the child's own gains not the parents'. The normal rules for working out capital gains tax apply – so, for example, the child can make £5,000 of gains in a tax year without paying tax.

Gains made by a trust

Trusts set up after 6 June 1978 pay capital gains tax at a flat rate of 30 per cent on net capital gains of over £2,500 which they make. This means that trusts are often liable for more capital gains tax than an individual. If a beneficiary becomes entitled to some or all of the assets of the trust – for example, when he reaches 18 – this counts as the trust disposing of the assets, and if there are gains, capital gains tax has to be paid by the trust (unless the trustees and beneficiary apply for *roll-over relief*).

25 Savings and retirement

In earlier chapters of this book, we've looked in detail at the various pension schemes which may be open to you. This information is crucial in working out how much you can expect from these sources. But that's not the end of the story – you need to work out how much extra (if anything) you need to save, to be moderately sure of an adequate income in retirement. And if you're already retired, you may be looking for ways in which you can boost your income.

Whether retirement is 20 years off, or coming up soon, the first step in sorting out your retirement finances is to look at how your income is likely to compare with your expenditure when you retire.

Of course, inflation could make a mockery of your retirement budgeting if you're looking a good many years ahead. Currently, though, the state retirement pension is increased regularly in line with rising prices. And the amount you can expect from an employer's pension – if based on final pay – should go up too, at least in the period up to retirement. But the buying-power of the income you can expect from any savings could be drastically reduced by inflation. The best you can probably do is to work out what you'll get (and what you'll need) in terms of today's prices and pensions. Then make regular checks – once a year, say – that you aren't going too far off course.

What you'll get   Your chief sources of income are likely to be some or all of:
- your state retirement pension
- a pension from your job (and from any earlier jobs)
- pensions from personal pension plans
- income from working after retirement
- income from any savings.

Your state retirement pension

Anyone who has worked for long enough (and paid enough NI contributions) is entitled to a *basic pension* – £32.85 a week for a single person, £52.55 for a married man, in November 1982. Employed people who are not contracted-out of the state scheme, and who retire after April 1979, may get an *additional pension* as well. People who were employed between April 1961 and April 1975 may also get a *graduated pension*. See Chapter 17.

The Table opposite shows for different levels of income, what state retirement pension (basic plus additional) you could expect with different lengths of time to go to retirement. The pension we give is worked out at today's rates – but state pensions are currently increased each year broadly in line with prices in general. As long as this continues, these pensions should have roughly the same buying-power in the future as now.

How much state retirement pension to expect [1]

tax year in which you'll retire	your earnings: typical yearly amount in today's money	your yearly state pension single person	married couple	married couple if each qualifies for own pension [2]
	£	£	£	£
1983–84	4,000	1,860	2,890	3,470
	6,000	1,990	3,010	3,600
(with 5 years	8,000	2,110	3,140	3,720
additional	10,000	2,240	3,260	3,850
pension)	15,000	2,330	3,350	4,160
1988–89	4,000	2,020	3,040	3,530
	6,000	2,270	3,290	3,780
(with 10 years	8,000	2,520	3,540	4,030
additional	10,000	2,770	3,790	4,280
pension)	15,000	2,950	3,970	4,910
1993–94	4,000	2,170	3,190	3,590
	6,000	2,550	3,570	3,970
(with 15 years	8,000	2,920	3,940	4,340
additional	10,000	3,300	4,320	4,720
pension)	15,000	3,570	4,590	5,650
1998–99 or later	4,000	2,320	3,350	3,650
	6,000	2,820	3,850	4,150
(with 20 years	8,000	3,320	4,350	4,650
additional	10,000	3,820	4,850	5,150
pension)	15,000	4,180	5,210	6,400

[1] Assuming you retire at age 65 (men) or 60 (women) and that you are not contracted-out of the state scheme. Includes the basic pension and any additional pension, but not the graduated pension. Amounts based on rates to apply from 24 November 1982. All the figures in the Table assume that you qualify for as much pension from the state as you possibly can, given your age and earnings. If you have gaps in your National Insurance contributions record, you may get a lower amount. If you are contracted-out of the state scheme, you'll get at least as much as is shown through your employer's scheme.
[2] Assuming husband and wife each earn half the amount shown in the *your earnings* column. If they don't, pension will be somewhat less – between amounts shown in this column and previous one.

A pension from your job

What you will get from an employer's pension scheme depends on how the scheme is set up. With *final pay schemes* you get a proportion (one-sixtieth, or one-eightieth, say) of your 'final pay' (as defined by your scheme) for each year you've been in the scheme. With *money purchase schemes*, your pension is the income that you and your employer's contributions can buy at the time you retire. See Chapter 17 for more details, and check with your employer how your scheme works, and approximately how much you could hope to get when you retire.

The problem with a pension from a job, is that though it may seem handsome when you first retire, it's likely to look less appealing after 10 years or so, if it hasn't increased in line with inflation. The Table overleaf shows the effect of inflation on the buying-power of your money.

Effect of inflation

yearly rate of inflation	what £1,000 will be worth		
	after 10 yrs	after 15 yrs	after 20 yrs
5%	£614	£481	£377
10%	£386	£239	£149
15%	£247	£123	£61
20%	£162	£65	£26
25%	£107	£35	£12

Many schemes have some pension increases built in. And some employers have, in the past, given special increases to help cope with inflation. But unless you belong to a scheme where the pension is index-linked (eg the Civil Service and other public sector schemes), you should allow for inflation in working out how well off you'll be after you retire.

If your scheme provides a lump sum in addition to your pension (or in place of part of your pension if you choose) deciding which to take isn't easy – see p158 for things to take into account.

It's unlikely that you'll stay in one job all your working life – and unfortunately, changing jobs is likely to mean you end up with less pension than if you'd stayed with one employer. You may get a *deferred pension* from the job you leave (based on the number of years you were in the scheme). This pension (except with schemes in the public sector) is unlikely to be increased to keep pace with inflation after you've left. So when taking a deferred pension into account, you should allow for the fact that inflation is likely to gradually erode its buying-power (use the Table on this page to adjust for the number of years you've got before you retire). For example, if your deferred pension is £2,000, and you have 20 years to go to retirement and you reckon inflation will average 15 per cent over that period, your deferred pension will be worth just £61 × 2,000 ÷ 1,000 = £122 in buying-power. Even if the rate of inflation were 5 per cent, it would be worth only £754.

With some pension schemes, you can arrange for a *transfer payment* from your old scheme into the new one you're joining. In return for this, you may get a fixed yearly addition (in £££) to whatever your pension from your new job will eventually be. Or you may be credited with years of membership in the new scheme – which would at least ensure that your pension was linked to your final pay.

Pensions from personal pension plans

If you're self-employed, or in a job but not in its pension scheme, you may be contributing to personal pension plans (see Chapter 18), and will get pensions from the insurance companies to which you've paid premiums. Check up with the companies (if they haven't told you already) how much pension your payments have so far earned you, and how much you'll get if you keep paying a certain amount into a plan each year. You'll have to adjust the figure you're given to allow for inflation between now and retirement – see above. To build up an adequate pension, you should aim to pay up to the maximum allowed for tax relief – see p178.

Working after retirement

Be wary of setting too much store on this. The economic situation may make jobs for people over retirement age hard to come by, your health may have deteriorated, or you may find yourself less and less inclined to go on working. So don't rely on this source of income to carry you through a major part of your retirement. And bear the *earnings rule* in mind – see p163. Note that if you do work after retirement age, you may be advised to put off drawing your state pension, and thereby building up more – see p163.

Income from savings

If you have money saved already, or plan to save in the future, you can add on to what you get in the way of pensions any income you'll get from investments. But bear in mind:

Widows – or other dependants

While planning your retirement finances, it's vital to check that your widow or other dependants wouldn't be left short should you die. Many employer's pension schemes provide a widow's pension (and possibly a lump sum too) on the death of the employee – whether before or after retirement. If your widow couldn't manage on this (together with any income from their job job, your savings, and state benefits) you need life insurance. This book doesn't cover this aspect of your family finances – for how to work out how much life insurance you need, see *Protection-only life insurance, Money Which?* December 1979, p681.

● if you invest your money for maximum safety, its value (except with a few investments – see p237) is not likely to keep pace with inflation – its buying-power, and that of the income you get from it, will fall over the years

● if you've accepted some degree of risk in the attempt to safeguard the buying-power of your money, you stand the chance of losing at least some of it. So it's sensible to make a pessimistic estimate of the income your investments will provide in, say, 20 years' time.

What you'll need   Around the time you retire, a shift in your spending pattern is very probable. You may be able to predict some of this change fairly easily, especially the part that relates to simply stopping work. You won't have to pay for fares to and from the office, for example, or for lunches at work. And you may also know that you'll spend more on particular hobbies – golf, gardening, or painting, say – when you have the time to give to them. You may also know that some of your current financial commitments – the mortgage, or school fees, for example – will have ended by the time you retire.

It's less easy to take into account the effects of simply growing older. In your late sixties, you may well want to spend more than you do now on, for example, staying warm, transport, labour-saving appliances, holidays (you may not want to rough it any more).

Giving realistic weight to this kind of age-related spending change is very hard – particularly if you're trying to look 20 or 30 years into the future. But it's still worth trying to allow for it when you work out your future spending needs: that way you can stand a better chance of coming closer to the truth than you do if you assume you'll spend your money the same way in your retirement as in your thirties or forties.

Balancing your   If you are looking ahead some time to retirement, you need to be
budget   thinking of ways of protecting your long-term savings against inflation, until the time comes when you'll actually need them.

The first three chapters of this book will help you in making your choices. If you're not buying a home already, this may be one of the best forms of long-term investment you could make – see Chapter 6. If you're already buying a home, moving to a better, more expensive one might pay.

If you're employed and there's a pension scheme at work, this is likely to be a worthwhile way of saving – and you could consider making additional voluntary contributions (see p158), especially in the last few years before retirement. Both your own and your employer's pension contributions are normally free from income tax. And they go into a special fund which doesn't have to pay income tax or capital gains tax. In addition, your pension is often linked to your pay when you leave your job, so giving you some protection against inflation until you retire.

If your employer doesn't have a pension scheme, or if you're self-employed, you should consider taking out a personal pension plan. This is, in effect, a pension scheme run by an insurance company for individuals rather than for groups of employees.

As with an employer's scheme, you get tax relief on your contributions, up to a certain limit. The fund your payments go into pays no income tax or capital gains tax. So you should get a good return on your money – but you won't be able to get it out before retirement.

Employed people who can choose whether to belong to their employer's scheme and who feel its benefits are poor, should check on whether they'd do better to go for a personal pension plan – though, of course, they then won't get any help through employers' contributions. Consider putting most of your other long-term savings into investments where your money at least stands a chance of maintaining its buying-power – such as index-linked National Savings Certificates, Save-As-You-Earn or British Government stocks, property bonds, commodity funds, alternative investments (eg stamps, silver). Be prepared to move your money around to take advantage of the investment opportunities of the day. Bear in mind the rate of tax you pay. Make sure your investments give you the best return – taking both income tax and capital gains tax into account (see p42).

Making ends meet in retirement

Your major sources of income in retirement are likely to be your pensions (from the state, and from any other schemes you were in) and the income from your savings. If you've already retired, there's likely to be little scope for building up extra savings to increase your income. And you may find that, because of inflation, an income which seemed adequate at the start of retirement, is looking on the low side now. The Table on p234 shows the devastating effects of inflation – bear this in mind when considering how much income you'll need over your retirement years.

Before checking on ways in which you could boost your income, consider ways of cutting your expenses. For example, check that you are claiming all the help that's available from social security (in the way of rate rebates, supplementary pension, and the like) or from your local authority (meals on wheels, home helps and the like). Check at your local social security office and Town Hall. Also make sure you're not paying more tax than you need – the current *Money Which?* Tax-Saving Guide should help. Look carefully at how you're spending your money *now* to see if there are any areas where you could cut back relatively painlessly.

You could also think about moving to a house which is cheaper

Tax after retirement

Like everybody else, the over-65s are liable for tax. But they can claim a higher personal allowance than younger people – so more of their income can be tax-free.

Age allowance

Anyone who is 64 or over before the start of the tax year (or whose wife is) can claim age allowance – whether or not they have retired – instead of the ordinary single person's or married man's allowance. For the 1982–83 tax year the full age allowance is £2,070 for a single person, £3,295 for a married man. But age allowance is reduced by two-thirds of the amount by which a person's 'total income' (see p43) exceeds a certain limit – £6,700 for the 1982–83 tax year. The allowance is never reduced below the level of the ordinary personal allowance, no matter how high 'total income' is. For the 1982–83 tax year, an elderly person with an income of not more than £7,457 if single, or £7,974 if married, could benefit from age allowance.

If your 'total income' is within the range where your age allowance is being reduced, bear in mind that each extra £ of taxable income you get will effectively be taxed at a fairly high rate – 50 per cent in the 1982–83 tax year. This might make investments where the return is not taxable (eg National Savings Certificates) worth considering – look carefully at investments with a ○ next to them in the Route Maps on pages 18 and 20.

See opposite for a complication which can arise if you cash in part of a life insurance policy.

Married women's pensions

If you're a married woman, a pension for which you qualify on your own contributions counts as your own earned income. This means that you can claim the wife's earned income allowance on it. For the 1982–83 tax year, up to £1,565 of your earnings (including any pension you earned in your own right) is tax free.

If you get a pension based on your husband's contributions, it normally counts as your husband's income, and wife's earned income allowance cannot be set against it. If you're entitled to a pension of your own but choose to get a (higher) pension based on your husband's contributions, you can count as your earnings the amount of pension you were entitled to on your own contributions.

to run – one with lower rates and fuel bills, or closer to shops, for example. But don't put off this decision for too long – it may be easier to make the move and establish new friends and social activities earlier in retirement.

If you've managed to cut down your expenses, you could either invest the money, or use some or all of it in ways which will cut costs later on – eg insulating your home, making repairs to your home. This sort of investment may not give you the best return on your money – but knowing that there'll be fewer large bills to meet later in retirement may be worth it in terms of peace of mind.

Boosting your income

More income from your investments

Check first that your investments are working as well for you as they can (taking into account the way you are taxed – see opposite). You should be looking for investments that stand a chance of maintaining their buying-power – either through an increasing income as time passes, or through capital growth with the possibility of withdrawing regular amounts to use as income. No investment can fully match these needs – so keep an eye on your investments to see how they're doing and likely to do. For general advice on planning your savings and brief details of a wide range of investments, see the first three chapters of this book.

National Savings Certificates (2nd Index-linked Issue) can protect at least part of your capital against inflation. The limit on the amount you can invest is £5,000 (£10,000 for a married couple). See p194 for details. To protect more of your savings against inflation, consider taking out an index-linked Save-As-You-Earn scheme (you don't have to be earning to qualify). You invest a regular monthly amount (from £4 to £50 over a five-year period). Details on p196. You could also consider index-linked British Government stocks (see Chapter 10). Whether you get a return greater or less than inflation depends on the price you buy at, whether you can hang on until redemption, or if not, the price you sell at.

An annuity is an investment designed especially for the elderly. You hand over your capital to an insurance company in return for a guaranteed income for the rest of your life – see Chapter 16.

Income from your home

You may be able to use your home to raise extra income in retirement. One way of doing this is to sell it and move to a cheaper one, chosen with an eye to lower running cost. This should leave you with a lump sum to invest.

If your home is of a convenient size and easy to run, you may feel there is no need for you to move. You could instead consider getting extra income through a home income scheme – which is specially designed for elderly people (the over-70s, say). See p154.

An alternative way to use your home to raise money – without moving out – is to let part of it, or to take in a lodger. Before you decide to try this however, get up-to-date information on your rights (and duties) as a landlord – in particular, what your rights are about getting your lodger or tenant out at some later date. The Department of the Environment publishes a series of leaflets which give the current rules – get them from your local Citizens' Advice Bureau. And remember that when you take a lodger or tenant you are going into business on a small scale: you should keep careful records of income and expenses, and keep an eye on changes in the law which may affect you. It would be prudent to get advice from a solicitor before becoming a landlord.

Gains on life insurance policies

If you've invested in a single-premium life insurance policy (see p136) and would like to cash part of it in, be careful. If you're getting age allowance there could be snags. Although any taxable gain you make when you cash in this type of life insurance policy is free of basic rate tax, it is counted as part of your investment income for the year. And increasing your income can mean you get less age allowance (see opposite) so pay more tax.

If you cash in part of a life insurance policy, for each year that you've held the policy you're allowed to cash in 5% of the premiums you've paid so far without it affecting your tax position at the time. If, for example, you invested £2,000 two years ago in a single-premium bond, your 'allowances' come to £2,000 × 2 × 5% = £200. If you cash in more than this, the excess is counted as a 'gain' in the year you make it, regardless of how much of it (if any) is in fact gain and how much is return of premiums. Cashing in £1,000, for example, would therefore lead to a 'gain' of: £1,000 − £200 = £800. This would be added to your 'total income' and could reduce your age allowance dramatically. So it's wise not to cash in more than the allowances you've built up – unless you cash in the whole of the policy (in which case only the actual gain is added to your income).

Index

Accountants 36, 85, 220
Accumulation trusts 221, 223, 230
Accumulation and maintenance trusts 221, 222, 231
Actuals, buying and selling 110
Additional voluntary contributions (AVCs) 21, 158, 235
Advice, professional investment 34–41
Age allowance 9, 51, 236
Age and investment 9
Alternative investments 10, 11, 14, 26, 70–7, 181, 236
and tax 72, 73
Aluminium, investing in 111
Annuities 9, 18–19, 23, 26–7, 45, 46, 66, 150–5, 158, 164, 167, 168, 170, 176, 177, 226, 227, 237
and tax 149, 152, 153, 154, 155
types of 150–1, 153, 154
Annuity, deferred 149, 150, 174
Annuity/endowment income bonds 149
Annuity trust schemes 227
Antique Collectors' Club, The 77
Antiques, investing in 10, 12, 72, 181
Associated Scottish Life Offices 41, 129
Association of Certified Accountants 41
Association of Independent Investment Managers 39
Association of Investment Trust Companies 41

Bank accounts see Deposit accounts, bank

Bank investment departments 40
Bank managers 38, 85
Bank of England 189, 191, 208
Banking Act 1979, 191
Banking Information Service 41
Bars, gold see Gold, investing in
Bond and Share Certificate Collectors' Society, The 77
Bonds and Stock Office 203
Bonds, British Savings 44, 47, 53
Bonds, busted 73
Bonds, family 185
Bonds, guaranteed see Bonds, income and growth
Bonds, income and growth 18–19, 28–9, 45, 46, 148–9, 181
and tax 148, 149
choosing 149
types of 149
Bonds, single-premium investment 14, 18, 19, 22, 24, 25, 32–3, 49, 133, 134, 136–41, 142, 146
equity 133, 134
managed 133, 134, 222
property 11, 50, 51, 91, 133, 134, 181, 236
Bonus, endowment policy 124–6, 128, 130
Bonuses, reversionary 168
Bonuses, terminal 168
British Association of Numismatic Societies 77
British Government stocks see Stocks, British Government
British Insurance Association 41
British Insurance Brokers Association 37, 41
British Philatelic Federation 77
British Savings Bonds 207

Building societies and Save-As-You-Earn 185, 197
and tax 45, 180, 184, 185
choosing 187–8
deposit accounts 186
escalator bonds 18–19, 26–7, 181, 182, 183
fixed notice shares 18–19, 21, 26–7, 181, 182, 183
interest 15, 44, 45, 46, 180, 182, 183, 184, 185, 186, 187
life insurance, linked to 20, 21, 23, 26–7, 52, 181, 182, 184–5, 193
monthly income shares 182
mortgages from 11, 18–19, 20, 21, 65, 68–9, 181, 187–8
ordinary shares 11, 18–19, 20, 21, 22, 23, 24, 26–7, 180, 181, 182, 183, 184, 186, 187, 192, 209, 219
subscription shares 20, 21, 26–7, 181, 182, 184, 185, 187, 193, 218, 219
term shares 18–19, 26–7, 92, 136, 148, 180, 181, 182, 183, 219
see also Friendly societies
Building Societies Association, The 41, 168, 180, 188
Building Societies Gazette 182, 187
Bullion, investing in gold 76; see also Gold, investing in

Capital gains tax 8, 14, 22, 27, 42, 49, 53–9, 72, 76, 90, 101, 120, 138, 139, 145, 156, 216, 217, 223, 231, 235, 236
and British Government

stocks 59, 107, 108
and homes 65, 66
and marriage 59
Capital growth from investing 13–14
Capital, net working 83
Capital transfer tax 14, 42, 55, 60–1, 147, 154, 217, 220, 221, 223, 227–8, 229, 230, 231
Cash funds 133, 168
Chartered Institute of Public Finance and Accountancy 119
'Chartism' 82
Chief Registrar of Friendly Societies 132, 188
Children, investments for 218–31
and tax 218, 220, 221, 222, 223, 230–1
covenants 223, 224–5
school fees 226–9
trusts 220–2
Citizens' Advice Bureau 237
Clawback 52, 130, 145
Cocoa, investing in 110, 111, 112, 113, 114, 115, 116
Coffee, investing in 110, 114, 115, 116
Coins, investing in 11, 70, 76, 77
Commission on insurance 129
Commodities 19, 28–9, 110–16, 181, 236
and tax 116
investing in 115–16
prices of 112–14
Commodity funds 28–9, 115–6
Commodity options 111
Composition fees 228
Contract note 86–7
Contracted-out pension schemes 159, 160, 161
Conveyancing fees 68
Copper, investing in 110, 111, 113, 114, 115, 116
Corporation of Mortgage Brokers and Life Assurance Consultants 41

Corporation loans and stocks see Local authority investments stocks
Coupon, British Government stock 104, 106
Covenants 223, 224–5
and tax 224, 225
Credit card borrowing 66
Currency, cost of foreign 216
Currency, gains made on 211

Daily Telegraph, The 215
Debentures 88, 90
Department of Trade 99, 100, 116, 132, 214
Deposit accounts, bank 18–19, 20, 21, 26–7, 47, 48, 181, 189–90, 191, 208, 214, 218, 219
and interest 15, 22, 189, 190
and tax 189, 214
Deposits, finance company 15, 18–19, 28–9, 45, 47, 189, 191, 219
and interest 191
and tax 191
Deposits, Cooperative Society 47
Diamonds, investing in 10, 26–7, 75
Directory of British Associations 77
Discretionary trusts 46, 221, 230, 231
Distributions, unit trust 100, 101
Dividend yield 88
Dividends 45, 78, 88, 90
Dollar premium 208
Double taxation agreements 217

Earnings, net relevant 173, 178–9
Endowment bonds, single-premium 149
Endowment policies 28–9, 51, 61, 124–32

and tax 126, 130
bonuses of 124, 127, 128, 132
cashing-in 130–31
choosing 132
flexible 124–6, 128–9, 130
non-profit 124, 125, 126
paid-up 130–31
with-profits 11, 21, 23, 124–6, 127, 128–9, 130, 132, 181, 222, 228
Endowment policy bonds, qualifying 149
Equity funds 133–4, 136, 138, 140, 146, 168
Equity-linked savings plans 138
Eurobonds 216
Exchange control regulations 208
Exchange rate of £ 208–9, 210–12
Extra interest accounts 183

Family income benefit policies 124
Fees, advisers' 35
Finance company deposits see Deposits, finance company
Financial Times, The 79, 108, 112, 134, 195, 215
Fixed-income investment 24–5, 45
Fixed-interest funds 133, 134, 168
Fixed notice of withdrawal accounts 190, 191
Fixed term accounts 190, 191
Fixed trusts 220–1, 230–1
Friendly societies 132, 141, 175, 185, 188
FT-Actuaries All-Share Index 83, 94, 99
Funds, offshore 214, 215
Futures, investing in 110, 111, 112, 116

Gearing 65, 67, 86
Gilt-edged securities see Stocks, British Government
Gilt fund, index-linked 177
Gold, investing in 26–7, 76, 77
Granny bonds see Retirement Issue, National Savings Certificates
Growth bonds see Bonds, income and growth
Guaranteed minimum pension (GMP) 161

Health and insurance 9
Home as investment 28–9, 62–9, 70
Home improvement and tax relief 66
Home income schemes 18–19, 23, 28–9, 154–5, 237
Homeloan Scheme 68, 69
Houses
bought with cash 64, 65
bought with mortgage 64, 65, 209
extra expenses in purchasing 68
mortgages for 68–9
prices of 62–4, 67

Income from investing 13
Income bonds see Bonds, income and growth
Income tax 42, 43–8
and overseas investment 217
Independent Schools Information Service 226
Index-linked investments 192–7
and tax 193, 195, 197
see also Stocks, British Government and National Savings Certificates, 2nd Index-linked Issue and Save-As-You-Earn
Inflation 10, 13, 18, 64, 65, 67, 73, 152, 153, 157, 164–5, 171–2, 177, 181, 210, 211, 212, 232, 233–4, 236, 237
see also Index-linked investments and Retail Price Index
Inspector of Foreign Dividends 217
Institute of Chartered Accountants 41
Insurance brokers 37, 154, 175, 176
Insurance Brokers Registration Council 41
Insurance, house 68
Insurance of alternative investments 72
Insurance Ombudsman Bureau 41
Interest and interest rates 15, 18, 24–5, 45, 46, 47, 103, 104, 118, 119, 120, 121, 124, 126, 130, 180, 182, 183, 184, 185, 186, 187, 189, 190, 191, 198–9, 200, 201–2, 206, 207, 214, 215
Interest in possession trusts see Fixed trusts
International Wine and

Food Society 77
Investment consultants 39, 82
Investment income surcharge 18, 20, 44, 46, 49, 223, 224, 230
Investment income, taxed before you get it 45–6
Investment income, taxed after you get it 45–6
Investment income, tax-free 42, 44
Investment Trust Year Book 215
Issue, bonus see, Scrip issue
Issuing Houses Association 40

Jewellery, investing in 12, 72
Jobbers 85, 90
Joint life policies 146, 177

Krugerrands 25, 76

Landlords and the Law 237
Land Registry fee 68
Law Society, The 41
Lead, investing in 110, 111
Letting property 237
Licensed deposit-taking institutions (LDTIs) 191
Life insurance 8, 9, 15, 20, 22, 23, 124, 127, 173, 174, 175, 219, 221, 223, 224–5, 226, 227, 228, 234, 237
and tax 42, 49–52, 56, 61, 136, 173, 184, 185, 221
endowment 124–32
equity linked 78
investment-type 22, 44, 226
linked to building societies 20, 21, 23, 26–7, 52, 181, 184–5, 193
protection-type 22, 124
subsidy on premiums for 51–2, 124, 126
term 8, 61, 124, 144, 145
unit-linked 52, 133–47, 229
whole life 61, 132
Life Offices' Association, The 41, 129
Limited editions, investing in 70, 74
Loan-bank facility 169, 172
Loan stock 88, 90, 127
Loans, bank 190
Loans for home purchase 25
Local authority bills 118

Local authority
investments 18–19
and tax 118, 119, 120, 122
interest on 118, 120, 122
loans 15, 24, 30–31, 117–19, 123, 127, 148, 181, 192, 219
stocks 30–31, 117, 120–21, 122, 123
yearling bonds 117, 120, 122, 123
London Commodity Exchange 111
London Gold Market 76, 77
London Metal Exchange 111

Managed funds 133, 134, 136, 137, 141, 168
Margin call 111
Married Women's Property Act 61, 221
Merchant banks 40
Mergers, company 90
Metals see Commodities and Individual entries
Money Management 99, 116, 132, 140, 154, 176, 214
Mortgage loans 118
Mortgage protection policies 51
Mortgage rate, recommended 168
Mortgages 11, 18–19, 20, 21, 42, 44, 65, 66, 68–9, 127, 154, 181, 187–8, 190
and tax 8, 65–6, 67

National insurance contributions 156, 160, 161, 232
National Savings Bank 15, 18–19, 20, 21, 22, 24, 30–1, 44, 47, 48, 191, 206–7, 218, 219
and tax 206, 207
investment accounts 207
ordinary accounts 206
National Savings Certificates 15, 19, 21, 30–1, 53, 148, 192, 198–202, 219, 236
and tax 44, 53, 199, 200, 236
National Savings Certificates, 2nd Index-linked Issue 13–14, 18, 21, 22, 23, 24, 28–9, 107, 148, 152, 181, 192, 193, 194–5, 196, 236, 237
and tax 44, 53, 195, 236
National Savings gift tokens 207, 219
National Savings stamps 207
National Savings Stock

Register 47, 107, 108, 109, 121
New issues 89
Nickel, investing in 111
Nil rate band (CTT) 60
Notes for Guidance on Retirement Annuity Relief 178

Oil, investing in 110, 114
Oil, North Sea 211, 212
Open-market option 167, 174, 176
Option mortgages 66, 154
Options 84, 90
Organisation of Petroleum Exporting Countries (OPEC) 114
Overdrafts 66
Overseas investment 208–17
and tax 217
bank accounts 214
Eurobonds 216
foreign currency funds 211, 215
government stocks 213, 215
investment trusts 215
life insurance 216
property 216, 217
shares 213, 215
unit trusts 214

Paid-up value 130, 144–5
Pensions
and tax 156, 158, 164, 165, 169, 171, 172, 174, 176–7, 178–9, 235
employer's 8, 21, 30–1, 42, 78, 156–9, 160, 161, 166, 232, 233–4
married women's 236
state 8, 30–1, 156, 157, 160–1, 232–3
Pension plans, personal 8, 10, 21, 23, 30, 31, 42, 78, 164–79, 232, 234, 235
Personal pension plans see Pension plans, personal
Physicals, buying and selling 110
Planned Savings 132, 176
Policyholders Protection Act 132, 141, 154, 175
Policyholders Protection Board 132, 175
Policy Market 154
Pooling shares 57
Port, investing in 73
Power of appointment trusts 221
Premium bond gift tokens 207
Premium bonds 30–1, 44, 203–5, 219

and tax 203
Premium facility, additional 138, 141
Price earnings ratio 88
Prior charges 88
Profit margin 83
Property, buying foreign 216
Property funds 133, 134, 136, 137, 140, 141, 146, 168
Public Works Loans Board 123

Quotel computer system 154, 176

Removal costs, house 68
Repayment Value chart 195
Retail Price Index 23, 62, 65, 107, 147, 160, 169, 177, 194, 195, 196, 197, 237
Retained profits 88
Retentions 88
Retirement and saving 232–7
Retirement Issue, National Savings Certificates 192, 193, 195
Return on capital employed 83
Rights issue 89–90
Roll-over relief 56, 72, 223, 231
Rooms to Let 237
Risk and investment 12
Rubber, investing in 110
Rugs, investing in 26–7

Save-As-You-Earn 21, 23, 28–9, 44, 53, 181, 182, 185, 192, 193, 196–7, 219, 236, 237
Save-As-You-Earn share option scheme 21, 30–1, 207
Savings accounts, bank 15
Savings Market, The 99, 140, 149, 154, 175
Savings plan, monthly 184
Savings plan, unit trust 101
Savings schemes,

regular 190
Section 226A policies 173, 174
School fees schemes 9, 226–9
and tax 227–8, 229
capital 226, 227–8
income 226, 228–9
Scrip issues 89
Scripophily 73
Self-Employed Pensions 175
Self-Employed Premium Certificate 178
Self-employment 8, 23, 37, 42, 161, 164, 165, 178–9, 234, 235; see also Pension plans, personal
Share certificates, collecting 73
Share exchange scheme, unit trust 101
Share-option schemes, savings related 90
Shares 11, 12, 18, 19, 22, 32–3, 70, 78–90, 91, 100, 101, 127, 138, 209, 212, 215, 219
and tax 56–8, 139, 215
beta analysis 83–4
buying 85–6, 87
chartism 82
fundamental analysis 83
new issues of 89–90
nominal value of 88
ordinary 88
preference 88, 90
selling 86, 87, 139
spreading the risk of 79–81
technical analysis 82
Silver, investing in 10, 11, 70, 74, 110, 111, 116, 236
Single-premium investment bonds see Bonds, single-premium investment
Solicitors 38, 85, 220
Sovereigns, dealing in 11, 70, 76
Spot price 110
Spread, the 138, 139, 146
Stamp duty 68
Stamps, investing in 10, 11, 26–7, 70, 74, 181, 236
Stockbrokers 36–7, 85–7, 108–9, 119, 121, 122, 216, 222

Stock certificates, collecting 73
Stock Exchange, The 36, 41, 73, 85, 86, 87, 89, 90, 101, 102, 106, 107, 117, 120, 121, 215
Stocks, British Government 11, 15, 18–19, 26–7, 45, 47, 53, 85, 90, 91, 92, 94, 100, 102–9, 120, 121, 122, 123, 127, 136, 151, 169, 180, 181, 192, 198, 208, 209, 215, 219, 227
and tax 59, 105, 107, 108
dated 102, 103–4, 106, 109
details of 106
index-linked 14, 18, 19, 22, 23, 28–9, 107, 152, 193, 236, 237
prices of 104–5, 109
returns from 105, 106
undated 102, 103, 104, 106, 109
Stocks, foreign Government 215
Students and covenants 224, 225
Subsidies on premiums 51–2, 124, 126, 142
Sugar, investing in 110, 113, 114, 115
Surveyor's fee 68
Switching funds 138, 140, 141, 146

Takeovers, company 90
Talisman system 87
Tax 8, 9, 13, 14, 18, 20, 22, 25, 27, 29, 31, 33, 42–61, 90, 236
after retirement 236, 237
and alternative investments 72, 73
and annuities 149, 152, 153, 154, 155
and bank deposits 189, 214
and British Government stocks 59, 105, 107, 108
and building societies 45, 180, 184, 185
and children 218, 220, 221, 222, 223, 230–1
and commodities 116
and covenants 224, 225

and endowment policies 126, 130
and Eurobonds 216
and finance company deposits 191
and foreign government stocks 215
and income and growth bonds 148, 149
and index-linked investments 193, 197
and investment trusts 215
and life insurance 42, 49–52, 54, 61, 136, 173, 184, 185, 221
and local authority loans 118, 119, 120, 122
and mortgages 8, 65–6, 67
and National Savings Bank accounts 206, 207
and National Savings Certificates 44, 53, 195, 199, 200, 236
and overseas investments 217
and pensions 156, 158, 164, 165, 169, 171, 172, 174, 176–7, 178–9, 235
and premium bonds 203
and property abroad 216
and Save-As-You-Earn share option scheme 207
and school fees schemes 227–8, 229
and shares 56–7, 58, 59, 139, 215
and trusts 221, 222, 230–31
and unit-linked life insurance 136, 138, 140, 145
and unit trusts 56–8, 101, 214
see also Capital gains tax, Capital transfer tax, Income tax
Tax-free investments 42, 44
Term insurance 8, 61, 124, 144, 145
Times, The 108
Tin, investing in 110, 111, 114
Top-slicing relief 50, 138, 140
Trustee Savings Bank

203, 219
Trust deeds 220, 221
Trustee status, building societies' 188
Trusts for children 220–2, 223
and tax 221, 222, 230–1
Trusts, investment 58, 78, 86
and tax 215

Ulster Savings Certificates 44
Unit-linked savings plans 21, 23, 32–3, 133, 138, 142–7, 181
and tax 142, 143, 145, 147
Unit Trust Association 41, 99, 100, 222
Unit Trust Year Book 98, 99
Unit trusts 12, 14, 18, 19, 21, 22, 23, 25, 32–3, 45, 46, 56–7, 58, 78, 83, 86, 91–101, 108, 115–16, 138, 181, 185, 208, 214, 219, 222
and choosing 96–8
and tax 56–7, 58, 101, 214
types of 94–5
Unit trusts, accumulation 58
United Terminal Sugar Market Association 111

Valuation fees, house 68
VAT 72, 73, 75, 76, 86

War Loan stock 45, 47, 102, 106
War Savings Certificates 198
Warrants, option 84, 90
Whole life insurance policies 61, 132
Withdrawal scheme, life insurance 141
Withdrawal schemes, unit trust 101

Yearling bonds see Local authority investments

Zinc, dealing in 110, 111